IMPROVING SCHOOLING FOR LANGUAGE-MINORITY CHILDREN

A Research Agenda

Diane August and Kenji Hakuta, *Editors*

Committee on Developing a Research Agenda
on the Education of Limited-English-Proficient
and Bilingual Students
Board on Children, Youth, and Families

Commission on Behavioral and Social Sciences and Education
National Research Council

Institute of Medicine

NATIONAL ACADEMY PRESS
Washington, D.C.   1997

NATIONAL ACADEMY PRESS • 2101 Constitution Avenue, NW • Washington, DC 20418

NOTICE: The project that is the subject of this report was approved by the Governing Board of the National Research Council, whose members are drawn from the councils of the National Academy of Sciences, the National Academy of Engineering, and the Institute of Medicine. The members of the committee responsible for the report were chosen for their special competences and with regard for appropriate balance.

This report has been reviewed by a group other than the authors according to procedures approved by a Report Review Committee consisting of members of the National Academy of Sciences, the National Academy of Engineering, and the Institute of Medicine.

Support for this project was provided by the U.S. Department of Education, as well as the Spencer Foundation, the Carnegie Corporation of New York, the Pew Charitable Trusts, The John D. and Catherine T. MacArthur Foundation, and the Andrew Mellon Foundation through a grant to Stanford University. The views expressed in this report do not necessarily reflect those of the sponsors.

Additional copies of this report are available from:

National Academy Press
2101 Constitution Avenue, N.W.
Washington, D.C. 20005
Call 800-624-6242 or 202-334-3313 (in the Washington metropolitan area). http://www.nap.edu

Printed in the United States of America.

First Printing, April 1997
Second Printing, May 1998

Contents

    LITERACY DEVELOPMENT AND CONTENT LEARNING   53

    State of Knowledge, 53
    Research Needs, 71
    References, 76

4   THE SOCIAL CONTEXT OF SCHOOL LEARNING   85

    State of Knowledge, 85
    Research Needs, 101
    References, 103

5   STUDENT ASSESSMENT   113

    State of Knowledge, 113
    Research Needs, 128
    Annex: Legislative Context for Standards and Assessment, 132
    References, 134

6   PROGRAM EVALUATION   139

    State of Knowledge, 139
    Research Needs, 157
    References, 159

7   STUDIES OF SCHOOL AND CLASSROOM EFFECTIVENESS   163

    State of Knowledge, 163
    Research Needs, 189
    Annex: Table 7-1, Studies of School and Classrooom Effectiveness, 197
    References, 244

8   PREPARATION AND DEVELOPMENT OF TEACHERS
    SERVING ENGLISH-LANGUAGE LEARNERS   251

    State of Knowledge, 251
    Research Needs, 266
    References, 270

9   ESTIMATING POPULATION PARAMETERS   275

    State of Knowledge, 275
    Research and Infrastructure Needs, 294
    Annex 1: National Surveys and Data Collection Efforts, 299
    Annex 2: Variables of Interest for Monitoring
       English-Language Learner Progress, 302
    References, 305

The National Academy of Sciences is a private, nonprofit, self-perpetuating society of distinguished scholars engaged in scientific and engineering research, dedicated to the furtherance of science and technology and to their use for the general welfare. Upon the authority of the charter granted to it by the Congress in 1863, the Academy has a mandate that requires it to advise the federal government on scientific and technical matters. Dr. Bruce Alberts is president of the National Academy of Sciences.

The National Academy of Engineering was established in 1964, under the charter of the National Academy of Sciences, as a parallel organization of outstanding engineers. It is autonomous in its administration and in the selection of its members, sharing with the National Academy of Sciences the responsibility for advising the federal government. The National Academy of Engineering also sponsors engineering programs aimed at meeting national needs, encourages education and research, and recognizes the superior achievements of engineers. Dr. William A. Wulf is interim president of the National Academy of Engineering.

The Institute of Medicine was established in 1970 by the National Academy of Sciences to secure the services of eminent members of appropriate professions in the examination of policy matters pertaining to the health of the public. The Institute acts under the responsibility given to the National Academy of Sciences by its congressional charter to be an adviser to the federal government and, upon its own initiative, to identify issues of medical care, research, and education. Dr. Kenneth I. Shine is president of the Institute of Medicine.

The National Research Council was organized by the National Academy of Sciences in 1916 to associate the broad community of science and technology with the Academy's purposes of furthering knowledge and advising the federal government. Functioning in accordance with general policies determined by the Academy, the Council has become the principal operating agency of both the National Academy of Sciences and the National Academy of Engineering in providing services to the government, the public, and the scientific and engineering communities. The Council is administered jointly by both Academies and the Institute of Medicine. Dr. Bruce M. Alberts and Dr. William A. Wulf are chairman and interim vice chairman, respectively, of the National Research Council.

Preface

This report is the culmination of a process that began in September 1994 at a planning meeting to determine whether there was a sufficient knowledge base to inform the development of a research agenda on the education of English-language learners. Nine experts in language development, cognitive development, bilingual education, immigrant education, minority child development, education evaluation, and student demographics discussed existing research that has informed the education of English-language learners and bilingual students and identified knowledge gaps and promising directions for a possible study.

In response to the suggestions resulting from this meeting, a committee was established under the Board on Children, Youth, and Families of the Commission on Behavioral and Social Sciences and Education (CBASSE) of the National Research Council (NRC) and the Institute for Medicine (IOM). Funding was provided by several offices within the U.S. Department of Education, the Office of Bilingual Education and Minority Languages Affairs, the Office of the Under Secretary, and the Office of Educational Research and Improvement. Funding was also provided by the Spencer Foundation, the Carnegie Corporation of New York, the Pew Charitable Trusts, The John D. and Catherine T. MacArthur Foundation, and the Andrew Mellon Foundation (through a grant to Stanford University).

Although this is the first NRC study on developing a research agenda on the education of English-language learners and bilingual students, it builds on three earlier NRC studies related to this topic.

Assessing Evaluation Studies: The Case of Bilingual Education Strategies (National Academy Press, 1992) recommended improving evaluation studies in

bilingual education, calling for a three-step process entailing exploratory or qualitative studies to identify important program features; the development of competing theories, leading to sharply distinct proposals for programs; and the creation
and assessment of these programs in tightly controlled comparative studies.

Cultural Diversity and Early Education: Summary of a Workshop (National
Academy Press, 1994) considered the scope and the quality of research evidence
on prekindergarten education of diverse populations of children. The report
stresses an urgent need for more research on this population, as well as better
coordination among agencies who fund this research. Some of the areas identified for future research include bilingual language instruction, effective educational practices, nonminority children as beneficiaries of cultural diversity, and
the community context of multicultural education.

*Research and Education Reform: Roles for the Office of Educational Re-
search and Improvement* (National Academy Press, 1992) addressed the question
of how federally sponsored education research might better contribute to improving education in the nation and makes recommendations for legislation to reau-
thorize the Office of Educational Research and Improvement. It identifies a
variety of obstacles, including the politicization of the research agenda; inadequate funding; lack of funding for investigator-initiated research; and various
internal problems, such as a weak advisory council and frequent turnover in top
administrative positions. Many of the report's recommendations were incorporated in the Educational Research and Improvement Act of 1994.

The charge to this committee, based in large part on the findings from the
planning meeting, was to review what is known about the linguistic, cognitive,
and social processes involved in the education of English-language learners;
identify issues that are worthy of more focused attention; examine the strengths
and weaknesses of various research traditions in the field; and make recommendations regarding research priorities, the research infrastructure, human resource
issues as they concern the supply and diversity of scientists and educational
personnel who work in this area, and the use of scientific evidence to inform and
improve policy and practice related to the education of English-language learners.

The committee began the task by dividing the research terrain into five
categories: language, literacy, learning, and social processes; assessment and
evaluation; school- and program-based studies of effective instruction; teacher
education and professional development; and national education statistics. Over
the course of four meetings, a number of subgroup meetings, and numerous
conference calls, the substantive issues in each of these areas were outlined and
discussed, and the relevant literature was reviewed. Review materials prepared
by committee members and staff, as well as background papers prepared by
others, guided the initial discussions and in some cases were incorporated into
draft chapters and reports. In cases in which the committee felt ill-equipped to
conduct a full-scale review, outside papers were commissioned (see below).

Infrastructure issues were addressed through a primary data collection effort, since published information in this area is not available. Study director Diane August, in consultation with committee member Carl Kaestle, gathered funding information from federal agencies and interviewed staff at these agencies, as well as staff in professional associations and directors of centers that conduct research on English-language learners. The results of their effort are presented in Appendix A.

At the beginning of the project the committee invited sponsors to share their goals for the project. We are grateful to Gilbert N. Garcia, from the Office of Educational Research and Improvement, and Eugene Garcia, formerly director of the Office of Bilingual Education and Minority Languages Affairs, for their thoughtful comments. We also thank Robert Siegler, Delia Pompa, and David Ramirez for participating on the committee at the beginning of the project.

The committee held one workshop and one open meeting. The workshop was designed to elicit advice from experts in educational research on language minority students and bolster the committee's knowledge base in certain areas, including social processes, effective schools and classrooms, and population estimates. The workshop participants prepared commissioned papers, which were discussed at the workshop. At the open meeting, advocates and representatives of professional organizations with a stake in bilingual education expressed their opinions and priorities. Several graduate students assisted with the project. They include Jennifer Merriman, who contributed to the section on subject matter learning in Chapter 3, and Joshua Rubin, who analyzed 1994 annual reports for foundations that fund substantial amounts of research for Appendix A and C. The committee is grateful to these presenters, consultants, readers, workshop participants, and technical reviewers for their contributions to our efforts; see Appendix D.

A few consultants deserve special recognition for their substantial contributions to various chapters: Claude Goldenberg for his work on effective schools and classrooms (Chapter 7), Miriam Gonzalez for her work on teacher education (Chapter 8), and Anne Hafner for her contribution on estimating population parameters (Chapter 9), and Lana Muraskin for her analysis of research supported through state departments of education in states with at least 6 percent English-language learner populations.

The committee wishes to acknowledge the support and assistance of officials from the federal and state agencies (see Appendix B) who graciously allowed us to interview them and provided us with background materials for our study of the infrastructure of research. Very special thanks are due to John Chapman from the U.S. Department of Education Budget Service for the many hours he spent helping us put together a table on Title VII funding for research over the last ten years.

The committee also benefited from the support of the staff of the Board on Children, Youth, and Families: Deborah Phillips's commitment to culturally diverse students made this project possible; Rosemary Chalk provided ongoing advice and encouragement; and Niani Sutardjo helped prepare the bibliography. Communications director Anne Bridgman was particularly helpful in the final stages of preparing the report and planning its dissemination. Special thanks are due to Carole Spalding, the project assistant, who provided the panel with excellent support in organizing the panel meetings, preparing agenda materials, and guiding the report from the first drafts to the published volume. We also thank editor Rona Briere, whose efforts contributed significantly to the presentation of the panel's views.

Most of all, thanks and acknowledgment of extraordinary effort are due to the members of the committee and our study director. In addition to participating in meetings and numerous conference calls and reading and reviewing hundreds of pages of studies and background materials, several members and staff took responsibility for the initial drafts of the chapters of this report. I thank Catherine Snow and Gaea Leinhardt for their work on Chapter 3; Lucinda Pease Alvarez, James Banks, and Catherine Snow for their work on Chapter 4; Richard Duran for his work on Chapter 5; David Kenny for his work on Chapter 6; Diane August and Donna Christian for their work on Chapter 7; and Alba Ortiz for her work on Chapter 8. Our work also benefited from the participation of Deborah Stipek, who served as a liaison between the committee and the Board on Children, Youth, and Families. Her expertise in education also contributed significantly to this report.

Kenji Hakuta, *Chair*
Committee on Developing a Research
Agenda on the Education of Limited-English-
Proficient and Bilingual Students

IMPROVING SCHOOLING FOR LANGUAGE-MINORITY CHILDREN

Executive Summary

OVERVIEW

American education has focused primarily on the needs of native English-speaking children. However, a large and growing number of students in U.S. schools come from homes where the language background is other than English, and are considered to be limited-English-proficient (LEP). These students are overwhelmingly from families with low incomes and lower levels of formal education. Thirty years ago these students were expected to "sink or swim" in a school environment that did not pay particular attention to their linguistic background. Since the 1970s, a variety of educational approaches to meeting the needs of English-language learners have been tried.[1] These approaches are designed to help these students develop proficiency in English, as well as learn the knowledge, skills, and attitudes that make up the curriculum. Impetus for these programs has come from a number of sources: Congress, the courts, state legislatures, departments of education, and various professional and advocacy groups. At first, these programs were not based on research, but relied on professional intuitions, political voices, and a moral conviction that something had to be done to reverse the pattern of poor academic outcomes for these students. What

---

[1]Throughout this report, the committee has elected wherever possible to use the term "English-language learners" (proposed by Rivera [1994]) rather than the term "LEP students." The committee believes that the former is a positive term, whereas the latter assigns a negative label. Moreover, we have chosen to forgo the editorially convenient practice of reducing English-language learners to an acronym.

1

little research existed focused on middle- and upper-middle-class Cuban exiles, populations of a different cultural background and generally of higher socioeconomic status than the typical English-language learner.

Beginning in the early 1970s and continuing to the present, a research base on English-language learner issues has been built in response to a number of circumstances. Major developments in basic research, especially in the areas of language and cognitive development, followed on the heels of the cognitive revolution of the 1960s and stimulated such research on English-language learners. The political controversy over bilingual education (i.e., use of the native language in instruction) led to a line of research aimed at evaluating the comparative effectiveness of bilingual education and other approaches using only English. Moreover, general concern with educational effectiveness led to research on English-monolingual populations aimed at identifying characteristics of schools that proved effective with respect to student outcomes, and this in turn stimulated parallel work to identify characteristics of effective programs for English-language learners. Efforts have also been made to incorporate English-language learners into large national surveys, such as the National Assessment of Educational Progress. These and other developments have resulted in a rich portfolio of research on English-language learners, ranging from basic processes to program evaluation and from program characteristics research to the collection of national statistics.

Almost 30 years after congressional passage of the Bilingual Education Act as Title VII of the Hawkins-Stafford Elementary and Secondary Education Act, we are now in a position to take stock of what we know and to consider ways of improving our knowledge building in this area. This task is of critical importance given the demographics of the school-age population. There has been an increase of almost 1 million English-language learners in U.S. public schools (grades K-12) in the last 10 years. As a consequence, these students make up approximately 5.5 percent of the public school student population. They are dispersed across the country, with about 6 percent of school districts serving student populations that are at least 40 percent English-language learners (Fleischman and Hopstock, 1993). Yet while the numbers of these students are increasing, their educational attainment remains low. For example, a recent Congressionally mandated study indicates that English-language learners receive lower grades, are judged by their teachers to have lower academic abilities, and score below their classmates on standardized tests of reading and math (Moss and Puma, 1995).

In this context, the Committee on Developing a Research Agenda on the Education of Limited-English-Proficient and Bilingual Students was formed and given the following charge:

• To review what is known about the linguistic, cognitive, and social processes involved in the education of these students.

• To examine the knowledge base on effective educational programming for these students and identify issues worthy of more focused attention.

• To review and identify the strengths and weaknesses of the traditional methodologies in this area.

• To make recommendations on research priorities in the field, the infrastructure supporting such research, human resource issues, and the use of scientific evidence to inform policy and practice in this area.

REVIEW OF SUBSTANTIVE AREAS

The committee reviewed research in a broad range of substantive areas, with a focus on how best to meet the academic and social needs of English-language learners. This report focuses on the following areas: how students learn a second language; how multiple languages are used and organized by bilingual children; how reading and writing skills develop in the first and second language; how information in specific content areas, such as mathematics and history, is learned and stored; how social and motivational factors affect learning in language-minority groups; how relations between different racial or ethnic groups are structured and moderated in school settings; how parents and communities influence and support learning; how student English proficiency and knowledge of content areas can be appropriately assessed; how programs can be evaluated with regard to achieving their goals; how school and classroom characteristics influence learning; how teacher education and professional development activities are structured to help teachers meet the needs of English-language learners; and how national education statistics include these students. For each of these areas, the following questions framed our inquiry: What do we know? How do we know it? What are promising research questions and methodologies that can advance research in this area?

The committee concluded that knowledge useful to the successful education of English-language learners has accumulated differentially across these areas. Some topics, such as second-language acquisition and discourse patterns in bilingual settings, have been characterized by a cumulative progression of theories and data. The challenge in these areas, then, is to extend the research to new languages, to new aspects of language, and to new subpopulations of research subjects. Other topics, such as the learning of academic content areas, have seen important developments in the mainstream research literature, but these insights have not been extended to language-minority populations. Others, such as program evaluation and effective schools, have seen significant activity, but a serious redirection of current efforts is warranted. Still others are plainly important, yet a major effort to address the fundamental issues for English-language learners has yet to be mounted; these topics include second-language literacy, intergroup relations, and the social context of learning. Finally, in the area of education statistics—an important tool in monitoring student and program characteristics, as well as educational outcomes for all students—progress in gathering systematic data on English-language learners and including these students in overall population estimates is seen as a major challenge for the immediate future.

These pockets of knowledge, once developed, could be combined to provide an elaborate, formal model of research and development. This is an ideal yet to be realized, but one that the committee sees as having great potential. We envision a model of instruction that is grounded in basic knowledge about the linguistic, cognitive, and social development of language-minority children. This model would be rich enough to suggest different programs for different types of students. It would take time to formulate such a model, and the participation of researchers from very different backgrounds would be required. Yet this model could serve as the basis for designing programs that would result in better outcomes for these students.

The envisioned model would be implemented in a small number of settings that would be carefully selected on the basis of student and school site characteristics. Throughout implementation, the process would be observed and described, and the implementation would be reworked. Once successful implementation had been demonstrated, the programs would be formally evaluated for outcomes. Some of these outcomes might include new and unexpected variables identified in the course of observing the implementation. The evaluation results would be used to confirm predictions of the general model. In addition, because the background characteristics of these programs could be related to the distribution of those characteristics nationally, hypotheses could be generated about the generalizability of the findings to new sites with similar and different characteristics. At this point, the programs could be disseminated as promising, and experimentation in other local sites encouraged. Once the model had been validated across a wide range of settings, the theory applied in creating effective programs could be used to guide professional development for teachers and other educators.

Such a picture linking theory and practice through empirical knowledge should be the long-term vision for a research agenda in the education of English-language learners.

REVIEW OF THE INFRASTRUCTURE THAT
SUPPORTS THE RESEARCH

In addition to our work in the above substantive areas, the committee investigated issues surrounding the infrastructure for research in this field. Our primary focus was on federal agencies, especially those in the Department of Education, but we also considered research by states and private foundations. Primary data for the analysis were interviews with key personnel and some award recipients and the background information they provided. At the federal level, questions related to the following topics guided the analysis: the organization and administration of the office, unit, or division; research related to the education of English-language learners that is funded; support for centers, laboratories, or other entities that conduct research on English-language learners; support for information services or resource centers that focus, at least in part, on these students; development of the research agenda; procedures that govern procurement, monitoring, accumulation of results, collaboration, dissemination, and linkages to policy and practice; obstacles to the sponsorship of research; promising efforts; and mechanisms to support the training of education rescarchers. A slightly abbreviated protocol was used with states. To generate information on foundation activity, we examined annual reports from 1994 and followed up this review with queries to all foundations included in this report.

Our infrastructure study revealed a number of serious obstacles to the development of an optimum research base in this field. A major factor has been the vulnerability of the agenda-setting process to external politics, as well as bureaucratic turf battles among various offices within the Department of Education. The Office of Bilingual Education and Minority Languages Affairs (OBEMLA), through its limited budget, has been the predominant voice for studies specific to English-language learners, as well as for the inclusion of these students in studies purporting to survey all students. However, OBEMLA's capacity to manage research has a mixed record. In addition, there has been a lack of staff capacity and interest among the other research offices and agencies for addressing the concerns of English-language learners. Thus, efforts at coordination and collaboration across offices have been extremely difficult to achieve, even though these students should be the concern of all offices that fund research in education. Other factors the committee identified as needing strengthening include the peer review process used to fund proposals; the processes available for monitoring research, accumulating knowledge, and developing consensus in given areas; and mechanisms for the dissemination of research results.

RESEARCH PRIORITIES: SUBSTANTIVE AREAS

In considering overall priorities for research, the committee applied four principles. These principles and the research priorities associated with each are summarized below.

Principle 1: Priority should be given to important topics to which insufficient attention has been paid, but for which there already exist promising theories and research methodologies so that sound research can be conducted in the immediate future.

Under this principle, the highest priorities are the topics of content area learning, second-language English literacy, intergroup relations, and the social context of learning:

• In the area of content learning, there exists very little fundamental research with English-language learners. Our review raised very important hypotheses about the nature of content area learning and knowledge, and the ways language learning and even the very structure of the two languages of bilinguals might interact with learning and knowledge representation.

• In second-language literacy, our review noted deep paradigmatic divisions, but identified important questions that are within the reach of research, such as the necessary basis for the development of second-language literacy and the optimal literacy instruction given the students' background.

• On the topic of intergroup relations, existing work has looked mainly at relations between African Americans and whites. This work has formed the basis for important theories of intergroup relations, such as social identity theory and the contact hypothesis. Such theories can be extended to look at language-minority/language-majority relations, as well as intraminority relations. At the same time, new theories may also be needed to account for the changed demographics of this country.

• Research that examines language-minority students in the context of their communities and homes has enhanced our understanding of the abilities and knowledge students bring to classrooms and the socialization practices that shape their development. On the basis of this work, many educators incorporate knowledge about students' homes and communities into their instruction to increase the students' academic potential. Much of the current knowledge is based on research using qualitative and interpretive frameworks. These methodologies need to be supported and amplified through studies using systematic sampling and quantitative measures.

Principle 2: Priority should be given to addressing important gaps in population coverage, such as certain age or language groups, for whom the applicability of current findings from a more limited population can be tested.

Under this principle, we identified specific questions that apply to hitherto understudied groups of students:

• Addressing the needs of young children in preschool programs requires a closer look at the relationship between the acquisition of English and native-language development.

• English acquisition, literacy development, content area learning, intergroup relations, and the social context of learning are all important issues to be addressed for older students with little or no formal education.

• Studies of older students formerly classified as having limited English proficiency would provide important insights into the needs of students who have been through special programs.

- Basic knowledge about the acquisition of English is needed for students with native languages other than Spanish.
- Knowledge is also needed about how to provide effective programming, assessments, and teacher education for English-language learners with disabilities.

Principle 3: Priority should be given to legitimate research questions that are of strong interest to particular constituencies, such as educators, policymakers, and the public at large.

Under this principle, we identified a number of questions that would be of concern to Congress, the administration, and state and local education administrators; the public and the media; advocates for equity; advocates for specific programs; foreign-language advocates; and teachers. The major areas of concern common to these groups are program evaluation and accountability, the extent to which students are acquiring English and progressing academically, and the characteristics of programs that promote student development.

Principal 4: Priority should be given to endeavors that would build the nation's capacity to conduct high-quality research on English-language learners and programs designed to serve their needs.

Under this principle, we identified areas of research in the cognitive sciences and approaches that would combine interpretive analysis and traditional positivistic paradigms, thus offering the potential to lure new researchers into the field. In addition, we identified the following areas as particularly promising ways of building cross-institutional bridges while also addressing vital issues: early childhood education and development, characteristics of effective practice, assessment, program evaluation, and teacher education and professional development. In the conduct of such research it is important to take contextual factors—such as the socioeconomic status of children's families and their ethnic background—into consideration.

RESEARCH PRIORITIES: RESEARCH INFRASTRUCTURE

Building the nation's infrastructure for research on the education of English-language learners requires more than promoting interesting and methodologically mixed research. As a result of our review of the federal, state, and foundation research infrastructure, the committee developed a number of recommendations for implementing our vision for the systematic development of research and practice in the education of English-language learners.

1. A new Department of Education Advisory Committee on Research on

English-language Learners should be established to oversee the development of a comprehensive system for integrating the review and synthesis of new knowledge into the agenda setting, funding, and dissemination of research on English-language learners. Further, this committee would be responsible for ensuring coordination and collaboration among offices within the department. Moreover, although its charge would be department-wide, it should also address and complement the work being funded outside the department. This committee should start by addressing topics we have identified as ripe for coordination: early childhood education, characteristics of effective practice, student assessment, program evaluation, teacher education, and the respective effects of limited English proficiency and poverty.

2. The Department of Education Advisory Committee on Research on English-language Learners should sponsor conferences and other activities jointly with other agencies to highlight the value of incorporating greater numbers of English-language learners into research conducted throughout the government and foundations. Perhaps necessary at some point would be a systematic inquiry by Congress into the extent of exclusion of English-language learners from federally funded research, followed by Congressional action if the situation should warrant. This action might include incentives for more work in this area.

3. Other areas the committee identified for strengthening include the peer review process used to fund proposals; the processes available for monitoring research, accumulating knowledge, and developing consensus in given fields; and mechanisms for the dissemination of research results. The National Educational Research Policy and Priorities Board is overseeing improvements in these areas. The proposed Advisory Committee on Research on English-language Learners should ensure that the funding and conduct of research on English-language learners are included in this department-wide agenda.

4. The efforts of the National Educational Research Policy and Priorities Board to improve the system of peer review of the Office of Educational Research and Improvement (OERI) should be augmented by two additional efforts. One would be to look at uses of peer review throughout the Department of Education, not just within OERI. Such an expansion would be within the board's authority to advise on research activities across the department. The other would address how to ensure expertise on English-language learner issues throughout the peer review process. This concern could be constructively addressed by the proposed Department of Education Advisory Committee on Research on English-language Learners.

5. The National Center for Education Statistics (NCES) should take the lead in population coverage issues. NCES should develop a common framework within which student and program data can be collected for national statistics. This framework could be extended to accommodate samples from all studies involving English-language learners and programs that serve them. NCES should also take the initiative to monitor the population representativeness of all funded

research conducted by federal, state, and private organizations, and report to the Advisory Committee on Research on English-language Learners regarding important gaps in coverage.

6. NCES should work with states and with all offices that collect data on English-language learners to implement a common definition of limited English proficiency. NCES should also lead an empirical effort to develop operational measures of limited English proficiency that can be used for a variety of purposes, ranging from large-scale assessment, such as the National Assessment of Educational Progress, to program-based and basic research studies, such as those funded through OERI. In addition, it should take the lead in developing procedures to incorporate English-language learners into large-scale assessments.

7. OBEMLA is the valid channel through which public-interest questions about English-language learners and programs that serve them are directed and filtered. OBEMLA should therefore take steps to identify itself as the conduit through which such public concerns are expressed. For example, OBEMLA could conduct consensus-building activities that would bring educators and advocates together with researchers to identify important questions for research investment. These areas for research could then be further developed in conjunction with the Advisory Committee on Research on English-language Learners.

8. OBEMLA provides major support for teacher education and professional development activities through Subpart 3 of Title VII. This report has shown a major need for research to improve the education of teachers who work with English-language learners. OBEMLA should take the lead in developing and evaluating approaches to the development of teachers who are specialists in teaching English-language learners, as well as those who are not specialists, but nevertheless teach a large number of such students. These approaches should be founded on a theoretically sound knowledge base regarding what and how teachers should be taught. Based on knowledge gained from this research, OBEMLA could take the initiative in working with the Office of Compensatory Education to develop guidance for professional development for teachers in Title I programs. OBEMLA could also work with the regional educational laboratories and comprehensive regional assistance centers that provide support to teachers whose classrooms include English-language learners. OBEMLA should develop consensus-building activities with the OERI institutes, especially the Students-at-Risk Institute, to identify priority areas for research that would be pursued by the institutes toward the end of improving teacher education. OERI should fund research in these areas.

9. Another important function for OBEMLA is in the development of researchers on English-language learner issues. OBEMLA already conducts a significant share of activities in this area through its Title VII Bilingual Fellowship Programs. OBEMLA should leverage this valuable source of support to attract education researchers who have not previously worked with this population, as well as to attract researchers who have traditionally not worked in the

area of education, for example by encouraging applications both from students in other educational fields and from students in institutions outside of schools of education. OBEMLA should also take a lead role in coordinating with other agencies and foundations in an effort to attract and develop fresh talent in this area.

10. A more long-term role for OBEMLA is to position itself so it can better utilize information on programs and their effectiveness from its Subpart 1 programs. Over the years, thousands of projects have been funded under Title VII basic programs. These programs constitute a tremendous opportunity—not yet realized—to implement theoretically driven interventions and assess their effects in different contexts. OBEMLA should work with the Planning and Evaluation Service of the Office of the Under Secretary to implement the recommendations for improving program evaluation presented in this report. To avoid problems that have arisen in the past, the staff capacity at OBEMLA should include researchers with expertise in the use of evaluation for purposes of program development.

11. Agencies in the Department of Education that have substantial responsibility for research on minority-language and English-language learner issues, such as OBEMLA, the Planning and Evaluation Service, and OERI (including the institutes, NCES, and ORAD), should allocate resources to train current staff and recruit staff with solid research experience so that there is substantive research expertise on English-language learners within the agencies. Agencies with incidental but important contact with such issues should find means to obtain the consultative expertise they need in a timely fashion.

12. States should make efforts to include English-language learners in data gathering, to disaggregate by language status where possible in reporting, to improve teacher education and development, and more generally to attend to research that will improve instructional interventions for these students. There are shared issues across states, and thus states would benefit from collaboration in these areas.

13. Foundations should develop mechanisms for providing technical assistance to school reform efforts to ensure that the needs of English-language learners are addressed. Foundations might fund projects that specifically address the educational needs of English-language learners, as well as support the development of local, state, and federal policies that would enhance their education. Finally, foundations can foster a more coherent research agenda on English-language learner issues by setting up and supporting communication in the form of ongoing networks or conferences among people who do not usually work together.

CONCLUSION

As this report shows, considerable knowledge about educating English-language learners and bilingual students has already accrued, and there are ways of strengthening and building upon this knowledge. Given the demographics of the school-age population, it is critical that we take stock of what we know and make recommendations for the next generation of research. It can be hoped that the paths to that end delineated by the committee can be followed with maximum intensity and minimum distraction through a strategic combination of theory, research, program development, evaluation, and monitoring.

REFERENCES

Fleischman, H.L., and P.J. Hopstock
  1993   Descriptive Study of Services to Limited English Proficient Students, Volume 1. Summary of Findings and Conclusions. Prepared for Office of the Under Secretary, U.S. Department of Education by Development Associates, Inc., Arlington, VA.
Moss, M., and M. Puma
  1995   Prospects: The Congressionally Mandated Study of Educational Growth and Opportunity. First Year Report on Language Minority and Limited English Proficient Students. Prepared for Office of the Under Secretary, U.S. Department of Education by Abt Associates, Inc., Cambridge, MA.
Rivera, Charlene
  1994   Is it real for all kids? *Harvard Educational Review* 64(1):55-75.

1

Overview

A large and growing segment of the population of students in the United States comes from homes where English is not the primary language spoken. Many of these students live in poverty, their families often do not have a deep history of formal education, and many are not yet proficient in English. At the same time, schools, and more generally the educational system, are not adequately prepared to respond to the rapidly changing student demographics. Such conditions combine and probably interact to produce educational outcomes that demand attention. Consider the following statistics:

- Among persons between the ages of 16 and 24 in 1989, 42 percent of those who reported difficulty with English had dropped out of high school, compared with 10.5 percent of those who spoke only English (McArthur, 1993).
- In 1992, in schools with high concentrations of poverty, almost 24 percent of third grade students with limited English proficiency had repeated a grade, compared with an overall grade retention rate of 15 percent (Moss and Puma, 1995).
- During the 1991-1992 school year, 9 percent of the students classified as limited-English-proficient were assigned to grade levels at least 2 years below age-grade norms (Fleischman and Hopstock, 1993).

The educational predicament of students of limited English proficiency has been a focus of policymakers and the courts for almost 30 years. According to federal law, and under many state laws, if students cannot participate meaningfully and equitably in the English-only school environment by virtue of their limited proficiency in English, they are eligible for special services. Programs to serve the needs of these students vary considerably. In some cases, students receive some proportion of their instruction in their native language. In others, they receive instruction exclusively through the medium of English, but the English is simplified, and the instructional context is enriched to make the content more understandable. In still others, the special help comprises instruction in English as a second language (ESL), with a primary focus on the development of English-language skills, rather than on the academic content areas. Determining the relative efficacy of this range of approaches has been the principal focus of the educational policy debate.

But the debate has also been shaped significantly by political factors that go beyond educational techniques. The modern roots of this debate can be traced to the Civil Rights movement of the 1960s and federal involvement in education at this time. As Epstein (1977) pointed out early in the debate, the question of bilingual education, especially those programs that espouse the development and maintenance of the ethnic language, can be framed in terms of whether to pursue "affirmative ethnicity" as an educational policy. The debate has also become an instantiation of related politically volatile issues, such as whether English should be constitutionally declared the official language of the United States (Crawford 1992), whether multiculturalism should be preserved (Graff, 1992; Hu-DeHart, 1995; Schlesinger, 1991), and whether national immigration policy needs to be changed (Brimelow, 1995). When ably used by politicians who wish to define themselves to voters or by the media when they wish to create controversy, the educational debate over how best to teach language-minority students is overwhelmed by these controversies.

PURPOSE OF THIS REPORT

The political issues outlined above cannot really be addressed by research; facts do not play a major role in these judgments. However, science and research are influenced by politics—from the research questions asked to the conduct of the studies and the way results are interpreted. Moreover, research in any highly controversial area invites suspicion and selective scrutiny from advocates of particular positions and must meet stringent demands to be credible and broadly accepted. The purpose of this report is to contribute to the construction of such a knowledge base in the education of students who are not fully English proficient by reviewing the state of knowledge and identifying a research agenda that will address the key knowledge gaps. We have endeavored to move beyond the narrow focus on language of instruction that has dominated the education and policy discussions.

CHARGE TO THE COMMITTEE

The formal charge to the Committee on Developing a Research Agenda on the Education of Limited English Proficient and Bilingual Students was as follows:

• Review what is known about the linguistic, cognitive, and social processes involved in the education of English-language learners (i.e., those who are not yet proficient in English but are in the process of second-language acquisition, as well as those who have become bilingual through the acquisition of English). As a result of this review, the committee will identify issues that are worthy of more focused attention.

• Review the methodologies traditionally used in this area, giving attention to the strengths and weaknesses of various research traditions.

• Make recommendations regarding research priorities that have promise for significantly advancing this field; the infrastructure that supports work in this area, including roles for public and private funders and academic institutions; human resource issues as they concern the supply and diversity of scientists and educational personnel who work in this area; and the use of scientific evidence to inform and improve policy and practice related to the education of English-language learners.

TERMINOLOGY

There are many labels for the students and programs under consideration in this report. The most commonly used term to refer to students who come from language backgrounds other than English and whose English proficiency is not yet developed to the point where they can profit fully from English-only instruction is *limited-English-proficient* (LEP). While we acknowledge the reality that this term has established itself in many critical areas, including national and state data collection efforts, federal and state education legislation, and court cases involving the rights of these students, we have elected to use the term proposed by Rivera (1994)—*English-language learners*. The committee feels that the latter is a positive term, whereas the former assigns a negative label. We use the term "LEP" when quoting another source, when citing such things as legal requirements, and when referring to issues rather than to children. Moreover, we have chosen to forego the editorially convenient practice of reducing English-language learners to an acronym.

Two other terms appear frequently in this report:

• *Bilingual students/programs/education*—Many of the programs intended to serve the needs of English-language learners use the students' native language as they acquire English. Thus the term *bilingual* is often used to refer to programs for these students generally. Yet this is really a misnomer for programs aimed at English-language learners, for two reasons: (1) the students are learning English and thus by definition are not yet bilingual, and (2) bilingualism is not the goal of these programs, but mainstreaming of the student into English-only programs. We therefore use the term *bilingual* to refer to an individual with a language background other than English who has developed proficiency in his or her primary language and enough proficiency in English not to be disadvantaged in an English-only school environment. We define *bilingual programs* in the background section later in this chapter.

• *Language-minority students*—This term refers to individuals from homes where a language other than English is actively used, who therefore have had an opportunity to develop some level of proficiency in a language other than English. A language minority student may be of limited English proficiency, bilingual, or essentially monolingual in English.

SCOPE OF THE REPORT

The primary focus of this report is on programs for English-language learners who are in the process of becoming proficient in English. The bulk of the advocacy, programmatic, and research emphasis has been on these students, rather than bilingual students, even though the potential for the development of bilingualism among language-minority students has always been acknowledged in the Bilingual Education Act. For example, in its most recent reauthorization, the act is explicit about the instrumental value of bilingualism: "As the world becomes increasingly interdependent and as international communication becomes a daily occurrence in government, business, commerce, and family life, multilingual skills constitute an important national resource which deserves protection and development" (Improving America's Schools Act, 1994, Section 7102(a)(10)). Despite such lofty aspirations, the primary focus of Title VII programs, as well as the relevant court deliberations, has been on providing meaningful and equitable access for English-language learners to the curriculum, rather than serving as an instrument of language policy for the nation through the development of their native languages (see Glenn, 1996, for a comparison of language policy regarding immigrant languages in other industrialized nations).

We note also that children develop within a broad set of environments and circumstances: in families, in neighborhoods, in classrooms and schools, and in societies. There is ample evidence of influence from each of these levels of environmental organization on child development, much of which cannot be adequately addressed in this report. For English-language learners, the important contextual issues include poverty, which as noted above is common among these students; attendance in underfunded schools; low social status accorded to members of certain ethnic and immigrant groups; familial stress; teacher expectations; and incompatibility between home and school environments, particularly related to first language, knowledge, skills, behavior, and ways of learning. These larger contextual issues are not directly addressed in this report, but form the foundation upon which the parameters we examine operate and interact.

Classrooms and schools, too, exist within complex environments, such as school districts and states; they are also influenced by federal policy, the media, and public opinion. A description of these contexts and factors and analysis of their impact on the education of English-language learners deserves serious attention by researchers. However, this committee saw the development of a research agenda in these areas as lying mostly beyond its charge. In the course of our work, we did address topics of key interest to policymakers, such as student assessment, program evaluation, and teacher education, but as an extension of our core charge: to review what we know about the linguistic, cognitive, and social processes involved in the education of English-language learners and develop recommendations for the next generation of research in these areas.

A final contextual parameter for this report is a set of assumptions shared by the members of the committee. They are as follows: (1) all children in the United States should be able to function fully in the English language; (2) English-language learners should be held to the same expectations and have the same opportunities for achievement in academic content areas as other students; and (3) in an increasingly global economic and political world, proficiency in languages other than English and an understanding of different cultures are valuable in their own right, and should be among the major goals for schools.

BACKGROUND

A detailed review of the history of programs, legislation, and court decisions related to English-language learners and bilingual students is provided in Appendix A. This section provides background information on the student population, the types of programs, the teachers, the educational outcomes, and the research addressed by this report.

The Students

According to the 1990 U.S. census, 6,322,934 school-aged (5-17) children, or about 14 percent of the total number of students in the U.S. population, lived in a home where a language other than English was spoken. Of these language-minority students, some subset were limited in their English proficiency. Based on the judgment of the respondents in the households sampled,[1] we can estimate

---

[1] Kominski (1989, cited in McArthur, 1993:4) looked at the validity of these categories in self-reporting English proficiency and found them "appropriate to use...as an aggregate measure to estimate the size of the limited-English-proficient population." The accuracy of parents' reports of their children's proficiency has not been investigated systematically, although one small-scale study showed that Mexican-American parents estimated their children's English proficiency better than their Spanish proficiency (Pease-Alvarez and Hakuta, 1993).

that 907,563 spoke English "not well or not at all," 1,480,680 spoke it "well," and 3,934,691 spoke it "very well."

According to a more direct estimate based on a nationally representative sample of school districts, the number of English-language learners in grades K-12 in the fall of 1991 was 2,314,079 (Fleischman and Hopstock, 1993, hereafter referred to as the Descriptive Study). This number represents an increase of almost 1 million students over the results of a survey conducted in 1984 using similar methodology.[2] Other estimates of the English-language learner population have ranged from 2.0 to 3.3 million because of the varying estimation methods used (Hopstock and Bucaro, 1993).

By far the largest proportion of English-language learners are native speakers of Spanish (73 percent). This is followed by Vietnamese (3.9 percent); Hmong (1.8 percent); Cantonese (1.7 percent); Cambodian (1.6 percent); Korean (1.6 percent); Laotian (1.3 percent); Navajo (1.3 percent); Tagalog (1.3 percent); and Russian, French Creole, Arabic, Portuguese, Japanese, Armenian, Chinese (unspecified), Mandarin, Farsi, Hindi, and Polish.

Geographically speaking, English-language learners are concentrated in a small number of large states. Of all the language-minority individuals enumerated in the 1990 census, 67 percent resided in just five states: California (30 percent), Texas (15 percent), New York (11 percent), Florida (6 percent), and Illinois (5 percent). English-language learners comprise proportionately high numbers in a small number of districts; in 1991, for example, 6 percent of districts served a student population that was at least 40 percent English-language learners (Descriptive Study). Recently, however, as the number of immigrants has increased, some have moved to smaller cities and suburban and rural areas, as well as to regions that have had few language minorities in the past, such as the midwest. This trend has been stimulated by a desire for employment and a lower cost of living (*Education Week*, September 11, 1996).

Most English-language learners are in the early elementary grades. Over half (53 percent) can be found in grades K-4. They make up a decreasing proportion of the total population in these grades: 8 percent of all kindergartners, down to about 6 percent of fourth graders.

As suggested earlier, English-language learners are also overwhelmingly from disadvantaged socioeconomic backgrounds. For example, 77 percent of English-language learners were eligible for free or reduced-price lunches, compared with 38 percent overall in the same schools. According to another study, known as Prospects (a Congressionally mandated evaluation of Chapter 1/Title I that follows longitudinally a nationally representative sample of students [Moss and Puma, 1995]), more than half of English-language learners in the first and third grade cohorts had family incomes under $15,000. A large percentage of

---

[2]Some of this increase is probably due to improvements in identification and reporting of English-language learners.

English-language learners attend schools where a high proportion (75-100 percent) of the other students are in poverty. Prospects found that 43 percent of first grade and 51 percent of third grade English-language learners attended such schools, compared with about 13 percent of the overall population. There are important qualitative differences between Hispanic and non-Hispanic language-minority groups. Although Prospects did not look separately at Spanish-speaking English-language learners, an analysis of the Current Population Survey from 1989 shows substantial family income differences within the non-English-language groups (McArthur, 1993). For example, 35 percent of families that spoke Asian/Pacific Island languages had incomes under $20,000, compared with 57 percent for Spanish speakers. There were parallel differences in parental educational attainment.

Program Definitions

The major dimensions used to define educational programs for English-language learners relate to native-language use, the mix of the students' linguistic backgrounds, and the goals of the program. However, most surveys of actual program characteristics show wide variation even within given nomenclatures. In addition, approaches do not exist in isolation, are in coexistence even within given schools, and are often combined in various ways depending on the availability of staff and resources. With these constraints in mind, we offer the following generic program labels and definitions. Note that the first two definitions refer to instructional approaches for teaching English, while the last four are program models that may include those approaches:

- *English as a second language (ESL)*—Students receive specified periods of instruction aimed at the development of English-language skills, with a primary focus on grammar, vocabulary, and communication rather than academic content areas.
- *Content-based ESL*—Students receive specified periods of ESL instruction that is structured around academic content rather than generic English language skills.
- *Sheltered instruction*—Students receive subject matter instruction in English, modified so that it is accessible to them at their levels of English proficiency.
- *Structured immersion*—All students in the program are English-language learners, usually though not always from different language backgrounds. They receive instruction in English, with an attempt made to adjust the level of English so subject matter is comprehensible. Typically there is no native-language support.
- *Transitional bilingual education*—Most students in the program are English-language learners. They receive some degree of instruction through the native language; however, the goal of the program is to transition to English as

rapidly as possible, so that even within the program, there is a rapid shift toward using primarily English.

   • *Maintenance bilingual education*—Most students in the program are English-language learners and from the same language background. They receive significant amounts of their instruction in their native language. Unlike transitional programs, these programs aim to develop English proficiency, but also to develop academic proficiency in the native language.

   • *Two-way bilingual programs*—About half of the students in these programs are native speakers of English, and the other half are English-language learners from the same language group. The goal of the program is to develop proficiency in both languages for both groups of students.

Data on program types are difficult to collect and interpret because program philosophy and objectives do not always translate into program practice. However, it is safe to say that ESL-only (with some variants of content-based ESL and sheltered instruction) and transitional bilingual education are the two prevalent models. A recent study found over 1600 schools that reported offering content ESL (content-based ESL and/or sheltered instruction) (Sheppard, 1995). Structured immersion programs are very few in number, as evidenced by the fact that a recent study examining the effects of structured immersion (Ramirez et al., 1991) had to select the universe of these programs. Maintenance programs are also relatively rare, while a recent survey of two-way bilingual programs, which are increasingly popular, identified just 182 schools nation-wide where this method is used (Christian and Whitcher, 1995).

Findings from the Descriptive Study suggest that about 33 percent of English-language learners are in ESL-only or immersion programs, while 57 percent are in some form of transitional bilingual program (9 percent have services classified as unknown). A different picture emerges from Prospects, which suggests a considerably smaller percentage of English-language learners receiving instruction in their native language; it estimates that reading and math were taught by a teacher using the native language in less than half of both the first and third grade cohorts. This discrepancy is notable, given that bilingual education is more prevalent in the lower than in the higher grades, and the Descriptive Study estimate is based on K-12, whereas Prospects is for grades 1 and 3. However, the studies are different in their sampling frames, missing data characteristics, timing, and questions employed. Most likely, Fleischman and Hopstock's category of "some L1" (L1 referring to the students' native language) included cases in which the L1 instruction was delivered by an instructional aide who spoke that language, rather than by the teacher.

The predominance of the transitional bilingual education model is underscored by one longitudinal analysis reported in Prospects (Exhibit 4.3), reporting data for the third grade cohort from the beginning and end of the year. At the beginning of the year, 71 percent of classroom teachers reported teaching primarily in the native language and 9 percent primarily in English. But by the end of the year, 14 percent reported teaching primarily in the native language and 40 percent primarily in English (another 37 percent reported that the language use varied from student to student).

The Descriptive Study used multiple regression to examine factors that predicted services involving native-language use. The strongest predictors were the availability of teachers who spoke the language and the percentage of English-language learners whose native language was Spanish. School poverty level was positively related to the likelihood of English-language learners' receiving instruction in their native language. Among the first grade cohort in Prospects, 70 percent of those in high-poverty schools received some math instruction in their native language, compared with 17 percent for those in medium- and low-poverty schools.

The Teachers

The Descriptive Study found that approximately 15 percent of all public school teachers in the country had at least one English-language learner in their class. Most of these teachers, about 66 percent, were mainstream classroom teachers serving some English-language learners; about 18 percent were mainstream classroom teachers serving primarily English-language learners. The study also found (p. 39) that "teachers of English-language learners hold regular elementary and secondary teaching certification; only small percentages are certified in bilingual education (10 percent) or ESL (8 percent). Forty-five percent hold Master's degrees or higher, while the remainder held Bachelor's degrees. Teachers of LEP students had a mean of four undergraduate mathematics and four undergraduate science courses; however, they averaged less than one mathematics course and less than one science course during their graduate training." About 42 percent of teachers of English-language learners spoke a non-English language that was the native language of one or more of those students. The study also found that only 55 percent of the teachers of English-language learners had taken relevant college courses or had received recent inservice professional development relating to the instruction of those students. Only about one-third of teachers of English-language learners had taken college courses concerning cultural differences and their implications for teaching such students.

Educational Outcomes

Data on educational outcomes are particularly difficult to obtain for the English-language learner population because their limited English proficiency constrains the validity of achievement measures administered in English.[3] For

---

[3]Recently, the National Center for Educational Statistics has made efforts to incorporate more of these students in its assessments (see Chapters 5 and 9).

example, the National Assessment of Educational Progress excludes students who have limited English proficiency and are judged incapable of taking the test in English. Similarly, in the National Educational Longitudinal Study of 1988 sample of eighth graders, 327 students identified as having limited English proficiency were included in the sample, but 3,831 students were eliminated because they were thought to be insufficiently proficient in English to complete the questionnaire or to take the tests. Thus, any estimate based on the sample of English-language learners who took the tests would likely be biased toward those most proficient in English.

The Prospects study provides some measure of achievement in the early grades. Students were tested either with the Comprehensive Test of Basic Skills (CTBS) or a similar test administered in Spanish, known as the SABE, offering English-language learners of Spanish-language background the opportunity to take the test in their native language if they were not judged adequately proficient in English. The CTBS results showed English-language learners performing considerably below general population norms in both reading and math. For example, the third grade cohort achieved at a mean percentile level of 24.8 percent in reading and 35.2 percent in math, compared with 56.4 and 56.8 percent, respectively, for all public school students. For those students who took the SABE, the mean percentile was somewhat but not much better, at 41.1 percent for reading and 35.2 percent for math. For both measures, performance was strongly related to the concentration of students from poor families in the school. The higher the concentration of poor families, the worse the student performance. The performance of English-language learners in schools with school poverty concentrations of 20-34 percent was not substantially different from the general population norm for all public school students. However, although there is an effect for poverty, limited English proficiency also plays a role in lowered scores, as indicated by differences between English-language learners and language-minority students (not currently limited-English-proficient) in high-poverty schools. For example, the third grade cohort of language-minority students in high-poverty (75-100 percent) schools scored at the 26.9 mean percentile, while English-language learners in these schools scored at the 15.5 mean percentile. Comparable figures for schools with 50-74 percent poverty were 43.7 mean percentile for language-minority students and 28.4 for English-language learners.

Prospects also examined student grades and teacher ratings of student ability and social and affective characteristics. English-language learners were less likely than all students to receive grades of excellent in reading or math. Teachers also rated such students lower than all students in their overall ability to perform in school and their overall achievement in school. However, teachers did not judge English-language learners to be different on a number of student affective characteristics, such as honesty, friendliness, happiness, self-esteem, ability to get along with teachers, and respect for authority. There were also no differences from the overall student population in school attendance, tardiness, and school suspensions.

Finally, drop-out rates for language-minority students provide one important indicator of educational outcomes for English-language learners. Data from the 1989 Current Population Survey show that 31.3 percent of Spanish speakers aged 16 to 24 were not enrolled in and had not completed high school, compared with 10.5 percent of English-only speakers. Figures for the other language groups were comparable to those for the English-only speakers. The difference between the Spanish-speaking and other language-minority groups is largely eliminated when one controls statistically for parental educational attainment (McArthur, 1993:Table 16).

To summarize, although incomplete, the data on student outcomes indicate distressing results for English-language learners, both short term as seen in test scores and teacher judgments and long term as seen in high school completion rates. Furthermore, other confounding factors—poverty level and level of parental educational attainment—are involved.

The Research

As discussed in Chapter 10 and Appendix A, recent federal policy with regard to educating English-language learners has been based on relatively little research, as a result of both the paucity of research and the predominance of politics. It has endorsed bilingual instruction, both through Title VII of the Elementary and Secondary Education Act of 1968 and the interpretation of the Supreme Court decision in *Lau v. Nichols*. The predominant justification for advocating bilingual education could be characterized as what one observer has called "a leap of faith" (Crawford, 1995). There was some documentation of the successful experiences in Dade County, Florida, serving the initial influx of Cuban refugees in the early 1960s (see Mackey and Beebe, 1977). Also influential were the comparative experiences with bilingual education in Canada, in which English-speaking children were immersed in French programs and emerged with functional bilingualism (Lambert and Tucker, 1972).

However, the students participating in the programs in Dade County in the 1960s and the French immersion programs in Canada were in many respects different from the majority of English-language learners. The students in the Dade County programs were children from the initial wave of Cuban refugees following Castro's revolution, children of the country's elite. The students in the Canadian immersion programs were children of the culturally dominant Anglophones who saw opportunity in their children's bilingualism and whose native language enjoyed a privileged status in the nation. Students with limited English proficiency in U.S. schools at large, to whom the laws were directed, came predominantly from low-income families. Except for studies from the early turn of the century based on theories about the genetic or experiential inferiority of eastern and southern European immigrants (see Hakuta, 1986), little was known about the education of English-language learners from poor and immigrant backgrounds and families of relatively low levels of formal educational history. American education research was thus faced with a significant challenge.

The response to this challenge came from three distinct and potentially complementary quarters. The first source of information was basic research on second-language acquisition and the development and functioning of bilingual children within the domains of literacy, cognition, and socio-emotional functioning—research that is essentially descriptive and not directly concerned with outcomes (see Chapters 2 through 4). By the late 1960s, major changes had taken place in theories of language, learning, and development. Behaviorism had collapsed and been replaced by cognitive theories that emphasized complex structures, computational models, and meaning. There was tremendous excitement and energy in the field that promised translation into practice. The founding of the National Institute for Education within the U.S. Department of Health, Education and Welfare in 1972 bespoke the faith placed in strong theory to guide education research, development, and practice. From this knowledge, it was hoped, would emerge effective programming for English-language learners.

The second source of information was program evaluation research (see Chapter 6). If a policy favors a certain type of program, such as the use of the student's native language in instruction, it makes sense to ask whether the programs that implement this policy are achieving the intended outcomes. Not surprisingly, the tug-of-war between bilingual and other programs that characterized the policy discussions of the 1970s and 1980s (see Chapter 6 and Appendix A) drove this research agenda. Usually, the outcomes of interest were (1) English-language proficiency (generally the primary focus) and (2) achievement in basic subject areas, usually as measured in English.[4] As is discussed later in this report, many of the early evaluation studies used quasi-experimental designs to compare bilingual and English-only treatments on these outcomes to test the validity of the policy favoring bilingual instruction.

Given the complexity of the issues related to educating English-language learners, as well as the failure of much basic research in bilingualism to address questions of policy and practice in bilingual education, basic research did not help inform practice. Nor did program evaluation research, which was narrowly focused on issues of language of instruction.

Gradually, a third line of research emerged that investigated the effectiveness of instructional programs and practices more broadly (see Chapter 7). One line of work described school and program environments to explore theories of teaching and learning. Another examined schools and classrooms determined to

---

[4]Although many advocates for language minority students favored a maintenance approach to bilingual education, this outcome was never seriously addressed by evaluation research, mostly because it was never a serious policy objective of either Title VII or the courts.

be effective based on nominations or student outcomes. Finally, studies were conducted to evaluate theoretically driven interventions. Some of these studies were quasi-experimental in nature.

There are many points of entry through which an organized research effort can illuminate and improve the education of English-language learners. The historical and policy contexts indicate a need to expand the questions addressed from simple English language acquisition to the teaching and learning of academic content. At the same time, the repertoire of research needs to be rich enough to support the changing demands of what constitutes appropriate action, given changes in student, teacher, and program characteristics. The research enterprise will have to be flexible and adaptable to new and unexpected changes, and will have to be exciting enough to draw first-rate talent to work creatively on the problems.

ORGANIZATION OF THIS REPORT

Chapters 2 through 9 review the state of knowledge and identify research needs in eight areas:

- Bilingualism and second-language learning (Chapter 2)
- Cognitive aspects of school learning, including literacy development and content area learning (Chapter 3)
- The social context of school learning (Chapter 4)
- Student assessment (Chapter 5)
- Program evaluation (Chapter 6)
- School and classroom effectiveness (Chapter 7)
- Preparation and development of teachers serving English-language learners (Chapter 8)
- Estimation of population parameters, or education statistics (Chapter 9)

This report is organized partly around the traditional distinction between basic and applied research, but is also structured to reflect specific areas of concern for educational policymakers. The first three chapters (Chapters 2-4) address basic research questions about bilingualism, second-language acquisition, literacy, content area learning, the social context of school learning, and intergroup relations. The next four chapters are organized around more practical issues: student assessment (Chapter 5), program evaluation (Chapter 6), school and classroom effectiveness (Chapter 7), and teacher education and development (Chapter 8). These topical issues were selected because they represent key areas of concern in the current discussions of educational reform. Chapter 9 analyzes issues involved in the collection of national education statistics. This important topic is given separate treatment because our recommendations are addressed primarily to one office: the National Center for Educational Statistics. Differing research traditions (cognitive aspects of school learning, program evaluation, and research on schooling and classroom effectiveness) are treated separately in individual chapters so the reader can get a sense of how the evidence from each tradition or data source is analyzed and how inferences are drawn. However, the reader should note there is some overlap among the kinds of studies cited in individual chapters.

Chapter 10 examines issues related to the infrastructure within which research on English-language learners and bilingual education is conducted. Important context for this discussion is presented in Appendix A (and the supporting information in Appendices B and C), which provides a comprehensive review of the history of research on English-language learners and examines the research infrastructure.

Finally, Chapter 11 presents the research priorities identified as a result of this study. Four principles guided the committee's identification of research priorities and provided coherence to our proposed agenda. These principles hold that priority should be given to the following: important topics to which insufficient attention has been paid, but for which there already exist promising theories and research methodologies; important gaps in population coverage, such as certain age or language groups, for whom the applicability of current findings from a more limited population can be tested; legitimate research questions that are of strong interest to particular constituencies, such as educators, policymakers, and the public at large; and endeavors that would build the nation's capacity to conduct high-quality research on English-language learners and programs designed to serve their needs.

REFERENCES

Brimelow, P.
 1995 *Alien Nation.* New York: Random House.
Christian, D., and A. Whitcher
 1995 *Directory of Two-Way Bilingual Programs in the United States.* Revised. Santa Cruz, CA, and Washington, DC: National Center for Research on Cultural Diversity and Second Language Learning.
Crawford, J.
 1992 *Language Loyalties: A Source Book on the Official English Controversy.* Chicago: University of Chicago Press.
 1995 *Bilingual Education: History Politics Theory and Practice.* Los Angeles: Bilingual Educational Services.
Education Week
 1996 Enrollment crunch stretches the bounds of the possible. *Education Week* (September 11):1.
Epstein, Noel
 1977 *Language, Ethnicity, and the Schools: Policy Alternatives for Bilingual-Bicultural Education.* Washington, DC: George Washington University.

Fleischman, H.L., and P.J. Hopstock
 1993   Descriptive Study of Services to Limited English Proficient Students, Volume 1. Sum-
        mary of Findings and Conclusions. Prepared for Office of the Under Secretary, U.S.
        Department of Education by Development Associates, Inc., Arlington, VA.
Glenn, C.L., with E.J. de Jong
 1996   Educating Immigrant Children: Schools and Language Minorities in 12 Nations. New
        York: Garland.
Graff, Gerald
 1992   Beyond the Culture Wars: How Teaching the Conflicts Can Revitalize American Educa-
        tion. New York: W.W. Norton.
Hakuta, K.
 1986   Minor of Language: The Debate on Bilingualism. New York: Basic Books.
Hopstock, P.J., and B.J. Bucaro
 1993   A Review and Analysis of Estimates of the LEP Student Population. Arlington, VA:
        Development Associates, Special Issues Analysis Center.
Hu-DeHart, E.
 1995   Ethnic studies in U.S. higher education: History, development and goals. Pp. 696-707 in
        J. Banks and C. McGee Banks, eds., Handbook of Research on Multicultural Education.
        New York: Macmillan.
Lambert, W.E., and G. R. Tucker
 1972   Bilingual Education of Children: The St. Lambert Experiment. Rowley, MA: Newbury
        House.
Mackey, William Francis, and Von Nieda Beebe
 1977   Bilingual Schools for a Bicultural Community. Miami's Adaptation to the Cuban Refu-
        gees. Rowley, MA: Newbury House.
McArthur, E.K.
 1993   Language Characteristics and Schooling in the United States, A Changing Picture: 1979
        and 1989. National Center for Education Statistics, Office of Educational Research and
        Improvement. Document number NCES 93-699. Washington, DC: U.S. Government
        Printing Office.
Moss, M., and M. Puma
 1995   Prospects: The Congressionally Mandated Study of Educational Growth and Opportu-
        nity. First Year Report on Language Minority and Limited English Proficient Students.
        Prepared for Office of the Under Secretary, U.S. Department of Education by Abt Associ-
        ates, Inc., Cambridge, MA.
Pease-Alvarez, L., and K. Hakuta
 1993   Perspectives from a North American Community. Keynote Address. Section on Lan-
        guage Attrition and Shift. Tenth World Congress of the International Association of
        Applied Linguistics. University of California at Santa Cruz and Stanford University.
Ramirez, D.J., S.D. Yuen, D.R. Ramey, and D.J. Pasta
 1991   Final Report: National Longitudinal Study of Structured-English Immersion Strategy,
        Early-Exit and Late-Exit Transitional Bilingual Education Programs for Language-Mi-
        nority Children. Volumes I and II. San Mateo, CA: Aguirre International.
Rivera, C.
 1994   Is it real for all kids? Harvard Educational Review 64(1):55-75.
Schlesinger, Arthur M., Jr.
 1991   The Disuniting of America. New York: Norton.
Sheppard, Kenneth
 1995   Content-ESL Across the USA: A Technical Report. Final report submitted to the Office
        of Bilingual Education and Minority Languages Affairs, U.S. Department of Education.
        Washington, DC: Center for Applied Linguistics.

BILINGUALISM AND SECOND-LANGUAGE LEARNING: SUMMARY OF THE STATE OF KNOWLEDGE

A review of the literature on bilingualism and second-language learning reveals the following key findings:

• Bilingualism is pervasive throughout the world, but varies according to the conditions under which people become bilingual, the uses they have for their various languages, and the social status of the languages. For example, some children learn two languages from the onset of language acquisition, while others begin to acquire a second language when they arrive in school.

• When socioeconomic status is controlled, bilingualism shows no negative effects on the overall linguistic, cognitive, or social development of children, and may even provide general advantages in these areas of mental functioning.

• Second-language acquisition is a complex process requiring a diverse set of explanatory factors. For example, second-language learning can be viewed as a linguistic and cognitive accomplishment, but social variables also affect language use and structure.

• An important dimension is the age and concomitant cognitive skills of the second-language learner. Because of their more advanced cognitive skills, older children acquire a second language at a more rapid rate than younger children.

• The degree of children's native-language proficiency is a strong predictor of their English-language development.

• Second-language abilities should be assessed in relation to the uses of language the learner will require, rather than in isolation as an abstract competence.

• Individual and group constraints such as age of learning, intelligence, attitudes, and personality have been examined in hopes of explaining individual differences in language learning. Age of learning and intelligence are related to certain aspects of second-language acquisition, but attitudes and personality are not promising explanations for the learning of English by language-minority students.

• Many bilinguals in the United States show a strong preference for English in a number of conversational situations, and this shift in preference results in a monolingual English upbringing for their children.

• Evidence from preschool programs reviewed in this chapter suggests that use of the child's native language does not impede the acquisition of English.

2

Bilingualism and Second-Language Learning

This chapter provides a broad overview of the findings of research on bilingualism and second-language learning and analyzes how theories in these areas have been reflected in thinking about the education of language-minority children in the United States. The literatures associated with these traditions are diverse in their methodologies and epistemologies and have undergone dynamic changes over the course of their history, extending back well over a century. They have developed largely independently from the educational and programmatic concerns that are the focus of this study, but they provide the fundamental science for the linguistic aspects of our inquiry. By necessity, a broad overview of these rich traditions involves a high level of synthesis. This review draws liberally from several existing general syntheses, which should be consulted for further details (Baetens-Beardsmore, 1986; Bialystok and Hakuta, 1994; Grosjean, 1982; Hakuta, 1986; Hamers and Blanc, 1989; Klein, 1986; Larsen-Freeman and Long, 1990; McLaughlin, 1984a, 1985; and Romaine, 1995).

STATE OF KNOWLEDGE

The following review of the state of knowledge in bilingualism and second-language learning begins by distinguishing the various types of bilingualism. It then briefly examines the consequences of bilingualism. The third section looks at linguistic aspects of acquiring a second language, while the fourth addresses individual differences in second-language acquisition. The phenomenon of language shift—in which ethnic minority groups shift their primary language to that of the dominant majority—is then examined. The final section reviews findings on educational conditions for second-language learning.

Types of Bilingualism

Bilingualism is pervasive throughout the world, but it varies according to (1) the conditions under which people become bilingual, (2) the uses they have for their various languages, and (3) the societal status of the languages. For example, in postcolonial Africa, students may be educated in English or French while another language is spoken in the home, and yet another (e.g., Swahili in eastern Africa) may be used in public encounters and institutional settings, such as the courts (Fishman, 1978). In officially bilingual countries such as Switzerland, children use one language at home and for most schooling, but, at least if middle class, are expected to acquire competence in at least one other official language; French and German are of equivalent social status and importance to success. Yet another set of conditions is created in bilingual households, where parents who are native speakers of two different languages choose to use both in the home. Finally, bilingualism is often the product of migration. Immigrants frequently continue to use their native language—which may be of low status and not institutionally supported—at home, and learn the dominant language of their new society only as required for work, public encounters, or schooling. The children of such families, for whom school is the primary social context, may end up fully bilingual, bilingual with the new language dominant, or having little knowledge of the parental language. They are the children of particular interest in this report.

A number of typologies of bilingualism have been offered. A major distinction among these typologies is that some focus their explanation at the individual and others at the societal level.

Individual Level

Weinreich (1953) distinguishes among compound, coordinate, and subordinate bilinguals, who differ in the way words in their languages relate to underlying concepts. In the compound form, the two languages represent the same concept, whereas in the coordinate form, the concepts themselves are independent and parallel. In the subordinate form, the weaker language is represented through the stronger language. These different forms are clearly related to the social circumstances in which the two languages are learned, but the distinction also reflects an individual's mental makeup. Weinreich's distinction led to a number of studies seeking behavioral differences reflecting this typology (e.g., Lambert et al., 1958). Though such attempts were essentially abandoned because of the difficulty of operationalizing the distinction, speculation that different bilingual experiences result in different cognitive and neural organization persisted. The emergence of procedures for seeing what prior stimuli facilitate the recognition of words presented later (called "lexical priming") has renewed interest in the possibility that we can tap the differential mental processes of the different types of bilinguals (Larsen et al., 1974).

A basic distinction at the individual level is that between simultaneous and sequential bilingualism: the former begins from the onset of language acquisition, while the latter begins after about age 5, when the basic components of first-language knowledge are in place (McLaughlin, 1984a). In the sequential type, a distinction is made between early and late bilinguals, according to the age at which second-language acquisition occurred (Genesee et al., 1978).

In general, research on distinctions among different types of bilingual individuals has failed to find consistent differences in task performance or processing variables. Much recent information-processing work has focused on the question of whether bilinguals process information in their two languages independently or interdependently—the findings not being related to any particular bilingual typology.

The above findings are important for discussion later in this report that addresses whether the linguistic outcomes of different types of education programs might result in qualitatively different types of individual bilinguals. They suggest, by and large, that bilingualism attained through different conditions of exposure will not be different in its fundamental cognitive organization.

Social Level

Typologies of bilingualism based on societal variables have focused mainly on the prestige and status of the languages involved. Fishman et al. (1966) draw a distinction between "folk" and "elite" bilingualism, referring to the social status of the bilingual group. The "folk" are immigrants and linguistic minorities who exist within the milieu of a dominant language and whose own language is not held in high esteem within the society. The "elite" are those who speak the dominant language and whose societal status is enhanced through the mastery of additional languages. As Fishman observes, "Many Americans have long been of the opinion that bilingualism is 'a good thing' if it was acquired via travel (preferably to Paris) or via formal education (preferably at Harvard) but that it is a 'bad thing' if it was acquired from one's immigrant parents or grandparents" (pp. 122-123).

Similarly, Lambert (1975) distinguishes "additive" from "subtractive" bilingualism. This distinction focuses on the effect of learning a second language on the retention of the native language. In additive bilingualism, the native language is secure, and the second language serves as an enrichment. Canadian French immersion programs for the English-speaking majority are a prime example of additive bilingualism. In subtractive bilingualism, the native language is less robust; society assumes that it will be used only temporarily until replaced by the dominant language as the group assimilates. Most immigrants to the United States, Canada, and Australia experience this latter form of bilingualism.

These broader social distinctions can help us understand how differences in individual-level bilingualism relate to cultural setting. As macro-level descriptions, they are difficult to test, but they help explain why programs that seem quite similar can have such divergent effects in different social settings—for example, why an immersion program in Canada succeeds in teaching French to English-speaking students who continue to maintain full proficiency in English and to function at a high academic level, while an immersion program to teach English to Spanish-speaking immigrants in the United States often results in both a shift to monolingualism in English and academic failure. (Immersion programs in both cases are sensitive to the fact that the students are all non-native speakers of the language; however, they differ considerably with respect to the populations they serve and their ultimate goals regarding the development of the native language.)

Consequences of Bilingualism

A commonly expressed fear about childhood bilingualism is that it could confuse the child, both linguistically and cognitively. This fear is rooted in an extensive literature on intelligence testing from the early 1900s (see Diaz, 1983, for a review), when psychometricians compared the performance of bilingual immigrant children and U.S.-born children on various measures of intelligence and found that the monolinguals outperformed the bilinguals. Two explanations for this discrepancy were offered: that the bilinguals (who at that time were predominantly from southern and eastern European countries) were genetically inferior to the western European monolinguals, or that the attempt to learn two languages caused mental confusion. This narrowly construed set of negative interpretations was captured well by noted psychologist Goodenough (1926). Observing a highly negative correlation between the extent to which different language groups used their native language in the home and the mean IQ scores for these groups, she concluded: "This might be considered evidence that the use of a foreign language in the home is one of the chief factors producing mental retardation as measured by intelligence tests. A more probable explanation is that those nationality groups whose average intellectual ability is inferior do not readily learn the new language" (p. 393).

The above literature has been largely discredited because of its failure to control for important variables, such as socioeconomic status, as well as the criteria used to select the bilingual samples (some studies, for example, used the students' last names as the basis for deciding whether they were bilingual). When such factors were controlled for, the results were reversed in favor of bilinguals. Indeed, Peal and Lambert (1962), widely credited for introducing important controls in monolingual-bilingual comparisons, describe a bilingual child as "a youngster whose wider experiences in two cultures have given him advantages which a monolingual does not enjoy. Intellectually his experience with two language systems seems to have left him with a mental flexibility, a superiority in concept formation, a more diversified set of mental abilities" (p. 20). Peal and Lambert's study gave rise to a large number of studies that selected bilinguals on a more considered basis. Generally, the results of these studies showed the bilingual groups to be superior on a variety of measures of cognitive skill, in particular, metalinguistic abilities (see Reynolds, 1991, for a review). Much research in this tradition employs between-group comparisons. To control for confounding factors in such comparisons, other studies have used within-group variation in the degree of bilingualism and looked at the predictive value of this variation for cognitive outcomes (Duncan and DeAvila, 1979; Galambos and Hakuta, 1988; Hakuta, 1987). Such studies continue to show positive relationships between degree of bilingualism and outcome measures.

Another tradition of research comes from case studies of individual children exposed to two languages at home. The earliest among these can be credited to the French linguist Ronjat (1913), but the seminal work even to this date is by Werner Leopold, who published a four-volume study of his German-English bilingual daughter Hildegard (1939, 1947, 1949a, 1949b). Ronjat's and Leopold's detailed studies of their own children gave rise to a rich tradition of linguists following their children around with notebooks (and later, tape recorders and video recorders). This literature has been reviewed most recently by Romaine (1995). Generally, the studies suggest that children can become productive bilinguals in a variety of language-use settings, though exposure to a language for less than 20 hours a week does not seem sufficient for a child to produce words in that language, at least up to age 3 (Pearson et al., in press). Very few cases of what might be considered language confusion are reported.

Linguistic Aspects of Second-Language Acquisition

The theoretical and empirical work in second-language acquisition serves as the basis for defining what one means by "proficiency" in a second language. Some researchers have defined it narrowly around the control of grammatical rules, others around the ability to use language in accomplishing cognitive tasks, and still others around the social and communicative aspects of language. This section describes how such broad definitions of language have influenced work on second-language acquisition. The theoretical assumptions underlying the construct of language proficiency have direct implications for the assessment of language proficiency, a topic addressed in Chapter 5.

Much of the research on second-language acquisition borrows heavily from the dominant paradigm in first-language acquisition, and thus has focused on the problem of how linguistic structures are acquired. Many studies, for example, have examined the acquisition of morphological and syntactic features of language that are fully in place in native speakers by the age of 5 or 6. Among these features are the grammatical aspects of language identified by Brown (1973) in his classic study of Adam, Eve, and Sarah, called Stage I through V speech; they include function words, sentence modalities, sentence embedding, and sentence coordination.

One important characterization of research on second-language acquisition relates to the researcher's definition of language. A narrow definition comes from formal linguistics, in particular from Chomsky's (1965) characterization of the logical problem of first-language acquisition as resolved by a "Language Acquisition Device" that enables the learner to derive abstract linguistic knowledge from limited linguistic input. By showing the end-state knowledge to be deep and abstract and demonstrating that this knowledge is not accessible through induction (i.e., observation of "surface data") or extrapolation from more general cognitive principles, one arrives at the logical conclusion that linguistic knowledge must be innate and highly specific to the task of language acquisition. This approach is typically taken by researchers with a background in formal linguistics (e.g., White, 1989; Schachter, 1990) or psychologists who subscribe strongly to linguistic nativism (e.g., Pinker, 1994). A broader view, typically taken by cognitive psychologists such as Bates (1976), Bialystok (Bialystok and Hakuta, 1994), and McLaughlin (1985), defines language to include vocabulary as well as pragmatic and communicative skills, aspects of language that are not considered by formal linguistics, and seeks explanations for language acquisition in general principles of learning and cognition. An even broader view emphasizes the social and interpersonal aspects of language and suggests that these aspects constrain language acquisition. Subscribers to this view include anthropologists (e.g., Gumperz, 1982) and sociolinguists (e.g., Preston, 1989). A view that combines the latter two perspectives is found in the literature on communicative, as opposed to linguistic, competence (Harley et al., 1990).

The literature generated by the above questions might be characterized as follows: each position has managed to find a domain of inquiry that legitimizes it, but the relationship among the various positions is far from specified. Thus, research in Universal Grammar (a formal linguistics perspective) has shown that even adults display the ability to learn aspects of language that are abstract and presumably unlearnable from general cognitive or social principles (Epstein et al., in press). This would suggest that a complete theory of second-language acquisition must account for induction of abstract rules from inadequate surface data. Research by those taking the cognitive and functionalist position has shown that on sentence processing tasks, second-language learners are sensitive to cognitively salient factors, such as the animacy of the subject of a sentence (in English, most subjects of sentences tend to be animate rather than inanimate). Thus, this view would argue that second-language learning can be regarded as a cognitive accomplishment. Those with a socioliguistic orientation, on the other hand, have pointed to examples where social variables affect language use and structure, that is, where socially useful phrases are learned first (e.g., Hatch, 1978), and bilinguals learn rules for code switching (e.g., Zentella, 1981) and for adjusting their language use to social circumstances (e.g., Bayley, 1991; Preston, 1989).

Thus we must conclude that second-language acquisition is a complex process requiring a diverse set of explanatory factors (Bialystok and Hakuta, 1994). Developing an inclusive theory of how a second language is acquired therefore necessitates moving beyond the description of plausible acquisition mechanisms for specific domains to an explanation of how those mechanisms work together to produce the integrated knowledge of a language that enables its use for communication.

A second important dimension of second-language acquisition is the extent of involvement of the native language in the acquisition process. Are native speakers of Spanish different from native speakers of Vietnamese in their acquisition of English? In the early 1960s, the answer would have been a definitive "yes," based on contrastive analysis theory (Lado, 1964). The 1970s saw an almost total rejection of the contrastive analysis approach and emergence of the view that second-language acquisition is accomplished through direct access to the language acquisition device, without mediation by the native language. This change was supported empirically by studies that examined the types of errors made by second-language learners and found that many errors could not be attributed to language transfer, and that many errors predicted by a simple transfer theory were absent. Also, a number of studies focusing on the acquisition of English morphology by learners from different language backgrounds demonstrated remarkable similarities in order of acquisition—suggesting that the target language has more effect than the first language on the course of acquisition (Bailey et al., 1974). The paradigm shift away from a focus on transfer was marked by the emergence of the notion of "interlanguage" (Selinker, 1972), conceived of as a linguistic system unique to each learner who has not yet achieved full competence in the second language.

Nonetheless, language transfer errors are frequent and have continued to fascinate researchers (Bialystok and Hakuta, 1994; Odlin, 1989). Even within the Chomsky-inspired Universal Grammar framework, language transfer, interpreted as "maintenance of first-language parameter settings," has gained momentum as an area of research. Finally, there is some interest in the possibility that language transfer would be more evident in the quantitative (speed of acquisition) rather than qualitative (e.g., types of errors and patterns of acquisition) aspects of second-language acquisition (Odlin, 1989), that is, that it takes longer to learn a language that is typologically very different from the native language than one that is relatively similar. For example, it would be easier for a native English speaker to learn French than Chinese.

A third dimension of importance is the age and concomitant cognitive skills of the second-language learner. The dominant first-language acquisition research paradigms equated first- and second-language learners, thus minimizing attention to those aspects of second-language acquisition that are unique to the more cognitively developed learner. In the early literature, for example, Hakuta (1976) noted that Uguisu, a 5-year old Japanese girl learning English, used connectives (*and, but, because,* etc.) much earlier in her English development than first-language learners do, and furthermore that she was less constrained by memory factors than first-language learners. Lightbown (1977) similarly attested to a lack of semantic constraints among second-language learners, presumably owing to their more advanced cognitive level. Such observations help explain why older children acquire a second language so much more quickly than younger children (e.g., Snow and Hoefnagel-Höhle, 1978).

Older language learners need to learn more complex linguistic structures in order to respond age-appropriately to the tasks for which they must use their second language. Snow (1987) suggests that older learners are more often faced with tasks in which various sorts of contextual support (e.g., helpful conversational partners, practice in talk about the topic) are unavailable. For example, adolescent immigrants in a submersion situation where they have no help in understanding the non-native language must produce language performances about complex and/or abstract topics with no conversational support at a much earlier stage of acquisition than preschool-aged immigrants. Furthermore, Snow's findings suggest that performance on highly supported or conversational tasks will not necessarily predict performance on less contextualized tasks. In one study of bilingual children, she showed that within either language, performance on contextualized tasks (such as face-to-face communication) was poorly related to that on less contextualized tasks (such as defining the meaning of a word) (Snow, 1987, 1990). Experience on a particular type of task within a specific language was more important than overall language proficiency in predicting performance on that task (see also Malakoff, 1988).

Cummins (1979, 1991) proposes a related task analysis that distinguishes two dimensions—degree of contextual support and degree of cognitive challenge. He argues that for a second-language speaker, performance on more conversationally supported and less challenging tasks (e.g., a chat with the English as a second language [ESL] teacher) will not predict performance on more challenging and autonomous tasks, test taking in particular, since the conversational abilities emerge first (Cummins and Swain, 1986). While both Cummins and Snow agree that language task analysis is crucial to prediction of academic performance from language proficiency, they disagree about whether second-language learning necessarily starts with conversational skills; in fact, a frequent feature of immigrant bilingualism is that seemingly more difficult tasks may be performed better in the second than in the first language. These views of language share the important claim that academic language is different from language use in other contexts, a claim related to an underlying view of language as an ability with many components, rather than a single accomplishment that cannot be analyzed. Both suggest that second-language abilities should be assessed in relation to the uses of language the learner will require, rather than in isolation as an abstract competence.

Individual Differences in Second-Language Acquisition

The most striking fact about second-language learning, especially as compared with first-language learning, is the variability in outcomes. Many individual and group variables have been examined in attempts to explain success or failure in second-language acquisition. This section reviews the literature on various individual differences in second-language acquisition. In looking at this literature, it is important to appreciate that the definition of the outcome of the second-language acquisition process has itself been variable, as discussed in the previous section (see also Chapter 5 on student assessment).

Age of Learning

One frequently cited factor is the age of the learner, with the assumption that younger learners acquire a second language more quickly and with a higher level of proficiency. Periodic reviews of this literature (Bialystok and Hakuta, 1994; Collier, 1987; Epstein et al., 1996; Harley and Wang, in press; Krashen et al., 1982; Long, 1990; Snow, 1987) have not supported this claim very well. Even though there is a critical period in the learning of a first language, this does not imply there is one for second-language learning. The following observations might be made:

- More mature learners generally make faster initial progress in acquiring morphological, syntactic, and lexical aspects of a second language.
- An increasing age of onset for second-language acquisition is correlated with declining ultimate attainment in the control of phonological, morphological, and syntactic aspects of language across age groups, beginning typically by age 6-7 in childhood and continuing into adulthood. In adult learners, this association between onset age and declining outcomes is most strongly manifested in oral aspects of second-language proficiency (maintenance of an accent).
- Some adult learners are nonetheless capable of near-native, if not native-like, performance in a second language, while some children are unsuccessful in achieving native-like performance.
- There is a general lack of evidence that acquisition processes differ across age groups, i.e., that radically different types of errors are made or that there is a different sequence to the acquisition of structures for learners of different ages (Harley and Wang, in press).

Many researchers have assumed that the best explanation for the age-related decline in oral ability with a second language is a biological one, based on a critical or sensitive period in brain development (Johnson and Newport, 1989, 1991; Oyama, 1976; Patkowski, 1980). However, the behavioral evidence is not consistent with evidence about periods of brain growth, and serious methodological problems have dogged even the most sound of existing studies (see Snow's 1987 review of critical period theory, and Bialystok and Hakuta's 1994 review of Johnson and Newport's study). For example, proficiency assessments often focus on tasks such as judgments about grammatical or morphological correctness—matters in which younger learners have likely received formal instruction. Also, younger immigrants are typically younger at testing; younger subjects have an advantage in any test that involves auditory attention. Studies in which the conditions of acquisition were as comparable as possible for younger and older learners (e.g., Genesee's 1981 study of early- versus late-immersion students) are less likely to show poorer ultimate performance for older learners.

Studies of age as a factor in the acquisition of English appropriate for academic use are consistent with the studies cited above in that children who start learning English in kindergarten in English-only educational settings take longer to achieve age-appropriate levels of performance on academic tasks than children who start in grades 2 through 6 (Collier, 1987). This age difference may simply reflect the general finding that initial acquisition is faster for older learners with more cognitive skills, but it has also been interpreted as supporting the claim that second-language acquisition is faster and easier if continued development in the first language is supported through mastery of the basic grammar in the first language, around age 6. Cummins (1979) has interpreted such findings as validating the importance of continued development of first-language grammar, although other researchers disagree (Rossell and Baker, 1996; Porter, 1990).

Intelligence

Another factor in second-language acquisition may be general intelligence. This factor has been addressed mainly in the arena of foreign-language learning in the classroom (Carroll, 1986; Gardner, 1983; Oller, 1981). For immigrant learners and those in immersion settings, second-language learning is evidently not impeded by learning disabilities or low intelligence to the extent it would be in formal learning settings (Bruck, 1982, 1984; see Genesee, 1992, for a review). In the field of bilingual education, second-language acquisition has not been tied to questions of general aptitude, although educational practitioners commonly observe that second-language acquisition is easier for students with a history of formal education and higher socioeconomic backgrounds. Furthermore, correlational studies that examine relative proficiencies in the two languages of bilingual children show that native-language proficiency is a strong predictor of second-language development (Cummins, 1984; Hakuta, 1987).

It should be noted that assessing the intelligence of second-language learners is a risky process. Whenever possible, such assessments should be conducted in the native language—though if the assessment is closely tied to school tasks, the child may display better performance in the school language. Koopmans (1991) showed that native Spanish-speaking third to fifth graders in bilingual programs—children who had lived in the United States an average of 11 years—performed better in Spanish on a logical reasoning task of a type rarely encountered in either home or classroom discourse. Malakoff (1988), on the other hand, showed that children at an international school performed better in the curricular than the home language on an analogies task, even at a very low level of general skill in the curricular language.

Attitudes

Studies investigating the predictive power of language attitudes and motivation for second-language acquisition have been limited, by and large, to students who study a foreign language that is generally used only in the classroom (Gardner and Lambert, 1972). Such studies have shown that a positive attitude and motivation are significant factors in predicting oral communicative skills in a second language, whereas language aptitude predicts proficiency in knowledge of grammar and vocabulary. It is therefore clear that attitude and motivation are important factors in second-language learning in some contexts. Yet the few studies that have looked at the importance of these factors in the acquisition of English among immigrants to the United States have had largely negative findings. For example, Hakuta and D'Andrea (1992) studied Mexican-American attitudes toward English and Spanish and administered tests of English and Spanish proficiency. Attitude had no predictive power for English proficiency, whereas a positive attitude toward Spanish predicted whether students continued to use that language as part of their sociolinguistic repertoire. In sociolinguistic settings such as the United States, it is likely that any variation in the attitudes of immigrant populations toward English will be largely overridden by the overwhelming importance of English to getting ahead in the society.

Personality

Many studies have attempted to isolate factors related to individual predisposition, over and above basic intelligence, toward second-language acquisition. Most of this work is focused on learning a foreign language rather than on learning a language in the society where it is used. A review of this literature shows a serious failure to address issues of construct validity (Bialystok and Hakuta, 1994). Given the inordinate difficulty of validly measuring personality constructs cross-culturally, this is probably not a very fruitful area for future research, although it will continue to be a source of speculation because of its intrinsic interest.

Language Shift

Language shift refers to the sociolinguistic phenomenon in which an ethnic group gradually moves its preference and use of language from its original ethnic language to the sociologically dominant language. Attempts to explain language shift range from macro-level population perspectives to micro-level analyses of language change within individual members of those communities.

Demographers and sociologists have tried to identify determinants of the vitality or imminent death of ethnic languages. Fishman et al. (1966) using an impressive variety of sources on language vitality in the United States, found rapid decline between 1940 and 1960 in the numbers of speakers of different languages. The only factor that consistently contributed to increasing those numbers was new immigration. In comparing data on language diversity in 35 nations, Lieberson et al. (1975) found that the amount of language loss occurring in the United States in a single generation would have taken about 350 years in other nations investigated. Analyzing data from the Survey on Income and Education, Veltman (1983, 1988) also found a consistent picture of rapid language shift in the United States. Most remarkably, even Spanish, the language for which geographical proximity and numbers of speakers favor maintenance, shows rapid loss, leading Veltman to conclude that in the absence of new immigration, the Spanish language will undergo rapid decline and extinction in the United States.

The shift from non-English to English that occurs may be both *intra-individual* and *intergenerational* in nature. That is, during the course of their lifetime, individuals shift their primary language preference from their native language to English, and ethnolinguistic communities in successive generations will likewise shift their linguistic preference. Ethnographic studies, as well as large-scale demographic information (Fishman et al., 1966; Lopez, 1978; Veltman, 1983), suggest that bilinguals in the United States show a strong preference for English in many conversational situations and that this preference is translated into a monolingual English upbringing for their offspring. In addition, though, consistent choice of English can lead to increased proficiency in English and decreased proficiency in the native language, even for an adult speaker (Seliger and Vago, 1991).

Studies of children provide evidence that there can be intra-individual loss of skills in the native language as gauged through academic achievement measures (Laosa, 1995; Merino, 1983), and cases of total loss of a first or dominant language by young children who do not persist in using it regularly are frequent (e.g., Burling, 1959). Every bilingual can document decreased ease and fluency in a long-neglected language, particularly with regard to vocabulary and complex grammar (e.g., Grosjean, 1982). However, studies that look at basic language proficiency identify highly robust aspects of the native-language grammar for students who have had the opportunity to develop the native language at home

(Hakuta and D'Andrea, 1992; Hakuta and Pease-Alvarez, 1994), with the clearest evidence of shift occurring in the domain of language choice, not proficiency. It is less clear what happens to children who are exposed to English and become dominant in it before their native language is fully established. Parental reports based on an informal sample suggest the native language can be stunted or lost (Wong Fillmore, 1991).

An understanding of basic questions about language maintenance and shift could well provide input needed to address practical issues such as the degree to which heritage languages can serve as a reservoir of bilingualism for the United States, the kinds of language instruction that would be useful to second-genera-tion minority language speakers, and whether there are risks associated with the loss of familial languages by young children.

Educational Conditions for Second-Language Learning

Often, interactions with peers and teachers provide the primary source of input to child second-language learners. For some children, this experience begins in preschool and child care environments; for all others, their first real exposure to English is in kindergarten. The nature of these linguistic environ-ments and their possible influences on English acquisition or on native-language maintenance or development have typically not been the focus of the basic re-search studies described thus far in this chapter. However, as theories of second-language acquisition have expanded to incorporate the social conditions under which learning takes place, there has been increased interest—over and above the concerns of program evaluation—in understanding the linguistic environment of the classroom setting and how it might relate to linguistic outcomes.

Some researchers have examined classrooms in trying to understand the opportunities they provide (or fail to provide) for students to contribute to con-versational exchanges involving their fellow students, as well as their teachers (e.g., Ellis, 1984). Proper accounting of what goes on linguistically in the class-room is important for a number of reasons. For example, such work would begin clarifying what might be meant by comprehensible input, a notion widely used by second-language acquisition researchers (Krashen, 1982; Long, 1983; Pica, 1987). The relevant classroom features include adjustments similar to those parents make when talking with young children, such as organizing talk around visible referents, using simple syntax, producing many repetitions and paraphrases, speaking slowly and clearly, checking often for comprehension, and expanding on and extending topics introduced by the learner. While researchers have exam-ined recurring features of classroom interaction hypothesized to be relevant to students' development of language (see van Lier, 1988), few studies have tried to link classroom communication and the learning of linguistic features, and those that have done so have not been successful (Ellis, 1995).

Other researchers have begun to offer detailed pictures of the relative uses of the student's two languages in elementary-grade bilingual classrooms (e.g., Enright, 1982; Milk, 1990; Shultz, 1975). Although these studies generally do not report outcome data with respect to English acquisition or native-language development, they have shown that English tends to predominate in terms of messages conveyed and frequency of use. For example, in her ethnographic study of mathematics teaching in five bilingual classrooms, Khisty (1995) found that teachers tended to use the students' native language, Spanish, as an "instrument to discipline, to call students' attention to the subject of the lesson, or to punctuate a statement" (p. 288). When providing mathematical explanations, teachers tended to revert to English, using only a scattering of Spanish words. However, Khisty found that these same teachers used Spanish consistently during reading and language arts instruction. Research on whether these conditions of use contribute optimally to the acquisition of English and/or maintenance of Spanish remains to be done.

A concern for documenting and understanding the factors that contribute to the diminished role of native languages in schools and classrooms has also framed classroom studies conducted in bilingual settings. Ethnographic research investigating bilingual programs has shown how social, cultural, and even political conditions may mediate the language-development goal and outcomes of the programs. For example, Pease-Alvarez and Winsler (1994) found that attitudes and beliefs favoring Spanish operate relatively independently from patterns of language choice in some classroom settings. Several other studies have shown how difficult it is to achieve the goal of dual language development and native-language maintenance in societies where assimilation toward the dominant group is the prevailing ideology. For example, Escamilla (1994) found that school-wide practices (e.g., language choice among faculty members and the language used for public displays and presentations in the school) contrasted with the school's official commitment to the development and support of both languages. Similarly, McCollum (1993) found that in a middle school two-way bilingual program, Spanish-background students used primarily English at school by choice. She interpreted her findings in terms of "cultural capital," arguing that students perceived English, not Spanish, as the language of power and responded accordingly.

Other studies have looked more generally at the effects of English-only and bilingual school environments on the overall language and cognitive development of English-language learners. Paul and Jarvis (1992), for example, compared English-language learners in bilingual and monolingual prekindergarten classrooms, and found positive outcomes for the children in the former classrooms on a criterion-referenced test, the Chicago Early Assessment and Remediation Laboratory (EARLY). An evaluation study of the Carpinteria Preschool Program, in which classroom activities were carried out exclusively in Spanish, shows similarly positive effects of first-language use on second-language acquisition (Campos, 1995). Even though their preschool program was conducted entirely in Spanish, by first grade almost half of the Carpinteria children were at level 5 (fluent English) on the Bilingual Syntax Measure, as compared with fewer than 10 percent of English-language learners from day care and other programs. Campos concluded that "there was no evident delay in the rate of English acquisition by the Carpinteria Preschool students, and they demonstrated competency in applying their English language skills. When compared with the language-minority comparison preschool group, they acquired English language fluency faster, transitioned out of bilingual education classrooms sooner, and achieved in English language classrooms and on English language standardized tests better. Clearly, first language development in their preschool program did not interfere or delay their second language learning. Instead the results suggest that they were better prepared to understand and utilize opportunities in their learning environment" (p. 46). Further, the investigators reported that these students had apparently maintained their bilingual skills and that almost all were expected to graduate from high school.

Such studies point to the importance of understanding the linguistic environments of institutional settings that serve as the primary base for second-language acquisition. These environments are best thought of as both dependent variables that are outcomes of larger social and cultural processes and independent variables that affect the linguistic attainment of the children. A wide variety of methodologies must be brought to bear on this problem, ranging from interpretive, ethnographic studies on the social and cultural ecology within which such programs exist, to more hypothesis-testing approaches that look at specific relationships between the linguistic environments and the linguistic attainments of English-language learners.

It is critically important to understand preschool environments for two major reasons. First, during the preschool years, language development itself is a major outcome of interest. The few studies reviewed suggest that the development of the native language and of English are interdependent, but additional work is needed in this area, particularly because the issue of native-language development through these programs promises to be just as controversial as what we have witnessed in the K-12 programs to date. Second, there are increasing calls for the expansion of high-quality preschool opportunities for all children (e.g., Carnegie Corporation, 1996). A critical ingredient in defining quality is the linguistic environment of these programs. This represents a window of opportunity where research can make a difference for a large number of programs and children.

RESEARCH NEEDS

2-1. Research is needed on the factors that account for variation in second-language acquisition. Variability in the degree of English acquisition can be attributable to variation in individual and group characteristics. More work is needed in particular on the latter factors.

Research on individual factors in second-language acquisition, including age of the learner, intelligence, and attitudes and motivation, has already yielded many answers. On the other hand, less is known about group effects, such as whether some groups of immigrants are more likely to acquire English rapidly or to higher levels than others, or whether certain sociolinguistic or educational conditions lead to more rapid acquisition of English than others. There has been insufficient research systematically relating rich information about the settings for learning English—such as how much direct instruction is provided, the order in which structures are taught, and the use of written versus oral modes for provision of input—to information about the rate and process of acquisition for individual learners. Furthermore, the individual factors that have been investigated may interact with group effects in ways that can yield new theoretical insights.

2-2. An important contribution to understanding variability in second-language acquisition would be an enhanced understanding of the components of English proficiency and how these components interact. Also important is the question of how proficiencies in the two languages of bilinguals are inter-related.

The above questions have a direct bearing on the appropriate assessment of English-language proficiency with respect to socially and academically valued outcomes (see also Chapter 5).

2-3. Assessment of second-language learners should involve analysis of unstructured, spontaneous speech in addition to more structured instruments. An important research goal is thus to create a common pool of spontaneous speech data for use by researchers.

The analysis of spontaneous speech could become systematized and routinely incorporated into the research culture if data sets were made widely available through the Internet. Such a system already exists in the field of child first-language acquisition through the Child Language Data Exchange System (MacWhinney, 1991). Expansion of this system to include data on second-language acquisition and bilingual children would greatly increase the vitality and productivity of the field.

2-4. It is essential to understand the interaction between language and other domains of human functioning.

Research reviewed here on the consequences of bilingualism has concluded that there are no negative consequences of learning two languages in childhood and that there are some positive correlations between bilingualism and general cognitive ability. This research should move beyond seeking macro-level effects and begin looking for more detailed and specific relationships between linguistic representations on the one hand and cognitive and social representations on the other. This recommendation is revisited in the discussion of content area learning and the recommendations in Chapter 3.

2-5. Macro-level questions about language shift in the United States have amply demonstrated the short-lived nature of non-English languages. Research is needed to help in understanding the dynamics of language shift.

Such research would include examining how messages concerning the value of native languages are conveyed, how children and youth understand such messages, what the effects are on the children's identities and their school achievement, and what the likelihood is of maintaining the native language while learning English. We need also to develop a more specific understanding of what is meant by language attrition, such as the relationship between language choice (choosing not to use one's native language) and the loss of language proficiency. Moreover, compared with current knowledge on the types of educational services provided to English-language learners to meet their needs in English, there is very little systematic information available on language programs for native-language development (such as courses in Spanish for Spanish speakers that are available in some high schools and universities). Finally, large-scale survey research is needed to determine Americans' attitudes toward both languages other than English and their speakers, and whether those attitudes are shared by the minority language speakers themselves.

REFERENCES

Baetens-Beardsmore, H.
1986   *Bilingualism: Basic Principles.* 2nd ed. Clevedon, England: Tieto.

Bailey, N., C. Madden, and S.D. Krashen
1974   Is there a "natural sequence" in adult second language learning? *Language Learning* 24:235-243.

Bates, E.
1976   *Language and Context.* New York: Academic Press.

Bayley, R.J.
1991   Variation Theory and Second Language Learning. Unpublished Ph.D. Dissertation, School of Education, Stanford University.

Bialystok, E., and K. Hakuta
1994   *In Other Words.* New York: Basic Books.

Brown, R.
1973   *A First Language: The Early Stages.* Cambridge, MA: Harvard University Press.

Bruck, M.
1982   Language-disabled children performance in additive bilingual education programs. *Applied Psycholinguistics* 3:45-60.

1984   Feasibility of an additive bilingual program for the language impaired child. In Y. LeBrun and M. Paradis, eds., *Early Bilingualism and Child Development.* Amsterdam: Swets and Zeitlinger.

Burling, R.
1959   The language development of a Garo and English speaking child. *Word* 15:45-68.

Campos, S.J.
1995   The Carpinteria Preschool Program: A long-term effects study. In E. Garcia and B. McLaughlin, eds., *Meeting the Challenge of Linguistic and Cultural Diversity in Early Childhood Education.* New York: Teacher's College.

Carnegie Corporation
1996   *Years of Promise. A Comprehensive Learning Strategy for America's Children.* New York: Carnegie Corporation.

Carroll, John B.
1986   Second language. Pp. 83-125 in R.F. Dillon and R.J. Sternbery, eds., *Cognition and Instruction.* Orlando, FL: Academic Press.

Chomsky, N.
1965   *Aspects of the Theory of Syntax.* Cambridge, MA: MIT Press.

Collier, Virginia P.
1987   Age and rate acquisition of second language for academic purposes. *TESOL Quarterly* 21(4):617-641.

Cummins, J.
1979   Cognitive/academic language proficiency, linguistic interdependence, the optimum age question and some other matters. *Working Papers on Bilingualism* 19:197-205.

1984   *Bilingualism and Special Education.* San Diego, CA: College Hill Press.

1991   Language development and academic learning. Pp. 161-75 in L.M. Malavé and G. Duquette, eds., *Language, Culture and Cognition.* Clevedon, England: Multilingual Matters.

Cummins, J., and M. Swain
1986   *Bilingualism in Education.* New York: Longman.

Diaz, R.M.
1983   Thought and two languages: The impact of bilingualism on cognitive development. *Review of Research in Education* 10:23-54.

Duncan, S., and E. DeAvila
  1979   Bilingualism and cognition: Some recent findings. *NABE Journal* 4:15-50.
Ellis, Nick C.
  1995   Psychology of foreign language vocabulary acquisition: Implications for CALL. *Computer Assisted Language Learning* 8(2):103-128.
Ellis, Rod
  1984   Communication strategies and the evaluation of communicative performance. *ELT Journal* 38(1):39-44.
Enright, Brian E.
  1982   Criterion-referenced Tests: A Guide to Separate Useful from Useless. Paper presented at the Annual International Convention of the Council for Exceptional Children, Houston, TX, April 11-16; Session T-27. University of North Carolina at Charlotte.
Epstein, S.D., D. Flynn, and G. Martohardjono
  1996   Second language acquisition: Theoretical and experimental issues in contemporary research. *Behavior and Brain Sciences* 19(4):677-758.
Escamilla, Kathy
  1994   The sociolinguistic environment of a bilingual school: A case study introduction. *Bilingual Research Journal* 18(1-2):21-47.
Fishman, J.A.
  1978   *Advances in the Study of Societal Multilingualism.* The Hague, The Netherlands, and New York: Mouton.
Fishman, J.A., V. Nahirny, J. Hofman, and R. Hayden
  1966   *Language Loyalty in the United States: The Maintenance and Perpetuation of Non-English Mother Tongues by American Ethnic and Religious Groups.* The Hague: Mouton.
Galambos, Sylvia Joseph, and Kenji Hakuta
  1988   Subject-specific and task-specific characteristics of metalinguistic awareness in bilingual children. *Applied Psycholinguistics* 9(2):141-62.
Gardner, R.C.
  1983   Learning another language: A true social psychological experiment. *Journal of Language and Social Psychology* 2:219-239.
  1985   *Social Psychology and Second Language Learning: The Role of Attitudes and Motivation.* London, England, and Baltimore, MD: E. Arnold.
Gardner, R.C., and W.C. Lambert
  1972   *Attitudes and Motivation in Second Language Learning.* Rowley, MA: Newbury House.
Gardner, R.C., R.N. Lalonde, and J. MacPherson
  1985   Social factors in second language attrition. *Language Learning* 5:519-540.
Genesee, F., J. Hamers, W.Lambert, L. Mononen, M. Seitz, and R. Starck
  1978   Language processing in bilinguals. *Brain and Language* 5:1-12.
Genesse, F.
  1981   A comparison of early and late second language learning. *Canadian Journal of Behavioral Sciences* 13:115-128.
  1992   Second/foreign language immersion and at-risk English-speaking children. *Foreign Language Annals* 25:199-213.
Goodenough, F.
  1926   Racial differences in the intelligence of school children. *Journal of Experimental Psychology* 9:388-397.
Grosjean, F.
  1982   *Life with Two Languages.* Cambridge, MA: Harvard University Press.
Gumperz, J.
  1982   *Discourse Strategies.* Cambridge, England: Cambridge University Press.

Hakuta, K.
  1976   A case study of a Japanese child learning English. *Language Learning* 26:321-351.
  1986   *Mirror of Language: The Debate on Bilingualism.* New York: Basic Books.
  1987   Degree of bilingualism and cognitive ability in mainland Puerto Rican children. *Child Development* 58(5):1372-1388.
Hakuta, K., and D. D'Andrea
  1992   Some properties of bilingual maintenance and loss in Mexican background high-school students. *Applied Linguistics* 13(1):72-99.
Hakuta, K., and L. Pease-Alvarez
  1994   Proficiency, choice and attitudes in Bilingual Mexican-American children. Pp. 145-164 in G. Extra and L. Verhoeven, eds., *The Cross-Linguistic Study of Bilingual Development.* Amsterdam: Netherlands Academy of Arts and Sciences.
Hamers, J., and M. Blanc
  1989   *Bilingualism and Bilinguality.* Cambridge, England, and New York: Cambridge University Press.
Harley, B., and W. Wang
  in   The critical period hypothesis: Where are we now? In A.M.B. de Groot and J.F. Kroll,
  press   eds., *Tutorials in Bilingualism: Psycholinguistic Perspectives.* Hillsdale, NJ: Erlbaum.
Harley, B., J. Cummins, and M. Swain
  1990   *The Development of Second Language Proficiency.* Cambridge, England, and New York: Cambridge University Press.
Hatch, E.
  1978   Discourse analysis and second language acquisition. In E. Hatch, ed., *Second Language Acquisition: A Book of Readings.* Rowley, MA: Newbury House.
Johnson, J. S., and E. L. Newport
  1989   Critical period effects in second-language learning: The influence of maturational state on the acquisition of English as a second language. *Cognitive Psychology* 21:60-99.
  1991   Critical period effects on universal properties of language: The status of subjacency in the acquisition of a second language. *Cognition* 39:215-258.
Khisty, Lena Licón
  1995   Making inequality: Issues of language and meanings in mathematics teaching with Hispanic students. Pp. 279-297 in W.G. Secada, E. Fennema, and L.B. Adajian, eds., *New Directions for Equity in Mathematics Education.* New York: Cambridge University Press.
Klein, W.
  1986   *Second Language Acquisition.* Cambridge, England: Cambridge University Press.
Koopmans, Matthijs.
  1991   Reasoning in two languages: An assessment of the reasoning ability of Puerto Rican elementary school children. *Linguistics and Education* 3:345-358.
Krashen, S.
  1982   *Principles and Practice in Second Language Acquisition.* Oxford: Pergamon.
Krashen, S., R. Scarcella, and M. Long, eds.
  1982   *Child-Adult Differences in Second Language Acquisition.* Rowley, MA: Newbury House.
Lado, Robert
  1964   *Language Teaching, A Scientific Approach.* New York: McGraw Hill.
Lambert, W.E.
  1975   Culture and language as factors in learning and education. Pp. 55-83 in A. Wolfgang, ed., *Education of Immigrant Students.* Toronto: Ontario Institute for Studies in Education.
Lambert, W., J. Havelka, and D. Crosby
  1958   The influence of language-acquisition contexts on bilingualism. *Journal of Abnormal and Social Psychology* 66:239-243.

Laosa, L.M.
   1995   *Longitudinal Measurements of English-language Proficiency Acquisition by Children Who Migrate to the United States From Puerto Rico.* Princeton, NJ: Educational Testing Service.

Larsen, J., T. Fritsch, and S. Grava
   1974   A semantic priming test of bilingual language storage and compound vs. coordinate bilingual distinction with Latvian-English bilinguals. *Perceptual & Motor Skills* 79:459-466.

Larsen-Freeman, D., and M. Long
   1990   *An Introduction to Second Language Acquisition Research.* London, England, and New York: Longman.

Leopold, W.
   1939   *Speech Development of a Bilingual Child: A Linguist's Record. Vol. 1: Vocabulary Growth in the First Two Years.* Evanston, IL: Northwestern University.
   1947   *Speech Development of a Bilingual Child: A Linguist's Record. Vol. 2: Sound Learning in the First Two Years.* Evanston, IL: Northwestern University.
   1949a *Speech Development of a Bilingual Child: A Linguist's Record. Vol. 3: Grammar and General Problems in the First Two Years.* Evanston, IL: Northwestern University.
   1949b *Speech Development of a Bilingual Child: A Linguist's Record. Vol. 4: Diary From Age Two.* Evanston, IL: Northwestern University.

Lieberson, S., G. Dalto, and M. Johnston
   1975   The course of mother-tongue diversity in nations. *American Journal of Sociology* 81:34-61.

Lightbown, Patsy M.
   1977   French L2 learners: What they're talking about. *Language Learning* 27(2):371-381.

Long, Michael H.
   1983   Linguistic and conversational adjustments to non-native speakers. *Studies in Second Language Acquisition* 5(2):177-193.
   1990   The least a second language acquisition theory needs to explain. *TESOL Quarterly* 24(4):649-666.

Lopez, D.E.
   1978   Chicano language loyalty in an urban setting. *Sociology and Social Research* 62:267-278.

MacWhinney, B.
   1991   *The CHILDES Project: Tools for Analyzing Talk.* Hillsdale, NJ: Erlbaum.

Malakoff, Marguerite E.
   1988   The effect of language of instruction on reasoning in bilingual children. *Applied Psycholinguistics* 9(1):17-38.

McCollum, Pamela
   1993   Learning to Value English: Cultural Capital in a Two-Way Bilingual Program. Paper presented at the annual meeting AERA, Atlanta, GA. Mississippi State University.

McLaughlin, Barry
   1984   *Second-language Acquisition in Childhood: Volume 1, Preschool Children.* Hillsdale, NJ: Erlbaum.
   1985   *Second-language Acquisition in Childhood: Volume 2, Schoolage Children.* Hillsdale, NJ: Erlbaum.

Merino, B.J.
   1983   Language loss in bilingual Chicago children. *Journal of Applied Developmental Psychology* 4:277-294.

Milk, R.
   1990   Preparing ESL and bilingual teachers for changing roles: Immersion for teachers of LEP children. *TESOL Quarterly* 24(3):407-426.

Odlin, T.
  1989   *Language Transfer: Cross-linguistic Influence in Language Learning.* Cambridge: Cam-
          bridge University Press.
Oller, J.W., Jr.
  1981   Language as intelligence. *Language Learning* 31:465-492.
Oyama, S.
  1976   A sensitive period for the acquisition of a nonnative phonological system. *Journal of
          Psycholinguistic Research* 5:261-285.
Patkowski, M.
  1980   The sensitive period for the acquisition of syntax in a second language. *Language Learn-
          ing* 30:449-472.
Paul, B., and C. Jarvis
  1992   The effects of native language use in New York City pre-kindergarten classes. Paper
          presented at the 1992 Annual Meeting of the American Educational Research Associa-
          tion, San Francisco, CA. ERIC Document ED351874.
Peal, E., and W.E. Lambert
  1962   The relation of bilingualism to intelligence. *Psychological Monographs: General and
          Applied* 76(546):1-23.
Pearson, B., S. Fernández, V. Lewedeg, and D. Oller
  in   The relation of input factors to lexical learning by bilingual infants (ages 8 to 30 months).
  press   *Applied Psycholinguistics* (18).
Pease-Alvarez, Lucinda, and Adam Winsler
  1994   Cuando el maestro no habla espanol: Children's bilingual language practices in the
          classroom. *TESOL Quarterly* 28(3):507-535.
Pica, Teresa
  1987   Second-language acquisition, social interaction, and the classroom. *Applied Linguistics*
          8(1):3-21.
Pinker, S.
  1994   *The Language Instinct.* New York: Morrow.
Porter, R.P.
  1990   *Forked Tongue: The Politics of Bilingual Education.* New York: Basic Books.
Preston, D.R.
  1989   *Sociolinguistics and Second Language Acquisition.* New York: Basil Blackwell.
Reynolds, A.
  1991   *Bilingualism, Multiculturalism, and Second Language Learning.* Hillsdale, NJ: Erlbaum.
Romaine, J.
  1995   *Bilingualism.* 2nd ed. Oxford, England: Blackwell.
Ronjat, J.
  1913   *Le développement du langage observé chez un enfant bilingue.* Paris: Champion.
Rossell, Christine, and Keith Baker
  1996   The educational effectiveness of bilingual education. *Research in the Teaching of En-
          glish* 30(1):385-419.
Schachter, J.
  1990   On the issue of completeness in second language acquisition. *Second Language Research*
          6:93-124.
Seliger, H., and R. Vago, eds.
  1991   *First Language Attrition: Structural and Theoretical Perspectives.* Cambridge and New
          York: Cambridge University Press.
Selinker, L.
  1972   Interlanguage. *International Review of Applied Linguistics* 10:209-230.

Shultz, N.W., Jr.
1975   *On the autonomy and comparability of linguistic and ethnographic description.* Lisse, Netherlands: Peter de Ridder.

Snow, C.E.
1987   Relevance of the notion of a critical period to language acquisition. Pp. 183-209 in M. Bornstein, ed., *Sensitive Periods in Development.* Hillsdale, NJ: Erlbaum.
1990   The development of definitional skill. *Journal of Child Language* 17:697-710.

Snow, C.E., and M. Hoefnagel-Höhle
1978   The critical period for language acquisition. *Child Development* 4:1114-1128.

van Lier, L.
1988   *The Classroom and the Language Learner.* London, England: Longman.

Veltman, C.
1983   *Language Shift in the United States.* New York: Mouton.
1988   *The Future of the Spanish Language in the United States.* New York City and Washington, DC: Hispanic Policy Development Project.

Weinreich, U.
1953   *Languages in Contact.* The Hague: Mouton.

White, L.
1989   *Universal Grammar and Second Language Acquisition.* Philadelphia, PA: Benjamins.

Wong Fillmore, L.
1991   When learning a second language means losing the first. *Early Childhood Research Quarterly* 6(3):323-346.

Zentella, A.C.
1981   Language variety among Puerto Ricans. Pp. 218-238 in C.A. Ferguson and S.B. Heath, eds., *Language in the USA.* New York: Cambridge University Press.

COGNITIVE ASPECTS OF SCHOOL LEARNING: SUMMARY OF THE STATE OF KNOWLEDGE

Research to date on the cognitive aspects of how children acquire literacy and content area knowledge in school has yielded the following key insights:

• Future successful readers typically arrive at school with a set of prior experiences and well-established skills conducive to literacy, including an understanding of literacy, abstract knowledge of the sound and structure of language, a certain level of vocabulary development, and oral connected discourse skills. In terms of English-language learners, there is considerable variability among ethnic or language groups in home literacy practices; some minimal ability to segment spoken language into phonemic units is a prerequisite to beginning to read, and bilingualism promotes this ability; English vocabulary is a primary determinant of reading comprehension; and there are positive correlations between English second-language oral proficiency and reading ability, particularly at higher grade levels, but not equally across all first-language groups.

• Early instruction is impacted by lack of explicit instruction in the local orthography, absence of background knowledge and skills acquired in highly literate environments, and lack of semantic support for decoding that comes from familiarity with the words one reads. With regard to reading instruction in a second language, there is remarkably little direct relevant research.

• Studies of the nature of what can be transferred from first- to second-language reading need to take into account not only the level of first-language reading, but also the level and content of the second-language reading material.

• English-language learners may encounter difficulties in reading because of limited access to word meanings in English and novel rhetorical structures.

• Different subjects have different core structures; there are multiple kinds of knowledge—knowledge of ideas and facts, as well as knowledge of how to do something; and prior knowledge plays a significant role in learning.

• The above five conclusions suggest that literacy assessments alone are not adequate measures for understanding specific subject matter knowledge; certain disciplines may lend themselves more easily to the transfer of knowledge across languages, depending on the structure of knowledge within the domain; attention to the subject matter specificity of learning and issues surrounding different classes of knowledge suggest the difficulty of providing high-quality instruction designed for English-language learners; and the way content learned in one language is accessed in a second is of concern since depth, interconnectness, and accessibility of prior knowledge dramatically influence the processing of new information.

3
Cognitive Aspects of School Learning: Literacy Development and Content Learning

Language-minority children in the United States are overrepresented among those performing poorly in school. An understanding of the cognitive challenges posed by learning to read and by acquiring new content knowledge, whether in a first or a second language, is a prerequisite to designing better instruction for these and indeed all children. Whereas the previous chapter focused primarily on acquisition of oral language skills, the focus in this chapter is on reading, writing, and subject matter knowledge. The emphasis is on research carried out from a cognitive perspective on the nature of the challenges inherent in learning to read or learning subjects such as math or history, and on the factors that facilitate success in learning. Most of this research has been conducted with monolingual English-speaking subjects, but nonetheless casts light on the process for second-language speakers and learners as well. It should be noted that while this chapter includes some discussion of optimal instruction in the area of reading, most of the discussion regarding instruction is included in Chapter 7, on studies of school and classroom effectiveness.

STATE OF KNOWLEDGE

The following review of the state of knowledge in cognitive aspects of school learning first examines literacy development and then content learning.

Literacy Development

Like work on language acquisition, research on literacy forms a continuum whose endpoints represent quite different definitions of the phenomenon. At one end of this continuum, literacy is defined as a psycholinguistic process involving component subprocesses such as letter recognition, phonological encoding, decoding of grapheme strings, word recognition, lexical access, computation of sentence meaning, and so on; at the other end, it is defined as a social practice of meaning construction with distinct characteristics among different groups. Of course, beliefs about effective literacy instruction correlate with these differing definitions. The psycholinguistic definition[1] identifies crucial subprocesses in reading; thus in general it tends to support the utility of explicit instruction about these subprocesses (e.g., phoneme-grapheme mapping, word-recognition strategies, identification of derivational morphological relations among words), as well as practice to achieve automatic processing of them. The social practice view assumes that participation in a community that uses literacy communicatively is the crucial precondition for becoming literate; thus this view is associated with instructional practices such as encouraging children to write with invented spelling, exposing children to books by reading aloud, having tapes available, providing classroom libraries, and promoting authentic reading experiences through the use of trade books rather than basal readers. In addition, researchers in the psycholinguistic tradition tend to accept an epigenetic view of reading, in which it is assumed that the learner's (and thus the teacher's) task is different at different stages of development, whereas the social practice view, deemphasizing as it does the individual learner's role, defines no such developmental reorganization.

There has been a vast amount of research related to literacy and literacy instruction. Here we can only provide examples of what has been learned in the various domains of literacy development, focusing on concepts that are relatively well established for first-language reading and their potential relevance for understanding literacy development among bilinguals and second-language learners. We examine in turn prerequisites for the successful acquisition of reading ability, optimal early reading instruction, reading as a developmental process, and psycholinguistic processes of skilled readers.

Prerequisites for the Successful Acquisition of Reading

It is clear that future successful readers typically arrive at school with a set of prior experiences and well-established skills conducive to literacy. The findings in this area are fairly consistent, though explanations of how those prerequisites function to foster literacy development are not. The key prerequisites include an

---

[1]There is some confusion in terminology in the field of literacy acquisition. Smith (1983) and Goodman (1968) have called their view of literacy, which in fact lies firmly on the social practice end of the continuum, "psycholinguistic" to emphasize their claim that literacy acquisition operates in the same way as language acquisition. We reserve the term "psycholinguistic" for views of reading that specify individual processes of graphological, phonological, lexical, or syntactic analysis.

understanding of literacy, abstract knowledge of the sound and structure of language, a certain level of vocabulary development, and oral connected discourse skills.

An Understanding of Literacy   Young children who come from literate households, who have been read to, and whose parents are highly educated and/or use literacy regularly are most likely to become successful readers. These findings clearly fit well with the view of literacy as a social practice; more psycholinguistically oriented researchers point out that participation in literacy-related practices provides opportunities for children to acquire specific knowledge about letters, language, and symbolic systems that are prerequisites to full literacy.

Remarkably little work has been done to describe literate practices in the homes of language-minority children. The work that has been carried out describes considerable variability within ethnic or language groups, though typically the comparison groups are all low-income and of low parental education (Langer et al., 1990; Teale, 1986; Teale et al., 1981). The uses of literacy, and thus the cultural meanings of literacy to which children are socialized, are conceptualized in this work as social rather than autonomous, just as book reading with young children is basically a social interaction in which the adult and the child construct the text together through a combination of reading and discussion. These social practices may generate expectations that conflict with school literacy practices.

Abstract Knowledge of the Sound Structure of Language   Alphabetic writing systems represent spoken words abstractly—the level of the phoneme, which is unpronounceable and thus accessible only at a relatively deep level of representation. Preschool children who have a sophisticated sense of phonemes—as demonstrated, for example, by the ability to rhyme, to name things that begin with a particular sound, to focus on similarities in sound rather than in meaning in grouping words, or to identify relations among words that differ by one phoneme—are likely to be successful at the early stages of reading. Moreover, while these skills clearly make reading acquisition easier, reading acquisition and the practice in phoneme analysis that comes with attempts at invented spelling in turn promote abstract knowledge about phoneme structure.

Evidence seems clear that some minimal ability to segment spoken language into phonemic units is a prerequisite to beginning to read in all alphabetic languages (Wagner and Torgeson, 1987) and that bilingualism promotes this ability (Bialystok, 1988, 1992, in press). No studies have been done that would clarify whether acquiring this ability in a first language is a sufficient basis for initial literacy instruction in a second language or whether the ability needs to be at least applied to the second language before literacy can be acquired—though evidence that phoneme segmentation transfers across languages under certain circumstances has been offered by Durgunoglu et al. (1993).

Vocabulary At every stage of reading development, vocabulary is a highly reliable correlate of reading ability (e.g., Koda, 1989a; Nagy, 1988; Stanovich, 1986). This relationship is easy to understand at later stages: reading involves confronting many relatively rare and sophisticated words, which are easier to read if already known and are also more likely to be acquired by children who read a great deal. At the early stages of reading, the relation of reading success to vocabulary may reflect the status of a child's vocabulary as an index of parental social class or educational level.

A limited number of studies have sought relationships between vocabulary knowledge and reading for English-language learners (see Fitzgerald, 1995, for a review). These studies converge on the conclusion that English vocabulary is a primary determinant of reading comprehension for such readers, and that those whose first language has many cognates with English have an advantage in English vocabulary recognition, but often do not fully exploit cognate relationships to optimize English vocabulary comprehension without target instruction (Garcia and Nagy, 1993).

Oral Connected Discourse Skills Considerable evidence is now accumulating that good readers arrive at school with greater ability to use oral language in ways that are adapted to the needs of nonpresent listeners, that linguistically mark relations across utterances, and that honor genre-specific rules for organizing discourse.[2] As the exact mechanism explaining the relationship of these studies to literacy is not known, there is as yet little basis for determining whether learners need to display these skills in the language in which they are learning to read, or whether possessing these skills in a first language is sufficient to support literacy acquisition in a second.

Learners show high correlations across these oral discourse skills between their two languages if both are used in educational settings (Velasco, 1989), but not if only the second language is used for schooling (Snow, 1990). For example, children in a bilingual program scored very similarly on a task of giving definitions in Spanish and English, even providing precisely the same information in many cases, whereas Spanish-speaking children being schooled only in English showed no correlation between their Spanish and English definitions. Presumably the second group had no chance at home to develop in Spanish the academic skills they were acquiring in English.

Effective use of comprehension strategies in reading both Spanish and English was found to be related to Spanish first-language oral proficiency in one

---

[2]Genre-specific rules include those defining the likely order of presentation of information in fictional stories (provision of background information, complicating events, a problem, a problem resolution, a conclusion) versus newspaper reports (the major event, then the complicating actions, then orienting information about place and characters involved).

study (Langer et al., 1990). High levels of skill in Spanish first-language reading facilitated English second-language reading (Moll and Diaz, 1985), and similarly, good writing in Spanish first language was found to be related to sophisticated writing in English second language (Lanauze and Snow, 1989), suggesting that second-language literacy may be able to build directly on high levels of oral language and literacy skills in the first language. A case study of an excellent Spanish-English bilingual reader (Jiménez et al., 1995) shows the use of similar strategies for identifying words and comprehending text in both languages, and the frequent use of information from the other language. A larger-scale study carried out by the same group (Jiménez et al., 1996) suggests that successful bilingual readers all used certain strategies for comprehending both Spanish and English texts: focusing on unknown words, using cognates as one source of knowledge, monitoring their comprehension, making inferences, and actively using prior knowledge. Unsuccessful readers focused much less on comprehension as their goal for reading.

There is considerable controversy about the level of second-language proficiency needed to support reading in that language. Wong Fillmore and Valadez (1986) argue that second-language reading for English-language learners should not be introduced until a fairly high level of second-language proficiency has been achieved. However, Anderson and Roit (1996), Gersten (1996), and others argue that instruction focused on second-language comprehension can be helpful to learners at all levels of second-language oral proficiency (even for those with learning disabilities [Klingner and Vaughn, 1996]), and in fact that support of second-language reading comprehension can generate gains in second-language oral skills (see also Elley, 1981).

In general, positive correlations have been found between English second-language oral proficiency and English second-language reading ability, particularly at higher grade levels, but not equally across all first-language groups (Devine, 1987; see Fitzgerald, 1995, for a review). The mixed findings may well reflect differences in oral language proficiency measures used across the various studies and in conditions for literacy acquisition. Oral language proficiency in face-to-face tasks may predict less well than performance in autonomous, connected discourse tasks, and older, already literate second-language learners acquiring English literacy through formal, foreign-language-type instruction may rely less on oral language as a route to literacy than those acquiring their initial literacy skills in the second language.

Optimal Early Reading Instruction

Perhaps the most controversial area in reading research is the question of how best to teach initial reading. The debate about the value of the whole-word method peaked with the publication of *Why Johnny Can't Read* (Flesch, 1955), and the controversy surrounding phonics/direct instruction methods versus whole-language methods has been addressed in *The Great Debate* (Chall, 1967, 1983) and *Beginning to Read* (Adams, 1990).[3] The controversy often extends beyond the interpretation of research results to the level of deeply personal conviction, a situation that persists in part because most children will learn to read under a wide variety of instructional procedures. In fact, a small percentage of children in literate societies learn to read with no instruction whatsoever—evidently seeking out for themselves information about how print represents sound and finding the task of applying that knowledge sufficiently easy and fun that they practice it extensively outside instructional contexts (Clark, 1976; Durkin, 1966).[4]

The spontaneous readers in the distribution are balanced by at least as many children who have persistent problems in learning to read, presumably because of some basic processing deficit in the identification of phoneme units, in the achievement of lexical access, or in some other area of symbolic processing. Of primary interest for present purposes, though, are the vast majority of children in the middle of the distribution, particularly the group of apparently normal children who nonetheless have problems learning to read and remain below grade level as readers throughout elementary school. This group of normal but at-risk children is composed overwhelmingly of children from low-income homes where the parents have relatively little education and of children who do not speak English as a first language. Hispanic children (a group that includes English monolinguals as well as Spanish-English bilinguals), for example, score well below their non-Hispanic peers in reading throughout the elementary school years and end up on average about 4 years behind in secondary school (Applebee et al., 1985, 1987, 1989). This is the group for which we are most interested in the effects of instruction.

The evidence is overwhelming that direct instruction in phoneme-grapheme mappings, word recognition strategies, and comprehension strategies is of value for this group of children (Adams, 1990). Many believe that such children are at considerable risk in classrooms that provide only a whole-language environment with no direct reading instruction, a conclusion supported by a meta-analysis conducted by Stahl and Miller (1989). They found that whole-language ap-

---

[3]The whole-word method involved teaching reading by having children acquire a large repertoire of sight words, without providing direct instruction in the regularities of English orthography. The phonics method focuses on teaching and providing practice in the orthographic system, i.e., sound-letter relationships, the rules governing the interpretation of orthographic cues such as the silent 'e', and the pronunciation of minor spelling patterns such as 'igh,' and 'ough.' The whole-language method emphasizes providing children with rich, authentic literacy experiences so they can discover the rules of English orthography themselves. Unlike the whole-word method, it does not involve teaching sight words.

[4]These claims that most children learn to read under any instructional regime and that 5-10 percent of children learn to read without formal instruction are based on studies of monolingual English speakers. We do not know whether similar claims can be made for bilinguals or for children learning to read in a second language in which they are not fully proficient.

proaches worked better with advantaged populations, though there were generally better outcomes for approaches that incorporated basal readers in the instruction, particularly for first graders (as opposed to kindergartners, who benefited more from whole-language approaches). Freppon and Dahl (1991) document the success of a kindergarten teacher who in the context of whole-language instruction helps children understand sound-symbol relations. It should of course be noted that these findings relate to English-language speakers, not to English-language learners.

Though the hard evidence favors direct instruction, it is also clear that many instructional methods associated with phonics-based instruction are unnecessary, of little value, or less useful than alternatives that incorporate some principles introduced by whole-language methods. Worksheets on which children practice identifying long versus short vowels, rhyming versus nonrhyming words, and words beginning with 'b' versus words beginning with 'd' are much less productive than forms of skill practice embedded in meaningful contexts (Anderson ct al., 1985). Authentic communication tasks, such as writing stories or journals, can serve as contexts for individualized phonics instruction that exploits the value of accurate representation of words for effective communication. The somewhat impoverished models of literature provided by many basal reading series can be supplemented or replaced by a judicious selection of trade books that provide engaging texts with literary value (see Elley and Mangubhai, 1983, for evidence of the value of high-interest reading in promoting second-language reading and language skills).

Instruction in small groups formed around children's reading levels has been shown to have a pernicious effect on some children's views of themselves as readers and on the quality of instruction available to the lower-level reading groups (Allington, 1978, 1980; Hoffman and Clements, 1984), though use of ability groups in the Success for All model has proven successful with both English and Spanish speakers (Slavin and Madden, 1994).

While one can cite research findings in support of the value of certain of these practices over others, only recently has anyone dared to express official sanction for the eclectic method of teaching reading—embedding direct instruction in component processes into meaningful, communicative, literate activities—that many experienced and successful teachers are in fact implementing in their classrooms (Adams and Bruck, 1995; Purcell-Gates, 1996).

With regard to reading instruction in a second language, there is remarkably little directly relevant research. Clearly one of the major intellectual stimuli to bilingual education programs has been the belief that initial reading instruction in a language not yet mastered orally to some reasonable level is too great a cognitive challenge for most learners. Studies of outcomes of bilingual programs, however, do not typically distinguish students who arrive at school already reading in their first language from those who learn to read only at school. The evidence that better academic outcomes characterize immigrant children who have had 2 to 3 years of initial schooling (and presumably literacy instruction) in their native countries (Collier and Thomas, 1989; Skutnabb-Kangas, 1979) is consistent with the claim that children should first learn to read in a language they already speak. However, it is clear that many children first learn to read in a second language without serious negative consequences. These include children in early-immersion, two-way, and English as a second language (ESL)-based programs in North America, as well as those in formerly colonial countries that have maintained the official language as the medium of instruction, immigrant children in Israel, children whose parents opt for elite international schools, and many others (see Christian, 1996; Feitelson, 1988).

What we know about early literacy acquisition suggests it is more likely than not to be successful under a wide variety of circumstances, but is nonetheless impacted by a long list of risk factors, including lack of explicit instruction in the local orthography, absence of the sort of background knowledge and skills acquired in highly literate environments, and unavailability of semantic support for decoding that comes from familiarity with the words one reads. Exposure to any one of these and other risk factors may have no impact on literacy achievement, though the coincidence of several may ensure a high rate of failure. The high literacy achievement of Spanish-speaking children in English-medium Success for All schools (Slavin and Yampolsky, 1992) that feature carefully designed direct literacy instruction suggests that even children from low-literacy homes can learn to read in a second language if the risk associated with poor instruction is eliminated.

Reading as a Developmental Process

There are rather different tasks and skills involved in reading at various points in the acquisition of skilled reading. These differences are great enough that Chall (1983) has claimed reading develops through distinct stages. Clearly, a stage theory meshes well with a direct instructional model, in which it is assumed that skills should be taught in a specific sequence. Whether or not one accepts a strict sequential stage notion, it is clear that in general, children learning to read face different challenges at different points in the process: learning about print versus nonprint, typically accomplished in the preschool years; learning to recognize and write letters; learning to decode words, which involves synthesizing phonological from graphemic sequences; reading relatively simple texts fluently; reading texts that include new information and unknown lexical items for comprehension; reading strategically, for specific information or purposes such as relaxation; and reading critically, to examine and compare the claims and arguments of different authors. The essential idea here is that the nature of reading skill needs to be defined somewhat differently at different points in its development, and thus that acquisition of prior skills does not always predict continued growth in reading ability; there are several points in development where novel skills need to be acquired.

The implications of this view for second-language learners are potentially enormous, as the task of learning to read in a second language is presumably quite different at different stages of first-language reading skill. Direct studies of the nature of what can be transferred from first- to second-language reading need to take into account not only the level of first-language reading, but also the level and content of the second-language material being read (as well as the nature of the orthographic [e.g., Koda, 1989b], linguistic, and rhetorical differences between the first and second languages).

Psycholinguistic Processes of Skilled Readers

Skilled readers are capable of reading with understanding in part because the component processes—letter recognition, word recognition, access to word meaning, syntactic parsing of the sentence—are fast and efficient (e.g., Adams, 1990). Efficiency is promoted in reading instruction by making provision for practice in reading to generate fluency or automatic processing of component processes (e.g., by introducing sustained silent reading periods in the classroom, or by providing opportunities for sufficient practice in oral reading). Even adult skilled readers process print in a largely bottom-up way, engaging in phonological encoding as part of the process of word recognition (Rayner and Pollatsek, 1989). Indeed, even readers of nonalphabetic languages such as Chinese seem to use phonological encoding for word recognition, suggesting that lexical storage is largely phonological in form (Hung and Tzeng, 1981; Perfetti and Zhang, 1991; Perfetti et al., 1992).

Thus the suggestion by Smith (1983), for example, that good reading involves top-down processing—in which understanding the smaller units is possible because the general message is accessible first—is a misrepresentation of normal skilled reading, though it comes closer to describing the process in which poor readers engage. Those whose skill with word recognition is limited can improve their comprehension by employing strategies such as reading the whole text for gist; self-monitoring for understanding; and using cues from titles, pictures, headings, and the like. Explicit instruction in comprehension strategies such as prediction, summarization, and questioning—for example, the widely used "reciprocal teaching" (Palincsar and Brown, 1984) or Berciter and Bird's (1985) think-aloud method—has been shown to be useful with poor first-language readers, and some evidence suggests it would also be useful with second-language readers who have comprehension difficulties (e.g., Barnett, 1989; Casanave, 1988; Cohen, 1990). Studies of the metacognitive strategies used by second-language readers of English (reviewed in Fitzgerald, 1995) reveal that such strategies are widely used and that the repertoire of those strategies includes some that may be specific to the second-language situation (such as using translation dictionaries or relying on information about cognates), but also many typical of first-language readers as well (asking questions, predicting, summarizing). Jiménez et al. (1996) found that good second-language readers focus much more on word meaning, presumably because this is a greater source of difficulty for them, than do good monolingual readers.

Some researchers studying instructional practices for reading have suggested that rather little attention is given to teaching or promoting comprehension strategies in classrooms with many language-minority students, even in the middle and later elementary grades when such instruction is important, because teachers tend to focus on word recognition and pronunciation (e.g., Gersten, 1996). On the other hand, literacy instruction for adult ESL learners focuses rather little on word recognition (Hilferty, 1996), despite the important role of word recognition skill in explaining variance in comprehension among this population (Carlo and Sylvester, 1996; Hilferty, 1996). A major obstacle to helpful research on reading instruction for language-minority children is the failure to recognize the existence of developmental changes in the reading process and in the speed and efficiency of second-language learning.

Skilled readers use syntactic information unconsciously to make the reading process more efficient, for example, by fixating on high-information items in the text (Rayner and Pollatsek, 1989). Since high-information items differ from language to language, this can lead to inefficient fixation patterns when reading in a second language (Bernhardt, 1987), thus perhaps disrupting the fluency that facilitates comprehension.

Skilled readers can tolerate a small proportion of unknown words in texts without disruption of comprehension and can even infer the meanings of those words from sufficiently rich contexts, but if the proportion of unknown words is too high, comprehension is disrupted. Word knowledge no doubt relates to reading comprehension both because encountering many unknown words slows processing and because lack of word knowledge indicates absence of the relevant background knowledge that is crucial in reading texts of any complexity. Educators who doubt the importance of relevant background knowledge to comprehension need only dip into the *Journal of Solid State Physics* for leisure reading to be convinced. Familiarity with content promotes reading comprehension when reading in either a second or a first language (Carrell, 1987; Johnson, 1981; see Fitzgerald, 1995, for a review), though knowledge of relevant background information may be less reliably indexed by second- than first-language vocabulary.

Comprehension is also supported by familiarity with macro structures present in texts. Knowing that paragraphs have topic sentences on which other sentences are meant to elaborate, being familiar with the basic principles of compare-and-contrast essays, and understanding the macro grammar of a typical story all aid the reader in integrating information across sentences. Of course, these macro structures are culturally determined, and knowing them is typically the product of a great deal of implicit learning, though direct instruction in these matters is provided in some classrooms. The importance of these macro-structural principles in promoting or impeding reading comprehension is clear to anyone who has compared a novel by James Michener with one by Isabel Allende or Kenzaburo Oe. The notions of plot and temporal sequence, of how much orientation is needed, and of how much interpretation should be supplied vary widely across these three writers, who are all, however, relatively mainstream within their own cultural-linguistic tradition. In general, passages organized in a familiar structure are easier to comprehend and recall for second-language readers (see Fitzgerald, 1995, for a review) than those exemplifying a novel rhetorical structure. There are clear first-language effects on the types of structures second-language readers find easy, presumably related to preferred macro-structural organization in the first language (Carrell, 1984; Hinds, 1983). Studies that have manipulated familiarity of both content and structure find that unfamiliar content is more disruptive to comprehension than unfamiliar structure (Carrell, 1987).

Content Learning

This section examines what we know about content learning in general and in relationship to English-language learners. We consider lines of research that have addressed learning and thinking in subject matter domains and what this research suggests for the tasks faced by teachers of second-language learners and their students. Considerable progress has been made over the last two decades in understanding the nature and processes of learning and acquiring knowledge of specified content information. This research has, for the most part, not concerned itself with issues of language per se, nor has it been incorporated into discussion about English-language learners. There are some notable exceptions, however. For example, research reviewed in Cocking and Mestre (1988) and discussed later in this chapter examines linguistic and cultural influences on learning mathematics. Fuson and Secada's (1986) study of particular mathematical topics and student learning extends our sense of the complexity of mathematical thinking and helps us interpret the teaching task with greater awareness. Work by Rosebery et al. (1992) and Chamot et al. (1992) is discussed in Chapter 7, on studies of school and classroom effectiveness.

We refer to the body of research that we review as "primary-language content learning." While it is clear that learning and understanding new content material in a second language pose specific linguistic difficulties not present in primary-language content learning, awareness of this body of research might well inform research on content learning in a second language. Expanding the systematic study of some of these issues to include English-language learners will inform and expand the theory as well.

The general perspective here is that of cognitive psychology. Cognitive theory, borrowing from the pioneering work of Piaget, provides educators a way of combining constructivism with systematic deep analyses of subject matter tasks. Cognitive analyses help reveal with special clarity a level of complexity in teaching and learning in subject areas. But cognitive psychology and cognitive science (cognitive psychology plus linguistics, philosophy, and artificial intelligence) also suggest a level of complexity in teaching and learning not anticipated by Piagetians, behaviorists, or even activity theorists (Cobb, 1994; Bruer, 1993; Resnick and Klopfer, 1989; Greeno and Simon, 1988; Simon and Kaplan, 1989; Wertsch, 1979).

Empirical research on teaching and learning has paralleled the evolution of educational theory (Bruer, 1993). As educational theory has expanded, so have the kinds of research questions posed. Most recently, research questions influenced by cognitive theory have focused on the relationship between structure of knowledge, meaning organization, and representations of tasks and resources: How does the structure of prior mathematical knowledge and representation influence student thinking about decimals (Heibert, 1986)? How do students juggle the multiple layers and constraints of geographical notation to reason with and from a map (Gregg, 1993)? How does self-explanation influence students' understanding and mental models of the circulatory system (Chi et al., 1994)? How do groups of students jointly construct effective explanations (Leinhardt, 1987)?

Seeking answers to these kinds of subject matter questions, as well to questions concerned with language acquisition and development, may generate important insights concerning the education of second-language students. Thus we suggest a program of research with second-language learners and their teachers that is extended to include cognitive approaches to subject matter learning, knowledge, and understanding. Because the "problem" for the English-language learner has been considered as almost entirely language-based, much of the research has focused on language acquisition issues. But learning school subject matter and work skills involves building intricate networks of concept relations, structuring and restructuring understandings, connecting them to other understandings, and practicing multiple skills in multiple environments. Therefore, more complex questions might fruitfully be asked about the nature of second-language students' learning, knowledge, and understanding of complex subject matter domains.

Discussion of complex questions of subject matter learning for English-language learners needs to be grounded in some assumptions about learning in general. The remainder of this section describes three assumptions drawn from cognitive analyses about school subject matter learning for primary-language content learning. These assumptions are context for much of the current research on school learning and apply to most students and most subject matter domains. First, we assume that different subjects have different core structures or epistemologies, thus making different demands on the learner. Second, we assume that there are multiple forms or kinds of knowledge—knowledge of facts and ideas, as well as knowledge of how to do something, for example. Third, we assume that prior knowledge plays a significant role in learning, not only in terms of where to start, but also in terms of the actual meanings attached to new information. The discussion of these assumptions offers some examples and considers what a program of cognitive research that considered subject matter learning for English-language learners might look like.

Subject Matter Specificity

Learning, knowledge, and understanding differ across subject matter. But these differences in subject matter are embedded in larger general similarities. Understanding, learning, and teaching earth science or social studies require the general ability to read English, to construct meaning, and to understand and follow spoken discussion. They also require general capabilities of inferencing, placing examples into overarching constructs, and building causal chains.[5] Knowledge varies both across and within subject matter areas: it varies across because subjects have different epistemological underpinnings and thus different arrangements of facts, concepts, notations, and patterns of reasoning; it varies within because some academic subjects have elaborate and importantly constraining notational systems (for example, algebraic and graphic systems). We now review several examples from the primary subject matter domains of mathematics, science, and history.

Analyses of mathematical learning and teaching have covered a variety of topics, from the earliest studies of counting (Briars and Siegler, 1984; Gelman and Meck, 1986), to models of addition and subtraction (Carpenter and Moser, 1982; Fuson, 1992; Resnick, 1992; Riley et al., 1983), to buggy algorithms[6] in subtraction (Brown and VanLehn, 1982), to descriptions of naive models of graphs (Leinhardt et al., 1990; Schoenfeld et al., 1993). These studies have extended our sense of the complexity of mathematical thinking and helped us interpret and undertake teaching tasks with greater awareness. Studies of counting (Briars and Seigler, 1984; Gelman and Gallistel, 1978; Gelman and Meck, 1986; Greeno et al., 1984) have focused on the inherent interaction between basic principled knowledge and procedural knowledge for specific mathematical tasks and operations. Research on buggy algorithms (Brown and VanLehn, 1982) shows that these errors are quite systematic and can be used generatively to understand the student's mental model that produces a procedural bug. In a very different kind of work, Lampert (1992) shows that to understand long-division problems, the student must grasp an underlying principle that includes fundamental multiplicative relationships.[7] These relationships are quite implicit and

---

[5]Between these bottom-up skills (Kintsch and van Dijk, 1978) and top-down schemas (Anderson and Pearson, 1984) lies a rather large domain of highly differentiated systems of knowledge, for which expertise also tends to be differentiated (Chi et al., 1982; Schwab, 1978; Stodolsky, 1988).

[6]Procedures that produce predictable errors.

[7]In one example, she describes posing two fundamental classes of division questions. First, given a specific number of groups (or people), how many belong in each group for a fixed number of

heavily dependent on linguistic nuances. Therefore, the efficiency of the algorithmic system may not be visible to all students, and the means of making the distinction visible must be developed with consideration for both linguistic and cultural issues.

Parallel research in science education exemplifies the epistemological differences among disciplines. Theories are fundamental to science. The task of learning science is, in part, to understand those theories deeply enough to be able to map them to extant data in order to explain a particular phenomenon (Ohlsson, 1992). Because of the disciplinary significance of theory, considerable educational research has been devoted to issues surrounding scientific theories, such as the difference between cohesive and fragmented intuitive scientific theories (diSessa, 1988), systems of errors (McKlosky, 1983), models of expert scientific problem solving (Chi et al., 1982; Simon et al., 1980), models of scientific discovery (Qin and Simon, 1990), theory articulation (Ohlsson, 1992), and concept interpretation (Reif, 1987).

One aspect of the study of science that can be especially difficult for students is the deceptive simplicity of many of the theories. Take, for example, the principle of acceleration: acceleration is the change in velocity over time. The formula (and theory) seems simple at first glance. However, in detailing how one determines the acceleration of any particular object, Reif (1987) shows the solution path as a progression through five separate substeps[8] and points out that "substantial complexities [are] hidden in the declarative specification of (the problem)...[and that] even some of the individual steps of the procedural specification involve complex sub-processes" (pp. 401-402). What might start out as a simple "plug the number into the formula" problem turns into a multilayered, means-end solution path, misleading students with its false impression of simplicity.

In the study of history, students must construct a coherent narrative or expository historical account that carries both multiple perspectives and a sense of layering—of event as it occurred, event as it was recorded, and event as it was interpreted (Leinhardt, 1994; Wineberg, 1994). History, as taught, usually lacks

---

items? For example, with 6 people and 48 apples, how many apples go to each person? Second, given a specific number per group, how many groups can be formed for a fixed number of items? For example, with 8 people per minivan and 48 people, how many minivans are needed? In the first case, the divisor (6 people) is a quantity, while the quotient is an intensive quantity (8 apples per person). In the second case, the divisor is an intensive quantity (8 per van), while the quotient is a quantity (6 vans). Both questions make use of the same algorithmic system to solve the problem, namely division, and both are part of the system of multiplicative structures. This consistency characterizes the efficiency of the mathematical discipline.

[8]These steps include (1) find the velocity of the particle at time t, (2) find the velocity of the particle at a slightly later time t', (3) find the change in velocity, (4) find the ratio of velocity to time, and (5) repeat the calculations until the ratio approaches a limiting value that is constant.

this sense of coherence. When asked to recall salient information from such texts, students tend to construct erroneous connections among the facts presented in an effort to make them coherent. McKeown and Beck (1994) found that if the texts were revised so less was presumed about the students' knowledge of the material (i.e., so that the actual text was more coherent), the students were better able to construct an accurate representation of the historical event, reason about the multiple perspectives involved, and construct an historical argument from the layered interpretations of particular events.

The point of the above discussion has been to emphasize the fundamental epistemological differences among subject matters. These differences necessitate highly differentiated systems of complex knowledge for both students and their teachers. While it is clear that at some level of abstraction, generalities across subject areas do exist, we believe these generalities are not sufficient to leapfrog the middle ground of differentiated knowledge. Further, we suggest that a better understanding of this middle ground can enhance our understanding of the nature of both primary-language content learning and content learning in a second language.

In light of the epistemological distinctions among the various subjects, it may be that certain disciplines lend themselves more easily to the transfer of knowledge across languages, depending on the structure of knowledge within the domain, but the particular domains to which this would apply to are not readily apparent. For example, it would appear at first glance that mathematics knowledge should be readily transferable from language to language. However, in light of the long-division example cited above and research in this area (Cocking and Chipman, 1988; Myers and Milne, 1988), we can see that some of the deepest principles of a particular domain (e.g., its efficiency) may be highly implicit and heavily dependent on language, and thus less accessible to an English-language learner. Because sophisticated knowledge in a given domain not only uses the terminology of that domain, but also builds upon gradually developing concepts—such as dividing among a group or grouping by a factor to determine the number of groups—learning such strands of content knowledge in one language and then shifting to another may be especially problematic.

We have asserted that there are substantial differences among subject matter areas. For the most part, studies of English-language learners and their teachers seem to have ignored these distinctions, identifying a central problem facing these students as learning enough general language to enter mainstream classrooms. We do not know what the advantages or complications are for English-language learners trying to learn the various disciplines themselves. However, we do suggest that it would be useful to learn how general language proficiencies interact with specific academic language proficiencies and with specific subject matter content. For example, in a study of writing and discourse about history by young adolescents, we have seen that gaining command of connecting words and phrases (e.g., *among, between, however, in spite of, in addition to*) is a requirement for building coherent arguments and a stumbling block if not mastered. This is not a vocabulary problem; it is a problem of logical relations that makes itself known through language (Young and Leinhardt, 1996). A study by Short (1994) indicates that integrating subject-specific terminology into language classes helps English-language learners better comprehend the subject matter (see Chapter 7).

Multiple Forms of Knowledge

Not only are there substantial differences among subject matter areas, but there are also different kinds of knowledge. One of the more common distinctions among types of knowledge is that between procedural knowledge (knowledge of actions and skills) and declarative knowledge (knowledge of concepts and principles) (Chi and Ceci, 1987; Heibert, 1986; Lampert, 1986; Scribner, 1984). One task facing the student is to integrate these two types of knowledge. This integration process will differ according to the generative power we expect students to develop from different subject matter information. Students of some disciplines, such as history, must develop arguments based on multiple forms of evidence, whereas students of other disciplines, such as science, are commonly asked to codify examples of complex phenomena. Thus, the underlying epistemologic foundation of the discipline dictates the nature of the required integration of procedural and declarative knowledge. Another distinction between types of knowledge is between knowledge of content and knowledge of that knowledge, referred to as metacognition. Brown (1980) discusses metacognition in terms of three features: knowing what you know and how well you know it, knowing what you need to know, and knowing the utility of active intervention. This self-awareness has been found to be a useful tool for learners across domains in that learners with such awareness are better able to organize the knowledge they have and identify that which they need to acquire.

We do not have much information about the English-language learner with respect to subject matter knowledge in these terms. (See Chapter 7 for a review of studies that examine the effect of instruction in metacognitive skills on subject matter learning of English-language learners.) However, issues of metacognition have been discussed for second-language learners in terms of the additive principle, which suggests these students have an advantage when learning new material.[9] The argument that metacognitive abilities facilitate learning by primary-

---

[9]It is striking how little research has been carried out on the metacognitive capacities of bilinguals, given the robust findings concerning their metalinguistic superiority. Bilinguals' abstract metalinguistic understanding of the structure of language may facilitate their learning of new material (Bialystok and Hakuta, 1994; Cummins, 1991; Diaz, 1986; Hakuta and Diaz, 1985; Peal and Lambert, 1962).

language content learners lends support to the claim of the additive principle. Note, however, that in considering metacognition, the assumed advantage for second-language learners when learning new material has been focused strictly on linguistic awareness; the findings do not generalize to utility for particular subject matter knowledge.

Prior Knowledge

The types and amount of knowledge available before encountering a new topic within a particular discipline affect how meaning is constructed. Theories about the structure of knowledge and knowledge acquisition have used similar metaphors for describing the structure of knowledge and the way the acquisition of new knowledge affects that structure (Case, 1993; Newell and Simon, 1972; Miller, 1993). The knowledge structure can be thought of as nodes of information, such as concepts, that are linked to each other in particular ways depending on how and what information has been learned. Links between concepts can be acquired, reconstructed, or deconstructed, and particular learning outcomes are determined jointly by what was known before (the unique pattern of nodes and links) and the effects of instruction (additions to or rearrangements of that pattern).

The issue of prior knowledge can be considered one of depth, interconnectedness, and access. Depth of knowledge refers to the number of linked concepts a student has in a domain. In math, for example, students' depth of knowledge will influence their recognition of a problem, their sense of meaning associated with the problem, their ability to perform the appropriate mathematical operations, and their ability to recognize a reasonable answer. It is often the case that neither students nor teachers recognize salient background knowledge in a mathematical or scientific domain. The extent to which concepts are interconnected reveals the coherence of a student's understanding of a particular domain. Finally, the existence of different kinds of knowledge poses a problem for both teaching and learning in that if the different types of knowledge are disconnected, they will be inert and unusable (Bereiter, 1984; Brown et al., 1983). A student may know *what* a long-division problem is, but not know *how* to solve it. Or a student may know how to solve a particular problem, but not when to use division procedures. The development of deep, interconnected, generative knowledge instead of shallow, fragmented, inert knowledge needs to be a continuous process for both teachers and their students, with the interaction between the two forms of knowledge being taught explicitly.

Thus the depth, interconnectedness, and accessibility of prior knowledge all dramatically influence the processing of new information (Chi and Koeske, 1983; McKeown et al., 1992; Pearson et al., 1979). Knowledge is a complex integrated network of information of various types: ideas, facts, principles, actions, and scenes. Prior knowledge is thus more than another chunk of information. It might facilitate, inhibit, or transform a new learning task. Students must connect their own prior knowledge with new information continuously, while teachers must understand how well students are making these connections (Lampert, 1992; Leinhardt, 1992).

With respect to second-language learners, then, a number of questions arise. Under what conditions is content learning affected by the fact that a superordinate category and its instantiation (e.g., commutivity and addition) are learned both tacitly and explicitly in one language, but are then to be used as a principle in a more complex instantiation in another language (e.g., addition of algebraic polynomials)? How are "errors" that have a language base handled in a second language (e.g., in English, the confusion of "north" with "up" on a page versus in real space)? Naturally, the potential for interference in terms of access is also of concern—although this may be a vocabulary issue. A problem may arise if base examples are introduced at a young age in the child's first language (e.g., for social studies, notions of community, roles, freedom, and power) and are to be built upon in the second language at a later age (e.g., in learning about the French Revolution). Does this affect the second-language learner, and how?

These questions are related to concerns about how and when instruction should be handled over time. In part, they raise issues of individual development over time, and in part issues of subject matter coherence and meaning over time. At this point, we know next to nothing about these questions. Do those conditions change with varying subject matter? These questions are analogous to questions of how bilinguals represent two languages—as one system or two (Bialystok and Hakuta, 1994:110). For example, under what conditions is content learning affected by whether the languages are independent or interdependent? An enhanced understanding of the nature of language (i.e., knowing that words help to differentiate concepts), if made explicit, could alleviate some confusion about literal translations between languages for specific concepts. Thus it would be pertinent, as argued by Hakuta (1986), to determine the extent to which the distinctions within and among concepts learned in a second language are similar to or different from those originally learned in the first language for each particular subject matter. Results from studies of primary-language content learning have rarely been included in the debates about when and how to introduce education in various subject matters in English to language-minority students. We do not know, for example, whether (especially for the older new arrival) time should be taken to review existing knowledge that is available in the first language in a way that recontextualizes it in the second language, or whether the new knowledge (e.g., Algebra II) should simply be supported with back references to salient ideas known in the first language but now used in the second (e.g., Algebra I). Aspects such as procedures for factoring a polynomial may be available in one language, while conceptual supports for meaningful understanding may be being discussed in another. We do not know how this affects learning and performance. The literature discussed here could be used to broaden the debate on content learning for English-language learners to address such issues.

RESEARCH NEEDS

Language-Literacy Relationships

3-1. Research is needed to answer the following questions: What is the nature of the relationship between language proficiency and literacy skill? Is that relationship the same across and within languages? Is there a level of oral language knowledge that is prerequisite to successful literacy acquisition? Is that level the same for learners of different first-language backgrounds, of different ages, of different levels of first-language literacy?

Questions about relationships between linguistic accomplishments and literacy achievement have long been a feature of work on literacy, but they have taken many different forms. Traditionally, work in this area has taken vocabulary or metalinguistic awareness to represent language. Some thinking has emerged from issues of dialect differences, questioning whether children are disadvantaged if the written code represents standard rather than vernacular oral forms. More recently, a number of studies have explored language ability defined more richly, attempting to use extended discourse skill as the language predictor.

Research in this area is particularly important because (1) teachers need guidance about the level of first- and of second-language proficiency at which literacy instruction in a second language can most efficiently be initiated; (2) if bilingual children are precocious in the metalinguistic skills that have been related to literacy, these skills should be built upon for successful literacy teaching; and (3) we need to understand the nature of the cognitive challenge faced by the many children in immersion or submersion situations for whom oral language and literacy skills are acquired in the second language simultaneously.

Relation of First- and Second-Language Literacy

3-2. Research is needed to examine the nature of the relationship between first- and second-language literacy skill. Is literacy knowledge represented the same way for monolingual and bilingual populations? Are literacy skills (and deficits) acquired in the first language directly transferred to the second, and if so, under what conditions? Is investment in first-language literacy training worthwhile for all combinations of first and second languages, for example, if orthographies differ radically or if the first language is a traditionally non-literate one? Does phoneme awareness transfer from one language to another, and if so under what circumstances (i.e., do the languages involved make a difference)?

As noted above, questions about the nature of literacy skill are the source of considerable controversy. There is good reason to believe that literacy is acquired through accretions of knowledge and accumulation of skill through practice, but there is also evidence that it is acquired in stage-like shifts to quite different levels of understanding. Similarly, there are those who (citing those children who are early spontaneous readers) argue that literacy is the product of natural developmental processes and others who (citing the 20-30 percent of children reading seriously below grade level) focus on the need for instructional intervention. While some evidence suggests that initial reading instruction in a weak language can be disadvantageous to long-term academic outcomes, there are also cases of children who learn to read initially in a second language and do well academically. We need to understand what characteristics differentiate these two groups of children so we do not put children into programs that threaten their chances for successful literacy acquisition. Furthermore, many non-English-speaking children arrive in American schools after having experienced some schooling and some literacy instruction in a native language. However, an insufficient attempt has been made to understand the cognitive processes underlying successful transfer of first-language literacy skill to the second language, the limitations on that transfer, the conditions that optimize positive and minimize negative transfer, or the differences between children who manage learning to read in a second language well and those who do not. Such information would make English literacy training for both child and adult immigrants much more efficient and effective.

Optimal Literacy Instruction

3-3. Research needs to investigate the optimal English literacy instruction for children of different ages, those with different native languages, those whose native language is not written, and those whose parents are not literate in English. Is there a single best way for all children, and if not, is there some way to identify child aptitudes so as to define optimal individualized instruction? What should the role of writing be in reading instruction, particularly for second-language learners?

Basic questions about optimal instruction and about the universality of optimal instruction versus the need for individualized teaching arise for second- as for first-language readers. The questions become acute as innovative teaching methods are introduced into mainstream classrooms. For instance, many primary classrooms are now using writing as a route to reading instruction; writing itself is now considered an important domain for literacy assessment and is increasingly being incorporated into content area instruction. The impact of such innovations on second-language learners is unknown.

Learning Language Through Literacy

3-4. An important question to be addressed is whether literacy can be used as a route to language learning, and if so, under what circumstances and with what consequences. Are there disadvantages with regard to language proficiency outcomes to acquiring a language with literate input from the very beginning? Is it possible for second-language learners to have highly developed literacy skills, but low or no oral language skills? If so, how do we incorporate these cases into our models of literacy acquisition and of language-literacy relationships? Are there consequences of second-language literacy acquisition for literacy and/or language functioning in the first language?

With young children, thinking has focused on issues such as how much oral language a child needs to know before literacy instruction should begin; with older second-language learners, it is possible that literacy can be a major source of language learning. It is unknown, though, how effective literacy is as a language-learning strategy, whether it has consequences for oral proficiency, or at what age or for what types of learners it works best. Since many English-language learners arrive in the United States after having acquired literacy in their first language, understanding how to use easily developed second-language literacy skills to promote oral proficiency safely and effectively is very important.

Learning Content with Limited English Proficiency

3-5. There are three key research questions that address how those with limited English proficiency learn content. First, what are the effects of limited English proficiency on the acquisition of content knowledge at a fine-grained level? Specifically, what are the consequences of acquiring beginning-level content knowledge in one language and then switching languages for higher levels of the content domain? Second, what levels of English proficiency are prerequisite to the capacity to profit from content area instruction in English? Third, are there modifications to the language used by teachers that can make complex subject matters accessible even to second-language beginners?

The research reviewed here makes clear that language interactions—questioning, expert explanations, discussions of alternative solutions, formulation of reasons for conclusions—contribute to the development of understanding of complex subject matter. Serious practical and ethical questions arise if these optimal methods for content area instruction are inaccessible to second-language speakers, who are thus excluded from participation in the best teaching practices. We need to know how early in the process of second-language acquisition speakers can profit from participation in challenging pedagogical conversations and whether simple modifications of the language used can speed that access. We need guidelines on how to provide second-language learners the opportunity for age-appropriate acquisition of content area material. These guidelines should take into account epistemological differences among subject matter areas.

Effects of English-Language Learners on Content Area Teachers

3-6. Several important research questions relate to the effects of English-language learners on teachers of specific subjects and their classrooms. How does the presence of a second language in the classroom affect the cognitive load for the content area teacher? Does a high proportion of language-minority children in a classroom have a negative effect on the classroom as a learning environment for native speakers of English, and if so, under what circumstances? How does the presence of second-language speakers or the use of a second language in the classroom affect the necessary balance between clear didactic presentation and less orderly generative classroom activity, such as discussion?

Teachers bear much of the burden of delivering effective education to language-minority students, and often with little access to information or training in how to do it optimally. Clearly, teaching complex subject matter to students of limited proficiency in the instructional language can place extra strain on teachers and may lead them into undesirable pedagogical practices. A good theory of what it means to make "linguistic modifications" in assessments or use "simplified English" in instruction would be useful to teachers. Researchers who have been looking at greater inclusion of English-language learners in large-scale assessments have tinkered with meeting this need, but with difficulty and quite narrowly. (Abedi, for example, simplified items using syntactic structures only and was unsuccessful in increasing performance.) A broader framework taking into account semantic, communicative, and sociolinguistic factors could be more useful. Such a theory could also provide a foundation for "sheltered instruction" programs.

Transfer of Content Knowledge from First to Second Language

3-7. Research is needed to identify the additive features of second-language knowledge/acquisition for cognition, for example, specific content area understanding, and to determine the extent to which learning complex material in a particular language requires having content-specific structures in that language. In other words, is content knowledge acquired in the first language automatically available to be built upon when learning in the second language?

It seems reasonable that content learners trying to construct powerful representations of their knowledge would find it advantageous to have access to two symbolic systems with which to construct those representations; thus one might expect that bilingual learners would have an advantage over monolinguals in this regard. Furthermore, if content knowledge acquired in the first language is available for use in the second, there is every reason to expect that language-minority children who arrive in the United States after years of rigorous schooling in their country of origin will display high academic achievement as soon as they learn English. Although most of the work on the academic performance of language-minority children emphasizes the risks to high achievement, the excellent accomplishments of immigrant children in national assessments of math and science suggest they may have an advantage in certain domains of learning, perhaps because of easy transfer or because of the cognitive consequences of bilingualism.

REFERENCES

Adams, M.J.
   1990   *Beginning to Read: Thinking and Learning about Print.* Cambridge, MA: MIT Press.
Adams, M., and M. Bruck
   1995   Resolving the "great debate." *American Educator* 19(2):10-20.
Allington, R.L.
   1978   Are Good and Poor Readers Taught Differently? Is That Why Poor Readers Are Poor
           Readers? Paper presented at AERA meeting, Toronto, April. State University of New
           York, Albany
   1980   Teacher interruption behaviors during primary grade oral reading. *Journal of Educa-
           tional Psychology* 72:371-377.
Anderson, R.C., and P.D. Pearson
   1984   A schema-theoretic view of basic processes in reading. Pp. 255-291 in P. D. Pearson, ed.,
           Handbook of Reading Research. New York: Longman.
Anderson, R.C., E.H. Hiebert, J.A. Scott, and I.A.G. Wilkinson
   1985   *Becoming a Nation of Readers: The Report of the Commission on Reading.* Washington,
           DC: National Institute of Education, U.S. Department of Education.
Anderson, V., and M. Roit
   1996   Linking reading comprehension instruction to language development for language minor-
           ity students. *Elementary School Journal* 96(3):295-310.
Applebee, A., J. Langer, and I. Mullis
   1985   *The Reading Report Card.* Princeton, NJ: Educational Testing Service.
   1987   *Learning to be Literate in America.* Princeton, NJ: Educational Testing Service.
   1989   *Crossroads in American Education.* Princeton, NJ: Educational Testing Service.
Barnett, M.A.
   1989   *More Than Meets the Eye: Foreign Language Reading. Language and Education:
           Theory and Practice.* Englewood Cliffs, NJ: ERIC.
Bereiter, C.
   1984   The limitations of interpretation (review of writing and the writer). *Curriculum Inquiry*
           4:211-216.
Bereiter, C., and M. Bird
   1985   Use of thinking aloud in identification and teaching of reading comprehension strategies.
           Cognition and Instruction 2:131-156.
Bernhardt, E.B.
   1987   Cognitive processes in L2: An examination of reading behaviors. Pp. 35-50 in J. Lantolf
           and A. Labarca, eds., *Research in Second Language Learning: Focus on the Classroom.*
           Norwood, NJ: Ablex.
Bialystok, E.
   1988   Levels of bilingualism and levels of linguistic awareness. *Developmental Psychology*
           24:560-567.
   1992   Attentional control in children's metalinguistic performance and measures of field inde-
           pendence. *Developmental Psychology* 28:654-664.
   in   The effects of bilingualism and biliteracy on children's emerging concepts of print. *De-*
   press   *velopmental Psychology.*
Bialystok, E., and K. Hakuta
   1994   *In Other Words.* New York: Basic Books.
Briars, D., and R.S. Siegler
   1984   A featural analysis of preschoolers' counting knowledge. *Developmental Psychology*
           20(4):607-618.

Brown, A.L.
  1980   Metacognitive development and reading. Pp. 453-481 in R.J. Spiro, B.C. Bruce, and W.F. Brewer, eds., *Theoretical Issues in Reading Comprehension*. Hillsdale, NJ: Erlbaum.

Brown, J.S., and K. VanLehn
  1982   Towards a generative theory of "bugs." Pp. 117-135 in T.P. Carpenter, J.M. Moser, and T.A. Romberg, eds., *Addition and Subtraction: A Cognitive Perspective*. Hillsdale, NJ: Erlbaum.

Brown, A.L., J.D. Bransford, R.A. Ferrara, and J.C. Campione
  1983   Learning, remembering, and understanding. Pp. 77-166 in J.H. Flavell and E.M. Markman, eds., Handbook of Child Psychology: Vol 3. *Cognitive Development*. 4th ed. New York: Wiley.

Bruer, J.T.
  1993   *Schools of Thought*. Cambridge, MA: MIT Press.

Carlo, M.S., and E.S. Sylvester
  1996   The Role of Low-Level Reading Components in Adult ESL Reading. Poster presented at the annual conference of the Society for the Scientific Study of Reading, April 1996, New York. Harvard University.

Carpenter, T.P., and J.M. Moser
  1982   The development of addition and subtraction problem-solving skills. Pp. 9-24 in T.P. Carpenter, J.M. Moser, and T.A. Romberg, eds., *Addition and Subtraction: A cognitive perspective*. Hillsdale, NJ: Erlbaum.

Carrell, Patricia L.
  1984   The effects of rhetorical organization on ESL readers. *TESOL Quarterly* 18(3):441-469.
  1987   Content and formal schemata in ESL reading. *TESOL Quarterly* 21(3):461-481.

Casanave, C.P.
  1988   Comprehension monitoring in ESL reading: A neglected essential. *TESOL Quarterly* 22:283-302.

Case, R.
  1993   Theories of learning and theories of development. *Educational Psychologist* 28:219-233.

Chall, J.S.
  1967   *Learning to Read: The Great Debate*. New York: McGraw-Hill.
  1983   *Stages of Reading Development*. New York: McGraw-Hill.

Chamot, A.U., M. Dale, J.M. O'Malley, and G. Spanos
  1992   Learning and problem solving strategies of ESL students. *Bilingual Research Journal* 16(3-4):1-33.

Chi, M.T.H., R. Glaser, and E. Rees
  1982   Expertise in problem solving. Pp. 7-75 in R.J. Sternberg, ed., *Advances in the Psychology of Human Intelligence, Vol 1*. Hillsdale, NJ: Erlbaum.

Chi, M.T.H., and R. Koeske
  1983   Network representation of a child's dinosaur knowledge. *Development Psychology* 19:29-39.

Chi, M.T.H., and S. Ceci
  1987   Content knowledge: Its role, representation, and restructuring in memory development. Pp. 91-142 in H.W. Reese, ed., *Advances in Child Development and Behavior, Vol. 20*. New York: Academic Press.

Chi, M.T.H., N. de Leeuw, M.H. Chiu, and C. LaVancher
  1994   Eliciting self-explanations improve conceptual understanding. *Cognitive Science* 18:439-477.

Christian, D.
    1996   Language development in two-way immersion: Trends and prospects. In James E. Alatis,
            Carolyn A. Straehle, Maggie Ronkin, and Brent Gallenberger, eds., *Georgetown Univer-
            sity Round Table 1996.* Washington, DC: Georgetown University Press.
Clark, M.M.
    1976   *Young Fluent Readers: What Can They Teach Us?* London, England: Heinemann.
Cobb, P.
    1994   Where is the mind? Constructivist and sociocultural perspectives on mathematical devel-
            opment. *Educational Researcher* 23(7):13-20.
Cocking, R.R., and S. Chipman
    1988   Conceptual issues related to mathematics achievement of language minority children. Pp.
            17-46 in R.R. Cocking and J.P. Mestre, eds., *Linguistic and Cultural Influences on Learn-
            ing Mathematics.* Hillsdale, NJ: Erlbaum.
Cocking, R.R., and J.P. Mestre
    1988   Considerations of language mediators of mathematics learning. Pp. 3-16 in R.R. Cocking
            and J.P. Mestre, eds., *Linguistic and Cultural Influences on Learning Mathematics.*
            Hillsdale, NJ: Erlbaum.
Cohen, E.G.
    1990   Teaching in multiculturally heterogeneous classrooms: Findings from a model program.
            McGill Journal of Education 26(1):7-23.
Collier, V.P., and W.P. Thomas
    1989   How quickly can immigrants become proficient in school English? *Journal of Educa-
            tional Issues of Language Minority Students* 5:26-38.
Cummins, J.
    1991   Language development and academic learning. Pp. 161-75 in L.M. Malavé and G.
            Duquette, eds., *Language, Culture and Cognition.* Clevedon, England: Multilingual
            Matters.
Devine, J.
    1987   General language competence and adult second language reading. Pp. 73-86 in J. Devine,
            P. Carrell, and D. Eskey, eds., *Research in Reading English as a Second Language.*
            Washington, DC: Teachers of English to Speakers of Other Languages.
Diaz, R.M.
    1986   Bilingual cognitive development: Addressing three gaps in current research. *Child De-
            velopment* 56:1376-1388.
diSessa, A.A.
    1988   Knowledge in pieces. Pp. 49-70 in G. Forman and P. Pufall, eds., *Constructivism in the
            Computer Age.* Hillsdale, NJ: Erlbaum.
Durgunoglu, A.Y., W. Nagy, and B. Hancin-Bhatt
    1993   Cross-language transfer of phonological awareness. *Journal of Educational Psychology*
            85(3):453-465.
Durkin, D.
    1966   *Children Who Read Early, Two Longitudinal Studies.* New York: Teachers College
            Press.
Elley, W.B.
    1981   A comparison of content-interest and structuralist reading programs in Niue primary
            schools. *New Zealand Journal of Educational Studies* 15(1):39-53.
Elley, W.B., and F. Mangubhai
    1983   The impact of reading on second language learning. *Reading Research Quarterly*
            19(1):53-67.
Feitelson, Dina
    1988   *Facts and Fads in Beginning Reading: A Cross-Language Perspective.* Norwood, NJ:
            Ablex.

Fitzgerald, J.
1995   English-as-a-second-language learners' cognitive reading processes: A review of research in the United States. *Review of Educational Research* 65:145-190.
Flesch, R.F.
1955   *Why Johnny Can't Read.* New York: Harper Row.
Freppon, P. A., and K. L. Dahl
1991   Learning about phonics in a whole language classroom. *Language Arts* 68 (March):190-197.
Fuson, K.C.
1992   Research on learning and teaching addition and subtraction of whole numbers. Pp. 53-187 in G. Leinhardt, R. Putnam, and R.A. Hattrup, eds., *Analysis of Arithmetic for Mathematics Teaching.* Hillsdale, NJ: Erlbaum.
Fuson, K.C., and W.G. Secada
1986   Teaching children to add by counting on with finger patterns. *Cognition and Instruction* 3:229-260.
Garcia, G.E., and W.E. Nagy
1993   Latino students' concept of cognates. Pp. 367-374 in D.J. Leu and C.K. Kinzer, eds., *Examining Central Issues in Literacy Research, Theory and Practice.* Chicago: National Reading Conference.
Gelman, R., and C.R. Gallistel
1978   *The Child's Understanding of Number.* Cambridge, MA: Harvard University Press.
Gelman, R., and E. Meck
1986   The notion of principle: The case of counting. Pp. 29-57 in J. Heibert, ed., *Conceptual and Procedural Knowledge: The Case of Mathematics.* Hillsdale, NJ: Erlbaum.
Gersten, R.
1996   Literacy instruction for language-minority students: The transition years. *The Elementary School Journal* 96(3):228-244.
Goodman, K.S.
1968   *The Psycholinguistic Nature of the Reading Process.* Detroit, MI: Wayne State University Press.
Greeno, J.G., M.S. Riley, and R. Gelman
1984   Conceptual competence and children's counting. *Cognitive Psychology* 16:94-143.
Greeno, J.G., and H.A. Simon
1988   Problem solving and reasoning. Pp. 589-672 in R.C. Atkinson, R.J. Hernstein, G. Lindzey, and R.D. Luce, eds., *Steven's Handbook of Experimental Psychology.* Vol. 2. New York: John Wiley & Sons.
Gregg, M.
1993   Learning Geographical Reasoning: Mapping the Course. Unpublished doctoral dissertation. University of Pittsburgh. College of Education, University of Alabama.
Hakuta, K.
1986   *Minor of Language: The Debate on Bilingualism.* New York: Basic Books.
Hakuta, K., and R.M. Diaz
1985   The relationship between degree of bilingualism and cognitive ability: A critical discussion and some new longitudinal data. Pp. 319-345 in K. Nelson, ed., *Children's Language.* 5th ed. Hillsdale, NJ: Erlbaum.
Heibert, J.
1986   *Conceptual and Procedural Knowledge: The Case of Mathematics.* Hillsdale, NJ: Erlbaum.
Hilferty, A.
1996   Coding Decoding: Predicting the Reading Comprehension of Latino Adults Learning English. Doctoral thesis, Graduate School of Education, Harvard University.

Hinds, J.L.
    1983   Contrastive rhetoric: Japanese and English. *Text* 3:183-195.
Hoffman, J.V., and R. Clements
    1984   Reading miscues and teacher verbal feedback. *The Elementary School Journal* 84:423-439.
Hung, D., and O. Tzeng
    1981   Orthographic variations and visual information processing. *Psychological Bulletin* 90:377-414.
Jiménez, R.T., G.E. Garcia, and P.D. Pearson
    1995   Three children, two languages, and strategic reading: Case studies in Bilingual/Monolingual Reading. *American Educational Research Journal* 32(Spring)(1):67-97.
    1996   The reading strategies of bilingual Latina/o students who are successful English readers: Opportunities and obstacles. *Reading Research Quarterly* 31(1):90-112.
Johnson, P.
    1981   Effects on reading comprehension of language complexity and cultural background of a text. *TESOL Quarterly* 15:169-181.
Kintsch, W., and T.A. van Dijk
    1978   Toward a model of text comprehension and production. *Psychological Review* 85(5):363-394.
Klingner, J.K., and S. Vaughn
    1996   Reciprocal teaching of reading comprehension strategies for students with learning disabilities who use English as a second language. *The Elementary School Journal* 96(3):275-294.
Koda, K.
    1989a   The effects of transferred vocabulary knowledge on the development of L2 reading proficiency. *Foreign Language Annals* 22(6):529-540.
    1989b   Effects of L1 orthographic representation on L2 phonological coding strategies. *Journal of Psycholinguistic Research* 18:201-222.
Lampert, M.
    1986   Knowing, doing, and teaching multiplication. *Cognition and Instruction* 4(4):303-342.
    1992   Teaching and learning long division for understanding in school. Pp. 189-219 in G. Leinhardt, R. Putnam, and R.A. Hattrup, eds., *Analysis of Arithmetic for Mathematics Teaching*. Hillsdale, NJ: Erlbaum.
Lanauze, M., and C.E. Snow
    1989   The relation between first- and second-language writing skills: Evidence from Puerto Rican elementary school children in bilingual programs. *Linguistics and Education* 1:323-340.
Langer, J.A., L. Bartolomé, O. Vasquez, and T. Lucas
    1990   Meaning construction in school literacy tasks: A study of bilingual students. *American Educational Research Journal* 27:427-471.
Leinhardt, G.
    1987   The development of an expert explanation: An analysis of a sequence of subtraction lessons. *Cognition and Instruction* 4(4):225-282.
    1992   What research on learning tells us about teaching. *Educational Leadership* 49(7):20-25.
    1994   History: A time to be mindful. Pp. 209-255 in G. Leinhardt, I.L. Beck, and C. Stainton, eds., *Teaching and Learning in History*. Hillsdale, NJ: Erlbaum.
Leinhardt, G., O. Zaslavsky, and M.K. Stein
    1990   Functions, graphs, and graphing: Tasks, learning, and teaching. *Review of Educational Research* 60(1):1-64.
McKeown, M., I. Beck, G.M. Sinatra, and J.A. Loxterman
    1992   The contribution of prior knowledge and coherent text to comprehension. *Reading Research Quarterly* 27:79-93.

McKeown, M., and I.L. Beck
  1994   Making sense of accounts of history: Why young children don't and how they might. Pp. 1-26 in G. Leinhardt, I.L. Beck, and C. Stainton, eds., *Teaching and Learning in History*. Hillsdale, NJ: Erlbaum.
McKlosky, M.
  1983   Intuitive physics. *Scientific American* (March):122-129.
Miller, P.A.
  1993   *Theories of Developmental Psychology*. 3rd ed. New York: W.H. Freeman.
Moll, L., and R. Diaz
  1985   Ethnographic pedagogy: Promoting effective bilingual instruction. Pp. 127-149 in E. Garcia and R. Padilla, eds., *Advances in Bilingual Education Research*. Tucson: University of Arizona Press.
Myers, D.E., and A.M. Milne
  1988   Effects of home language and primary language on mathematics achievement: A model and results for secondary analysis. Pp. 259-293 in R.R. Cocking and J.P. Mestre, eds., *Linguistic and Cultural Influences on Learning Mathematics: The Psychology of Education and Instruction*. Hillsdale, NJ: Erlbaum.
Nagy, W.
  1988   *Teaching Vocabulary to Improve Reading Comprehension*. Urbana, IL: National Council of Teachers of English.
Newell, A., and H.A. Simon
  1972   *Human Problem Solving*. Englewood Cliffs, NJ: Prentice-Hall.
Ohlsson, S.
  1992   The cognitive skill of theory articulation: A neglected aspect of science education? *Science & Education* 1:181-192.
Palincsar, A.S., and A.L. Brown
  1984   Reciprocal teaching of comprehension-fostering and comprehension-monitoring activities. *Cognition and Instruction* 1(2):117-175.
Peal, E., and W.E. Lambert
  1962   The relation of bilingualism to intelligence. *Psychological Monographs: General and Applied* 76(546):1-23.
Pearson, D.P., J. Hansen, and C. Gordon
  1979   The effect of background knowledge on young children's comprehension of explicit and implicit information. *Journal of Reading Behavior* 11(3):201-209.
Perfetti, C.A., and S. Zhang
  1991   Phonological processes in reading Chinese characters. *Journal of Experimental Psychology: Learning, Memory, and Cognition* 17:633-643.
Perfetti, C.A., S. Zhang, and I. Berent
  1992   Reading in English and Chinese: Evidence for a "universal" phonological principle. Pp. 227-248 in R. Frost and L. Katz, eds., *Orthography, Phonology, Morphology, and Meaning*. Amsterdam: Elsevier.
Purcell-Gates, V.
  1996   Process teaching with explicit explanation and feedback in a university-based clinic. In E. McIntyre and M. Pressley, eds., *Balanced Instruction: Strategies and Skills in Whole Language*. Norwood, MA: Christopher-Gordon.
Qin, Y., and H.A. Simon
  1990   Laboratory replication of scientific discovery processes. *Cognitive Science* 14:281-312.
Rayner, K., and A. Pollatsek
  1989   *The Psychology of Reading*. Englewood Cliffs, NJ: Prentice Hall.
Reif, F.
  1987   Interpretation of scientific or mathematical concepts: Cognitive issues and instructional implications. *Cognitive Science* 11:395-416.

Resnick, L.B.
1992   From protoquantities to operators: Building mathematical competence on a foundation of everyday knowledge. Pp. 373-429 in G. Leinhardt, R. Putnam, and R.A. Hattrup, eds., *Analysis of Arithmetic for Mathematics Teaching.* Hillsdale, NJ: Erlbaum.

Resnick, L.B., and L.E. Klopfer
1989   *Toward the Thinking Curriculum: Current Cognitive Research.* Alexandria, VA: Association for Supervision and Curriculum Development.

Riley, M.S., J.G. Greeno, and J.I. Heller
1983   Development of children's problem-solving ability in arithmetic. Pp. 153-196 in H.P. Ginsberg, ed., *The Development of Mathematical Thinking.* New York: Academic Press.

Rosebery, A. S., B. Warren, and F. R. Conant
1992   Appropriating scientific discourse: Findings from language minority classrooms. *The Journal of the Learning Sciences* 2(1):61-94.

Schoenfeld, A.H., J.P. Smith, and A. Arcavi
1993   Learning: The microgenetic analysis of one student's evolving understanding of a complex subject matter domain. Pp. 55-176 in R. Glaser, ed., *Advances in Instructional Psychology.* Vol. 4. Hillsdale, NJ: Erlbaum.

Schwab, J.J.
1978   Education and the structure of the disciplines. In I. Westbury and N.J. Wilkof, eds., *Science, Curriculum, and Liberal Education: Selected Essays.* Chicago: University of Chicago Press.

Scribner, S.
1984   Studying work intelligence. Pp. 9-40 in B. Rogoff and J. Lave, eds., *Everyday Cognition: Its Development in Social Context.* Cambridge, MA: Harvard University Press.

Short, D.J.
1994   Expanding middle school horizons: Integrating language, culture, and social studies. *TESOL Quarterly* 28(3):581-608.

Simon, H.A., and C. Kaplan
1989   Foundations of cognitive science. Pp. 1-47 in M.I. Posner, ed., *Foundations of Cognitive Science.* Cambridge, MA: MIT Press.

Simon, H.A., J. H. Larkin, J. McDermott, and D.P. Simon
1980   Models of competence in solving physics problems. *Cognitive Science* 4:317-345.

Skutnabb-Kangas, Tove
1979   *Language in the Process of Cultural Assimilation and Structural Incorporation of Linguistic Minorities.* Arlington, VA: National Clearinghouse for Bilingual Education.

Slavin, R., and R. Yampolsky
1992   *Success for All. Effects on Students with Limited English Proficiency: A Three-year Evaluation.* Report No. 29. Baltimore, MD: Center for Research on Effective Schooling for Disadvantaged Students, The Johns Hopkins University.

Slavin, R., and N. Madden
1994   Lee Conmigo: Effects of Success for All in Bilingual First Grades. Paper presented at the annual meeting of the American Educational Research Association, New Orleans. Center for Social Organization of School, Johns Hopkins University.

Smith, F.
1983   *Understanding Reading.* 3rd ed. New York: Holt, Rinehart and Winston.

Snow, C.E.
1990   The development of definitional skill. *Journal of Child Language* 17:697-710.

Stahl, S.A., and P.D. Miller
1989   Whole language and language experience approaches for beginning reading: A quantitative research synthesis. *Review of Educational Research* 59(1):87-116.

Stanovich, K.
   1986   Matthew effects in reading: Some consequences of individual differences in the acquisition of literacy. *Reading Research Quarterly* 21:360-407.
Stodolsky, S.
   1988   *The Subject Matters: Classroom Activity in Mathematics and Social Studies.* Chicago: University of Chicago Press.
Teale, W.H.
   1986   Home background and young children's literacy development. In W. Teale and E. Sulzby, eds., *Emergent Literacy: Writing and Reading.* Norwood, NJ: Ablex.
Teale, W.H., E. Estrada, and A. Anderson
   1981   How preschoolers interact with written communication. In M. Kamil, ed., *Directions in Reading: Research and Instruction.* Washington, DC: The National Reading Conference.
Velasco, P.
   1989   The Relationship of Oral Decontextualized Language and Reading Comprehension in Bilingual Children. Doctoral thesis, Graduate School of Education, Harvard University.
Wagner, R.K., and J.K. Torgeson
   1987   The nature of phonological processing and its causal role in the acquisition of reading skills. *Psychological Bulletin* 101:192-212.
Wertsch, J.V.
   1979   From social interaction to higher psychological processes: A clarification and application of Vygotsky's theory. *Human Development* 22:1-22.
Wineberg, S.
   1994   The cognitive representation of historical texts. Pp. 85-136 in G. Leinhardt, I.L. Beck, and C. Stainton, eds., *Teaching and Learning in History.* Hillsdale, NJ: Erlbaum.
Wong Fillmore, L., and C. Valadez
   1986   Teaching bilingual learners. Pp. 648-685 in M.C. Wittrock, ed., *Handbook of Research on Teaching.* 3rd ed. New York: Macmillan.
Young, K.M., and G. Leinhardt
   1996   *Writing from Primary Documents: A Way of Knowing in History.* Tech. Report No. CLIP-96-01. Pittsburgh, PA: University of Pittsburgh, Learning Research and Development Center.

THE SOCIAL CONTEXT OF SCHOOL LEARNING: SUMMARY OF THE STATE OF KNOWLEDGE

Research based on the premise that schooling must be analyzed from social as well as cognitive perspectives has yielded a number of important insights:

• In classroom learning situations, negotiation occurs within at least two domains: the rules for how to talk in the classroom and the construction of actual content knowledge through talk. The implications for English-language learners are that negotiating these matters is much more difficult in a second language, and negotiated rules are likely to be heavily influenced by culture.

• Language-minority students may be treated differently from mainstream students as a result of forces both within and outside of school that implicitly and explicitly promote and sustain the perspectives and institutions of the majority.

• While achievement motivation is an important factor in helping explain school success, it does not explain differences in success among language-minority groups or between immigrant and mainstream groups.

• The dialects spoken by children influence teacher perceptions of their academic ability, the students' learning opportunities, evaluations of their contributions to class, and the way they are grouped for instruction. The languages students speak also influence perceptions of their academic ability and their learning opportunities.

• Research on cooperative learning indicates that students of color and white students have a greater tendency to make cross-racial friendship choices after they have participated in interracial cooperative learning teams, and the academic achievement of students of color is increased when cooperative learning activities are used. Cooperative learning activities also increase student motivation and self-esteem and help students develop empathy.

• Research indicates that curriculum interventions—multi-ethnic and -racial lessons and materials—have positive effects on the ethnic and racial attitudes of students.

• Evidence suggests that like all students, immigrant and language-minority children benefit from actions taken in the home to promote child academic achievement. Such activities can be classified as monitoring, communication, motivational, and protective. However, these actions may not be visible to school personnel, who thus assume parents are uninvolved in their children's learning.

4

The Social Context of School Learning

Whereas the previous chapter reviewed cognitive aspects of literacy and content learning, this chapter examines research related to a variety of social factors involved in school learning. It is clear that children may arrive at school ready to learn in a number of different ways. One way is to have high levels of language, emergent literacy, and world knowledge acquired at home or in preschool. Equally important, though, is readiness in the emotional, social, and motivational realms: the ability to adapt to the new constraints of the classroom, the social skills that are needed to participate effectively in classroom discourse, and the self-esteem and sense of agency required to work hard and learn intentionally. School learning is a social as well as a cognitive process, one influenced by the relationships between student and teacher and among students. Furthermore, what children learn at school is not exclusively academic content; schools are designed to make children productive citizens who are respectful of the diversity of their society. While there has been a great deal of research on the social and motivational determinants of school success for mainstream children, attention to these matters with regard to language-minority children has focused more on issues of mismatch between the social rules these children bring from home and those that obtain in the classroom. In this chapter, we identify some of the salient themes in research on social factors as related to academic achievement for language-minority children.

STATE OF KNOWLEDGE

This section reviews the findings of research on social factors in school learning in five areas: the social nature of knowledge acquisition, the issue of differential treatment of ethnic minority students, cultural differences in the motivation to achieve, children's social and group relationships, and parental involvement in children's school learning

The Social Nature of Knowledge Acquisition

Were we to focus only on issues examined in the previous chapter, such as the nature of understanding across subject matter, the various forms of knowledge learners possess, and the way prior knowledge influences the acquisition of new knowledge, we would be ignoring a vital aspect of school learning: the fact that most learning occurs in a social context in which individual actions and understandings are negotiated by the members of a group. There are two theoretical perspectives on the locus of this negotiation. The individual perspective is based on the idea of constructivism—that individuals actively construct meanings from interaction with the world around them, an idea traced back to Piaget's (1970) theories of cognitive development (see Chapter 3). In contrast, the social perspective is based on sociocultural theories of learning that emphasize the role of social interaction with more knowledgeable others (Vygotsky, 1978) and activity-oriented work in a social setting (Leont'ev, 1981). While there has been a tradition of debate over the relative accuracy of these perspectives in depicting learning processes, recent work suggests it may be more profitable to determine when and how the two perspectives might work together to describe student learning (Bereiter, 1994; Cobb, 1994).

We focus here not on this debate, but on the context of negotiation as related to the social nature of learning. We propose that in a classroom learning situation, negotiation occurs within at least two domains: the rules for how to talk in the classroom and the construction of actual content knowledge through talk. It is from the interpretation of these negotiations that students construct their own knowledge and understanding. However, it is typically the teacher who, either implicitly or explicitly, initiates negotiation across these dimensions.

Negotiating How to Talk

The process of negotiating the way classroom participants will talk about subject matter is of concern for researchers from a sociocultural perspective because participation in situated cultures of practice is assumed to be an important influence on an individual's academic performance. Thus, students who understand that a teacher's question about a text requests an explanation for their interpretation rather than the literal interpretation itself will participate more effectively in that classroom's practice. Research on learning outside the classroom has demonstrated the extent to which context influences the nature of such learning for any given individual (Brown et al., 1989; Carraher et al., 1985; Lave et al., 1984; Resnick, 1987; Scribner, 1984). Classroom participants similarly negotiate how they will talk about the subject matter at hand (Wertsch, 1979, 1990; Vygotsky, 1978; Cobb et al., 1993; Moll and Whitmore, 1993; Lampert, 1990). To date, these issues have not been addressed systematically in the study of student learning across subject matter domains. However, they have obvious implications for second-language education, in part because negotiating these matters is much more difficult in a second language and in part because the negotiated rules are likely to be heavily influenced by culture.

Ideally, conclusions about cultural mismatch in the negotiation of talk are based on observations of children both at home and at school. One such study was conducted by Philips (1983) in the homes and classrooms of Native American students. Using an ethnographic approach to the study of language-use practices among Warm Springs Indian children, Philips identified and described the different participant structures to which the children had access in home, community, and school settings. She found that the children's verbal participation was much greater in classrooms whose participant structures were similar to those used routinely in their homes and community. Similarly, in her ethnographic study of how language is learned by African American and white children in the rural south, Heath (1983) showed that certain language-use patterns characteristic of the African American community differed from those used by white teachers—both in their homes and in their classrooms to structure talk—in the schools the African American children attended.

Both Gee (1988a, 1988b) and Michaels (1991) have focused on the social meaning of children's own discourse forms, both as effective ways of expressing their own intentions and as forms that lead to miscommunication with and negative reactions from teachers. Michaels analyzed the sharing-time turns of an African-American child, identifying the culturally specific pattern of story telling she used and the ways it violated the rules for sharing time imposed by the teacher (see also Gee, 1985, 1990). The mismatches identified by Gee and Michaels make access to full participation in educational interactions more difficult for the speakers of the less-valued discourse forms.

Other studies leading to conclusions about cultural mismatch have been conducted exclusively in classroom settings; these are of the type Cazden (1986:446) identifies as the "culturally different case," that is, comparison with an assumed mainstream pattern of interaction. For example, Au and Mason (1981) focus their comparisons on the discourse of two teachers—one who had little experience with Polynesian children and one who had a long history of working with them. The latter teacher's reading lessons were characterized by discourse patterns that resembled those identified in studies of native Hawaiian teachers (Au, 1980) and children (Boggs, 1985). This teacher's students engaged in the kinds of collaborative and overlapping talk that are characteristic of talk story, a native Hawaiian joint story-telling event. The students taught by this teacher performed better on several verbal measures related to academic engagement and reading ability (amount of academically engaged time, number of reading-related and correct responses to teachers' questions, and number of idea units and logical inferences) than the students of the other teacher. Gutierrez et al. (1995) demonstrate how particular classroom communities evolve, and illustrate how the schooling practices of an urban school serve to marginalize rather than accommodate the linguistic, social, and cultural capital of its diverse student population.

Other studies focusing on enactments of sociocultural pedagogy in schools and classrooms have investigated efforts to incorporate into classrooms features of learning and talking that are characteristic of the homes and communities of English-language learners. Perhaps the most well-known such effort to make classroom instruction culturally responsive is the Kamehameha Early Education Program (Au and Mason, 1981), which incorporated the talk story format discussed above into literacy instruction, with positive results.

Negotiating Knowledge

In addition to negotiation of the rules for classroom talk, social practices for talking about a particular subject matter are negotiated by the participants, who thus are able to discuss the subject in a routine, predictable way. For example, studies have demonstrated that students' text comprehension is improved when the classroom participants, both teachers and students, take an active role in constructing their understanding of the text through the techniques of questioning the author (Beck et al., in press) and reciprocal teaching (Palincsar and Brown, 1984; Palincsar et al., 1993). Expert explanations have been found to facilitate student learning in history and mathematics for students of both low and high ability (Leinhardt, 1993). To participate in an explanation, students must understand the goals of the explanation and their role in attaining those goals. Students have the opportunity to learn the subject matter content through negotiations about that content during classroom discourse.

Using the classroom as a social arena for the public examination of ideas accomplishes three important things: (1) students gradually gain competence in using terminology and in connecting actions and concepts within a discipline; (2) in the course of dialogue, students naturally build on or refute old ideas as these are merged with new knowledge; and (3) actions of discussion, proof, and explanation are merged with networks of concepts and principles that are part of a particular subject matter. The examination of classroom discourse has informed research in primary-language content learning (see Chapter 3) by focusing on how social interaction influences the nature of learning by classroom students.

A recent volume of *Linguistics and Education* (6:1, 1994) focuses on the efforts of researchers, most of whom are participants in the Santa Barbara Classroom Discourse Group, working in classrooms of Spanish/English bilingual students in the elementary and middle grades. As the editors state in their introduction to the volume, these studies contribute to our understanding of "the ordinary discursive and social practices in an everyday setting—classrooms and how these practices contribute to the construction of knowledge in classrooms" (p. 234). A central notion underlying these studies is that classroom discourse is both the process by which knowledge is constructed and the source of specific content, as well as the content of students' knowledge production. Implicit in each study is the view of a dialectical process in which participants' interactions both shape and are shaped by a range of contextual forces. It is this notion of dialectic and the way it contributes to the construction of knowledge that is implicit in the situated view of learning and the learner set forth in these studies.

Many studies that focus on teaching and learning literacy in classrooms include an examination of the issues associated with a particular pedagogical perspective or practice. Several of these studies have helped extend our under-standing of the conditions that have led to variations in the way a particular approach is applied. For example, in her ethnographic study of journal sharing in nine different bilingual classrooms, Gutierrez (1992, 1994) found that teachers shared one of three "scripts" or pedagogical views of writing. Based on Gutierrez's 1992 descriptions, only one of these scripts provided enriched con-texts for literacy learning in line with the tenets of sociocultural theory outlined above, that is, "contexts that give students both assistance and the occasions to use and write elaborated and meaningful discourse" (p. 259).

A number of researchers have focused on a discussion format known as instructional conversation that is grounded in the Vygotskian notions of assisted performance (e.g., Goldenberg and Gallimore, 1991; Rueda et al., 1992; Saunders et al., 1992; Patthey-Chavez and Goldenberg, 1995), as used in classrooms serv-ing language-minority students. Instructional conversation contrasts markedly with the traditional teacher-fronted and skills-based approaches to instructional discourse most often available to language-minority students. Studies of this approach have shown that it is characterized by a thematic focus, teachers' efforts to build upon students' previous verbal contributions and experiences, and direct teaching. Although the use of this approach in classroom settings has not been linked to formal assessment of student learning, evidence of learning may be gleaned from an examination of the instructional conversations themselves. For example, as teachers become more proficient with the format, student talk in-creases, as measured by the percentage of total turns they take and the mean turn length (Patthey-Chavez and Goldenberg, 1995; Dalton and Sison, 1995).

Similarly, research by Warren and Rosebery in two bilingual science class-rooms has focused on the nature of the scientific discourse used by students and teachers and the extent to which students appropriate scientific ways of knowing and reasoning. This research has tended to be quite detailed, focusing on a specific device or pattern. For example, in a recent article, Warren and Rosebery (1995) examine the role of argumentation in one of the classrooms. As they state in their introduction to this work, the intent of the study is to further articulate sociocultural theory on how science can be learned in classroom settings, using

Bakhtin's notion of dialogism as a filter for understanding this discourse sequence.[1] (From a Bakhtinian perspective, utterances within a social context are imbued with multiple meanings and subject to evaluation, revision, and refinement.) In their analysis of argumentation in a bilingual Haitian Creole science class, Warren and Rosebery (1995) focus on students' disagreements over scientific claims, how these disagreement sequences shape the students' scientific understanding, and more specifically what it means for a claim to be accountable to evidence. This interpretive approach to the analysis of a single discussion yields insights into how norms of scientific practice, as well as elements of scientific thinking, can be jointly constructed by students engaged in meaningful acts of inquiry.

What distinguishes Warren and Rosebery's research from many other interpretive studies is the attention they pay to student learning (Rosebery et al., 1992). During interviews conducted in September and June, students were asked to think aloud about how they would research and explain two scientific dilemmas. The researchers' quantitative analyses revealed that the students had increased their appropriate uses of content knowledge and hypothesis statements by the time of the June interviews. Their qualitative analyses showed that the students were better able to reason in terms of larger explanatory frameworks by June. Students who had solved problems with simplistic, unexplained conjectures in September were using their scientific understandings to generate hypotheses and experiments by the end of the school year.

The work of Moll and his colleagues (Moll et al., 1992) at the University of Arizona represents an important and all-too-rare collaboration between researchers and teachers aimed at utilizing community-based knowledge in classroom settings. Drawing on the principle that "the students' community represents a resource of enormous importance for educational change and improvement," teachers and researchers involved in his work have interviewed parents and other community members to identify the information and skills or "funds of knowledge" that are available to Mexicano households through an elaborate set of social networks that connects each household to other households and institutions. Teacher-researchers participating in the project then organize their curriculum around this information and these skills. In addition, they call upon the expertise of community members in their efforts to incorporate community-based knowledge sources into their curriculum.

Ethnographic research that situates the school experiences of language-minority children within the context of culture, community, and society has

---

[1]When describing their intent, Warren and Roseberry (1995:1) state: "We intend to illustrate how our perspective on learning in science is emerging through contact with socioculturally based theoretical perspectives and with the everyday experiences of teachers and students as they work to build sense-making communities in their classrooms."

provided a rich and complex portrayal of variations in the range of social contexts and circumstances that influence academic performance. While much of this research has focused on those factors implicated in the difficulties students encounter in school, its overall message situates the issue of academic achievement within the context of the social environments in which students participate, consistent with the view that knowledge is socially constructed.

Differential Treatment

While cultural mismatch is one explanation for the relatively poor academic performance of language-minority children, another avenue of research, known in the literature as differential treatment studies, starts from the assumption that some of those children may not be socialized toward academic achievement. This literature has contributed to the view that language-minority students, along with other ethnic minority students, are treated differently from mainstream students as a result of forces both within and outside of school that implicitly and explicitly promote and sustain the perspectives and institutions of the majority. Ogbu, a primary contributor to this view (Ogbu, 1978; Ogbu and Matute-Bianchi, 1986), has focused on how societal forces have contributed to socialization and acculturation patterns that ultimately influence minority students' academic achievement. Other researchers have concentrated on schools and classrooms when investigating the interaction among cultural, societal, and school influences on student achievement.

Like cultural mismatch studies, differential treatment studies focus on different kinds of comparisons, including those within a single classroom (e.g., Moll and Diaz, 1987) and those within the context of an entire school population (e.g., Gibson, 1988; Suarez-Orozco and Suarez-Orozco, 1995; Tuan, 1995; Harklau, 1994). As Losey (1995) reports, some of the early differential treatment studies include large-scale studies with many subjects, while more recent research has tended to take the form of ethnographic or qualitative accounts of a classroom or school. The latter studies have shown how schools engage in a number of practices that favor the status quo by enabling middle- and upper-class English-speaking students to progress through an educational pipeline that is often inaccessible to low-income ethnic minority students, including those who are deemed to have limited English proficiency. Studies that compare the experiences of language-minority students who have been successful in school with those who have had difficulties have provided important insights into the complex role played by culture and discrimination in the academic experiences of these students.

Despite the vivid and complex picture provided by these studies, it is often difficult to assess the degree to which differential treatment actually explains the circumstances faced by the groups under study. One major problem is operationalizing the term "underachievement" or "lower achievement" as used to characterize the groups under study. Studies seldom rely on individually assessed data on learning outcomes, particularly as pertains to the students being studied, because such data are seen as part of the positivistic paradigm with which the researchers contrast themselves. Instead, general descriptions of student underachievement (i.e., percentage of dropouts in a given ethnic group, average grade point) or information about the amount and nature of student participation (e.g., total amount of student talk) are used. Assessments of student learning tied to teachers' instructional goals are almost always lacking in these studies.

Another related problem is the inability to determine whether a given set of circumstances is really the cause of the difficulty students encounter in school. This problem is most apparent in the mismatch studies, which leave an important question unanswered: Which of the differences are the important ones for explaining student underachievement? The qualitative designs used in these studies do not establish causal connections between particular discontinuities and student learning. For most researchers working within this tradition, of course, this criticism is not a valid concern.

Cultural Differences in Achievement Motivation

A major nexus of hypotheses about the relatively poor academic performance of language-minority (and English-speaking ethnic minority) children implicates cultural differences in achievement motivation—the set of beliefs children hold about how and why to do well in school. The notion that achievement motivation may vary culturally has been supported by cross-national studies (e.g., Stevenson et al., 1990; Stevenson et al., 1986) showing that Asian children believe high achievement is the result of effort, whereas American children believe it is the result of innate ability. In the United States, however, these ethnic differences are eliminated or even reversed: second-generation Korean American children attribute success to ability more than do European American children (Choi et al., 1994), and high achievers across a variety of ethnic groups (African American, Latino, Indochinese American, and European American, all low-income) attribute their success to their high innate ability (Bempechat et al., in press).

Further analysis of the achievement motivation of Latino and Indochinese immigrant children suggests they have similar perceptions of parental socialization strategies and similar theories of educational success and failure. Nonetheless, the Indochinese immigrants were found to perform better than the Latino children (Bempechat and Williams, 1995). Moreover, Suarez-Orozco and Suarez-Orozco (1995) found that adolescents of Mexican descent showed higher academic achievement and orientation to academic achievement in the immigrant group than in later generations. One aspect of assimilation seems to be a lowering of academic goals, perhaps because of incorporation into a caste-like minority status or peer stigmatization of high achievement (Ogbu, 1995). It may be that Asian immigrants are less susceptible to the negative consequences of assimilation because, as voluntary immigrants, they place their faith in schools as agents of improvement (DeVos, 1978).

The above findings suggest that while achievement motivation is an important factor in helping to explain school success, it does not explain differences in success among language-minority groups or between immigrant and mainstream groups.

Children's Social and Group Relationships

Research by Harrison (cited in Garcia, 1993) indicates that the dialects spoken by students influence teacher perceptions of their academic ability, the students' learning opportunities, evaluations of their contributions to class, and the way they are grouped for instruction. The languages students speak also influence perceptions of their academic ability and their learning opportunities (Ryan and Carranza, 1977). Language can be the basis as well for categorization and the formation of ingroups and outgroups, especially within an institutional context in which the languages spoken have unequal status. Languages are often symbols of group boundaries and are therefore the sources of intergroup conflicts and tensions (Giles, 1977; Issacs, 1992). The following subsections examine studies of these issues in four areas: social identity theory, or the minimal group paradigm; the contact hypothesis; cooperative learning and interracial contact; and curriculum interventions.

Social Identity Theory: The Minimal Group Paradigm

Whenever ingroups and outgroups form, stereotypes, prejudice, and discrimination develop. Consequently, it becomes necessary for educators to design and implement strategies for improving intergroup relations. Social psychological theory and research addressing what is known as social identity theory or the minimal group paradigm indicate that when mere categorization develops, individuals favor the ingroup (their own group) over the outgroup and discriminate against the outgroup (Rothbart and John, 1993; Smith and Mackie, 1995). This phenomenon can occur in situations involving no prior historical conflict and animosity, competition, or physical differences—indeed no important differences at all. Writes Tajfel (1970:98-99), "Whenever we are confronted with a situation to which some form of intergroup categorization appears directly relevant, we are likely to act in a manner that discriminates against the outgroup and favors the ingroup." In a series of studies, Tajfel and colleagues (Tajfel, 1970; Billig and Tajfel, 1973) produced considerable evidence to support the postulate that individuals are likely to evaluate the ingroup more positively than the outgroup and to treat the ingroup more favorably, even when the differences between the groups are minimal, contrived, and insignificant. Language can become the basis for such categorization when some students speak a particular language and others do not, although little of the existing research on intergroup relations examines variables related to language. Lacking such research, we must glean from existing research those policies and practices which can help improve intergroup relations in linguistically, culturally, and racially diverse classrooms.

The minimal group paradigm is more helpful in explaining the development of ingroup-outgroup boundaries than in suggesting practices for reducing them. One implication of the paradigm is that to increase positive intergroup contact, the salience of group characteristics should be minimized, and a superordinate group with which students from different cultural and language groups can become identified should be constructed. In a classroom characterized by language diversity, group salience is likely to be reduced to the extent that all students become competent in the same languages. For example, in a classroom with both Anglos and Mexican Americans, group salience is increased if only the Mexican American students speak Spanish. However, if both Anglo and Mexican American students become competent in both English and Spanish, this bilingual competency can be the basis for the formation of a superordinate group to which all of the students belong.

Two-way bilingual programs, in which students from two different language groups learn both languages, may provide an effective way of reducing group salience and constructing a superordinate group identity. As an example, 300 students were enrolled in the Amigos two-way elementary school bilingual program in Cambridge, Massachusetts, in 1993 (Lambert and Cazabon, 1994). Half of the students enrolled in the program were native Spanish speakers and half native English speakers. Each language was used as the medium of instruction for half of the school day. Lambert and Cazabon found that the students in the program formed close friendships with members of both their own and the other group.

The Contact Hypothesis

Most of the work in social psychology related to race relations has been guided by the contact hypothesis and related research that emerged out of the events surrounding World War II. The rise of Nazi anti-Semitism and its devastating consequences motivated social scientists in the post-war years to devote considerable attention to theory and research related to improving intergroup relations. The contact hypothesis that guides most of the research and theory in intergroup relations today emerged from the classic work by Williams (1947) and Allport (1954). The hypothesis explains the conditions that must exist in interaction situations among different racial and ethnic groups in order for the interactions to result in positive rather than negative attitudes.

Allport (1954) states that contact between groups improves intergroup relations when the contact is characterized by four conditions: (1) equal status, (2) cooperation rather than competition, (3) sanctioning by authorities, and (4) interpersonal interactions in which people become acquainted as individuals. Stephan and Stephan (1996) describe the latter condition as "individualized contact." Writes Allport (1979/1954:281):

> Prejudice (unless deeply rooted in the structure of the individual) may be reduced by equal status contact between majority and minority groups in the pursuit of common goals. The effect is greatly enhanced if this contact is sanctioned by institutionalized supports (i.e., by law, custom, or local atmosphere), and provided it is of a sort that leads to the perception of common interests and common humanity between members of the two groups.

It should also be noted, however, that despite its significant influence on theory and practice, the contact hypothesis has a number of limitations. Pettigrew (1986:171) suggests that it is a theory "of modest scope derived to explain a particular and limited set of conflicting empirical findings in an applied area of interest—changes in intergroup attitudes as a function of intergroup contact under varying conditions." Moreover, most intergroup research related to classrooms was conducted in the 1970s and 1980s, and almost none of it in the 1990s. Thus, most of the research on race relations and cooperative groups was conducted using African Americans and whites as subjects. Race relations changed in significant ways during the 1980s and 1990s, however, when large numbers of students from Asia and Latin America entered the nation's classrooms.[2] Nevertheless, to improve intergroup relations in the nation's schools, educators must use the best theories available. The contact hypothesis is a theory that can be used to help educational practitioners improve intergroup relations in linguistically and culturally diverse classrooms.

Cooperative Learning and Interracial Contact

Since 1970, investigators have accumulated an impressive body of research on the effects of cooperative learning groups and activities on students' racial attitudes, friendship choices, and achievement. Much of this research has been conducted as well as reviewed by investigators such as Aronson and colleagues (Aronson and Bridgeman, 1979; Aronson and Gonzalez, 1988), Cohen and colleagues (Cohen, 1972, 1986; Cohen and Roper, 1972; Cohen and Lotan, 1995), Johnson and Johnson (1981, 1991), Slavin (1979, 1983, 1985), and Slavin and Madden (1979). Schofield (1995) has written an informative review of this

---

[2]Between 1981 and 1990, about 67 percent of the immigrants that entered the United States came from Mexico and nations in Central America and Asia; less than 10 percent came from Europe (Hansen and Bachu, 1995).

research, most of which has been conducted using elementary and high school students as subjects (Slavin, 1983, 1985).

The research on cooperative learning and interracial contact that has been conducted since 1970 is grounded in the theory of intergroup relations developed by Allport (1954). The results of this research lend considerable support to the postulate that if the conditions stated by Allport are present in the contact situations, cooperative interracial contact in schools has positive effects on both student interracial behavior and academic achievement (Aronson and Gonzalez, 1988; Slavin, 1979, 1983). In his review of 19 studies of the effects of cooperative learning methods, Slavin (1985) found that 16 showed positive effects on interracial friendships. In a more recent review, Slavin (1995) also describes the positive effects of cooperative groups on cross-racial friendships, racial attitudes, and behavior.

Most of this research supports the following postulates: (1) students of color and white students have a greater tendency to make cross-racial friendship choices after they have participated in interracial cooperative learning teams (Aronson and Bridgeman, 1979; Slavin, 1979); and (2) the academic achievement of students of color, such as African Americans and Mexican Americans, is increased when cooperative learning activities are used, while the academic achievement of white students remains about the same in both cooperative and competitive learning situations (Aronson and Gonzalez, 1988; Slavin, 1985). Investigators have also found that cooperative learning methods increase student motivation and self-esteem (Slavin, 1985) and help students develop empathy (Aronson and Bridgeman, 1979).

An essential characteristic of effective cooperative learning groups and methods is that the students experience equal status in the contact situation (Allport, 1954). Cohen (1972) points out that in an initial contact situation, both African American and white students may attribute higher status to whites that may perpetuate white dominance. Cohen and Roper (1972) designed an intervention to change this expectation for African American and white students. She also implemented a project in bilingual classrooms made up largely of children of Hispanic background with a small proportion of white, African American, and Asian children (Cohen and Intili, 1981; Cohen, 1984a, 1984b). Mixed groups of children worked together in learning centers on math and science activities; bilingual versions of the materials were available.

The research by Cohen and Roper (1972) indicates that equal status between groups in interracial and interethnic situations must be constructed by teachers, rather than assumed. If students from diverse racial, ethnic, and language groups are mixed without structured interventions that create equal-status conditions in the contact situation, racial and ethnic categorization and conflict are likely to increase. In a series of perceptive and carefully designed studies that span two decades, Cohen and colleagues (Cohen, 1984a, 1984b; Cohen and Roper, 1972; Cohen and Lotan, 1995) have consistently found that contact among different groups without deliberate interventions to increase equal status and positive interactions will increase rather than reduce intergroup tensions. Cohen (1994) has developed practical guidelines and strategies that can be used by teachers and other practitioners to create equal status within racially, culturally, and linguistically diverse classrooms.

There is a great deal of discussion but little agreement about what constitutes equal status in intergroup contact situations. Some researchers interpret equal status to mean equal socioeconomic status. For example, in his summary of favorable and unfavorable conditions that influence interracial contact, Amir (quoted in Hewstone and Brown, 1986:7) describes the following as an unfavorable condition: "contact between a majority and a minority group, when the members of the minority group are of lower status or are lower in any relevant characteristics than the members of the majority group." Yet Cohen and Roper (1972) interpret equal status differently. Although the African American and white students in their study were from different social-class groups, the researchers created equal status in the classroom by modifying the students' perceptions of each racial group. They accomplished this by assigning the African-American students a task that increased their status in the classroom. Cohen and Roper applied a social-psychological, rather than a socioeconomic, view of equal status.

Curriculum Interventions

The representations of different ethnic, racial, and language groups that are embedded in curriculum materials and textbooks and within the activities and teaching strategies of instructors privilege some groups of students (thus increasing their classroom status) and erode the status of others by reinforcing their marginal status in the larger society. Studies of textbooks indicate that the images of groups they project reflect those which are institutionalized within the larger society (Sleeter and Grant, 1991). If we view status from a social-psychological perspective, as do Cohen and Roper (1972), a multicultural curriculum that includes representations of diverse groups in realistic and complex ways can help equalize the status of all groups within the classroom or school. Only a few studies of curriculum intervention are reviewed here; see Stephan (1985) and Banks (1993, 1995) for more comprehensive reviews.

Since the 1940s, several curriculum intervention studies have been conducted to determine the effects of multi-ethnic and -racial lessons and materials, role playing, and other kinds of simulated experiences on the attitudes and perceptions of students. The limitations of these studies are similar to those that characterize most intergroup relations studies, such as those on categorization (Tajfel, 1970) and cooperative groups (Slavin, 1985). Most curriculum intervention studies are related to African Americans and whites, are of rather short duration, involve little follow-up, rarely measure the actual behavior of the subjects, use a variety of measures that have low intercorrelation, and have used interventions that are often not well defined so that it is difficult for the studies to be replicated by other researchers (Banks, 1995).

Despite the limitations of these studies, however, they provide guidelines that can help educators improve intergroup relations in the nation's classrooms and schools. In a study conducted by Litcher and Johnson (1969), white second grade children developed more positive racial attitudes after using multi-ethnic readers. However, when Litcher et al. (1973) replicated this study using photographs instead of readers, the children's racial attitudes were not significantly changed. The investigators suggested that the shorter length of the latter study (1 month versus 4) and the different racial compositions of the two communities in which the studies were conducted could help explain why there were no significant effects on the children's racial attitudes in the second study. (The community in which the second study was conducted had a much higher percentage of African American residents than did the community in which the first was conducted.)

The effects of a simulation on the racial attitudes of third graders were examined by Weiner and Wright (1973). They divided a class into orange and green people. The children wore colored armbands that designated their group status. On one day of the intervention, the students who wore orange armbands experienced discrimination; on the other day, the children who wrote green armbands were the victims. On the third day and again 2 weeks later, the children expressed less-prejudiced beliefs and attitudes.

The effects of multi-ethnic social studies materials and related experiences on the racial attitudes of 4-year-old African American children were examined by Yawkey and Blackwell (1974). The children were divided into three groups. The students in group 1 read and discussed the materials. The group 2 students read and discussed the materials and also took a related field trip. The students in group 3 experienced the traditional preschool curriculum. The interventions in groups 1 and 2 had a significant, positive effect on the students' racial attitudes toward African Americans and whites.

Research indicates that curriculum interventions such as plays, folk dances, music, and role playing can also have positive effects on the ethnic and racial attitudes of students. Four plays about African Americans, Chinese Americans, Jews, and Puerto Ricans increased racial acceptance and cultural knowledge among fourth, fifth, and sixth graders in the New York City schools (Gimmestad and DeChiara, 1982). McGregor (1993) used meta-analysis to integrate findings of 26 studies and examine the effects of role playing and antiracist teaching on reducing prejudice in students. He concluded that role playing and antiracist teaching "significantly reduce racial prejudice, and do not differ from each other in their effectiveness" (p. 215).

With particular relevance to language-minority children, two-way bilingual programs have been shown to foster friendships across ethnic lines, as well as high self-esteem among both the language-minority and language-majority children (Cazabon et al., 1993; Lambert and Cazabon, 1994). The Lambert and Cazabon (1994) study of third-graders who had been in a two-way program since kindergarten found that the children expressed a preference for multi-ethnic classrooms. Of course, such attitudes may be less a product of the program than a reflection of the home experiences of children whose parents chose such a program.

Parental Involvement in Children's School Learning

There may be differing views between home and school regarding parents' appropriate role in the education of their children. Parents may feel that school subjects are the responsibility of the teacher, that the parent is responsible only for sending the child to school ready to learn. American schools, on the other hand, value a certain amount of parental participation in education and may unwittingly punish parents who fail to contribute in the culturally prescribed way (see Hidalgo et al., 1995).

Much research has emphasized the parental role in ensuring children's academic achievement (Epstein, 1990, 1992). Parents are seen as providing their children with motivational resources, including self-esteem, agency, and self-control (e.g., Connell and Wellborn, 1990), and as helping to instill in them high expectations and good work habits (Entwisle and Alexander, in press). Parents often establish partnerships with their children's schools, thus extending school learning effectively into the home and reinforcing academic values outside school (Henderson, 1987; Dornbusch and Ritter, 1988). Positive effects of such partnerships have been found with both low- and middle-income populations, as well as populations of different racial/ethnic groups (Comer, 1986; Delgado-Gaitan, 1990; Epstein and Dauber, 1991; Dauber and Epstein, 1993; Hidalgo et al., 1995; Robledo Montecel, 1993).

Studies describing parental involvement in immigrant and language-minority families can be classified according to Epstein's types or categories of involvement. The first type covers actions taken in the home to promote child academic achievement; much evidence suggests that immigrant and language-minority children benefit from this form of parental involvement. For example, ethnographic work reveals that Puerto Rican parents use four different strategies—monitoring, communication, motivational, and protective—to promote their children's academic success (Hidalgo et al., 1995). Monitoring strategies are actions related to the academic learning of the child; communication strategies are processes that aim to foster open, nurturing family relationships; motivational strategies stimulate the child's interest in school; and protective strategies are actions geared to maintaining child safety.

Chinese American parents display two patterns of parental involvement based on, among other things, whether they are recent immigrants. Siu's (1995) longitudinal ethnographic study found that immigrant Chinese American parents tightly structured their children's learning environment because the parents were often unfamiliar with the school and its ways. These parents tried to ensure their children's academic success by engaging in such tasks as assigning additional homework. The Chinese American parents who themselves had experienced schooling in the United States allowed their children more choices, placing less emphasis on regulated academic work and more on independence and creativity. Siu labels these two parental involvement approaches low- and high-security patterns, respectively.

Vélez-Ibañez and Greenberg's (1992) qualitative work with Mexican-American families defines domains of knowledge transmitted by families to their children, which, borrowing from Moll (1992), they call "funds of knowledge." Mexican American families express a preference for social networks in which families operate to form clusters of social relations: "...these networks form social contexts for the transmission of knowledge, skills, information, and assistance, as well as cultural values and norms" (Moll et al., 1990:4). Funds of knowledge are reaffirmed and maintained through the interchange of information within the social relational framework.

In her qualitative study of 59 Puerto Rican families of high- and low-achieving students, Diaz-Soto (1988) found that "parents acted as facilitators within an organized framework of expectations" (p. 19). Diaz-Soto found a number of recurrent themes in the homes of high achievers: language (parents used both Spanish and English in communicating with their children), aspirations (parents held high expectations for their children's future careers), discipline (parents employed consistent controlling strategies), and protectiveness ("parents always knew where their children were") (p. 12).

These and related studies reveal parental behaviors that foster child learning. However, those behaviors may not be visible to school personnel, and the learning may not be highly valued at school, either. Teachers' notions of desirable parent involvement include coming to conferences, responding to notes, and participating in the classroom—notions that may be foreign to immigrant parents (Allexsaht-Snider, 1992; Matsuda, 1989). Explicit information from teachers about their expectations for parental involvement may well not be communicated to parents (Delgado-Gaitan, 1990, 1993; Glenn, 1996) in the absence of explicit programs such as parent centers designed to promote the exchange of such information (Johnson, 1993, 1994; Rubio, 1995). Two-generation literacy programs (McCollum, 1993), parent training seminars (Smith, 1993), and Epstein's program Teachers Involve Parents in Schoolwork (Epstein et al., 1995) have all been demonstrated to help align parental involvement with teacher expectations.

RESEARCH NEEDS

Curriculum Interventions

4-1. Research is needed to examine what innovative classroom organizations and interventions, such as curriculum content, can influence children's views of themselves and of members of other ethnic groups, promoting cross-ethnic friendships and positive regard.

There is some evidence, both from experimental studies and from educational experiments such as desegregation and two-way bilingual programs, that it is possible to promote healthy cross-ethnic relationships as well as positive self-identities for children from minority groups. These demonstrations, however, have been few and limited in the range of groups they have involved. Fostering full participation as a productive citizen in a society that is characterized by racial, ethnic, and linguistic diversity requires incorporating positive intergroup relations into our goals for school outcomes and assessing the best ways of achieving this end.

4-2. There is a need for research on academic learning, including both literacy learning and content area learning, that incorporates information about the social and motivational factors known to affect outcomes. Does excellent instruction take into account home-school mismatches or simply teach children the school discourse effectively? Does promoting parent-school contact affect children's learning by increasing motivation, by changing teacher attitudes, or by enabling parents to help their children more effectively? Can we devise programs that directly affect children's motivation to succeed in order to examine secondary effects on their academic outcomes?

We argue that fully understanding the nature of school achievement for language-minority children, as for native English speakers, requires operating with a model that incorporates both cognitive and social/motivational factors known to be of importance. Future research should attempt at least to acknowledge the relevance of the full array of factors, and if possible to assess the contributions of both cognitive and social/motivational processes in ensuring school success.

Status Differences Among Children's Language

4-3. There are two important questions for research regarding status differences among various languages. First, what are the consequences of such differences for children's intergroup and interpersonal relations? Second, how do teachers' perceptions of the status of children's languages influence their interactions with, expectations of, and behavior toward the children?

Most of the current intergroup studies conceptualize problems of intergroup relations as African American/white, with African Americans often viewed as "the problem." Myrdal and colleagues (Myrdal et al., 1944) titled their study, which was destined to become a classic, *An American Dilemma: The Negro Problem and Modern Democracy.* Today we realize that intergroup problems in the United States are much more complex than African American/white. Studies are needed to examine intergroup relations both across and within ethnic groups, e.g., Mexican Americans/African Americans and Mexican Americans/Puerto Rican Americans.

Nonobtrusive studies that examine intergroup relations in natural settings are also needed. Most existing intergroup studies are laboratory or curriculum interventions that have a highly limited focus. It is difficult to generalize some of the findings of these studies to the world of classrooms and schools.

In addition, studies are needed to describe the extent to which language-minority students are stigmatized because of their language characteristics and how those characteristics affect their self-perceptions and classroom status. Studies are also needed to develop interventions that can help raise the status of language-minority students in classrooms and schools.

New paradigms and theories that can guide research and practice in intergroup relations need to be conceptualized and tested empirically. Existing paradigms and theories, such as social identity theory and the contact hypothesis, need to be seriously examined in light of the important demographic changes that have occurred in U.S. society within the last two decades. These paradigms and theories were developed during a time when race relations problems in the United States were different in important ways. Although they are the best we have to guide interventions at this time, thoughtful funding of field-initiated research is likely to attract a new generation of scholars into intergroup relations research— many from racial and language-minority communities—who are most likely to develop new paradigms, theories, and findings that are more appropriate for a new century.

Home-School Alignment in Instructional Practices

4-4. Research needs to address the alignment between home and school. Are there classroom structures and practices that are particularly familiar to language-minority children and thus promote their learning by minimizing home-school mismatches? Are there procedures for inducting language-minority children into novel classroom and instructional interactions that promote their learning of English and of subject matter?

Novel instructional practices are often seen as universally desirable, rather than as possibly more helpful for some subgroups of children than others. Careful attention to the kinds of instructional interactions that occur in the homes of language-minority children is needed, as well as much more work on analyzing the nature of the classroom organization and of instructional interactions in classrooms that serve these children successfully.

Academic Socialization in Language-Minority Homes

4-5. Research is needed to examine the nature of socialization practices in the homes of language-minority children with regard to both content (e.g., exposure to literacy, opportunities for participation in substantive conversations) and socialization in ways of learning (e.g., through observation versus participation, in a relationship of collaboration versus respectful distance from the expert).

Enough research has been done on cultural differences in home socialization practices with regard to school learning that we know these differences exist. We have, however, almost no information about these issues for many of the ethnic groups that are now well represented among America's language-minority children. We have some knowledge of these socialization practices among families of Mexican descent, but know almost nothing about them among Puerto Rican, Santo Domingan, Central American, Vietnamese, Cambodian, Haitian, or Cape Verdean families. Much more basic descriptive work is needed, both as input to understanding the factors that operate in academic achievement and as input to the education of teachers who will have these children in their classrooms.

REFERENCES

Allport, G.W.
    1954/   *The Nature of Prejudice.* 25th anniversary ed. Reading, MA: Addison-Wesley.
    1979
Allexsaht-Snider, M.
    1992   Bilingual Parents Perspectives on Home-School Linkages. Paper presented at the annual meeting of the American Educational Research Association, April 20-24, San Francisco, CA. School of Teacher Education, University of Georgia.
Aronson, E., and D. Bridgeman
    1979   Jigsaw groups and the desegregated classroom: In pursuit of common goals. *Personality and Social Psychology Bulletin* 5:438:446.
Aronson, E., and A. Gonzalez
    1988   Desegregation, jigsaw, and the Mexican-American experience. Pp. 301-314 in P.A. Katz and D.A. Taylor, eds., *Eliminating Racism: Profiles in Controversy.* New York: Plenum.
Au, Kathryn Hu Pei
    1980   Participation structures in a reading lesson with Hawaiian children: Analysis of a culturally appropriate instructional event. *Anthropology and Education Quarterly* 11(2):91-115.
Au, Kathryn Hu Pei, and Jana M. Mason
    1981   Social organizational factors in learning to read: The balance of rights hypothesis. *Reading Research Quarterly* 17(1):115-152.

Banks, James A.
    1993   Multicultural education for young children: Racial and ethnic attitudes and their modifi-
           cation. Pp. 236-250 in B. Spodek, ed., *Handbook of Research on the Education of Young
           Children.* New York: Macmillan.
    1995   Multicultural education: Its effects on students' racial and gender role Attitudes. Pp.
           617-627 (Ch. 34) in *Handbook of Research on Multicultural Education.* New York:
           Macmillan.
Beck, I. L., M.G. McKeown, J. Worthy, C.A. Sandora, and L. Kucan
    in   Questioning the author: A year-long implementation to engage students with text. *The
    press   Elementary School Journal.*
Bempechat, J., N. Jimenez, and S. Graham
    in   Motivational influences in the achievement of poor and minority children. *Journal of
    press   Child and Youth Care Work.*
Bempechat, J., and W. Williams
    1995   Parental Influences on Achievement Cognition: The Development of a Parental Educa-
           tion Socialization Measure. Paper presented at SRCD, Indianapolis, April.
Bereiter, C.
    1994   The limitations of interpretation (review of writing and the writer). *Curriculum Inquiry*
           14:211-216.
Billig, M., and H. Tajfel
    1973   Social categorization and similarity in intergroup behaviour. *European Journal of Social
           Psychology* 3:27-52.
Boggs, S.
    1985   *Speaking, Relating, and Learning: A Study of Hawaiian Children at Home and School.*
           Norwood, NJ: Ablex.
Brown, J., A. Collins, and P. Duguid
    1989   Situated cognition and the culture of learning. *Educational Researcher* 18(1):32-42.
Carraher, T. N., D.W. Carraher, and A.D. Schliemann
    1985   Mathematics in the streets and in schools. *British Journal of Developmental Psychology*
           3:21-29.
Cazabon, M., W. Lambert, and G. Hall
    1993   *Two-way Bilingual Education: A Progress Report on the Amigos Program.* Research
           Report #7. Santa Cruz, CA, and Washington, DC: National Center for Research on
           Cultural Diversity and Second Language Learning.
Cazden, C.
    1986   Classroom discourse. Pp. 432-463 in Merlin C. Wittrock, ed., *Handbook of Research on
           Teaching.* New York: Free Press
Choi, E., J. Bempechat, and H. Ginsburg
    1994   Educational socialization in Korean-American children: A longitudinal study. *Journal of
           Applied Developmental Psychology* 15:313-318.
Cobb, P.
    1994   Where is the mind? Constructivist and sociocultural perspectives on mathematical devel-
           opment. *Educational Researcher* 23(7):13-20.
Cobb, P., T. Wood, and E. Yackel
    1993   Discourse, mathematical thinking, and classroom practice. Pp. 91-119 in E. Forman, N.
           Minick, and C. A. Stone, eds., *Contexts for Learning: Sociocultural Dynamics in
           Children's Development.* New York: Oxford University Press.
Cohen, E.G.
    1972   Interracial interaction disability. *Human Relations* 25:9-24.

1984a Talking and working together: Status, interaction, and learning. Pp. 171-186 in P. Peterson, L. C. Wilkinson, and M. Hallinan, eds., *The Social Context of Instruction.* New York: Academic Press.

1984b The desegregated school: Problems in status power and interethnic climate. Pp. 77-96 in N. Miller and M. B. Brewer, eds., *Groups in Contact: The Psychology of Desegregation.* New York: Academic Press.

1986 *Designing Groupwork: Strategies for Heterogeneous Classrooms.* New York: Teachers College Press.

1994 *Designing Groupwork: Strategies for the Heterogeneous Classroom, 2nd ed.* New York: Teachers College Press.

Cohen, E.G., and J.K. Intili
1981 *Interdependence and Management in Bilingual Classrooms.* Final Report. National Institute of Education Grant. Stanford, CA: Center for Educational Research.

Cohen, E.G., and R.A. Lotan
1995 Producing equal-status interaction in the heterogeneous classroom. *American Educational Research Journal* 32:99-120.

Cohen, E.G., and S.S. Roper
1972 Modification of interracial interaction disability: An application of status characteristic theory. *American Sociological Review* 37:643-657.

Comer, James P.
1986 Parent participation in the schools. *Phi Delta Kappan* 67(6):442-446.

Connell, J., and J. Wellborn
1990 Competence, autonomy, and relatedness: A motivational analysis of self-system analyses. Pp. 43-77 in M.R. Gunnar and L.A. Sroufe, eds., *Self-Process and Development.* The Minnesota Symposia on Child Psychology. Vol. 23. Hillsdale, NJ: Erlbaum.

Dalton, S., and J. Sison
1995 *Enacting Instructional Conversation with Spanish-speaking Students in Middle School Mathematics.* Educational Research Report No. 12. Santa Cruz, CA, and Washington, DC: National Center for Research on Cultural Diversity and Second Language Learning.

Dauber, S.L., and J.L. Epstein
1993 Parents' attitudes and practices of involvement in inner-city elementary and middle schools. Pp. 53-71 in N. Chavkin, ed., *Families and Schools in a Pluralistic Society.* Albany, NY: SUNY Press.

Delgado-Gaitan, Concha
1990 *Literacy for Empowerment: The Role of Parents in Children's Education.* New York: Falmer Press.

1993 Parenting in two generations of Mexican American families. *International Journal of Behavioral Development* 16(3):409-427.

DeVos, G.
1978 Selective permeability and reference group sanctioning: Psychological continuities in role degradation. Pp. 7-24 in Y. Yinger and S. Cutler, eds., *Competing Models of Multiethnic and Multiracial Societies.* New York: American Sociological Association.

Diaz-Soto, Lourdes
1988 The home environment of higher and lower achieving Puerto Rican children. *Hispanic Journal of Behavioral Sciences* 10(2):161-168.

Dornbusch, S.M., and P.L. Ritter
1988 Parents of high school students: A neglected resource. *Educational Horizons* 66:75-77.

Entwisle, D.R., and K.L. Alexander
in Family type and children's growth in reading and math over the primary grades. *Journal*
press *of Marriage and the Family.*

Epstein, J.
    1990   School and family connections: Theory, research, and implications for integrating so-
            ciologies of education and family. In D. Unger and M. Sussman, eds., *Families in Com-
            munity Settings: Interdisciplinary Perspectives*. New York: Haworth Press.
    1992   School and family partnerships. Pp. 1139-1152 in M. Alkin, ed., *Encyclopedia of Educa-
            tional Research*. 6th ed. New York: MacMillan.
Epstein, J., and S. Dauber
    1991   School programs and teacher practices of parental involvement in inner-city elementary
            and middle schools. *Elementary School Journal* 91(3):289-303.
Epstein, J., T.L. Connors, and K. Salinas
    1995   Five-Year Review: Research on Families, Communities, Schools, and Children's Learn-
            ing. Paper presented at the annual meeting of the American Educational Research Asso-
            ciation, San Francisco, CA.
Garcia, E.E.
    1993   Language, culture, and education. Pp. 51-98 in L. Darling-Hammond, ed., *Review of
            Research in Education*. Vol. 19. Washington, DC: American Educational Research
            Association.
Gee, J.P.
    1985   The narrativization of experience in the oral style. *Journal of Education* 167:9-35.
    1988a   Discourse systems and aspirin bottles: On literacy. *Journal of Education* 170(1):27-40.
    1988b   Dracula, the vampire lestat, and TESOL. *TESOL Quarterly* 22(2):201-225.
    1990   *Social Linguistics and Literacies: Ideology in Discourses*. London: Falmer.
Gibson, M.A.
    1988   *Accommodation Without Assimilation: Sikh Immigrants in an American High School*.
            Ithaca: Cornell University Press.
Giles, Michael W.
    1977   Percent black and racial hostility: An old assumption reexamined. *Social Science Quar-
            terly* 58(3):412-417.
Gimmestad, B.J., and E. DeChiara
    1982   Dramatic plays: A vehicle for prejudice reduction in the elementary school. *Journal of
            Educational Research* 76(1):45-49.
Glenn, C.L., with E.J. de Jong
    1996   *Educating Immigrant Children: Schools and Language Minorities in 12 Nations*. New
            York: Garland.
Goldenberg, C., and R. Gallimore
    1991   Local knowledge, research knowledge, and educational change: A case study of first-
            grade Spanish reading improvement. *Educational Researcher* 20(8):2-14.
Gutierrez, K.D.
    1992   A comparison of instructional contexts in writing process classrooms with Latino chil-
            dren. *Education and Urban Society* 24(2):244-262.
    1994   Language borders: Recitation as hegemonic discourse. *International Journal of Educa-
            tional Reform* 3(1):22-36.
Gutierrez, K.D., J. Larson, and B. Kreuter
    1995   Cultural tensions in the scripted classroom. The value of the subjugated perspective.
            Urban Education 29(4):410-442.
Hansen, C.A., and A. Bachu
    1995   Foreign born population, 1994. Current Population Reports. Bureau of the Census.
            Washington, D.C.: U.S. Department of Commerce.
Harklau, Linda
    1994   Tracking and linguistic minority students: Consequences of ability grouping for second
            language learners. *Linguistics and Education* 6(3):217-244.

Heath, S.B.
　1983　*Ways with Words: Language, Life, and Work in Communities and Classrooms.* New York: Cambridge University Press.
Henderson, A.
　1987　*The Evidence Continues to Grow: Parent Involvement Improves Student Achievement.* Columbia, MD: National Committee for Citizens in Education.
Hewstone, M., and R. Brown
　1986　Contact is not enough: An intergroup perspective on the 'contact hypothesis.' Pp. 1-44 in M. Hewstone and R. Brown, eds., *Contact and Conflict in Intergroup Encounters.* New York: Basil Blackwell.
Hidalgo, Nitza M., J. Bright, S.F. Sui, S. Swap, and J. Epstein
　1995　Research on families, schools, and communities: A multicultural perspective. Pp. 498-524 in J. A. Banks and C.A. Banks, eds., *Handbook of Research on Multicultural Education* (Chapter 28). New York: Macmillan.
Isaacs, H.R.
　1992　Language as a factor in inter-group conflict. Pp. 466-478 in J. Crawford, ed., *Language Loyalties: A Source Book on the Official English Controversy.* Chicago: University of Chicago Press.
Johnson, V. R.
　1993　*Parent/Family Centers in Schools: Expanding Outreach and Promoting Collaboration.* Center Report 20. Baltimore, MD: Center on Families Communities Schools and Children's Learning.
　1994　*Parent Centers in Urban Schools: Four Case Studies.* (Center Report 23.) Baltimore: Center on Families Communities Schools and Children's Learning.
Johnson, D.W., and R.T. Johnson
　1981　Effects of cooperative and individualistic learning experiences on interethnic interaction. *Journal of Educational Psychology* 73:444-449.
　1991　*Learning Together and Alone.* (3rd ed.) Englewood Cliffs, NJ: Prentice-Hall.
Lambert, W., and M. Cazabon
　1994　*Students' Views of the Amigos Program. Research Report #11.* Santa Cruz, CA, and Washington, DC: National Center for Research on Cultural Diversity and Second Language Learning.
Lampert, M.
　1990　When the problem is not the question and the solution is not the answer: Mathematical knowing and teaching. *American Educational Research Journal* 27(1):29-63.
Lave, J., M. Murtach, and O. de la Rocha
　1984　The dialectic of arithmetic in grocery shopping. Pp. 67-116 in B. Rogoff and J. Lave, eds., *Everyday Cognition: Its Development in Social Context.* Cambridge, MA: Harvard University Press.
Leinhardt, G.
　1993　Instructional explanations in history and mathematics. Pp. 5-16 in W. Kitsch, ed., *Proceedings of the Fifteenth Annual Conference of the Cognitive Science Society.* Hillsdale, NJ: Erlbaum.
Leont'ev, A.N.
　1981　The problem of activity in psychology. In J.V. Wertsch, ed., *The Concept of Activity on Social Psychology.* Armonk, NY: Sharpe.
Linguistics and Education
　1994　*Linguistics and Education* 5 (whole issue).
Litcher, J.H., and D.W. Johnson
　1969　Changes in attitudes toward Negroes of White elementary school students after use of multiethnic readers. *Journal of Educational Psychology* 60:148-152.

Litcher, J.H., D.W. Johnson, and F.L. Ryan
   1973   Use of pictures of multiethnic interaction to change attitudes of White elementary school students toward Blacks. *Psychological Reports* 33:367-372.

Losey, Kay M.
   1995   Mexican American students and classroom interaction: An overview and critique. *Review of Educational Research* 65(3):283-318.

Matsuda, M.
   1989   Working with Asian parents: Some communication strategies. *Topics in Language Disorders* 45-53.

McCollum, Pamela
   1993   Learning to Value English: Cultural Capital in a Two-Way Bilingual Program. Paper presented at the AERA annual meeting, Atlanta, GA. Mississippi State University.

McGregor, J.
   1993   Effectiveness of role playing and antiracist teaching in reducing student prejudice. *Journal of Educational Research* 86(4):215-226.

Michaels, S.
   1991   Sharing time. *Language in Society* 10:423-447.

Moll, L.C.
   1992   Bilingual classroom studies and community analysis: Some recent trends. *Educational Researcher: Special Issue on Bilingual Education* 21(2):20-24.

Moll, L.C., and S. Diaz
   1987   Changes as the goal of educational research. *Anthropology and Education Quarterly* 18:300-311.

Moll, L.C., C. Vélez-Ibañez, and J. Greenberg
   1990   *Community Knowledge and Classroom Practice: Combining Resources for Literacy Instruction. A Handbook for Teachers and Planners.* Tucson: Arizona University, Tucson College of Education.

Moll, L.C., C. Amanti, D. Neff, and N. Gonzalez
   1992   Funds of knowledge for teaching: Using a qualitative approach to connect homes and classrooms. *Theory into Practice* 31(2):132-141.

Moll, L.C., and K.F. Whitmore
   1993   Vygotsky in classroom practice: Moving from individual transmission to social interaction. Pp. 19-41 in E. Forman, N. Minick, and C.A. Stone, eds., *Contexts for Learning: Sociocultural Dynamics in Children's Development.* New York: Oxford University Press.

Myrdal, G., with R. Sterner, and A. Rose
   1944   *An American Dilemma: The Negro Problem and Modern Democracy.* New York: Harper and Row.

Ogbu, J.U.
   1978   *Minority Education and Caste: The American System in Cross-Cultural Perspective.* New York: Academic Press.
   1995   Understanding cultural diversity and learning. Pp. 582-593 in J.A. Banks and C.A.M. Banks, eds., *Handbook of Research on Multicultural Education.* New York: Macmillan.

Ogbu, J.U., and M.E. Matute-Bianchi
   1986   Understanding sociocultural factors: Knowledge, identity, and school adjustment. Pp. 73-142 in *Beyond Language: Social and Cultural Factors in Schooling Language Minority Students.* Los Angeles: Evaluation, Dissemination, and Assessment Center, California State University.

Palincsar, A.S., and A.L. Brown
   1984   Reciprocal teaching of comprehension-fostering and comprehension-monitoring activities. *Cognition and Instruction* 1(2):117-175.

Palincsar, A.S., A.L. Brown, and J. Campione
    1993   First-grade dialogues for knowledge acquisition and use. Pp. 43-57 in E. Forman, N. Minick, and C. A. Stone, eds., *Contexts for Learning: Sociocultural Dynamics in Children's Development*. New York: Oxford University Press.
Patthey-Chavez, G., and C. Goldenberg
    1995   Changing instructional discourse for changing students: The instructional conversation. Pp. 205-230 in R. Macías and R. García Ramos, eds., *Changing Schools for Changing Students: An Anthology of Research on Language Minorities, Schools and Society*. Santa Barbara, CA: University of California Linguistic Minority Research Institute.
Pettigrew, T. P.
    1986   The intergroup hypothesis reconsidered. Pp. 169-195 in M. Hewstone and R. Brown, eds., *Contact and Conflict in Intergroup Encounters*. New York: Basil Blackwell.
Philips, S.U.
    1983   *The Invisible Culture: Communication in Classroom and Community on the Warm Springs Reservation Indian Reservation*. New York: Longman.
Resnick, L.
    1987   Learning in school and out. *Educational Researcher* 16:13-20.
Robledo Montecel, M.
    1993   *Hispanic Families as Valued Partners: An Educator's Guide*. San Antonio, TX: Intercultural Development Research Association.
Rosebery, A., B. Warren, and F.R. Conant
    1992   Appropriating scientific discourse: Findings from language minority classrooms. *The Journal of the Learning Sciences* 2(1):61-94.
Rothbart, M., and O.P. John
    1993   Intergroup relations and stereotype change: A social-cognitive analysis and some longitudinal findings. Pp. 32-59 in P.M. Sniderman, P.E. Telock, and E.G. Carmines, eds., *Prejudice, Politics, and the American Dilemma*. Stanford, CA: Stanford University Press.
Rubio, O.
    1995   'Yo soy voluntaria:' Volunteering in a dual-language school. *Urban Education* 29(4):396-409.
Rueda, R., C. Goldenberg, and R. Gallimore
    1992   *Rating Instructional Conversations: A Guide*. Educational Practice Report, No. 4. Washington, DC: Center for Applied Linguistics.
Ryan, E.B., and M.A. Carranza
    1977   Ingroup and outgroup reactions to Mexican American language varieties. Pp. 59-82 in H. Giles, ed., *Language, Ethnicity and Intergroup Relations*. New York: Academic Press.
Saunders, W., C. Goldenberg, and J. Hamann
    1992   Instructional conversations beget instructional conversations. *Teaching and Teacher Education* 8:199-218.
Schofield, J.W.
    1995   Improving intergroup relations. Pp. 635-646 in J. A. Banks and C.A.M. Banks, eds., *Handbook of Research on Multicultural Education*. New York: Macmillan.
Scribner, S.
    1984   Studying working intelligence. Pp. 9-40 in B. Rogoff and J. Lave, eds., *Everyday Cognition: Its Development in Social Context*. Cambridge, MA: Harvard University Press.
Siu, Sau-Fong
    1995   *Final Report, Center on Families, Communities, Schools and Children's Learning, Volume Two: Patterns of Chinese American Family Involvement in Young Children's Education*. Boston, MA: Wheelock College.

Slavin, R.E.
  1979 Effects of biracial learning teams on cross-racial friendships. *Journal of Educational Psychology* 71:381-387.
  1983 *Cooperative learning.* New York: Longman
  1985 Cooperative learning: Applying contact theory in desegregated schools. *Journal of Social Issues* 41:45-62.
  1995 Cooperative learning and intergroup relations. Pp. 628-634 in J.A. Banks and C.A.M. Banks, eds., *Handbook of Research on Multicultural Education.* New York: Macmillan.
Slavin, R.E., and N.A. Madden
  1979 School practices that improve race relations. *American Educational Research Journal* 16(2):169-180.
Sleeter, C.E., and C.A. Grant
  1991 Race, class, gender, and disability in current textbooks. Pp. 78-110 in M.W. Apple and L.K. Christian-Smith, eds., *The Politics of the Textbook.* New York: Routledge.
Smith, C.
  1993 Parents and teachers in partnership. *Gifted Child Today* Nov/Dec:16-19.
Smith, E.R., and D.M. Mackie
  1995 *Social Psychology.* New York: Worth.
Stephan, W.G.
  1985 Intergroup relations. Pp. 599-658 in G. Lindzey and E. Aronson, eds., *The Handbook of Social Psychology.* Vol. 2, 3rd ed. New York: Random House.
Stephan, W.G., and C.W. Stephan.
  1996 *Intergroup Relations.* Madison, WI: Brown and Benchmark.
Stevenson, H.W., S.Y. Lee, and J.W. Stigler
  1986 Mathematics achievement of Chinese, Japanese, and American children. *Science* 231:693-699.
Stevenson, H.W., Chuansheng Chen, and David H. Uttal
  1990 Beliefs and achievement: A study of black, white, and Hispanic children. *Child Development* 61(2):508-523.
Suarez-Orozco, C., and M. Suarez-Orozco
  1995 *Transformations: Migration, Family Life, and Achievement Motivation Among Latino and White Adolescents.* Stanford, CA: Stanford University Press.
Tajfel, H.
  1970 Experiments in intergroup discrimination. *Scientific American* 223(5):96-102.
Tuan, Mia
  1995 Korean and Russian students in a Los Angeles high school: Exploring the alternative strategies of two high-achieving groups. In Ruben G. Rumbaut and Wayne A. Cornelius, eds., *California's Immigrant Children: Theory, Research, and Implications for Educational Policy.* University of California, San Diego: Center for U.S.-American Studies.
Vélez-Ibáñez, Carlos G., and James B. Greenberg
  1992 Formation and transformation of funds of knowledge among U.S.-Mexican households. *Anthropology and Education Quarterly* 23(4):313-335.
Vygotsky, L.S.
  1978 *Mind in Society: The Development of Higher Psychological Processes.* Cambridge, MA: Harvard University Press.
Warren, B., and A.S. Rosebery
  1995 This question is just too, too easy! Perspectives from the classroom on accountability in science. In L. Schauble and R. Glaser, eds., *Innovations in Learning: New Environments for Education.* Hillsdale, NJ: Erlbaum.

Wertsch, J.V.
1979   From social interaction to higher psychological processes: A clarification and application of Vygotsky's theory. *Human Development* 22:1-22.
1990   The voice of rationality in a sociocultural approach to mind. Pp. 111-126 in L.C. Moll, ed., *Vygotsky and Education: Instructional Implications and Applications of Sociohistorical Psychology*. New York: Cambridge University Press.
Weiner, M.J., and F.E. Wright
1973   Effects of undergoing arbitrary discrimination upon subsequent attitudes toward a minority group. *Journal of Applied Social Psychology* 3:94-102.
Williams, R.M.
1947   *Reduction of Intergroup Tensions*. New York: Social Science Research Council.
Yawkey, T.D., and J. Blackwell
1974   Attitudes of 4-year old urban black children toward themselves and whites based upon multi-ethnic social studies materials and experiences. *The Journal of Educational Research* 67:373-377.

STUDENT ASSESSMENT:
SUMMARY OF THE STATE OF KNOWLEDGE

From the literature on student assessment, the following key findings can be drawn:

• Several uses of assessment are unique to English-language learners and bilingual children. They include identification of children whose English proficiency is limited, determination of eligibility for placement in specific language programs, and monitoring of progress in and readiness to exit from special language service programs.

• English-language learners are assessed for purposes that extend beyond determination of their language needs, including placement in categorically funded education programs such as Title I, placement in remedial or advanced classwork, monitoring of achievement in compliance with district- and/or state-level programs, and certification for high school graduation and determination of academic mastery at graduation.

• It is essential that any assessment impacting children's education strive to meet standards of validity (whether inferences drawn are appropriate to the purposes of the assessment) and reliability (whether assessment outcomes are accurate in light of variations due to factors irrelevant to what the assessment was intended to measure).

• States and local districts use a variety of methods to determine which students need to be placed in special language-related programs and monitor students' progress in those programs. Administration of language proficiency tests is the most common method. Achievement tests in English are also frequently used.

• Regardless of the modality of testing, many existing English-language proficiency instruments emphasize measurement of a limited range of grammatical and structural skills.

• States use a variety of procedures to assess student academic performance, including performance-based assessments and standardized achievement tests, and states are in various stages of incorporating English-language learners into these assessments.

• To a large extent, the field lacks instruments appropriate for assessing very young English-language learners, as well as English-language learners with disabilities.

• The standards-based reform movement has major implications for the assessment of English-language learners.

5

Student Assessment

This chapter addresses the issue of assessing the language proficiency and subject matter knowledge and skills of English-language learners.[1]

STATE OF KNOWLEDGE

Assessment plays a central role in the education of English-language learners and bilingual children. Teachers generally use assessments to monitor language development in students' first or second language and track the quality of their day-to-day subject matter learning. In addition, assessments are used to place students in special programs and to provide information used for accountability and policy analysis purposes. The research issues related to these roles have much in common.

Several uses of assessment at the classroom and school levels are unique to English-language learners and bilingual children, while others also apply to students generally. Uses unique to English-language learners and bilingual children include the following:

- Identification of children whose English proficiency is limited

---

[1]The standards for assessing reading and writing developed by the International Reading Association and the National Committee of Teachers of English, as well as those currently in development by Teachers of English to Speakers of Other Languages for assessing English proficiency, are consistent with and supportive of the model of assessment emerging from the review in this chapter.

• Determination of eligibility for placement in specific language programs (e.g., bilingual education or English as a second language [ESL])
• Monitoring of progress in and readiness to exit from special language service programs

Uses of assessment that extend beyond English-language learners include the following:

• Placement in categorically funded education programs, such as special education, gifted and talented, and Title I programs
• Placement in remedial or advanced academic course work
• Monitoring of achievement in compliance with school district and/or state-level assessment programs
• Certification for high school graduation and determination of academy mastery at graduation

In addition, the federal government sponsors a variety of assessments, such as the National Assessment of Educational Progress, to measure the performance and progress of U.S. students. Additional discussion of the National Assessment of Educational Progress and other large-scale assessments in relation to English-language learners is included in Chapter 9.

The remainder of this section begins by looking at issues of validity and reliability associated with student assessment. The next two subsections review uses of assessment that are unique to English-language learners and issues involved in assessing language proficiency. This is followed by two subsections that examine uses of assessment that extend beyond English-language learners and those associated with the assessment of subject matter knowledge. One additional set of assessment issues is then explored—those associated with assessing special populations, including very young second-language learners and English-language-learners with disabilities. The chapter ends with a discussion of standards-based reform and its implications for the design and conduct of student assessments.

Validity and Reliability Issues

It is essential that those using any assessment impacting children's education strive to meet standards of validity and reliability (American Educational Research Association, American Psychological Association, and National Council on Measurement in Education, 1985). Validity concerns whether the inferences drawn from assessment outcomes are appropriate to the purposes of the assessment. It encompasses use of an assessment to measure current achievement and ability relative to specific performance criteria, as well as the potential for future achievement, and to investigate the underlying competencies that theory indicates should be tapped by an assessment. Reliability concerns the accuracy of assessment outcomes in light of the variations in those outcomes that are due to factors irrelevant to what the assessment was intended to measure. Such factors might include characteristics of the individual, the fact that the assessment represents only a sample of a larger universe of assessment items, and inconsistency of the scoring of performance on an assessment (such as a constructed response test) from scorer to scorer and across an individual's scoring of the same assessment. The issue of reliability is made more complex because these factors may interact in ways that are not readily measured for their impact on performance (Cronbach et al., 1995). The validity and reliability of assessments can be investigated using a wide range of psychometric and statistical procedures, as well as experimental and qualitative studies of assessment performance.

Garcia and Pearson (1994:343-349) examine assessment and diversity across a wide range of subject matters and test types. They highlight potential problems for English-language learners that result from the "mainstream bias" of formal testing, including a norming bias (small numbers of particular minorities included in probability samples, increasing the likelihood that minority group samples are unrepresentative), content bias (test content and procedures reflecting the dominant culture's standards of language function and shared knowledge and behavior), and linguistic and cultural biases (factors that adversely affect the formal test performance of students from diverse linguistic and cultural backgrounds, including timed testing, difficulty with English vocabulary, and the near impossibility of determining what bilingual students know in their two languages).

The ensuing discussion of assessment as applied to English-language learners and bilingual children inherently involves questions about the validity and reliability of assessments and their appropriateness for these children. It is also important to note that assessment practices have social and educational consequences that should be considered in an ongoing program of validity research (Messick, 1988).

Assessment Purposes Unique to English-Language Learners

There are many purposes for assessments of language proficiency, including placing students in special services, monitoring their progress, predicting educational outcomes, and exiting students from special language services. According to four recent surveys, states and local districts use a variety of methods to determine which language-minority students have limited English proficiency, to place these students in special language-related programs, and to monitor the progress of the students in such programs (August and Lara, 1996; Cheung et al., 1994; Fleishman and Hopstock, 1993; Rivera, 1995). These methods include home language surveys, registration and enrollment information, observations, interviews, referrals, grades, and classroom performance and testing (Cheung et al., 1994). However, administration of language proficiency tests in English is the most common method (Fleishman and Hopstock, 1993). Fleishman and Hopstock found that 83 percent of school districts with English-language learners used English-language proficiency testing, either alone or in combination with other techniques, to determine which language-minority students were of limited English proficiency. Similarly, such tests were used by 64 percent of school districts for assigning English-language learners to specific instructional services in schools and by 74 percent of school districts for reclassifying students once they have developed English proficiency.

Achievement tests in English are also frequently used by school districts and schools to help identify English-language learners, assign them to school programs, and reclassify them when English proficient (Fleischman and Hopstock, 1993). Specifically, 52 percent of school districts and schools across the country use such tests to help identify English-language learners, 40 percent use them to help assign students to specific instructional programs within a school, and over 70 percent use them for reclassification purposes (as reported in Zehler et al., 1994).

There is a great deal of variability across school districts in the way assessments are used for the above purposes. This is because many states, while providing guidance to the districts on assessment procedures for students with limited English proficiency, allow them considerable flexibility in choosing assessment methods, assessment instruments (usually from a menu of state-approved instruments), and cutoff scores for these instruments (August and Lara, 1996).[2]

Issues in Assessing Language Proficiency

Regardless of the modality of testing, many existing English-language proficiency instruments emphasize measurement of a limited range of grammatical and structural skills. Test items are frequently designed to assess a specific discrete language skill, though some tests and test items involve assessment of a number of discrete skills simultaneously. In part, emphasis on assessment of

---

[2]Of the 25 states that have assessment requirements for determining which language-minority students are of limited English proficiency, 22 specify English proficiency tests. Of these 22 states, 8 also specify achievement tests, and 3 specify English proficiency tests and below-average performance based on grades or classwork. When assessment is used for program placement, similar procedures are used. In the other states, it is up to individual districts to set these policies. In some states, native-language proficiency assessments are required (Arizona, Hawaii, Utah, California, Texas, New Jersey) or recommended. The only information regarding methods for reclassifying students from language assistance programs (Cheung and Soloman, 1991) indicates that language tests are the most frequently used method (required in 36 percent of states, recommended in 30 percent), followed by content area tests (required in 34 percent of states, recommended in 11 percent). Other methods recommended for determining program exit include observations and interviews. About one-third of states reported having no state requirement regarding exit criteria.

grammatical and structural control of a language is a legacy from first-language acquisition studies. First-language acquisition research was dominated, especially in the 1970s, by arguments between empiricists and nativists who used morphology and syntax as the primary battleground for framing our scientific understanding of language acquisition (Bialystok and Hakuta, 1994).

During the 1970s and 1980s, new models of bilingual language competence emerged from the fields of linguistic pragmatics, interactional sociolinguistics, and cognitive studies of discourse processing. These perspectives, which were better attuned to the language demands faced by language-minority students in everyday settings (Rivera, 1984), examined how children acquire competence in using language to accomplish purposeful functions arising in social interaction (e.g., Wong Fillmore, 1982) and how language practices are tied to ongoing participation in classroom activities, referred to as authentic assessment (e.g., Gutierrez, 1995). As a consequence of these new models of language competence, Valdez Pierce and O'Malley (1992) recommend assessment procedures for monitoring the language development of language-minority students in the upper elementary and middle grades that reflect tasks typical of the classroom or real-life settings. As examples, they cite oral interviews, story retellings, simulations/situations, directed dialogues, incomplete story/topic prompts, picture cues, teacher observation checklists, and student self-evaluations. They also describe a portfolio assessment framework for monitoring the development of English-language learners. Authentic assessments are both more difficult to administer and less objectively scored than traditional assessments, but they do reflect the important view that language proficiency is multifaceted and varies according to the task demands and content area domain (see Chapter 2). Widespread implementation of practical assessments based on this viewpoint has been slow to emerge and is an important area for further research. One promising approach has been developed by Royer and Carlo (1991). They report on the utility of a sentence verification technique test (which basically involves reading or listening to a passage and then marking sentences as to whether they correctly reflect the information in the passage). The authors suggest the passages can be developed locally, based on curricular material familiar to the student. This form of assessment is relatively easy to develop in any language, and the reliability and validity data appear strong.

However, in pursuing new assessments of language proficiency for English-language learners and bilingual children, we should not ignore existing language assessment methods that focus on discrete language skills, even though there are differing beliefs about which components are most critical. For example, evidence exists throughout the cognitive and psycholinguistic research literature that routinization of basic language recognition and production skills is associated with greater fluency in language use at the level of spoken and written discourse (McLaughlin, 1984). Thus the assessment of these skills is a legitimate endeavor, though it is important to recognize that such assessments may have good predictive ability because they are tapping an ability correlated with a variety of language proficiencies, not because they constitute language proficiency.

In summary, the major purpose of English-language proficiency testing has been to determine placement in special language programs, monitor students' progress while in these programs, and decide when students should be exited from these programs. Most measures used not only have been characterized by the measurement of decontextualized skills, but also have set fairly low standards for language proficiency. Ultimately, English-language learners should be held to high standards for both English language and literacy, and should transition from special language measures to full participation in regularly administered assessments of English-language arts.

Assessment Purposes That Extend Beyond English-Language Learners

The assessment policies discussed in this section are related to determining eligibility for federal assistance and monitoring student progress at the state and district levels.

Title I is by far the largest federal program serving English-language learners. Yet past practice in using tests to assess eligibility for such programs raises a number of issues. For example, in documenting district policies, Strang and Carlson (1991) found that many English-language learners were not being served through Title I because districts required students to be English proficient before they could be served. However, those English-language learners who met the English proficiency requirements also scored above the cut-off on English achievement tests used for Title I selection.

New Title I assessment policy is currently being discussed because of changes in the law (see Kober and Feuer, 1996). Those changes provide for the participation of all students, including English-language learners, in assessments to determine whether they are meeting performance standards and for reasonable adaptations of these assessments to accomplish this end. According to the law, English-language learners are to be included in assessments to the extent practicable, in the language and form most likely to yield accurate and reliable information on what they know and can do, including their mastery of skills in target subject matter areas, not just English. The law now further requires that each state plan identify the languages other than English that are present in the participating student population and indicate the languages for which yearly student assessments are not available and are needed. States are required to make every effort to develop such assessments and may request assistance from the Secretary of the Department of Education if linguistically accessible assessment measures are needed (see August et al., 1995).

Assessment is particularly important for purposes of selecting eligible students for services in Title I targeted assistance programs, whereby Title I services are made available to a subset of the students "on the basis of multiple, educationally related, objective criteria established by the local educational agency and supplemented by the school" (Section 1115). The current policy guidance provided by the U.S. Department of Education does not elaborate on how this might be accomplished for English-language learners, and leaves it up to local districts to select those eligible students "most in need of special services." In the absence of adaptations to assessments, including assessments conducted in the native language, as well as methods for determining how English-language learners compare with other students on educational needs, a large proportion of English-language learners may not be served through Title I.

Surveys of state-wide assessment systems (August and Lara, 1996; Rivera, 1995) show that states use a variety of measures to assess student performance, including performance-based assessments and standardized achievement tests, and that states are in various stages of incorporating English-language learners into these assessments. August and Lara (1996) found that only 5 states require English-language learners to take state-wide assessments required of other students;[3] 36 states exempt English-language learners from such assessments, although 22 of those states require these students to take the assessments after a given period of time (usually 1-3 years). Some states base their assessment decision on the proficiency level of their English-language learners; of these, a few leave it up to local districts to determine which students have enough English proficiency to participate in the state-wide assessments. Finally, some states use multiple criteria to excuse students from state-wide assessments, including number of years in English-speaking classrooms, language proficiency scores, school achievement, and teacher judgment.

States use a variety of approaches to assess students that have been exempted from the state-wide assessments. Hafner (1995) reports that 55 percent of states allow modifications in the administration of at least one of their assessments to incorporate English-language learners. The most common modifications are extra time (20 states), small-group administration (18 states), flexible scheduling (16 states), simplification of directions (14 states), use of dictionaries (13 states), and reading of questions aloud in English (12 states). Other accommodations include assessments in languages other than English, availability of both English and non-English versions of the same assessment items, division of assessments into shorter parts, and administration of the assessment by a person familiar with the children's primary language and culture (Rivera, 1995).

Some states also provide guidance to scorers on evaluating the work of English-language learners. Hafner (1995) reports that 10 percent of states give special training on evaluating the work of English-language learners, and 10 percent give directions in their manuals. Some training entails the development of scoring rubrics and procedures for constructed response items that are sensi-

---

[3]In 3 of these states, however, English-language learners may be exempted under certain conditions.

tive to the language and cultural characteristics of English-language learners. The Council of Chief State School Officers recently developed a Scorer's Training Manual (Wong Fillmore and Lara, 1996) to be used by states and local education agencies to aid in the scoring of English-language learners' answers to open-ended mathematics questions. In collaboration with the National Center for Educational Statistics and the Educational Testing Service, this manual will be piloted using the work of English-language learners who participated in the 1996 National Assessment of Educational Progress math assessment to see how well it prepares scorers to assess the work of those students accurately.

Clearly, classroom teachers also assess students to determine how well they are grasping coursework and to inform instructional practice (see Chapter 7). Innovations at the classroom level include an assessment process that is multiple referenced and incorporates information about the students in a variety of contexts obtained from a variety of sources through a variety of procedures (Genesee and Hamayan, 1994). Navarette et al. (1990) describe innovative assessment procedures that include unstructured techniques (e.g., writing samples, homework, logs, games, debates, story telling) and structured techniques (e.g., criterion-referenced tests, cloze tests, structured interviews), as well as a combination of the two (portfolios). In addition, students are assessed in their native language to better determine their academic achievement and ensure appropriate coursework (Genesee and Hamayan, 1994). Information on student background characteristics such as literacy in the home, parents' educational backgrounds, and previous educational experiences is collected and provides essential information that helps put the assessment results in context.

Issues in Assessing Subject Matter Knowledge

A central issue in assessing subject matter knowledge is determining what knowledge is intended for assessment. This issue is discussed in detail in the later section on standards-based reform. In the discussion in this section, we assume that the developers of an assessment have decided what to assess and examine the difficulties involved in incorporating English-language learners and bilingual children into assessments intended for their English-proficient peers.

As noted in the *Standards for Educational and Psychological Tests,* every assessment is an assessment of language (American Educational Research Association, American Psychological Association, and National Council on Measurement in Education, 1985). This is even more so given the advent of performance assessments requiring extensive comprehension and production of language.[4]

---

[4]For example, the performance description for *mathematical communication*, one of seven mathematical performance areas for elementary school children, requires the student to "use appropriate mathematical terms, vocabulary, and language based on prior conceptual work; show ideas in a variety of ways including words, numbers, symbols, pictures, charts, graphs, tables, diagrams, and

The English-language proficiency levels of students affect their performance on subject area assessments given in English. For example, Garcia (1991) found that the English reading test performance of Spanish-speaking Hispanic students was adversely affected by their unfamiliarity with vocabulary terms used in the test questions and answer choices. In fact, interview data demonstrate that the presence of unknown vocabulary in the questions and answer choices was the major linguistic factor that adversely affected the Hispanic children's reading performance.[5] Alderman (1981) found that the relationship between test scores on *Prueba de Aptitud Academica* (a Spanish version of the SAT developed for use with native Spanish speakers) and English SAT scores increased with higher English proficiency test scores for native Spanish-speaking high school students. This study indicated that aptitude can be seriously underestimated if the test taker is not proficient in the language in which the test is being given.

Given that the English proficiency level of students affects their performance on assessments administered in English and that recent assessments require high levels of English proficiency, research is needed to develop assessments and assessment procedures appropriate for English-language learners. One strategy under active investigation is the use of native-language assessments. Approximately 75 percent of English-language learners come from Spanish-language backgrounds. For some of these students, it is realistic to develop native-language assessments. However, in doing so, it is desirable to keep in mind the difficulties involved in developing native-language assessments that are equivalent to the English versions. Such difficulties include problems of regional and dialect differences, nonequivalence of vocabulary difficulty between two languages, problems of incomplete language development and lack of literacy development in students' primary languages, and the extreme difficulty of defining a "bilingual" equating sample (each new definition of a bilingual sample will demand a new statistical equating). Minimally, back-translation should be done to determine equivalent meaning, and ideally, psychometric validation should be undertaken as well.[6]

The challenge of using native-language assessments or bilingual versions is illustrated by the results of research on developing and administering mathemat-

---

models; explain clearly and logically solutions to problems, and support solutions with evidence, in both oral and written form; consider purpose and audience when communicating; and comprehend mathematics from reading assignments and from other sources" (New Standards, 1995). Quite clearly, this assessment of mathematical skills is also an assessment of language proficiency.

[5]Garcia (1991) also found that the Hispanic students' English reading test performance was adversely affected by their limited prior knowledge of certain test topics, their poor performance on the implicit questions (which required use of background knowledge), and their tendency to interpret the test literally when determining their answers. These findings have implications for the schooling of English-language learners (see Chapters 3 and 7).

[6]Hambleton and Kanjee (1994) recommend validating the translated version with empirical evidence using item response theory.

ics test items only in Spanish or in side-by-side Spanish-English format as part of the National Assessment of Educational Progress field test of mathematics items (Anderson et al., 1996). Spanish-language items were translations of English-version items. This research found substantial psychometric discrepancies in students' performance on the same test items across both languages, leading to the conclusion that the Spanish and English versions of many test items were not measuring the same underlying mathematical knowledge. This result may be attributable to a lack of equivalence between original and translated versions of test items and needs further investigation.

Another strategy to make assessments both comprehensible and conceptually appropriate for English-language learners might entail decreasing the English-language load through actual modification of the items or instructions. This would not be a straightforward task, however. While some experts recommend reducing nonessential details and simplifying grammatical structures (Short, 1991), others claim that simplifying the surface linguistic features will not necessarily make the text easier to understand (Saville-Troike, 1991). When Abedi et al. (1995) reduced the linguistic complexity of National Assessment of Educational Progress mathematics test items in English, they reported only a modest and statistically unreliable effect in favor of the modified items for students at lower levels of English proficiency.

Other strategies for incorporating English-language learners into assessments include those mentioned earlier, such as extra time, small-group administration, flexible scheduling, reading of directions aloud, use of dictionaries, and administration of the assessment by a person familiar with the children's primary language and culture (Rivera, 1995). Additional possibilities include making test instructions more explicit and allowing English-language learners to display their knowledge using alternative forms of representation (e.g., showing math operations on numbers and knowledge of graphing in problem solving). Almost no research has been conducted to determine the effectiveness of these techniques, however.

Another issue in assessment of subject matter knowledge for English-language learners is the errors that result from inaccurate and inconsistent scoring of open-ended or performance-based measures. There is evidence that scorers may pay attention to linguistic features of performance unrelated to the content of the assessment. Thus, scorers may inaccurately assign low scores for performance in which English expression (either oral or written) is weak. This obviously confounds the accuracy of the score enormously.[7] Absent training, different scorers probably will rate the same student work very differently.

---

[7]Interestingly, Lindholm (1994) found highly significant and positive correlations between standardized scores of Spanish reading achievement and teacher-rated reading rubric scores, as well as between the standardized reading scores and students' ratings of their reading competence, for native English-speaking and native Spanish-speaking students enrolled in a bilingual immersion program.

Issues in Assessing Special Populations

Very Young Second-Language Learners

Assessing young children's development in meaningful ways is already surrounded by a great deal of controversy and concern among the preschool education community. As Meisels (1994:210-211) states:

> ...measurement in preschool is marked by recurrent practical problems of formulation and administration....Many measurement techniques used with older children are inappropriate for use with children below school age, or even below grade 3. For example, the following methods are extremely unlikely to yield valid information about normative trends in development: paper and pencil questionnaires, lengthy interviews, abstract questions, fatiguing assessment protocols, extremely novel situations or demands, objectively-scored, multiple choice tests, isolated sources of data. None of these methods are consistent with principles of developmentally appropriate assessment.

If none of these practices are appropriate for young children in general, their inappropriateness for children from different linguistic and/or cultural backgrounds can certainly be taken as a given.

For these reasons, McLaughlin et al. (1995:7-8) have called for a special set of guidelines to be used in assessing bilingual preschool children. These guidelines include the following:

- Developmental and cultural appropriateness
- Awareness of the child's linguistic background
- An approach that allows children to demonstrate what they can do
- Involvement of parents and family members, teachers, and staff, as well as the child

Using these guidelines, McLaughlin et al. recommend what they call "instructionally embedded assessment," in which teachers make a plan about what, when, and how to assess a child; collect information from a variety of sources, including observations, prompted responses, classroom products, and conversations with family members; develop a portfolio; write narrative summaries; meet with family and staff; and finally, use the information to inform curriculum development. And this is a recursive process that begins again once it has been completed for any individual child. An assessment system of this sort is, of course, extremely time-consuming and necessitates reform in several areas, including use of time, professional staff development, accountability, and relationships with parents. It may, however, be the only meaningful way teachers can assess young second-language learners.

Children with Disabilities

The field still lacks instruments appropriate for assessing English-language learners with disabilities. This problem is exacerbated by the lack of assessment personnel with expertise in evaluating linguistically and culturally diverse learners. Among the most commonly recommended approaches to nondiscriminatory assessment are the use of nonverbal measures (e.g., the Performance Scale of the Weschler Intelligence Scales for Children [WISC], the Leiter International Performance Scale); translation of instruments into the student's native language; culture-free, culture-fair tests; culture-specific tests; and pluralistic assessments (Shinn and Tindal, 1988). Shinn and Tindal caution, however, that many of these alternative assessment instruments have inadequate psychometric properties and may not provide a comprehensive picture of students' skills and abilities. For example, even so-called nonverbal tests have a verbal component (e.g., instructions for item completion are usually required). With regard to translation of instruments into the student's native language, this is difficult to do well; moreover, some English-language learners may not be literate in their native language. Furthermore, if norms for native-language test versions are not available, assessment personnel may interpret results using English norms, a practice that may give inaccurate results. And because learning occurs in environmental contexts, it is not possible to develop culture-free or culture-fair tests. The practical strategy may be to train assessment personnel rather than await the development of norm-referenced instruments appropriate for English-language learners.

The literature does identify several promising practices in assessment of English-language learners with disabilities that may be useful as well for inclusion of all English-language learners in local and state assessments. Tharp and Gallimore (cited in Durán, 1989) recommend a process of assisted performance in which the teacher first assesses the student's learning performance and then aids the learner in attaining new competencies. Durán also recommends the use of dynamic assessment (e.g., Feuerstein's [1979] Learning Potential Assessment Device), which also involves a test-train-test cycle during which a student's response to a criterion problem is evaluated, and feedback is given to help improve performance. Lewis (1991) recommends the use of the Kaufman Assessment Battery for Children because it separates the mental processing scores from the achievement scores and because it includes a training component to ensure that the student understands the task. He suggests that this approach accommodates different cognitive processing styles, an advantage in assessing diverse cultural groups. He suggests that Feuerstein's dynamic assessment approach and the Kaufmann Assessment Battery for Children are more advantageous than instruments like the Weschler Intelligence Scales for Children-Revised (WISC-R) because they deemphasize factual information and learned content and focus instead on problem-solving tasks.

Because of the myriad of factors that must be considered in distinguishing linguistic and cultural differences from disabilities, ecological models of assessment are recommended so that learning problems are examined in light of contextual variables affecting the teaching-learning process, including the interaction of teachers, students, curriculum, instructional variables, and so forth. Assessors must consider the student's native- and English-language skills, select appropriate measures for assessing skills across languages, and interpret outcomes in light of factors such as the student's age and cultural and experiential background (Cloud, 1991).

Standards-Based Reform

The standards-based reform movement has major implications for English-language learners, especially in the area of assessment. This section first provides background information about standards-based reform and then examines the implications for English-language learners.

Background

The standards-based reform movement commonly refers to three types of standards: content, performance, and opportunity-to-learn standards (McLaughlin and Shepard, 1995). Content standards address what students should know, what schools should teach, and what instruction should be about. Such standards in a broad range of subject matters, such as language arts, mathematics, science, social studies, history, geography, foreign language, art, and physical education, are being developed through the efforts of a number of educational stakeholder institutions at the national, state, and local community levels and subject matter professional groups. Well-publicized efforts of this sort include the mathematics content standards developed by the National Council of Teachers of Mathematics (1989) and the controversial language arts standards developed by the International Reading Association and the National Council of Teachers of English (see the discussion of literacy in Chapter 3). More recently, these efforts have also included the development of model standards by the Teachers of English to Speakers of Other Languages (1996) to guide instruction and assessment of English skills and knowledge for non-English-background children and adults.

Content standards are critical to the assessment and evaluation process. In essence they operationalize an implicit theory of what education can be about for children. While content standards begin to specify broad curriculum goals, performance standards are intended to specify concrete examples and explicit definitions of what students must know and be able to do to demonstrate that they are proficient in the skills and knowledge framed by content standards (McLaughlin and Shepard, 1995). The emphasis of performance standards is on evidence that provides information about the degree of mastery or proficiency shown by students in a content area. Performance standards address the question: "How good is good enough (New Standards, 1995)?

Opportunity-to-learn standards define the level and availability of programs, staff, and other resources sufficient to enable all students to meet challenging content and performance standards (McLaughlin and Shepard, 1995).

The passage of Goals 2000 and the reauthorization of the Elementary and Secondary Education Act (now called the Improving America's Schools Act) in 1994 set in legislation many of the tenets of standards-based reform (see Annex 5-1). Goals 2000 provided resources to states and local districts for developing standards and assessments and implementing state and local improvement initiatives. The Improving America's Schools Act adopted the standards-based framework most conspicuously in its Title I compensatory education programs, which serve a large number of English-language learners (Moss and Puma, 1995). The state plan, the local education agency plan, a demonstration of yearly progress, and school improvement plans are all framed around standards and their assessment. Title VII was also framed around standards, with greater emphasis on school- and district-wide programs to include English-language learners in systemic improvement efforts focused on attaining performance standards.

Efforts to develop performance standards and assessments tied to those standards have been spearheaded by such groups such as New Standards (1995) and the Council of Chief State School Officers (1992), as well as by numerous states and consortia of school districts. Assessments based on performance standards can employ a variety of assessment techniques, including familiar standardized multiple-choice test items; brief constructed response exercises, such as fill-in items; extended constructed response problem-solving exercises, such as essays and written or oral explanations; projects; and aggregations of student work in the form of portfolios or collections of student work. Regardless of the technique employed, however, all such assessments aspire to "faithfully reflect important learning goals.... Individual assessment tasks should elicit the kinds of demonstrations and applications of knowledge ultimately expected of students; and the complete assessment should represent the extent and range of knowledge expected" (McLaughlin and Shepard, 1995:52).

Individual states or other education agencies responsible for a standards-based system develop specifications that serve as guidelines for the creation of performance assessments.[8] The actual development and technical study of assessments are then undertaken by the state or other appropriate education agencies, or alternatively by test publishers sanctioned to perform such work. Collec-

---

[8]The term "performance assessment" is sometimes used in an ambiguous manner. On some occasions, it is used to refer to any form of assessment pertinent to performance standards. For example, a multiple-choice question requiring recall of a key fact or concept might be consistent with a performance standard tied to a content standard. On other occasions, the term is used to denote assessment exercises requiring constructed responses or complex open-ended performances.

tively, all of these groups bear professional and scientific responsibility for investigating the validity and reliability of assessment systems for all children, including English-language learners and bilingual students (American Educational Research Association, American Psychological Association, and National Council on Measurement in Education, 1985).

Implications for English-Language Learners

Both Goals 2000 and the Improving America's Schools Act state explicitly that all students, including English-language-learners, are expected to attain high standards. For example, program accountability provisions in both Title I and Title VII are framed around the need to demonstrate that students in these programs are meeting state and local performance standards for all students (see Annex 5-1). The demonstration of results has been a particularly complex issue for English-language learners because of the unavailability of assessments suited to their needs, as discussed previously.

Issues of validity and reliability in assessing the subject matter knowledge and skills of English-language learners were discussed earlier in this chapter. Another assessment issue related to standards-based reform is how to define adequate yearly progress for English-language learners. The new Title I law, for example, requires that adequate yearly progress be defined in a manner that "...is sufficient to achieve the goal of all children served under [this part in] meeting the State's proficient and advanced levels of performance, particularly economically disadvantaged and LEP students." Yearly progress as defined by the law pertains to the progress of districts and schools, measured by the aggregation of individual student scores on assessments aligned with performance standards. According to the law, the same high performance standards that are established for all students are the ultimate goal for English-language learners as well.

On average, however, English-language learners (especially those with limited prior schooling) may take more time to meet these standards. Therefore, additional benchmarks might be developed for assessing the progress of these students toward meeting the standards. Moreover, because English-language learners are acquiring English-language skills and knowledge already possessed by students who arrive in school speaking English, additional content and performance standards in English-language arts may be appropriate. Recently, Teachers of English to Speakers of Other Languages has developed model content standards to guide the instruction and assessment of English skills and knowledge for such students.

Another issue related to adequate yearly progress has to do with districts' obligation to determine whether schools served by Title I funds are progressing sufficiently toward enabling all children to meet the state's student performance standards. According to the law, adequate progress is defined as that which results in continuous and substantial yearly improvement of each district and school, sufficient to achieve the goal of having all children—particularly the economically disadvantaged and English-language learners—meet the state's proficient and advanced levels of performance. To determine whether English-language learners are meeting these standards, assessment results will have to be disaggregated by English proficiency status. Some states, such as Florida, Hawaii, Louisiana, Maine, Ohio, and Washington, report disaggregating data by English proficiency status (August and Lara, 1996). However, research is needed to determine how best to accomplish this in statistically sound ways, especially in light of alternative assessment procedures used with English-language learners.

Because of the difficulties in assessing English-language learners, it may be important to assess their access to necessary resources and conditions, such as adequate and appropriate instruction. However, defining and assessing these conditions is a very difficult task. Although there has been substantial work in defining some conditions, such as content coverage and time for mainstream students (Carroll, 1958; Leinhardt, 1978), the research base for defining the most important and effective resources and conditions for English-language learners is very weak (see Chapter 7). However, many English-language learners find themselves in poor schools and do not have access to the basics of education necessary for success in school. A good start would be to define and assess these essential resources (e.g., textbooks, course offerings, accessibility of information) while continuing research into other aspects of school life, such as effective school-wide and classroom attributes.

In terms of improving opportunities to learn for English-language learners, another strategy would be to encourage the development and evaluation of methods to help school staff monitor progress in improving schooling through systematic attempts to compare their school's performance against certain quality indicators.[9] This notion is further elaborated in Chapter 7.

RESEARCH NEEDS

A relatively small number of student assessment research needs stand out as candidates for highest priority given our existing knowledge base. To address these needs, there must be coordination with the research findings on the linguistic and cognitive development of children (see Chapters 2 and 3).

Issues in Assessing Language Proficiency

5-1. Research is needed on how assessments of children's language proficiency in their primary language and English can be improved so they are

---

[9]California, for example, has a Program Quality Review System that relies on peer review. Additional benchmarks could include school-wide and classroom factors that are known to improve the performance of English-language learners.

consistent with research findings on first- and second-language acquisition and literacy development.

Existing English-language proficiency instruments emphasize measurement of a limited range of frequently discrete language skills, such as grammar and syntax. Assessments of language proficiency need to be broadened to reflect findings from research in such fields as linguistic pragmatics, interactional sociolinguistics, and cognitive studies of discourse processing that better reflect the language demands placed on language-minority children in everyday contexts (although existing methods for assessing discrete skills should not be ignored).

New research on language proficiency, building on research on social factors in school learning highlighted in the previous chapter, should attend to issues such as sensitivity to bilingualism as a social phenomenon and should take into account the potential impact of bilingualism on language proficiency assessment (Valdes and Figueroa, 1994). We need to know more about how community language use affects the development of proficiency in two languages (see Chapter 2). Verhoeven (1996), for example, has found that immigrant children may acquire a less-developed knowledge of grammar in their first language as a result of their limited exposure to use of that language in their new communities. Acquiring language in a bilingual community may lead to variations in both the first and second languages that incorporate grammatical, lexical, and idiomatic features from the other language.

5-2. Research is needed on how to use assessments to determine levels of proficiency in different aspects of English required for English-language learners to participate in English-only instruction. What are the measurement issues associated with the determination of these aspects? How do these proficiency requisites vary by subject and grade?

Although many states and local districts have established performance standards for exit from special language assistance programs, these standards have not been validated by tracking student performance in mainstream classrooms. Proficiency requisites may vary by subject since some content areas are more dependent on language than others (for example, reading versus math). They will vary by age since language becomes less contextualized in the upper grades.

Issues in Assessing Subject Matter Knowledge

5-3. Research on the assessment of subject matter knowledge needs to address the following questions. First, how do students' levels of English proficiency affect their performance on subject area assessments given in English? Second, how does verbal facility with a first language affect performance on assessments in the native language? Third, how does the language used for instruction affect performance on assessments in the native language?

Research to date (Alderman, 1981) has found that a student's aptitude in a subject can be significantly underestimated if the test is administered in a language in which the student has limited proficiency. Further research is needed to explore this relationship.

With regard to the question of how facility with a first language affects performance on assessments in that language, it is not appropriate to approach this issue as a question of "proficiency" in the native language; such an approach makes neither theoretical nor empirical sense since native speakers acquire proficiency in a first language through their early socialization and additional capacity for proficiency through biological maturation. Instead, the key issues in assessment surround children's familiarity with the kind of language used on an assessment in the first language. For example, we need to investigate how well children understand assessment instructions in their first language—a peculiar usage of language that depends on previous experience with tests of the sort being administered. Research is also needed on how the language used for instruction affects assessment performance in a primary language. For example, do students with communicative competence in their native language but schooling in English perform better when assessed in English than when assessed in their native language? What effect do native language proficiency, years of schooling in English, and difficulty of subject matter assessed have on their performance?

5-4. Research is needed to develop assessments and assessment procedures that incorporate more English-language learners. Further, research is needed toward developing guidelines for determining when English-language learners are ready to take the same assessments as their English-proficient peers and when versions of the assessment other than the "standard" English version should be administered.

This research should include attention to the language and performance demands of assessments and assessment instructions that are separate from the content and domain under assessment. It should also include investigation of the effect of any modifications on the validity and reliability of the assessment. We need to understand better the interaction between the performance of English-language learners and the nature of the assessment. That is, do certain assessment formats (e.g., multiple choice versus constructed response) make it more difficult or easier for such students to express subject matter knowledge?

Criteria are needed as well for determining which English-language learners should take which form of an assessment—an unmodified English version, a native-language version, a modified English version, an English assessment with support, or some other alternative assessment mode (see August and McArthur, 1996).

5-5. Research is needed to address inaccurate and inconsistent scoring of open-ended or performance-based measures of the work of English-language learners. How can errors resulting from such inaccurate and inconsistent scoring be reduced?

We need to understand the mechanisms by which the filter of English can influence scorers' accuracy and consistency and ways in which the scoring of English-language learner assessments can be improved.

Standards-Based Reform

5-6. Research needs to address whether it is possible to establish common, standard benchmarks for subject matter knowledge and English proficiency for English-language learners within a valid theoretical framework; what these benchmarks might be; and how the benchmarks for English proficiency might be related to performance standards for English-language arts.

5-7. Research is needed to determine whether in the context of school and district outcomes, English-language learners are making progress toward meeting proficient and advanced levels of performance. How can the outcomes of nonstandard administrations/alternative assessments be incorporated into district- and state-wide accountability systems and reporting requirements?

5-8. Research is needed into how opportunities to learn can be evaluated.

Standards-based reform has contributed to a redefinition of the role of assessment that has implications for English-language learners. These policies call for the inclusion of these students in assessments, for assessments that are systematically linked to standards systems at the district and state levels, and for evaluations of programs at the school site and district levels to ensure that students are meeting the standards. Although current policy does not require assessments of school and classroom conditions and resources that make it possible for students to meet new standards, educators concerned with helping language-minority children are interested in assessing these opportunities to learn.

ANNEX:
LEGISLATIVE CONTEXT FOR STANDARDS AND ASSESSMENT

Legislation passed by Congress in recent years contains several consistent themes regarding student assessment, program evaluation (see Chapter 6), and standards with respect to English-language learners. These themes provide important opportunities for directed research to guide the policy process. Legislative language expressing these themes can be found in Goals 2000 (P.L. 103-227), Title I (Helping Disadvantaged Children Meet High Standards) and Title VII (Bilingual Education Programs) of the Improving America's Schools Act of 1994 (P.L. 103-382), and the Reauthorization of the Office of Educational Research and Improvement (Title IX of P.L. 103-227). The themes might be encapsulated as follows:

- Standards and assessments are to fully include English-language learners.
- Innovative ways of assessing student performance are encouraged, including modifications to existing instruments for English-language learners.
- Programs are to be evaluated with respect to whether they meet "challenging" performance standards, rather than on a normative or comparative basis.
- Evaluations are to be useful for program improvement as well as program accountability.

The following subsections summarize key provisions of the major legislation.

Department of Education Organization Act of 1994

According to Section 216(b)(3) of this act:

The Secretary shall ensure that limited-English-proficient and language-minority students are included in ways that are valid, reliable, and fair under all standards and assessment development conducted or funded by the Department.

Goals 2000

Goals 2000 provides resources to states and communities to develop and implement systemic education reforms aimed at helping all students meet challenging academic and occupational standards. The law defines "all students" as meaning "students or children from a broad range of backgrounds and circumstances, including among others, students or children with limited English proficiency."

The law authorizes grants to states and local education agencies (LEAs) to help defray the cost of developing, field testing, and evaluating assessment systems that are aligned with state content standards. It sets aside a portion of funds for developing assessments in languages other than English.

Goals 2000 further authorizes federal grants to state education agencies (SEAs) for the purpose of developing a state plan to improve the quality of education for all students. Development of the state plan is to include establishment of teaching and learning standards and assessments aligned with these standards, as well as strategies for program improvement and accountability.

Title I

The law requires states to develop or adopt a set of high-quality yearly assessments, including assessments in at least reading or language arts and math, to be used as the primary means of determining the yearly performance of each LEA and school served under Title I in enabling all children to meet the state's student performance standards. (If states are using transitional assessments, they must devise a procedure for identifying LEAs and schools for improvement, and this procedure must rely on accurate information about the academic progress of each LEA and school.)

The law states that the same assessments must be used to measure the performance of all children. It specifies that assessments must be aligned with challenging content and student performance standards; provide coherent information about student attainment of such standards; be used for purposes for which such assessments are valid and reliable; measure the proficiency of students in the academic subjects in which a state has adopted challenging content and student performance standards; administered at some time during grades 3 through 6, 6 through 9, and 10 through 12; and involve multiple up-to-date measures of student performance. The assessments are to provide for the participation of all students; reasonable adaptations and accommodations for students with diverse learning needs; and the inclusion of English-language learners, who are to be assessed, to the extent practicable, in the language and form most likely to yield accurate and reliable information on what they know and can do, so that their mastery of skills in subjects other than English can be determined.

Furthermore, the law states that adequate and yearly progress must be defined in a manner that is consistent with guidelines established by the Secretary of Education, resulting in continuous and substantial yearly improvement of each LEA and school; such improvement must be sufficient to achieve the goal of enabling all children served under this part of the legislation to meet the state's proficient and advanced levels of performance, particularly economically disadvantaged students and English-language learners. Moreover, progress must be linked primarily to performance on the assessments carried out under this section of the legislation, while also being established in part through the use of other measures.

Title VII

The law clearly indicates the purposes of evaluations for programs funded under Subpart 1 (Bilingual Education Capacity and Demonstration Grants): "(1) for program improvement, (2) to further define the program's goals and objectives, and (3) to determine program effectiveness."

Evaluations are to address student achievement using state student performance standards (if any), including data comparing English-language learners and other students on school retention, academic achievement, and gains in English (and where applicable, the non-English language) proficiency. The evaluations are also required to incorporate "program implementation indicators that provide information for informing and improving program management and effectiveness," including information on the curriculum and professional development. In addition, evaluations must describe the relationship of activities funded under Title VII to the overall school program and activities conducted through other sources.

Evaluations have consequences for comprehensive school grants and system-wide improvement grants. These programs are to be terminated if students "are not making adequate progress toward achieving challenging State content standards and challenging State student performance standards," and "in the case of a program to promote dual language facility, such program is not promoting such facility" (Sections 7114(b)(2) and 7115(b)(2)).

Subpart 2 of Title VII authorizes funds for data collection, dissemination, research, and program evaluation through grants, contracts, and cooperative agreements. Current or recent recipients of program grants may conduct longitudinal research to monitor the students. Funds are also made available for activities to promote the adoption and implementation of "programs that demonstrate promise of assisting children and youth of limited English proficiency to meet challenging State standards."

REFERENCES

Abedi, J., C. Lord, and J. Plummer
   1995   *Language Background Report.* Graduate School of Education, National Center for Research on Evaluation, Standards, and Student Testing. Los Angeles: University of California at Los Angeles.
Alderman, D.
   1981   Language proficiency as a moderator variable in testing academic aptitude. *Journal of Educational Psychology* 74:580-857.
American Educational Research Association, American Psychological Association, and National Council on Measurement in Education
   1985   *Standards of Educational and Psychological Testing.* Washington, DC: American Psychological Association.
Anderson, N.E., F.F. Jenkins, and K.E. Miller
   1996   NAEP Inclusion Criteria and Testing Accommodations. Findings from the NAEP 1995 Field Test in Mathematics. Washington, DC: Educational Testing Service.

August, Diane, and Julia Lara
  1996   *Systemic Reform and Limited English Proficient Students.* Washington, DC: Council of Chief State School Officers.
August, Diane, Kenji Hakuta, Fernando Olguin, and Delia Pompa
  1995   *LEP Students and Title I: A Guidebook for Educators.* Washington, DC: National Clearinghouse for Bilingual Education.
August, Diane, and Edith McArthur
  1996   Proceedings of the Conference on Inclusion Guidelines and Accommodations for Limited English Proficient Students in the National Assessment of Educational Progress (December 5-6, 1994). National Center for Education Statistics, Office of Educational Research and Improvement, U.S. Department of Education, Washington, DC.
Bialystok, E., and K. Hakuta
  1994   *In Other Words.* New York: Basic Books.
Carroll, John B.
  1958   Communication theory, linguistics, and psycholinguistics. *Review of Educational Research* 28(2):79-88
Cheung, Oona M., and Lisa W. Soloman
  1991   *Summary of State Practices Concerning the Assessment of and the Data Collection about Limited English Proficient (LEP) Students.* Washington, DC: Council of Chief State School Officers
Cheung, Oona M., Barbara S. Clements, and Y. Carol Mieu
  1994   *The Feasibility of Collecting Comparable National Statistics about Students with Limited English Proficiency.* Washington, DC: Council of Chief State School Officers.
Cloud, N.
  1991   Educational assessment. Pp. 219-245 in E.V. Hamayan and J.S. Damico, eds., *Limiting Bias in the Assessment of Bilingual Students.* Austin, TX: Pro-Ed.
Council of Chief State School Officers
  1992   *Recommendations for Improving the Assessment and Monitoring of Students with Limited English Proficiency.* Washington, DC: Council of Chief State School Officers.
Cronbach, L., R. Linn, R. Brennen, and E. Haertel
  1995   *Generalizability Analysis for Educational Assessments.* Los Angeles: Center for Research on Evaluation, Standards and Student Testing and Center for the Study of Evaluation, University of California.
Durán, Richard P.
  1989   Assessment and instruction of at-risk Hispanic students. *Exceptional Children* 56(2):154-158.
Feuerstein, R.
  1979   *The Dynamic Assessment of Retarded Persons.* Baltimore, MD: University Park Press.
Fleischman, H.L., and P.J. Hopstock
  1993   Descriptive Study of Services to Limited English Proficient Students, Volume 1. Summary of Findings and Conclusions. Prepared for Office of the Under Secretary, U.S. Department of Education by Development Associates, Inc., Arlington, VA.
Garcia, G.E.
  1991   Factors influencing the English reading test performance of Spanish-speaking Hispanic children. *Research Reading Quarterly* 26(4):371-392.
Garcia, G.E., and P.D. Pearson
  1994   Assessment and diversity. *Review of Research in Education* (20):337-391.
Genesee, F., and E.V. Hamayan
  1994   Classroom-based assessment. In F. Genesee, ed., *Educating Second Language Children: The Whole Child, the Whole Curriculum, the Whole Community.* New York: Cambridge University Press.
Gutierrez, K.
  1995   Unpackaging academic discourse. *Discourse Processes* 19(1):21-37.

Hafner, A.
   1995   Assessment Practices: Developing and Modifying Statewide Assessments for LEP Students. Paper presented at the annual conference on Large Scale Assessment sponsored by the Council of Chief State School Officers, June 1995. School of Education, California State University, Los Angeles.
Hambleton, R.K., and A. Kanjee
   1994   Enhancing the validity of cross-cultural studies: Improvements in instrument translation methods. In T. Husen and T.N. Postlewaite, eds., *International Encyclopedia of Education* (2nd edition). Oxford, UK: Pergamon Press.
Kober, Nancy L., and Michael J. Feuer
   1996   *Title I Testing and Assessment. Challenging Standards for Disadvantaged Children. Summary of a Workshop.* Board on Testing and Assessment, National Research Council. Washington, DC: National Academy Press.
Leinhardt, G.
   1978   Educational opportunity: Opportunity to learn. Pp. 15-24, Chapter III in *Perspectives in the Instructional Dimensions Study: A Supplemental Report from the National Institute of Education.* Washington, DC: National Institute of Education.
Lewis, J.
   1991   Innovative approaches in assessment. In R.J. Samuda and S.L. Kong, J. Cummins, J. Pascual-Leone, and J. Lewis, eds., *Assessment and Placement of Minority Students.* Toronto, Canada: C.J. Hogrefe.
Lindholm, K.
   1994   Standardized Achievement Tests vs. Alternative Assessment: Are Results Complementary or Contradictory? Paper presented at the American Educational Research Association, New Orleans, April. School of Education, San Jose State University.
McLaughlin, B.
   1984   *Second-Language Acquisition in Childhood,* 2d ed. Hillsdale, NJ: Erlbaum.
McLaughlin, B., A. Blanchard, and Y. Osanai
   1995   *Assessing Language Development in Bilingual Preschool Children.* NCBE Program Information Guide Series, No. 22. Washington, DC: National Clearinghouse for Bilingual Education.
McLaughlin, M.W., and L.A. Shepard
   1995   *Improving Education Through Standards-Based Reform.* Stanford, CA: The National Academy of Education.
Meisels, S.
   1994   Designing meaningful measurements for early childhood. Pp. 202-222 in B. Mallory and R. New, eds., *Diversity and Developmentally Appropriate Practices: Challenges for Early Childhood Education.* New York: Teachers College Press.
Messick, Cheryl K.
   1988   Ins and outs of the acquisition of spatial terms. *Topics in Language Disorders* 8(2):14-25.
Moss, M., and M. Puma
   1995   Prospects: The Congressionally Mandated Study of Educational Growth and Opportunity. First Year Report on Language Minority and Limited English Proficient Students. Prepared for Office of the Under Secretary, U.S. Department of Education by Abt Associates, Inc., Cambridge, MA.
National Council of Teachers of Mathematics
   1989   *Curriculum and Evaluation Standards for School Mathematics.* Reston, VA: National Council of Teachers of Mathematics.
Navarette, C., J. Wilde, C. Nelson, R. Martinez, and G. Hargett
   1990   *Informal Assessment in Educational Evaluation: Implications for Bilingual Education Programs.* Program Information Guide No. 13. Washington, DC: National Clearinghouse for Bilingual Education.

New Standards
  1995   *Performance Standards. English Language Arts, Mathematics, Science, and Applied Learning.* Volumes 1, 2, and 3. Consultation Drafts. Washington, DC: National Center for Education and the Economy.
Rivera, Charlene
  1984   *Communicative Competence Approaches to Language Proficiency Assessment: Research and Application.* Multilingual Matters 9. Rosslyn, VA: InterAmerican Research Associates.
  1995   *How We Can Ensure Equity in Statewide Assessment Programs?* Findings from a national survey of assessment directors on statewide assessment policies for LEP students, presented at annual meeting of the National Conference on Large Scale Assessment, June 18, 1995, Phoenix, AZ. The Evaluation Assistance Center East. Washington, DC: George Washington University Institute for Equity and Excellence in Education.
Royer, J., and M. Carlo
  1991   Assessing the language acquisition progress of limited English proficient students: Problems and a new alternative. *Applied Measurement in Education* 4:85-113.
Saville-Troike, Muriel
  1991   *Teaching and Testing for Academic Achievement: The Role of Language Development.* Focus, Occasional Papers in Bilingual Education, No. 4. Washington, DC: National Clearinghouse for Bilingual Education.
Shinn, M.R., and G.A. Tindal
  1988   Using student performance data in academics: A pragmatic and defensible approach to non-discriminatory assessment. Pp. 383-407 in R.G. Jones, ed., *Psychoeducational Assessment of Minority Group Children: A Casebook.* Berkeley, CA: Cobb and Henry.
Short, D.
  1991   *How to Integrate Language and Content Instruction: A Training Manual.* Washington, DC: Center for Applied Linguistics.
Strang, E. William, and Elaine Carlson
  1991   *Providing Chapter 1 Services to Limited English-Proficient Students.* Final Report. Rockville, MD: Westat.
Teachers of English to Speakers of Other Languages (TESOL)
  1996   *ESL Standards for Pre-K-12 Students.* Washington, DC: Center for Applied Linguistics.
Valdes, Guadalupe, and Richard A. Figueroa
  1994   *Bilingualism and Testing: A Special Case of Bias.* Norwood, NJ: Ablex.
Valdez Pierce, L., and J.M. O'Malley
  1992   *Performance and Portfolio Assessment for Language Minority Students.* NCBE Program Information Guide Series. Washington, DC: National Clearinghouse for Bilingual Education.
Verhoeven, L.
  1996   Early bilingualism, cognition, and assessment. Pp. 276-291 in M. Milanovic and N. Saville, eds., *Performance Testing, Cognition and Assessment.* Cambridge, England: Cambridge University Press.
Wong Fillmore, L.
  1982   Language minority students and school participation: What kind of English is needed? *Journal of Education* 164:143-156.
Wong Fillmore, L., and Julia Lara
  1996   *Summary of the Proposal Setting the Pace for English Learning: Focus on Assessment Tools and Staff Development.* Washington, DC: Council of Chief State School Officers.
Zehler, Annette M., Paul J. Hopstock, Howard L. Fleischman, and Cheryl Greniuk
  1994   *An Examination of Assessment of Limited English Proficient Students.* Special Issues Analysis Center, Task Order Report, March 28, 1994. Arlington, VA: Development Associates, Inc.

PROGRAM EVALUATION:
SUMMARY OF THE STATE OF KNOWLEDGE

The following key points can be drawn from the literature on program evaluation:

• The major national-level program evaluations suffer from design limitations; lack of documentation of study objectives, conceptual details, and procedures followed; poorly articulated goals; lack of fit between goals and research design; and excessive use of elaborate statistical designs to overcome shortcomings in research designs.

• In general, more has been learned from reviews of smaller-scale evaluations, although these, too, have suffered from methodological limitations.

• It is difficult to synthesize the program evaluations of bilingual education because of the extreme politicization of the process. Most consumers of research are not researchers who want to know the truth, but advocates who are convinced of the absolute correctness of their positions.

• The beneficial effects of native-language instruction are clearly evident in programs that are labeled "bilingual education," but they also appear in some programs that are labeled "immersion." There appear to be benefits of programs that are labeled "structured immersion," although a quantitative analysis of such programs is not yet available.

• There is little value in conducting evaluations to determine which type of program is best. The key issue is not finding a program that works for all children and all localities, but rather finding a set of program components that works for the children in the community of interest, given that community's goals, demographics, and resources.

• Five general lessons have been learned from the past 25 years of program evaluation:

—Higher-quality program evaluations are needed.
—Local evaluations need to be made more informative.
—Theory-based interventions need to be created and evaluated.
—We need to think in terms of program components, not politically motivated labels.
—A developmental model needs to be created for use in predicting the effects of program components on children in different environments.

6

Program Evaluation

Of the types of programs for English-language learners reviewed in Chapter 1, the most commonly studied are those that use the native language for some period of time for core academics (i.e., transitional bilingual education programs) and those that do not use the native language in any regular or systematic way (i.e., English as a second language [ESL] and its variants, such as structured immersion and content-based ESL, as well as "submersion programs"). During the 1970s and 1980s, the federal government and advocates were keenly interested in determining which of these two models is more effective. Program evaluations were intended to provide a definitive answer to this question. This chapter examines what we know from program evaluations conducted to date and identifies research needs in this area. Note that this chapter focuses on evaluation of various models for educating English-language learners, Chapter 7 reviews studies of school and classroom effectiveness, and makes recommendations regarding research to improve educational programming for English-language learners and studies of the processes related to program development, implementation, and dissemination.

STATE OF KNOWLEDGE

This section begins by reviewing national-level evaluations of programs for English-language learners. It then examines reviews of smaller-scale program evaluations. This is followed by a discussion of the politicization of program evaluation. The final subsection addresses the future course of program evaluation, presenting five lessons learned that can lead to better, more useful evaluations.

National Evaluations

There have been three large-scale national evaluations of programs for English-language learners. Although these studies provided some information about the education of English-language learners, they were of limited utility for the evaluation of programs. Nonetheless, it is instructive to review them so we can avoid the mistakes of the past, as well as benefit from what was learned. This section also summarizes the findings of a National Research Council report (Meyer and Fienberg, 1992) that reviews two of these studies.

American Institutes for Research (AIR) Study

The American Institutes for Research (Dannoff, 1978) conducted the first large-scale national evaluation of programs for English-language learners, commonly referred to as the AIR study. The study compared students enrolled in Title VII Spanish/English bilingual programs and comparable students (in terms of ethnicity, socioeconomic status, and grade level) not enrolled in such programs. In the AIR study, 8,200 children were measured twice during the school year on English oral comprehension and reading, math, and Spanish oral comprehension and reading. Generally, the results from this study showed that students in bilingual education programs did not gain more than students not in such programs.

The study was the subject of a great deal of criticism, the major criticism addressing the strength of the treatment control group comparison (Crawford, 1995). Nearly three-quarters of the experimental group had been in bilingual programs for 2 or more years, and the study measured their gains in the last few months. Additionally, about two-thirds of the children in the control group had previously been in a bilingual program; these children did not represent a control group in the usual sense of the term. Thus, the AIR study did not compare bilingual education with no bilingual education.

In part because of the ambiguity of the conclusions from the AIR study, two major longitudinal studies were commissioned by the U.S. Department of Education in 1983 to look at program effectiveness. The hope was that these studies would provide definitive evidence, one way or the other, about the effectiveness of bilingual education. These two studies are reviewed below.

Longitudinal Study

The National Longitudinal Evaluation of the Effectiveness of Services for Language Minority Limited English Proficient Students (Longitudinal Study)

(Development Associates, 1984; Burkheimer et al., 1989) was conducted by Development Associates, with Research Triangle Institute as a prime subcontractor. The study had two distinct phases. The descriptive phase, which examined the variety of services provided to English-language learners, was designed as a four-stage stratified probability sample. First-stage units were states; second-stage units were school districts, counties, or clusters of neighboring districts or counties; third-stage units were schools; and fourth-stage units were teachers and students.[1] A total of 342 schools were identified, but only 86 agreed to participate in the study. Because of this low participation rate, the sample cannot be considered nationally representative. Nonetheless, the descriptive phase of the Longitudinal Study provided one of the most comprehensive reports on the services received by English-language learners. Some of the major findings were as follows:

- The vast majority of English-language learners came from economically disadvantaged families.
- English-language learners were at risk educationally, with most performing below grade level.
- Most instruction of the children was in English or in some combination of English and the native language.

The goal of the second phase of the study was a longitudinal follow-up to determine the relative effectiveness of programs. The focus was on 25 schools from the first phase, with students from kindergarten to fifth grade being followed over 3 years (Burkheimer et al., 1989). Students in the sample consisted of six distinct groups—three types of students sampled in two cohorts. The English-language learners' group consisted of virtually all students in the respective cohort who were classified as having limited English proficiency by local criteria. The English-proficient group consisted of students who were receiving special services because they were placed in classes with English-language learners. The comparison group consisted of children considered English proficient who had never received such special services.

Because the schools were initially selected for the follow-up phase on the basis of having representative populations of interest and not on the basis of program differences, there was not much variation in the programs represented in this phase. Moreover, some of the schools had no children in the control group.

---

[1]The target population of students consisted of elementary-age language minority students/English-language learners receiving special language-related services from any source of funding. The sample included the 10 states with at least 2 percent of the national estimated target population, and an additional 10 states were selected as a stratified random sample of the remaining states, with selection probability proportional to the estimated size of the elementary-grade target population in the state.

In an attempt to compensate for the weakness of the study design, elaborate statistical techniques were used. Given these limitations, one should be cautious about interpreting the study findings. The major findings can be summarized as follows (Burkheimer et al., 1989):

• Assignment of English-language learners to specific instructional services reflects principally local policy determinations. To a much more limited extent (mainly in the lower grades), assignment may be based on "deliberate" (and apparently criterion-driven) placement of students in the specific services for which they are ready.

• Too heavy a concentration in any one aspect of the English-language learner's education can detract from achievement in other areas.

• The yearly achievement of English-language learners in math and English-language arts is facilitated by different approaches, depending on student background factors. For example, students who are relatively English proficient are better able to benefit from English-language arts instruction given in English, whereas students who are weak in English and/or strong in their native language show better yearly English-language arts achievement when instructed in their native language.

• In the later grades, proficiency in mathematics when tested in English seems to require proficiency in English. This is not the case in the lower grades.

• Like assignment to specific services for English-language learners, exit from those services reflects both local policy determination and specific criterion-driven exit rules related to reaching certain levels of proficiency/achievement in English.

• Children are more likely to be exited from English-language learner services if those services are similar to those that would be expected for English-proficient students.

Immersion Study

The Longitudinal Study of Immersion and Dual Language Instructional Programs for Language Minority Children (Immersion Study) (Ramirez et al., 1991), conducted by Aguirre International, was a much more focused study of program alternatives than the Longitudinal Study. It attempted a quasi-experimental longitudinal comparison of three types of programs: English-only immersion, early-exit bilingual (also known as transitional bilingual), and late-exit bilingual (also known as maintenance bilingual). The study took place at nine sites, but five of these had only one of the three types of programs (Ramirez et al., 1991). In fact, the late-exit bilingual program was completely confounded with site. Despite sophisticated statistical models of growth, the conclusions from the study are seriously compromised by the noncomparability of sites.

The major findings of the comparison of program types were summarized by the U.S. Department of Education (1991). After 4 years in their respective programs, English-language learners in immersion strategy and early-exit programs demonstrated comparable skills in mathematics, language, and reading when tested in English. There were differences among the three late-exit sites in achievement level in the three subjects: students at the sites with the most use of Spanish and the most use of English ended sixth grade with the same skills in English language and reading; students at the two late-exit sites that used the most Spanish showed higher growth in mathematics skills than those at the site that abruptly transitioned into almost all English instruction. Students in all three programs realized a growth in English-language and reading skills that was as rapid or more so than the growth that would be expected for these children had they not received any intervention.

National Research Council Report

Both the Longitudinal and Immersion studies were reviewed by a National Research Council panel of the Committee on National Statistics (Meyer and Fienberg, 1992). The primary focus of the panel's report is on determining whether the statistical methods used in those studies were appropriate. The report draws important lessons learned from these major efforts, including the following:

• The formal designs of the Longitudinal and Immersion studies were ill suited to answering the important policy questions that appear to have motivated them.
• Execution and interpretation of these studies, especially the Longitudinal Study, were hampered by a lack of documentation of the study objectives, the operationalizing of conceptual details, actual procedures followed, and changes in all of the above.
• Because of the poor articulation of study goals and the lack of fit between discernible goals and research design, it is unlikely that additional statistical analyses of the data would yield results central to the policy questions these studies were originally intended to address.
• Both the Longitudinal and Immersion studies suffered from excessive attention to the use of elaborate statistical methods intended to overcome the shortcomings in the research designs.
• Although the samples in the Immersion study were followed longitudinally, later comparisons are not considered valid because of sample attrition.

Quite clearly the Longitudinal and Immersion studies did not provide decisive evidence about the effectiveness of bilingual programs. However, according to the National Research Council report, findings from the comparisons that were most sound with respect to study design and sample characteristics indicate that kindergarten and first grade students received academic instruction in Spanish had higher achievement in reading than comparable students who received academic instruction in English.

In general, more has been learned from smaller-scale program evaluations, to which we now turn, than from these multi-million-dollar studies.

Reviews of Smaller-Scale Evaluations

This section examines five key reviews of smaller-scale program evaluations: Baker and de Kanter (1981), Rossell and Ross (1986) and Rossell and Baker (1996), Willig (1985), and the U.S. General Accounting Office (U.S. GAO) (1987).

Baker and de Kanter (1981)

Still by far the most influential review of studies in bilingual education, despite its age, is that of Baker and de Kanter (1981). This review, which was based on earlier reviews by Engle (1975) and Zappert and Cruz (1977), was in turn used as a basis for other reviews that are both critical (e.g., Rossell and Ross, 1986; Rossell and Baker, 1996) and supportive (e.g., Willig, 1985) of bilingual education. Since the study was conducted, it has become increasingly difficult to find comparison groups because of judicial decisions (see Appendix A); thus, the Baker and de Kanter review is more current than might be presumed.

Baker and de Kanter located about 150 evaluations of programs designed for English-language learners. To be included in the review, a study essentially had to either employ random assignment of children to treatment conditions or take measures to ensure that children in the treatment groups were equivalent. Baker and de Kanter rightly rejected studies that had no comparison group. Of the studies initially located, only 28 satisfied their criteria. Other reviews of the literature have also found a disappointing percentage of studies (only about 10 percent [Lam, 1992]) to be methodologically adequate. We return to the issue of the poor quality of program evaluation later in this chapter.

Baker and de Kanter (1981:1) drew the following conclusion from their review: "The case for the effectiveness of transitional bilingual education is so weak that exclusive reliance on this instruction method is clearly not justified." It is important to realize that Baker and de Kanter were not evaluating whether bilingual education was effective, rather whether there was sufficient research basis to justify transitional bilingual education over alternative forms of instruction. They adopted the conservative strategy of defining a "sufficient research basis" as showing that transitional bilingual education was significantly better statistically than a comparison program.

Rossell and Ross (1986) and Rossell and Baker (1996)

Rossell and Ross (1986) and Rossell and Baker (1996) used the Baker and de Kanter (1981) review as the basis for their review of the research literature. Working from Baker and de Kanter (1981), as well as Baker and Pelavin (1984), they considered studies that evaluated alternative second-language programs. Their review included only studies of "good quality," which was defined as having random assignment to programs or statistical control for pretreatment differences between groups when random assignment was not possible. Rossell and Ross (1986:413) drew the following conclusion: "The research...does not support transitional bilingual education as a superior instruction for increasing the English language achievement of limited-English-proficient children." Rossell and Baker (1996:7) came to essentially the same conclusion: "Thus the research evidence does not support transitional bilingual education as a superior form of instruction for limited English proficient children."

Despite these conclusions, both reviews state that a small number of studies support the view that transitional bilingual education is beneficial. Both reviews suggest that structured immersion is a more promising program. In such a program, instruction is in the language being learned (i.e., English), but the teacher is fluent in the students' native language.[2]

Willig (1985)

Willig (1985) conducted a meta-analysis of the studies reviewed by Baker and de Kanter (1981). Meta-analysis provides a quantitative estimate of the effect of an intervention. Willig made several significant improvements to the Baker and de Kanter review (Secada, 1987). First, she eliminated five studies conducted outside of the United States (three in Canada, one in the Philippines, and one in South Africa) because of the significant differences in the students, the programs, and the context in those studies. She also excluded one study in which instruction took place outside the classroom.

Second, as is required in meta-analysis, and in contrast with previous reviews, she quantitatively measured the program effect in each study, even if it was not statistically significant. To make these measurements, she had to eliminate seven more of the studies reviewed by Baker and de Kanter because they did not provide sufficient data to perform the necessary calculations.[3] Thus, her

---

[2]The second language used in these programs is always geared to the children's language proficiency level at each stage so that it is comprehensible. The native tongue is used only in the rare instances when the students cannot complete a task without it. The student thus learns the second language and subject matter content simultaneously. Immersion programs in which the second language is not the dominant language of the country typically include at least 30 to 60 minutes of native-language arts, and in some cases become bilingual programs early on.

[3]Recent work by Bushman and Wang (1996) does permit the combining of quantitative and qualitative results.

major conclusions are based on 16 studies, from which she computed about 500 effect size measures. (An effect size is a measure of program benefit relative to another program.) Her overall conclusion is quite different from that of Baker and de Kanter (1981): "positive effects for bilingual programs...for all major academic areas" (p. 297). However, it should be noted that Willig was asking a fundamentally different question than Baker. While Baker was asking whether bilingual education should be mandated, Willig was asking a more modest question: Does bilingual education work? As she notes, she did *not* compare transitional bilingual education programs with other programs, such as ESL and sheltered instruction, in part because neither she nor Baker could find many evaluations that made such a comparison. She only contrasted program versus no-program studies. Against that standard, Willig concluded that bilingual education does work (better than not having anything in place). In addition, Willig's results indicate that the better the technical quality of the study—for example, if a study used random assignment as opposed to creating post hoc comparison groups—the larger the effects. These results raise an interesting possibility: that the "effectiveness" debate may really be a debate carried on at the relatively superficial level of a study's technical quality.

The Willig (1985) meta-analysis does, however, have drawbacks. Most problematic, it employs the questionable practice of including the same study more than once in the analysis. Willig used a complicated weighing procedure to compensate for this problem, but she may not have been entirely successful in this effort. While the practice of using the same study more than once is quite common in meta-analysis, it does seriously compromise the validity of the inferential statistical analysis.

Willig (1985) has also been criticized for controlling for variables "which partly eliminated the actual treatment effect" (Rossell and Baker, 1996:25). It may have been necessary to control for those variables.[4] However, because there were small numbers of studies for some levels of these control variables, Willig's estimate of effect became quite unstable after adjustment for these variables. It should be noted, however, that her unadjusted effects parallel her adjusted effects.

U.S. General Accounting Office (1987)

In the mid-1980s, Augustus Hawkins, Chairman of the Education and Labor Committee of the House of Representatives, asked GAO to evaluate the effectiveness of bilingual education programs. Perhaps to complete the report promptly, GAO surveyed 10 experts in the field and presented conclusions in the

---

[4]Variables included the following: research design (random assignment versus correlational); type of measure (e.g., language versus mathematics, raw scores versus percentiles); language of measurement (English versus not English); and type of score (e.g., d versus derived d).

form of "7 of the 10 believe that...." Most of the experts surveyed looked quite favorably upon educational policy that encourages the use of native-language instruction and were relatively critical of structured immersion. Moreover, most questioned the value of "aggregate program labels" (e.g., immersion or transitional bilingual education).

The U.S. GAO (1987) report is problematic because it attempts to find a consensus. While it is likely that the report captures the dominant view of the experts surveyed, there is not really a strong consensus about what is best for the education of English-language learners. If different experts had been chosen, different conclusions would have been drawn.

Summary of the Reviews

The beneficial effects of native-language instruction are clearly evident in programs that have been labeled "bilingual education," but they also appear in some programs that are labeled "immersion" (Gersten and Woodward, 1995). There appear to be benefits of programs that are labeled "structured immersion" (Baker and de Kanter, 1981; Rossell and Ross, 1986); however, a quantitative analysis of such programs is not yet available. Based primarily on the Willig (1985) meta-analysis, the committee accepts the conclusion of the previous National Research Council panel (Meyer and Fienberg, 1992:105), noted earlier: "the panel still sees the elements of positive relationships that are consistent with empirical results from other studies and that support the theory underlying native language instruction."

However, for numerous reasons, we see little value in conducting evaluations to determine which type of program is best. First, the key issue is not finding a program that works for all children and all localities, but rather finding a set of program components that works for the children in the community of interest, given the goals, demographics, and resources of that community. The focus needs to be on the proper contexts in which a program component is most effective and conversely, the contexts in which it may even be harmful. Second, many large-scale evaluations would likely suffer from the problem encountered in some previous national evaluations: the programs would be so loosely implemented that the evaluation would have no clear focus. Third, programs are not unitary, but a complex series of components. Thus we think it better to focus on components than on programs. As we argue later, successful bilingual and immersion programs may contain many common elements. Our view is shared by Ginsburg (1992:36): "...focusing evaluations on determining a single best method of language instruction for non-English-speaking children was probably the wrong approach to take."

Politicization of Program Evaluation

It is difficult to synthesize the program evaluations of bilingual education because of the extreme politicization of the process. Research always involves compromises, and because no study is perfect, every study has weaknesses. What has happened in this area of research is that most consumers of the research are not researchers who want to know the truth, but advocates who are convinced of the absolute correctness of their positions. Advocates care mainly about the results of a study. If its conclusions support their position, they note the study's strong points; if not, they note its weak points. Because there are studies that support a wide range of positions, advocates on both sides end up with plenty of "evidence" to support their position. Policymakers are justifiably troubled by the inability of the research evidence to resolve the debate.

A related issue is that very quickly a new study gets labeled as pro- or anti-bilingual education. What is emphasized in the debate is not the quality of the research or insights about school and classroom attributes that contribute to or hinder positive student outcomes, but whether the study is consistent with the advocate's position. Because advocacy is the goal, very poor studies that support an advocated position are touted as definitive. Consider two different examples.

In general, we are quite positive about the California Case Studies (discussed below, as well as in the next chapter). The project was never designed to be an evaluation, and funding that might have been used for evaluation was cut. Nonetheless, there have been attempts to document the effectiveness of this bilingual project; see especially the studies presented in Krashen and Biber (1988). Yet results of these studies are presented with very little documentation. For example, sample sizes are frequently not presented for the means given, and often there are no controls for socioeconomic status. As presented, the studies would not stand the test of evidence if they were submitted to a peer-reviewed journal.[5] To their credit, Krashen and Biber (1988) admit the data do not "rigorously test" (p. 31) the effectiveness of bilingual education, but others have ignored these qualifications.

Advocates of bilingual education are not alone in presenting less than scientifically acceptable evidence. Recently, extensive publicity has been given to an evaluation of the New York City bilingual program (Board of Education of the City of New York, 1994). That study compared the exit rates (how long children stayed in the program) and achievement of students in ESL and bilingual programs. The comparisons made between the two programs were seriously confounded with native language: most of the students in the bilingual program had Spanish as a native language, while the students in ESL had other language backgrounds. Ironically, the New York City study carefully documented the

---

[5]Rossell and Baker (1996) arrive at a similar appraisal.

native-language confound, but made no attempt to control for this variable or for other confounds (e.g., socioeconomic status). In the preface, the authors describe the results of the study as "preliminary" and "ongoing." Yet advocates and the media accepted the conclusions of the report. The New York City evaluation has been heralded by advocates as providing "hard evidence" (Mujica, 1995) because it makes bilingual education look ineffective. Again study quality is ignored if the results support the advocate's position.

The politicization of this research area has a further harmful consequence. The hope is that evaluations will enter the policy debate as "principled arguments" (Abelson, 1995). However, because investigators very quickly become labeled as advocates of one position or another (even if they do not see themselves that way), the basis of their arguments is not perceived as principle but as politics. Scientists are seen as advocates.

The Future Course of Evaluation

It is easy to criticize previous program evaluations, but we need to realize that program evaluation was in its infancy when many of these studies were initially undertaken. During the past 25 years, the model of program evaluation has evolved considerably. There are several key elements in the current model (see Fetterman et al. [1995] for one such formulation). First, the initial focus is not on comparing programs, but on determining whether a given program is properly implemented and fine tuning it so it becomes more responsive to the needs of children, the school, and the community. Once the program has been established, a summative evaluation with control groups is recommended. Second, instead of being a top-down process, the evaluation is more participatory, guided by students, staff, and the community (Cousins and Earl, 1992). Third, qualitative as well as quantitative methods are used (see Chapter 4).

Although program evaluation to date has yielded disappointing results, it would be a serious mistake to say we have learned nothing from the enterprise. We see that five general lessons have been learned from the past 25 years of program evaluation:

1. Higher-quality program evaluations are needed.
2. Local evaluations need to be made more informative.
3. Theory-based interventions need to be created and evaluated.
4. We need to think in terms of components, not politically motivated labels.
5. A developmental model needs to be created for use in predicting the effects of program components on children in different environments.

The following subsections expand on these five lessons.

Lesson 1: Higher-Quality Program Evaluations

The following factors are critical to high-quality program evaluations: program design, program implementation, creation of a control group, group equivalence, measurement, unit of analysis, power, and missing data.

Program Design   A program should have clearly articulated goals. Although scientific research can play a role in determining intermediate goals, program goals are generally determined by the school community. For instance, some communities may place a premium on students maintaining a native language, whereas others may prefer to encourage only the speaking of English. Once the program goals have been set, curriculum must be found or created, staffing requirements determined, and training procedures developed. The program should be designed using basic theory (see the discussion of lesson 3 below), but should also be practical enough to be implemented in the schools.

Program Implementation   Many programs created for English-language learners by government, schools, researchers, and courts have not been implemented. Implementation difficulties are often due to the improper training and background of teachers (see Chapter 8). An evaluation without evidence of successful implementation is an evaluation of an unknown quantity.

Demonstration of program implementation requires more than examining the educational background of teachers and the completion of forms filled out by administrators. While interviews with teachers and students can provide an approximate fix on what is actually being delivered, the best approach is to observe what teachers and students do in the classroom (see Chapter 7). Examining program implementation offers several advantages. First, it encourages thinking of the program not as unitary (e.g., bilingual education), but as a series of components; one can then determine whether each of these components has been implemented (see the discussion of lesson 4 below). Second, it allows for the measurement of processes that would otherwise not be measured, such as opportunity to learn. Third, if the implementation data are measured for the same children for whom outcome data are measured, it is possible to analyze the process by which program features are translated into outcomes.

Creation of a Control Group   Even when a program has clearly articulated goals, is based on sound theory, and is adequately implemented, a program evaluation is of little value if one does not know what experiences the children in the control group have had. Identifying control groups may be difficult. Because of legislative, judicial, and educational constraints, an untreated group may be difficult to find. Moreover, the researcher should not assume that just because children are not currently receiving an intervention, they never have. The current and past experiences of children in the control group need to be carefully documented.

One might suppose that an emphasis on standards precludes the need for a control group. While it may be important to examine whether students meet performance standards, we still need to know whether a program improves performance over what was achieved under a previous program. Moreover, given the economic background of most English-language learners (see Chapter 1) and the likely heavy English load in most testing (see Chapter 5), the use of standards could create an unduly pessimistic appraisal of these children. While high standards are the ultimate goal, they will likely have to be reached gradually.

Group Equivalence   Program evaluation involves comparison of an experimental and a control group. These two groups should be demographically and educationally equivalent. Equivalent groups are guaranteed by random assignment. Because of legislative, judicial, and administrative constraints, random assignment of students to conditions may not generally be feasible; nonetheless, we urge vigilance in attempting to find opportunities for random assignment.

Because random assignment will often not be feasible, other ways must be found to ensure that the groups are similar. As recommended by Meyer and Fienberg (1992), if the control group students can be selected from the same school, there is a greater likelihood of equivalence. If another classroom, school, or school district must be chosen, it should be as similar as possible to the treated units.

Researchers need to ascertain whether the groups are equivalent before the intervention begins. The best way to do this is to measure the children in both groups to obtain a baseline measure. Ideally, there should be little or no difference at baseline.[6] If there are differences, statistical analysis can be used to make groups more similar,[7] but it cannot be expected to make them truly equivalent.

Measurement   We will not review here all of the difficult issues of student assessment discussed in Chapter 5. However, we note that longitudinal assessment of English-language learners virtually guarantees that different tests will be taken by different groups of children, making it necessary to equate the tests. The timing of measurement is important. The baseline or pretest measure should occur before the program begins, and the post-test should occur after the program has been completed and its potential effects are evident (see the earlier discussion

---

[6]Ensuring equivalence by matching individual scores at the pretest only appears to create equivalence (Campbell and Stanley, 1963).

[7]There is considerable controversy about to how to adjust statistically for baseline differences (e.g., Lord, [1967]). This controversy reinforces the point that the presence of baseline differences seriously compromises the persuasiveness of the evaluation.

of the AIR study). A long interval from pretest to post-test will increase the amount of missing data in the sample (see below).

Unit of Analysis   Even when there is random assignment, the child is generally not the unit assigned to the intervention, but rather the classroom, the school, or sometimes the district. A related issue is that children affect each other's learning in the classroom, and indeed, several recent educational innovations (e.g., cooperative learning) attempt to capitalize on this fact. Consideration then needs to be given to whether the child or some other entity is the proper unit of analysis.

Power   This factor concerns the probability of detecting a difference between treatment and control groups if there actually is one. Program evaluations must be designed so that there is sufficient power. In many instances, there may be insufficient resources to achieve an acceptable level of power. For instance, there may be only 50 children eligible for a study, but to have a reasonable chance of getting a significant result may require more subjects. Even if there are sufficient resources, the study may be too large to manage.

Missing Data   Typically, evaluations are longitudinal, and in longitudinal research, missing data are always a serious concern. Given the high mobility of English-language learners, attrition is an especially critical issue in these types of evaluations (Lam, 1992). A plan for minimizing and estimating the effect of missing data should be attempted. To some extent, the use of growth-curve modeling (Bryk and Raudenbush, 1992) and the computation of individual change trajectories can alleviate this problem.

Summary   Clearly, program evaluations are difficult. The above discussion indicates that there are often tradeoffs: to maximize one aspect of a study, another must be reduced. Although research always involves compromises and limitations, there must still be some minimum degree of quality for the research to be informative. Therefore, sometimes the most prudent choice is not to conduct a program evaluation, but to devote research efforts to determining whether a program is successfully implemented in the classroom and identifying the process by which the program leads to desirable outcomes (see the discussion of lesson 2). At the same time, researchers and policymakers still need to be creative in recognizing opportunities for evaluation.

Lesson 2: More Informative Local Evaluations

American education has always been characterized by local control, and the current trend is for this to intensify. Evaluations are increasingly emphasizing local involvement as well (Fetterman et al., 1995).

Contemporary evaluation methods can assist local educators in planning, implementing, and assessing programs. Evaluation needs to be viewed as a tool for program improvement, not as a bureaucratic obligation. Local evaluation efforts need to focus on methods for improving program design and implementation (Ginsburg, 1992; Meyer and Fienberg, 1992). Lam (1992:193) makes the following recommendation: "It seems reasonable to urge local educators and administrators to use the majority of the evaluation budgets for formative purposes—that is, to document and guide full implementation of the program design, including the analysis of problems arising when the school's capacity to actually implement the proposed program is being developed." Title VII legislation explicitly encourages this type of evaluation (Section 7123b).

Federal and state governments might monitor local evaluations more closely. School districts that present evidence for successfully implemented models should receive grants for outcome evaluation. While we do not believe in enforcing standardization across sites in these evaluations, there should be attempts to encourage collaboration that would allow pooling of results. There are successful examples in other areas of human resource evaluation in which there is local control, but comparable measures and designs are used to allow for data aggregation.

It should also be noted that both large-scale and local evaluations have their limitations. With smaller-scale evaluations, it is easier to monitor the effort, keep track of implementation, and institute procedures to minimize missing data. However, small evaluations are plagued with insufficient sample sizes and sometimes insufficient program variation. Moreover, results in one community may not be generalizable to other communities. Just as national evaluations were oversold in the 1970s and 1980s, we do not wish now to oversell local evaluations.

We expect program effects to interact with site and community characteristics.[8] Although some site effects will be random and inexplicable, others will be systematic. If enough sites can be studied, an understanding of the necessary conditions for successful programs can be developed. One statistical technique that is ideally suited for the analysis of within-site effects is hierarchical linear modeling (Bryk and Raudenbush, 1992), which can be used to test whether there are site interactions and what factors can explain them. Basically, any technique that permits conditioning on content variables will help.

Lesson 3: Creation and Evaluation of Theory-Based Interventions

Programs should be designed so they are consistent with what is known about basic learning processes. The studies and programs described in this sec-

---

[8]A good example of effects varying by site is presented by Samaniego and Eubank (1991). They tested basic theory using the California Case Studies (see below) in four school districts, and results varied considerably across sites.

tion are based on a theory of second-language learning and its relationship to student achievement and successful educational practice. The theory is tested through implementation in a classroom setting. While none of the examples described here is perfect, each has aspects that are exemplary.

California Case Studies   In 1980, the California State Department of Education applied a theory-based model for bilingual education (Gold and Tempes, 1987). The program, which came to be known as the California Case Studies, was a collaborative effort among researchers, local educators, and the California State Department of Education. The program began with a declaration of principles (see Chapter 7), many of which are based on research results reviewed in Chapters 2 through 4. Five elementary schools serving large numbers of Spanish-speaking students were selected for participation in the program. In the program, students are provided with substantial amounts of instruction in and through the native language; comprehensible second-language input is provided through both ESL classes and sheltered classes in academic content areas; and teachers attempt to equalize the status of second-language learners by treating English-language learners equitably, using cooperative learning strategies, enrolling language majority students in second-language classes, and using minority languages for noninstructional purposes.

While this program is exemplary in its application of principles based on well-established basic research and its collaborative effort between educators and researchers, very few of its results have been published in peer-reviewed journals.[9] An exception to this is the work of Gersten and colleagues (Gersten, 1985; Gersten et al., 1984; Gersten and Woodward, 1995).

Immersion Programs   In a series of studies, Gersten and colleagues (Gersten, 1985; Gersten et al., 1984; Gersten and Woodward, 1995) have tested the effectiveness of immersion programs. The program they developed is a blend of ideas from bilingual and immersion programs, hence their use of the term "bilingual immersion."[10]   Gersten and Woodward (1995:226) define this program as follows: "This approach retains the predominant focus on English-language instruction from the immersion model but tempers it with a substantive 4-year Spanish language program so that students maintain their facility with their native language" (p. 226).

In a major 4-year study (Gersten and Woodward, 1995), 228 children in El Paso, Texas, were placed in either bilingual immersion (as defined above) or

---

[9]The program was never intended as an evaluation, and funding was cut at the end of the project, which made evaluation more difficult.

[10]Although Gersten and Woodward label this program "bilingual immersion," it should not be confused with two-way bilingual programs (also called "bilingual immersion programs," in which students are provided with subject matter instruction in their native language[s]).

transitional bilingual programs. Children were followed from fourth through seventh grades. While differences found in language and reading ability in the early years favored the bilingual immersion approach, those differences seemed to vanish in the later years. However, almost all of the bilingual immersion children had been mainstreamed by the end of the program, while nearly one-third of the transitional bilingual children had not.[11]

Two-Way Programs Two-way bilingual or two-way immersion programs integrate language-minority and language-majority students for instruction in and through two languages—the native language of the language minority students and English.

The rationale for two-way programs as an effective model for all students comes from principles underlying bilingual education for language-minority students and foreign-language immersion for English-speaking students. The blending of these two approaches is predicted to result not only in high achievement for both groups of students, but also in improved cross-cultural understanding as a benefit of positive interactions in the classroom (see Chapter 4).

Despite the fairly elaborate theoretical justification for two-way programs, there has not been uniformity in the programs that have been implemented. The California State Department of Education developed a model in the mid-1980s, which was implemented in several schools and became the basis for one of the primary variants of two-way programs (referred to as "90-10" because 90 percent of instruction is provided in the non-English language in the first years of the program). Although the approach may be defined generally as the integration of students from two different language backgrounds in a classroom where both languages are used for instruction, there is currently tremendous variability in program implementation (Christian, 1994). While flexibility is clearly needed to adapt any program to local conditions, there has been little research directed at understanding the consequences of programmatic decisions. Moreover, there are likely to be requirements that must be satisfied before a two-way program can be instituted. Several key parameters of variation include proportion of students from the two language backgrounds in the classroom, amount of instructional time provided in the two languages, practices related to screening students and admitting newcomers to a cohort after the first year, language choice for initial literacy instruction, language use in the classroom, and whether students enter the program on a voluntary basis or are assigned by school personnel.

In a review of evaluation studies of two-way programs, Mahrer and Christian

---

[11]The statistical analysis of the data from this program by Gersten and Woodward (1995) has been less than optimal. Generally, analysis of variance is not appropriate for longitudinal studies. Moreover, growth curve analysis (Bryk and Raudenbush, 1992) can often provide a much more detailed picture of process. However, correcting these statistical problems would probably not result in major changes in the study's conclusions.

(1993) found a great deal of variation in both the assessments used and the outcomes. Many programs showed evidence of positive language proficiency and academic achievement outcomes for both native and non-native English speakers, but most of these studies used designs in which there was no comparison group. When comparison groups are available, evaluations typically show that English-language learners in two-way programs outperform those in other programs.

Summary   Very often there is a fine line between theory- and advocacy-based program evaluations. Some of the examples in this section might be considered advocacy based. We see an important difference between theory- and advocacy-based programs. First, the former type of program is grounded in a theory about the learning of a second language and its relationship to student achievement, not solely in a social or political philosophy. Second, the educational curriculum is designed to implement the theory in a school setting. Third, the educational outcomes of children are used to test the theory; the program evaluation tests both the basic theory and the educational intervention.

Lesson 4: Thinking in Terms of Components, Not Political Labels

Historically, programs are described as unitary; a student is either in a program or not. The current debate on the relative efficacy of immersion and bilingual education has been cast in this light. However, as noted above, we need to move away from thinking about programs in such broad terms and instead see them as containing multiple components—features that are available to meet the differing needs of particular students. Thus two students in the same program could receive different elements of the program. Moreover, programs that are nominally very different—especially the most successful ones—may have very similar characteristics (see Chapter 7). These common characteristics include the following:

- Some native-language instruction, especially initially
- For most students, a relatively early phasing in of English instruction
- Teachers specially trained in instructing English-language learners

Lesson 5: Creation of a Developmental Model

A general formal model is needed to predict children's development of linguistic, social, and cognitive skills. The foundation of this model would be derived from basic research reviewed in Chapters 2 through 4, including theories of linguistic, cognitive, and social development. The model would predict exact nonlinear growth trajectories for the major abilities—not only the mean or typical trajectories, but also their variability. It would be flexible enough to allow for the introduction of a second language and would explicitly address possible transfer and interference for different first languages, as well as educational issues for new immigrants.

Learning takes place in specific environments, and these would be explicitly considered in the model as well. The environment would serve as a moderator that accelerates or decelerates the child's development. Among the school environment variables would be classroom composition, teachers, and school climate. Family and community variables would also serve as moderators. From a policy perspective, the most important moderators would be program inputs, for example, bilingual education and English immersion—not in an idealized sense, but in terms of instructional practices, such as percentage of first-language instruction. Moreover, the model would predict interactions between the effectiveness of program features and student and environmental characteristics.

The creation of such a model would require collaboration among basic researchers, statisticians, and educators. It would likely occur in stages. The model would be so complex that it would have to be computer simulated. It should be able not only to explain results that are currently well established, but also to make predictions about results that have not yet been obtained and those that are unexpected. The model would be much too large to be testable in its entirety, but should be specific enough to be testable in narrow contexts.

A research effort geared toward developing such a model is that of Thomas and Collier (1995).[12] Using data from the immersion studies discussed above and data collected since then from other school districts, Thomas and Collier sketch approximate growth curves for different programs. The model we envision would be much more extensive in that it would predict individual (as opposed to program) growth, as well as interactions between programs and child characteristics. Moreover, we would hope that programs in the model would be replaced by program features (see lesson 4).

RESEARCH NEEDS

The research needs identified in this section are different in nature from those presented in Chapters 2 through 5 and 7 through 9. The reason for this is that research is not needed on evaluation per se; rather, program evaluations need to be conducted differently if we are to learn from the programs and practices we implement. Our recommendations for improving the conduct of program evaluations correspond to the lessons presented above.

---

[12]Findings from this study are not discussed in this report because the study had not been completed or published prior to the report's publication.

Lesson One

6-1. To ensure high-quality program evaluations, attention is needed to the following factors: program design, program implementation, creation of a control group, group equivalence, measurement, unit of analysis, power, and missing data.

Lesson Two

6-2. Local evaluation efforts should focus initially on formative purposes— documenting and guiding full implementation of the program design. Once successful implementation has been demonstrated, outcome evaluations can be conducted. Finally, if enough sites can be studied, an understanding of necessary conditions for successful programs can be developed.

6-3. Local evaluations need to focus first on determining whether programs are properly implemented and on fine tuning those programs so they become more responsive to the needs of children, the school, and the community. Only once a program has been documented as established should a summative evaluation with control groups be undertaken. Both quantitative and qualitative methods are needed to accomplish a total program evaluation.

6-4. Mandated Title VII evaluations should be monitored more closely. School districts that present evidence for successfully implemented models could receive grants for outcome evaluation. Alternatively, the Department of Education could provide competitive grants or contracts for technically skilled outsiders to conduct local evaluations of their efforts across various sites. Results might be pooled for sites where the characteristics of the programs are similar, these programs have been successfully implemented, and outcomes are similar to provide more generalizable evidence of effectiveness.

6-5. Broadly conceived assessment should be built into the educational process to assist in the monitoring of the progress of students, teachers, programs, classrooms, and schools.

Lesson Three

6-6. Educational practice in general and program evaluation in particular require the specification of explicit goals, a set of instructional practices and curriculum, and methods for implementing those practices in the schools and classrooms.

6-7. Basic researchers need to develop curriculum and instructional techniques following from theoretically grounded research and theory. Collaborating with school systems, the researchers would then implement and test these models in the schools.

Lesson Four

6-8. We recommend evaluations that are locally conceived, based, and conducted. Evaluations of the relative efficacy of broad programs that are loosely implemented in a wide range of settings are likely to yield little information about what interventions are effective.

Lesson Five

6-9. An interdisciplinary formal model of development should be formulated to predict the growth of individual children's skills and the moderation of that growth as a function of program features.

REFERENCES

Abelson, R.P.
  1995   *Statistics as Principled Argument.* Hillsdale, NJ: Erlbaum.
Baker, K.A., and A.A. de Kanter
  1981   *Effectiveness of Bilingual Education: A Review of the Literature.* Washington, DC: U.S. Department of Education.
Baker, K.A., and S. Pelavin
  1984   Problems in Bilingual Education. Paper presented at annual meeting of American Educational Research Association, New Orleans, LA. American Institutes for Research, Washington, DC.
Board of Education of the City of New York
  1994   Educational Progress of Students in Bilingual and ESL Programs: A Longitudinal Study, 1990-1994. New York.
Bryk, A.S., and S.W. Raudenbush
  1992   *Hierarchical Linear Models: Applications and Data Analysis Methods.* Newbury Park, CA: Sage.
Burkheimer, Jr., G.J., A.J. Conger, G.H. Dunteman, B.G. Elliott, and K.A. Mowbray
  1989   *Effectiveness of Services for Language-minority Limited-English-proficient Students.* 2 vols. Technical Report. Research Triangle Park, NC: Research Triangle Institute.
Bushman, B.J., and M.C. Wang
  1996   A procedure for combining sample standardized mean differences and vote counts to estimate the population standardized mean difference in fixed effects models. *Psychological Methods* 1:66-80.
Campbell, D.T., and J.C. Stanley
  1963   Experimental and quasi-experimental designs for research in teaching. In N.L. Gage, ed., *Handbook of Research on Teaching.* Chicago: Rand-McNally.
Christian, D.
  1994   *Two-Way Bilingual Education: Students Learning Through Two Languages.* Education Practice Report No. 12. Santa Cruz, CA, and Washington, DC: National Center for Research on Cultural Diversity and Second Language Learning.
Cousins, J.B., and L.M. Earl
  1992   The case for participatory evaluation. *Educational Evaluation and Policy Analysis* 14:397-418.

Crawford, J.
1995 *Bilingual Education: History Politics Theory and Practice.* Los Angeles: Bilingual Educational Services.

Dannoff, M.N.
1978 *Evaluation of the Impact of ESEA Title VII Spanish-English Bilingual Education Programs.* Technical Report. Washington, DC: American Institutes for Research.

Development Associates
1984 *Overview of the Research Design Plans for the National Longitudinal Study of the Effectiveness of Services for Language Minority Students.* Arlington, VA: Development Associates.

Engle, P.
1975 The use of the vernacular language in education. *Bilingual Education* Series No. 2. Washington, DC: Center for Applied Linguistics.

Fetterman, D.M., S.J. Kaftarian, and A. Wandersman, eds.
1995 *Empowerment Evaluation: Knowledge and Tools for Self-Assessment and Accountability.* Thousand Oaks, CA: Sage.

Gersten, Russell
1985 Structured immersion for language minority students: Results of a longitudinal evaluation. *Education Evaluation and Policy Analysis* 7(3):187-196.

Gersten, Russell, and John Woodward
1995 A longitudinal study of transitional and immersion bilingual education programs in one district. *Elementary School Journal* 95(3):223-239.

Gersten, Russell, R. Taylor, J. Woodward, and W.A.T. White
1984 *Structured English Immersion for Hispanic Students in the U.S.: Findings from the Fourteen-year Evaluation of the Uvalde, Texas, Program.* Technical Report 84-1, Follow Through Project. Eugene: University of Oregon.

Ginsburg, A.L.
1992 Improving bilingual education programs through evaluation. Pp. 31-42 in *Proceedings of the Second National Research Symposium on Limited English Proficient Student Issues: Focus on Evaluation and Measurement.* Vol. 1. OBEMLA. Washington, DC: U.S. Department of Education.

Gold, T., and F. Tempes
1987 A State Agency Partnership with Schools to Improve Bilingual Education. Paper presented at the annual meeting of the American Educational Research Association, Washington, DC. California State Department of Education.

Krashen, S., and D. Biber
1988 *On Course: Bilingual Education's Success in California.* Sacramento: California Association for Bilingual Education.

Lam, Tony C.M.
1992 Review of practices and problems in the evaluation of bilingual education. *Review of Educational Research* 62(2):181-203.

Lord, F.M.
1967 A paradox in the interpretation of group comparisons. *Psychological Bulletin* 68:304-305.

Mahrer, C., and D. Christian
1993 *A Review of Findings from Two-Way Bilingual Education Evaluation Reports.* Santa Cruz, CA. and Washington, DC: National Center for Research on Cultural Diversity and Second Language Learning.

Meyer, M.M., and S.E. Fienberg, eds.
  1992   *Assessing Evaluation Studies: The Case of Bilingual Education Strategies.* Panel to Review Evaluation Studies of Bilingual Education, Committee on National Statistics, National Research Council. Washington, DC: National Academy Press.

Mujica, B.
  1995   Findings of the New York City longitudinal study: Hard evidence on bilingual and ESL programs. *READ Perspectives* 2:7-34.

Ramirez, D.J., S.D. Yuen, D.R. Ramey, and D.J. Pasta
  1991   *Final Report: National Longitudinal Study of Structured-English Immersion Strategy, Early-Exit and Late-Exit Transitional Bilingual Education Programs for Language-Minority Children, Vol. 1 and 11, Technical Report.* San Mateo, CA: Aguirre International.

Rossell, Christine H., and Keith Baker
  1996   The educational effectiveness of bilingual education. *Research in the Teaching of English* 30(1):7-74.

Rossell, Christine H., and J. Michael Ross
  1986   The social science evidence on bilingual education. *Journal of Law and Education* 15(4):385-419.

Samaniego, F., and L. Eubank
  1991   *A Statistical Analysis of California's Case Study Project in Bilingual Education* TR #208. Intercollegiate Division of Statistics. Davis: University of California.

Secada, Walter G.
  1987   This is 1987, not 1980: A comment on a comment. *Review of Educational Research* 57(3):377-384.

Thomas, W., and V. Collier
  1995   *Language Minority Student Achievement and Program Effectiveness.* Washington, DC: National Clearinghouse for Bilingual Education.

U.S. Department of Education
  1991   *The Condition of Bilingual Education in the Nation: A Report to the Congress and the President.* Office of the Secretary. Washington, DC: U.S. Department of Education, Washington, DC.

U.S. Government Accounting Office
  1987   Bilingual Education: A New Look at the Research Evidence. Briefing report to the Chairman, Committee on Education, Labor, House of Representatives, GAO/PEMD-87-12BR. Washington, DC.

Willig, A.C.
  1985   A meta-analysis of selected studies on the effectiveness of bilingual education. *Review of Educational Research* 55(3):269-317.

Zappert, L.T., and B.R. Cruz
  1977   *Bilingual Education: An Appraisal of Empirical Research.* Berkeley, CA: BAHIA Press.

**STUDIES OF SCHOOL AND CLASSROOM EFFECTIVENESS:
SUMMARY OF THE STATE OF KNOWLEDGE**

The literature on school and classroom effectiveness provides the following key findings:

• The studies reviewed here provide some evidence to support the "effective schools" attributes identified nearly 20 years ago, with at least two important qualifications:

—The studies challenge the conceptualization of some of those attributes, for example, the idea that implementing characteristics of effective schools and classrooms makes schools and classrooms more effective.

—The studies suggest that factors not identified in the effective schools literature may be important as well if we are to create schools where English-language learners, indeed all students, will be successful and productive. Examples of such factors are a focus on more than just basics, ongoing staff development, and home-school connections.

• The following attributes are identified as being associated with effective schools and classrooms: a supportive school-wide climate, school leadership, a customized learning environment, articulation and coordination within and between schools, some use of native language and culture in the instruction of language-minority students, a balanced curriculum that incorporates both basic and higher-order skills, explicit skills instruction, opportunities for student-directed activities, use of instructional strategies that enhance understanding, opportunities for practice, systematic student assessment, staff development, and home and parent involvement.

• Although suggestive of key attributes that are important for creating effective schools and classrooms, most studies reviewed here cannot give firm answers about any particular attribute and its relationship to student outcomes. For example, the nominated schools designs do not report data on student outcomes and are thus inconclusive. Prospective case studies lack comparison groups, so that changes in student outcomes may be due to extraneous factors. And while quasi-experimental studies that focus on an entire program provide the strongest basis for claims about program or school effects, they make direct claims only about the program or school effect overall. Claims about the effects of specific components must, in general, rest on other studies that examine those components explicitly.

7

Studies of School and Classroom Effectiveness

Whereas Chapter 6 focuses on program evaluations, in which instructional language issues are paramount, this chapter focuses on empirical studies that attempt to identify school- and classroom-level factors related to effective schooling for English-language learners from early education programs through high school. Although instructional language issues are important in the research described in this chapter, they do not dominate. The research reviewed here is categorized according to four distinct methodologies: effective schools research, nominated schools research, prospective case studies, and quasi-experiments. Thus the chapter begins with a description of these methodologies. The chapter then summarizes the studies of each type reviewed and presents some observations on the features on these studies. Next is a detailed discussion of 13 attributes identified by the studies as being associated with effective schools and classrooms. The final section examines the methodological strengths and limitations of the four types of studies. Although different approaches to a review of this sort are possible, the present review is organized according to methodology because the committee believes the study findings should be viewed in light of the methodologies used to generate them. For example, some findings are richer in detail but less generalizable than others. Moreover, it is important to highlight the various methodologies because strengthening and integrating them is necessary if school and classroom research is to be improved.

STATE OF KNOWLEDGE

Beginning in the 1970s, and largely in response to findings by Coleman et al. (1966), Jencks et al. (1972), and others suggesting that differences in student outcomes were due largely to factors outside the control of schools, a group of studies appeared that challenged this conclusion by identifying effective schools and the characteristics that made them effective (e.g., Edmonds, 1979; Rutter et al., 1979; Weber, 1971; see especially Purkey and Smith, 1983). This research yielded what became (with some variations) a familiar list of "effective schools" characteristics, which included the following:

- Strong leadership, particularly instructional, by the principal
- High expectations for student achievement
- Clear school-wide focus on basic skills
- A safe, orderly school environment
- Frequent assessment of student academic progress

Despite early and ongoing criticism (e.g., Scott and Walberg, 1979; Stedman, 1985, 1987), effective schools research has evolved over the past two decades (Bliss et al., 1991), flourishing and even turning into a national movement. In terms of sheer numbers, it is now perhaps the most successful of the dozens of ideas informing school reform efforts nation-wide. According to *Education Week* (1995), more than 2,000 school districts—15 percent of the nation's 14,500—report using effective school research.[1]

In the 1990s, there has been a significant change in the way "effective" schools are identified, particularly in efforts to uncover effective schooling dimensions for English-language learners. Instead of designating schools as effective on the basis of measures of student learning or achievement, investigators now typically use a "nominated" schools design.[2] As in the previous effective schools research, current investigators attempt to identify schools or programs that are "exemplary." However, rather than being identified on the basis of outcome measures, schools are identified in accordance with the professional judgments of knowledgeable educators. Independent measures of student achievement are not in the data set reported by most of these investigators. In schools or classrooms with large numbers of English-language learners, this is often the case because investigators could not find adequate student achievement data to verify the validity of the nominations (Berman et al., 1992, 1995).[3] However, in some instances, investigators have asked nominated schools to pro-

---

[1]This figure might actually indicate diminished influence of the effective schools movement in the 1990s. A 1989 General Accounting Office survey estimated that 41 percent of U.S. school districts had programs based on effective schools research in 1988 (Bliss et al., 1991).

[2]However, there is still effective schools research that relies on student outcomes; moreover, not all research prior to the 1990s used student outcomes to determine school or classroom effectiveness.

[3]For example, Berman et al. (1992:6) found that "language proficiency results were of questionable validity, subject to sources of unreliability and not comparable; schools did not consistently assess LEP students on California assessment tests or had little accumulated data as a result of high transiency or poor attendance."

vide information that corroborates their effectiveness[4] or have attempted to verify the quality of nominees by examining "proxies" for student achievement in nominated classrooms, such as academic learning time (Tikunoff, 1983).

Prospective case studies and quasi-experiments represent a different approach to studying effective schooling. Instead of finding schools that are already "effective" or have been nominated as such, prospective studies attempt to document changes in school-wide programs or classrooms and the effects of these changes on student achievement. In the ideal situation, the changes are based on strong theory. In the discussion of program evaluation in Chapter 6, we note many problems with large-scale efforts that have provided very little "bang for the buck." Among the prescriptions suggested are small-scale evaluations of the implementation of theory-based programs. The prospective case study approach to studying school and classroom effectiveness comes close to this ideal.

An example of the prospective case study approach is the Case Studies in Bilingual Education project (Gold and Tempes, 1987), a collaborative effort during the mid-1980s between the California State Department of Education and five elementary schools serving large numbers of Spanish-speaking students. Applying theoretical models for the education of English-language learners and for the implementation of school-wide change, schools developed and carried out changes in curriculum, instruction, and organization to promote higher levels of academic achievement for Spanish-speaking English-language learners. Although the effects of the instructional program have been somewhat more mixed than is often reported (Samaniego and Eubank, 1991), the project appears to have been extremely successful overall and led to the development of a Title VII Academic Excellence Program, based on one of the California Case Study schools (Eastman), entitled Project MORE.

A quasi-experimental design (Cook and Campbell, 1979) is generally defined as a research design that approximates the control of randomized design. We define the term somewhat differently: a quasi-experimental design employs comparison schools or classrooms and measured outcomes. Thus our use of the term is meant to convey designs that afford stronger conclusions than those typically used in effective or nominated schools research or prospective case studies. Quasi-experimental studies also begin with a school(s) or classroom(s) that is not more effective and perhaps even less effective than one or more comparable schools or classrooms. Investigators and educators implement a

---

[4]For example, to be considered for inclusion in the Descriptive Study of Significant Features of Exemplary Special Alternative Instructional Programs (Tikunoff, 1983), applicants had to describe their programs and provide evidence of exceptional student performance in some combination of the following areas across at least 2 successive years: relative gains in English-language proficiency, in academic performance, and in special language programs before students were exited, and extent to which grade promotion requirements were met while participating in or after exiting the program.

change or intervention predicted to improve student outcomes. Student outcomes (pre and post) are measured at the target and comparison schools or classrooms to determine the effects of the change or intervention. Because of the existence of a comparison site, the quasi-experimental approach offers the strongest basis for claiming that what was done at a target site produced changes in student achievement.

Studies Reviewed

For this review of the literature on studies of school and classroom effectiveness, studies that met the following criteria were included: (1) the school population(s) or classroom(s) studied included substantial numbers of English-language learners, and (2) investigators made some attempt (or at least claim) to identify school- or classroom-level factors, including instruction, associated with positive outcomes (or good programs) for these students.[5] Studies that examined the relationship between student knowledge/skills and task demands on literacy and learning are reviewed in Chapter 3. In general, these studies did not examine school and classroom factors that promote learning; rather, they focused on student and task attributes and their relationship to learning.

Other school-based efforts besides those examined here have aimed at improving outcomes for English-language learners, but there is insufficient information about them to permit an analytic review. For example, the Academic Excellence Program (funded by Title VII) identifies effective programs serving English-language learners. To be designated an Academic Excellence Program, a program must provide evidence that it has improved outcomes for these students and propose a plan for disseminating the program to other schools around the country. The Academic Excellence Programs represent a diverse array of curricular and instructional approaches that include, for example, content-based English as a second language (ESL), computer-assisted writing, two-way bilingual education, gifted and talented education, transitional bilingual education, programs for recent immigrants, and interactive computer technologies. Dis-

---

[5]A broad search was done to locate relevant articles and books for this review: The search focused initially on Education Resources Information Center (ERIC) documents dating back to 1985, using limiters relevant to the topics of interest. Very few studies were located, and as a result, indexes from the following journals were searched back to 1985 for relevant studies: *Educational Researcher, TESOL Quarterly, Journal of Educational Issues of Language Minority Students, Journal of the National Association for Bilingual Education, Urban Education, Language and Education, Equity and Choice, American Educational Research Journal, Review of Educational Research, Educational Leadership, Harvard Educational Review, Applied Linguistics, Bilingual Research Journal, Read Perspectives,* and *Journal of Reading Behavior.* All reference lists from useful retrieved documents were checked for additional sources, and an effort was made to obtain relevant studies. Finally, experts on the education of English-language learners were consulted regarding books and reports that might be of interest.

semination efforts generally involve school-wide adoption (e.g., awareness, training, technical assistance, follow-up; see Wilson et al., 1994) or "restructuring" (Wilson et al., 1994). Thus, the programs as originally developed and their dissemination to new sites probably involve school- and classroom-level factors that would be relevant to this review. At the moment, however, such information is not readily available and therefore could not be incorporated here.

In addition, there are many national school reform networks. We reviewed the work of 13 of these projects[6] and found that very few have provided empirical evidence on issues of successful schooling for English-language learners (see Chapter 10). In part this is because many of these projects remain unevaluated or do not specifically examine outcomes for these students. For example, Chasin and Levin (1995) provide a case study of an "accelerated school" (elementary level) where 13 different languages are spoken, but they do not report the English-learning status of English-language learners, address concerns that are specific to these students' educational experiences, or report changes in outcomes for these students.

As a result of our literature search, we identified reports of 33 studies for inclusion in this review; these studies and reports are identified in Annex Table 7-1. Most of the studies fall into one of four design categories (Annex Table 7-1, column 4): effective schools/classrooms design (6 studies); nominated schools/classrooms design (7 studies); prospective case study design (5 studies); and quasi-experimental or experimental design (13 studies). There are also 2 studies that do not fall into a design category.

Effective Schools Research

The basic design and logic of effective schools research still inform efforts to discover principles or processes that can be used to improve schooling opportunities and outcomes for "at-risk" students. However, the design has become more of a hybrid, relying on both student outcomes and nomination. More recent studies examine attributes of effective classrooms rather than schools. Some of these studies are reviewed in this section. Although most of these studies do not focus on English-language learners, our review found some studies involving such students: one pure effective schools study (Carter and Chatfield, 1986), three studies that rely on both nomination and student outcomes (Edelsky et al., 1983; Garcia, 1990a; Moll, 1988), and two studies (Mace-Matluck et al., 1989;

---

[6]These networks include the Accelerated Schools Project, Center for Educational Renewal, Coalition of Essential Schools, Core Knowledge Foundation, Effective Schools Networks, National Board for Professional Teaching Standards, National Paideia Center, New American Schools Development Corporation, New Standards Project, School Development Program ("Comer Schools"), and Success for All.

Wong Fillmore et al., 1985) that examine the relationship between current schooling practices and the language and/or reading achievement of students who began their instruction in bilingual education classrooms. We include the latter studies in this category because their goal is to identify attributes of effective classroom instruction by examining correlations among student background information, instructional practices, and student outcomes.

Nominated Schools Research

Nominated schools studies included in this review are Lucas et al. (1990), Berman et al. (1992, 1995), and Tikunoff et al. (1991). Nominated classrooms studies include Tikunoff (1983), Pease-Alvarez et al. (1991), and Gersten (1996). A study that explores the replicability and stability of features identified in the initial study of nominated classrooms (Tikunoff, 1983) is also reviewed.

Prospective Case Studies

We reviewed five prospective case studies that document student change as a result of a theory-driven intervention. One is the Case Studies in Bilingual Education project (Gold and Tempes, 1987) mentioned earlier. A second explores the extent to which reciprocal teaching of question generation, summarizing, and predicting using students' primary language improves reading comprehension in that language; it also explores how these strategies are used in second-language reading (Hernandez, 1991). A third study examines the effects of a collaborative inquiry approach to science on learning by language-minority students (Rosebery et al., 1992). A fourth study examines strategies used by classroom teachers to facilitate students' comprehension of subject matter and improve their academic language skills (Short, 1994). A fifth (Cohen, 1984) examines the effect of status on peer interaction in activity centers structured to promote science and math learning; it also investigates the relationship between peer interaction and learning.

Quasi-Experimental Research

Our review includes thirteen examples of quasi-experimental or experimental research on school- and classroom-level factors associated with schooling outcomes for English-language learners. Five of these studies are adaptations of Success for All for English-language learners. Success for All is an intervention program from the Johns Hopkins Center for Research on the Education of Students Placed at Risk that focuses on helping students attain high levels of reading proficiency in elementary school. The Success for All studies are reported in Dianda and Flaherty (1995), Slavin and Madden (1994, 1995), Slavin and

Yampolsky (1992), and Calderon et al. (1996).[7] Although four of the Success for All studies could have been reviewed here as one (as synthesized and reported in Slavin and Madden, 1995), they are in fact different studies replicated in different school contexts and settings. Two other quasi-experimental studies included here (Goldenberg and Gallimore, 1991; Goldenberg and Sullivan, 1994) are also fairly detailed case studies. Each describes the issues and dynamics of change at a single elementary school with a large Latino population, and each makes pre-post comparisons of student achievement with that in comparable schools in the district.

Finally, five quasi-experimental studies and an experimental study examine the effects of classroom interventions on English-language learners through use of comparison and control groups. The first quasi-experimental study explores the effect of metacognitive reading strategy training on the reading performance and student reading analysis strategies of third grade bilingual students (Muniz-Swicegood, 1994). The second examines the effect of thematically integrated mathematics instruction on achievement, attitudes, and motivation in mathematics among school students of Mexican descent, many of whom have limited English proficiency (Henderson and Landesman, 1992). The third explores the effect of curriculum content and explicit teaching of learning strategies on students' metacognitive awareness and their learning of content and knowledge (Chamot et al., 1992). The fourth investigates effective strategies for teaching literature to transition students (Saunders et al., 1996). The fifth investigates the effectiveness of a Spanish version of reading recovery entitled Descubriendo La Lectura (Escamilla, 1994). The experimental study investigates the effects of a "culturally appropriate" reading program on the reading performance of Hawaiian children (Tharp, 1982).

Other Studies

Two studies do not fall in any of the above categories. One (Minicucci and Olsen, 1992) is an exploratory study that examines 27 secondary schools; its purpose is descriptive. The other study (Fisher et al., 1983) explores the replicability and stability of features identified in the initial study of nominated classrooms (Tikunoff, 1983). It assesses replicability by studying a second sample of classrooms (89 at 8 sites) serving different ethnolinguistic groups, as well as by examining classrooms that have not been nominated as successful. It examines the stability of the instructional process by studying teachers and students for a second academic year in different settings.

---

[7]The Calderon et al. (1996) study encompasses only one aspect of Success for All—Bilingual Cooperative Integrated Reading and Composition (BCIRC).

Observations on Studies of Effectiveness

Annex Table 7-1 identifies the important features of the 33 studies, including the school- and classroom-level attributes investigators claim are related to effective, or exemplary, schooling for English-language learners (as discussed in the next section). Several general observations can be made about this collection.

First, this is a heterogeneous group of studies representing levels of schooling from prekindergarten to high school, employing at least four different types of designs (as discussed above), and ranging from single-classroom and -school studies to a study of nine different "exemplary programs" in a total of 39 schools. By far the greatest number of schools has been studied within the nominated schools research design.

Second, school- and classroom-level factors associated with varying outcomes for English-language learners have received less attention than have other areas of research on these students. Clearly, the issue of language of instruction (whether English-language learners should be taught in their native language, and if so, to what extent) has dominated the research agenda (see Chapter 6). There have also been qualitative and ethnographic studies that have examined social context, language distribution, classroom interaction, and sociocultural enactments of classroom pedagogy (see Chapters 2, 3, and 4). Although these studies provide rich descriptions of educational environments, many do not relate practice to learning outcomes.

Third, although many non-English languages found in U.S. schools appear to be represented in these studies, by far the most commonly found is Spanish. This of course reflects the reality that approximately three-fourths of English-language learners are Spanish speaking. Most of the studies were conducted in schools that were predominately Latino. However, some sites within larger studies had substantial numbers of non-Spanish-speaking English-language learners. Only a few studies—Slavin and Yampolsky (1992) (Asian), Wong Fillmore et al. (1985) (Chinese), Rosebery et al. (1992) (Haitian-Creole), and Tharp (1982) (Hawaiian)—targeted non-Spanish-speaking English-language learners.

Fourth, as previously mentioned, by far the greatest number of schools and classrooms studied have been within the nominated schools design. These studies, as well as a few in the other categories, do not report student achievement data.[8] The absence of outcome data does not mean that a study is uninformative.

---

[8]In their report on the California Case Studies, Gold and Tempes (1987:7) explicitly state that their project "was *not* designed as an experiment" and that they "carefully avoided efforts to set up premature or unreasonable comparisons." However, achievement data on the California Case Studies have been reported in various papers and publications (e.g., Krashen and Biber, 1988). Samaniego and Eubank (1991) conducted a more objective and rigorous secondary analysis of achievement data at four of the five sites. Three other studies included in this review (Lucas et al., 1990; Tikunoff,

Indeed, these studies are filled with interesting and useful data about programs, staff, students, community, and, more generally, the very complex and challenging circumstances in which students and teachers must function. They also provide what in many cases are highly compelling accounts of dedicated educators working to create engaging, meaningful, and responsive settings for student learning. However, they do not link these settings to indicators of student outcomes, at least not in any explicit way.

Finally, as noted above, these studies report a wide range of school- and classroom-level attributes related to effectiveness (see columns 7 and 8 of Annex Table 7-1). These attributes, summarized in the following section, can be conceptualized and categorized in many different ways. It is important to keep in mind, however, that the attributes discussed here represent concepts refracted through at least two sets of lenses (the original investigators' and this committee's), that the empirical bases for making strong causal claims vary considerably and are sometimes unknown, and that there are caveats associated with some of the attributes. For example, different attributes may be more or less important for different age groups or different ethnic groups. Therefore, none of these individual attributes should be considered necessary or sufficient conditions for the schooling of English-language learners.

Attributes of Effective Schools and Classrooms

Based on the findings of the 33 studies reviewed, effective schools and classrooms have the following attributes[9] : a supportive school-wide climate, school leadership, a customized learning environment, articulation and coordination within and between schools, some use of native language and culture in the instruction of language-minority students, a balanced curriculum that incorporates both basic and higher-order skills, explicit skills instruction, opportunities for student-directed activities, use of instructional strategies that enhance understanding, opportunities for practice, systematic student assessment, staff development, and home and parent involvement. Each of these attributes is discussed in the following subsections.

1983; Tikunoff et al., 1991) report that some indicators of student outcomes informed the selection of the "effective" or "exemplary" sites, but neither these data nor the criteria used by investigators are reported. Of the remaining studies, one was exclusively exploratory (Minicucci and Olsen, 1992) and makes no claim of trying to explain how effective programs came to be; the studies by Berman et al. (1992, 1995), Pease-Alvarez et al. (1991), and Gersten (1996) neither report outcome data nor apparently used student outcomes to inform the selection of nominated sites. With the exception of Short (1994), which is more of an exploratory study, the prospective and quasi-experimental studies report student outcome data.

[9]Note that not all studies include all attributes, but the general attributes appear in many of the studies.

Supportive School-wide Climate

Teachers', students', and parents' beliefs, assumptions, and expectations for themselves and for each other probably exert a powerful influence on student learning opportunities and student outcomes (Rutter et al., 1979). It is not surprising, then, that a supportive school-wide climate, sometimes called school "ethos," is an attribute of effective schools for English-language learners. Such a climate is explicitly cited or can easily be inferred from almost all the studies reviewed.

Carter and Chatfield (1986), Moll (1988), Lucas et al. (1990), Tikunoff (1983), Tikunoff et al. (1991), Berman et al. (1992, 1995), and Minicucci and Olsen (1992) report that a positive school-wide climate was a feature of the effective or exemplary schools they studied. The schools varied in their particular manifestations of such a climate, but overall emphasized three things—value placed on the linguistic and cultural background of English-language learners, high expectations for their academic achievement, and their integral involvement in the overall school operation. The schools studied by Lucas et al. (1990:8) "celebrated diversity." For example, although they made English literacy a primary goal, they also encouraged students to enhance their native-language skills in classes for those students who spoke Spanish. Moreover, a number of teachers and counselors had made an effort to learn to speak Spanish. Moll (1988:467) notes that "in contrast to the assumption that working-class children cannot handle an academically rigorous curriculum, or in the case of limited English proficient students, that their lack of English fluency justifies an emphasis on low-level skills, the guiding assumption in the [effective] classrooms analyzed seemed to be the opposite: that the students were as smart as allowed by the curriculum." One school studied by Berman et al. (1995) had a house structure whereby each house was named for a California State University campus with which it forged a partnership—but the continuously reinforced message was that high levels of learning and achievement were expected of all students. Integral involvement of English-language learners also characterizes effective schools and classrooms. Berman et al. (1995) found that school restructuring enabled the exemplary schools to design and adapt programs that best suited the needs of English-language learners—and all students.

How does a school climate, or ethos, change from being "not conducive" to being "conducive" to high levels of achievement for English-language learners? Unfortunately, the studies do not offer much guidance here. Gold and Tempes (1987) report that teachers at their case study sites received training in Teacher Expectations and Student Achievement, a program designed to boost teachers' expectations for their students, which in turn is assumed to boost student achievement. Gold and Tempes also report that steps were taken to improve the perceived status of language-minority students—administrator and teacher support for use of Spanish at school, cross-cultural activities, and cooperative learning.

Yet we do not know whether and how these attempts to influence school climate directly affected the climate, in turn affecting achievement. Only Goldenberg and Sullivan (1994) address this question directly and prospectively. They claim that changes in school climate were the result of a complex process aimed at improving student achievement, begun by identifying school-wide goals and expectations for students, followed by consistent, visible, multiple, and long-term efforts to work toward those goals. Teachers responded positively to the more meaningful and substantive focus at the school.

Although the logic of attempting to change school climate through staff development and training to improve student achievement is supported by research on teacher expectations, an alternative hypothesis may merit attention: that school climate is at least as much a reflection of student achievement as an influence on it (Jussim, 1986). In other words, it may be that teachers hold high expectations when they have students who achieve, and conversely that they hold low expectations when students do not achieve. If this formulation is valid, it suggests that one important way to raise teacher expectations is to raise student achievement by creating structures at a school and helping teachers acquire skills and knowledge needed to be more successful with students, rather than by exhorting teachers to raise their expectations. Goldenberg and Gallimore (1991), for example, report that first grade reading expectations at the school they studied seemed to increase as a result of changes in first grade reading achievement, not as a result of training to raise expectations. Comer (1980) also describes how improved expectations followed the establishment of successful practices, which in turn raised expectations.

School Leadership

Consistent with findings of the effective schools research that began two decades ago, school-level leadership appears to be a critical dimension of effective schooling for English-language learners. At least half of the studies reviewed name leadership, often the principal's, as an important factor; the role of leadership can also be inferred from several of the other studies that do not explicitly cite it. A clear statement of the role of leadership comes from Tikunoff et al. (1991:10): "Without exception, exemplary SAIPs [Special Alternative Instructional Programs] came about because someone assumed leadership for planning, coordinating, and administering the programs." Both Carter and Chatfield (1986) and Lucas et al. (1990) name the principal's leadership as one of the elements that helps explain the effective or successful schools they studied. The principal is seen as playing a key role in many ways, for example, making the achievement of English-language learners a priority, providing ongoing direction and monitoring of curricular and instructional improvement, recruiting and keeping talented and dedicated staff, involving the entire staff in improvement efforts, and providing a good physical and social environment. Goldenberg and

Sullivan's (1994) model identifies "leadership" as one of the four change elements; in this model, there are two crucial dimensions of leadership that help propel and maintain change—providing support and exerting pressure.

An important exception can be found in the Success for All studies, which do not name leadership as an important attribute. In fact, in another report (Slavin et al., 1995), Slavin and associates seem to suggest that, except for the operational role apparently played by the program facilitator, school-level leadership may not be particularly critical for success. Despite the fact that several schools discontinued use of the Success for All model following a change in principal, Slavin et al. say that many other schools "have survived changes of superintendents, principals, facilitator, and other key staff..." (p. 30). The implication is that personal leadership is far less critical for school reform and improvement than is having an effective program in place.

This position contrasts with that of Carter and Chatfield (1986). In discussing the implications of their effective schools study, they comment that school districts should reexamine policies requiring principals to move every few years. They give the example of an effective principal who was transferred because of such a policy. "If it is true (and we think it is) that three years is the minimum amount of time required to approach [school] effectiveness, then such policy should be questioned" (p. 230). The Success for All data would suggest that if an effective program is in place, principal changes (presumably within some limits) should not matter.

More generally, Success for All is an important exception to much of the literature on school change since its developers make strong claims about the exportability of the program, which has very specific materials, manuals, and structures, to a wide range of schools, students, staffs, and communities. Indeed, the program seems to stand independently of the personnel called upon to implement it. This stance is atypical of the school change literature as a whole, and some suggest that the Success for All program does not require a strong principal because leadership comes from a charismatic and dynamic individual outside the school (Robert Slavin, the developer of Success for All), teachers provide this leadership, and the program is very structured and limited to language arts and reading instruction. (We return to this issue later in the chapter.)

Customized Learning Environment

Staff in effective schools and classrooms design the learning environment to reflect school and community contextual factors and goals while meeting the diverse needs of their students. Many researchers have noted that there is no one right way to educate language-minority students; different approaches are necessary because of the great diversity of conditions faced by schools. They recommend that local staff and community members identify the conditions under which one or some combination of approaches is best suited and then adapt models to match their particular circumstances. Berman et al. (1992) state that they cannot identify which of the major approaches to educating English-language learners is most effective under all conditions and claim that different approaches are necessary because of the great diversity of conditions. Their 1995 study reports that "rather than using a single model for all LEP students, teachers adjusted curriculum, instruction, and use of primary language to meet the varying needs of students" (p. 13). Tikunoff et al. (1991) found that the form of an exemplary Structured Alternative Instructional Program and the nature of its success build upon and are influenced by its context. Moll (1988) observes that effective teachers hold similar views about teaching, but create their own instructional programs that are attuned to the needs of their students. Samaniego and Eubank (1991) found the same to be the case in verifying the California Case Studies. In their study of effective secondary schools, Lucas et al. (1990) found that language-minority students are more likely to achieve when a school's curriculum responds to their individual and differing needs by offering variety in three areas: the skills, abilities, and knowledge classes are designed to develop (i.e., native-language development, ESL, subject matter knowledge); the degrees of difficulty and sophistication among available classes (i.e., advanced as well as low-level classes); and the approaches to teaching content (i.e., native-language instruction, content ESL, and specially designed instruction in English). Berman et al. (1995) found that successful schools also plan for the needs of newcomers (newly arrived students who immigrated to this country after the early elementary grades) and include in the design of their programs strategies to meet their needs.

Articulation and Coordination Within and Between Schools

Effective schools are characterized by a smooth transition between levels of language development classes (e.g., between content-based ESL and sheltered instruction) and coordination and articulation between special second-language programs and other school programs, as well as between levels of schooling. Short (1994) found collaboration between language and content teachers that involved identifying the language and academic difficulties and demands of particular subjects for English-language learners, ensuring close articulation between program components, and integrating ESL and content area instruction. Slavin and Yampolsky (1992) describe the central concept underlying the Success for All program as all of the school's personnel working together to ensure the success of every child; this includes ESL teachers, who teach reading and closely integrate instruction in English with the requirements for success in the regular program, especially reading. Minicucci and Olsen (1992) document coordination and articulation between the ESL/bilingual education department and other departments and between different grade levels. Berman et al. (1995) found that effective transition from special language instruction to mainstream classes was gradual, carefully planned, and supported with activities designed to ensure students' success at mastering complex content in English. Saunders et al. (1996) found that their strongest evaluation results came from project schools where students were exposed to the programs' instructional components beginning in second grade and then participated in two years of transition activities to prepare them for English-only classrooms; this included explicit connections between learning English and students' prior learning and experiences in Spanish. Calderon et al. (1996) combined Cooperative Integrated Reading and Composition (CIRC) strategies (e.g., heterogeneous learning teams that work together to help each other learn academic material) with innovative transitional and ESL strategies as students began to transition from Spanish to English reading.

Use of Native Language and Culture

The advantages of native-language use are a prominent theme among these studies, either explicitly (e.g., Henderson and Landesman, 1992; Hernandez, 1991; Muniz-Swicegood, 1994; Lucas et al., 1990; Berman et al., 1995; Rosebery et al., 1992, Tikunoff, 1983; Pease-Alvarez et al., 1991; Calderon et al., 1996) or implicitly (Carter and Chatfield, 1986, and Goldenberg and Sullivan, 1994, both of which took place in school settings where there was a firm commitment to bilingual education). Even those studies that report on Special Alternative Instructional Programs, where most instruction takes place in English, cite teachers' use of students' native languages to clarify and elaborate on points they are making in English (Tikunoff et al., 1991). Moreover, findings from a study of nine Special Alternative Instructional Programs (Lucas and Katz, 1994:545) indicate that even in exemplary programs designed to provide instruction primarily in English, the classrooms were "multilingual environments in which students' native languages served a multitude of purposes and functions. Across sites, native language use emerged as a persistent and key instructional strategy realized in very site-specific ways."

Mace-Matluck et al. (1989:209) suggest that correlation patterns between English and Spanish reading measures indicate that "a child's knowledge and skills associated with decoding are related across the two languages, as are those associated with overall reading ability, but to a lesser degree." As a result, they conclude that "reading is a single process and that reading knowledge and skills gained in one language can be transferred, if the necessary conditions are met, to reading in another known language." Further, they state that "the practice of teaching children to read initially in their stronger language appears to be educationally sound." However, they cite Moll et al. (1981), who caution that learning is primarily situation specific; generalizability to other situations depends on whether the environment is organized to provide similar features that will facilitate its applicability to a different setting.

Nevertheless, several sites examined in these studies do not feature native-language programs. One of the Success for All sites, for example, has a largely

Asian population, and instruction is all in English. In addition, while some of the Spanish-speaking students in the Success for All studies are in primary-language programs, some are in sheltered English programs. Success for All has significant and important effects on the achievement of English-language learners, regardless of whether they are in a primary-language or sheltered English program. However, Spanish-speaking students in the Spanish-language Success for All program do better when tested in Spanish than do Spanish-speaking students in the English-language Success for All program when tested in English (to the extent achievement across two languages can be directly compared). This is not surprising, since we would expect that in the short run, reading achievement in one's native language would be superior to reading achievement in a second language, holding constant the instructional program.

We do not yet know whether there will be long-term advantages or disadvantages to initial literacy instruction in the primary language versus English, given a very high-quality program of known effectiveness in both cases. The question will not likely be resolved by the Success for All studies since there were probably pre-existing differences between students in the primary-language and sheltered English programs. Although the Success for All studies are unlikely to contribute to the debate on language of instruction, however, they do show that this program model is highly effective in both primary-language and sheltered English/ESL contexts.

Similarly, most of the studies cited in this review can contribute little direct knowledge to important questions about adapting instructional programs to students' home culture (e.g., sociolinguistic patterns, cognitive styles). These studies take place in contexts where the students' home culture is valued and seen as a resource to build upon, rather than a liability to remediate. Most of the studies report some aspect of home culture validation, accommodation, or inclusion in their effective sites. For example, Wong Fillmore et al. (1985) found that instructional practices and settings work differently for different groups of children and that conditions and experiences must be tailored to the characteristics of each group. Tharp (1982) found that small-group reading lessons structured to capitalize on the pre-existing cognitive and linguistic abilities of Hawaiian children were successful in teaching the children to read. He attributes some of the success of the program to the fact that the reading lessons resembled a major speech event in Hawaiian culture—talk story (see Chapter 4).

Again, Success for All presents a challenging counterpoint. There is nothing in the Success for All literature indicating that cultural validation or cultural accommodation per se is an important element of the program or, indeed, that culture plays any direct role at all (aside from language). Success for All is an intensive, prescriptive, well-conceptualized program designed to help as many children as possible leave third grade reading at grade level. Except for the important language adaptation (including somewhat different strategies for teaching Spanish and English reading), the program is no different for African American students in Baltimore than for Latinos in bilingual education or sheltered English programs in California or for Cambodians in an ESL program in Philadelphia (Slavin et al., in press). Of course, it is possible that cultural adaptations were taking place in the Success for All schools studied (as a result of the programs or not), but this factor was not examined.

Thus, the studies reviewed do not answer a question that has dominated research and professional and public discourse about educating English-language learners: What role should home language and culture play in the education of these students? The studies reviewed here can, at best, make an oblique contribution to this debate, in part because there are no rigorous studies that have controlled for interactions among student background (e.g., prior schooling in the native language, age), ways in which the first and second languages are used, and other instructional variables (e.g., overall quality of schooling). To illustrate the complexity of this issue, we cite a study on reading and bilingual students (Mace-Matluck et al., 1989) in which enrollment in Spanish reading programs was generally found to be negatively associated with acquired English literacy skills, but much of the relationship was due to entry-level differences in oral language skills. However, there was some indication of relatively superior English literacy skills at fourth grade exit for those students with longer enrollments in such Spanish reading programs. See Chapters 5 and 6 for further discussion of assessment and methodological issues.

Balanced Curriculum

Some schools focus primarily on curriculum "beyond basic skills." For example, the 1995 Berman et al. study features schools (grades 4-8) that emphasize "meaning-centered thematic curriculum." In contrast with Carter and Chatfield's (1986) classic "effective schools" description, Berman et al. (1995) do not even mention basic skills, objectives, and testing. Pease-Alvarez et al. (1991) note that the effective kindergarten teachers they studied involved their students in a wide range of meaningful activities or experiences focused on a particular concept, rather than exclusively emphasizing basic skills.

In much of the quasi-experimental research, however, classroom teachers combine basic and higher-order skills. In the Success for All schools, there is a balance between instruction in basic and higher-order skills at all grade levels. Story Telling and Retelling (STaR) is used in prekindergarten, in kindergarten, and early in first grade. Beyond the Basics is the name of the program in grades 2-6. The programs focus on comprehension, thinking skills, fluency, pleasure reading, and the use of increasingly complex material. Cooperative learning is used throughout the grades. Success for All's strong outcomes make the balance of these two levels of instruction very compelling. Both Goldenberg and Gallimore (1991) and Goldenberg and Sullivan (1994) report that the schools they worked with and studied included a "balanced" literacy program in which key skills and subjects such as phonics, word recognition, specific comprehension skills, and writing conventions were taught. However, they argue that early reading achievement improved at those schools partly because teachers incorporated language and meaning-based approaches into a system that had previously relied on basic decoding skills as the only avenue for learning to read.

Explicit Skills Instruction

The studies reviewed indicate that effective teachers for English-language learners use explicit skills instruction for certain tasks, mostly (though not always) to help students acquire basic skills.[10] Wong Fillmore et al. (1985) suggest that quality explicit skills instruction is important for all students, but especially for Hispanic students. In the Significant Bilingual Instructional Features study (Tikunoff, 1983), a measure of effectiveness is active teaching, defined in part as "instruction, in which the teacher sets and articulates learning goals, actively assesses student progress, and frequently makes class presentations, illustrating how to do assigned work" (p. 4). Many of the studies that report actual student achievement (Carter and Chatfield's [1986] effective schools study; Goldenberg and Gallimore [1991]; Escamilla [1994]; and Goldenberg and Sullivan's [1994] and Slavin and Yampolsky's [1992] quasi-experiments) also report that the schools involved had substantial amounts of time available for explicit skills instruction.

Opportunities for Student-Directed Activities

The studies reviewed indicate that teachers supplement explicit skills instruction, characteristic of the initial effective schools research, with student-directed activities. Berman et al. (1995) found that effective teachers provide English-language learners with adequate opportunities to produce oral and written English, and emphasize an exchange of ideas in an intellectual conversation. Moll (1988:466-467) observes that teachers nominated as effective emphasize "the creation of classroom contexts in which children learn to use, try out, and

---

[10]The value of explicit skills instruction is corroborated by other researchers. According to Sternberg (1986), explicit skills instruction is highly effective for some tasks (i.e., teaching subject matter knowledge, knowledge of hierarchical relationships among bits of information, and knowledge of valid strategies in science, and enhancing beginning readers' ability to decode and use process strategies [e.g., summarize, clarify, question, predict] so that they better comprehend what they have read). Executive processes such as comprehension monitoring can also be taught through explicit skills instruction if developmentally appropriate for the student. Rosenshine and Stevens (1986) argue that explicit teaching is highly effective for well-structured skill and knowledge domains such as math computation, explicit reading comprehension strategies, map reading, and decoding.

manipulate language in the service of making sense or creating meaning. The role of the teacher is to provide the necessary support and guidance so that children through their own efforts assume full control of the purposes and uses of oral language." Pease-Alvarez et al. (1991) found that effective kindergarten teachers encourage collaborative/cooperative interactions among students. Rosebery et al. (1992) and Henderson and Landesman (1992) also used a collaborative inquiry approach to successfully teach middle and high school language-minority students science and math, respectively. Cohen (1984) implemented a bilingual curriculum combined with complex instruction—a method of small-group learning featuring open-ended discovery on conceptual tasks.

Other prospective and quasi-experimental studies demonstrate the effectiveness of interventions that combine explicit skills instruction and student-directed work. Muniz-Swicegood (1994) used teacher modeling of comprehension strategies, teacher activation of student prior knowledge before reading, and a gradual shift of responsibility to students for carrying on the activities of the teacher to teach third grade Spanish-dominant students metacognitive reading strategies. Hernandez (1991) used a similar intervention to help Spanish-speaking seventh grade students improve their reading comprehension. In the Success for All studies, children were explicitly taught letter sounds, sound blending, word recognition skills, writing skills, and comprehension (metacognitive) strategies. However, they were also engaged in student-directed activity, such as cooperative learning and peer tutoring. CIRC and Bilingual CIRC (Calderon et al., 1996) combine explicit skills instruction in reading comprehension with cooperative learning, partner reading, and checking. The same is true for Saunders et al. (1996:30): "Like teachers described elsewhere (Gersten, 1996), teachers and advisors in our project saw the need to be comprehensive, to synthesize across rather than put in opposition various approaches to teaching and learning (directed lessons and instructional conversation, literature, and basals, writing projects and dictations)."

Instructional Strategies That Enhance Understanding

Effective teachers of English-language learners use specially tailored strategies to enhance understanding. This is important for students who are instructed in their second language. Dianda and Flaherty (1995:8) find that providing students with metacognitive skills they can use to "think about and prepare for a task, monitor themselves as they complete the task, and evaluate the outcomes helps language-minority students deal with context-reduced tasks." The Success for All reading and language arts program teaches students why, when, and how to use metacognitive strategies. Muniz-Swicegood (1994) employs instruction in self-generated questioning strategies; Hernandez (1991) teaches and models comprehension strategies, such as question generating, summarizing, and predicting, to Spanish-speaking students, thus significantly improving their Spanish reading comprehension; Chamot et al. (1992) use explicit instruction in learning strategies.

The use of routines to minimize the dependence on language is also helpful. Edelsky et al. (1983) note that the effective teacher they observed used routines for such purposes as writing projects, literature study, conferencing procedures, and science experiments. Sometimes she used written cues to make part of a routine or process explicit. Calderon et al. (1996) postulate that because students learned the CIRC process, protocols, and reading and learning strategies in Spanish first, these were easily transferable to the ESL content.

The studies reviewed also note strategies to help make instruction comprehensible to English-language learners: adjusting the level of English vocabulary and structure so it is appropriate for the students given their current level of proficiency in English; using explicit discourse markers such as "first" and "next"; calling attention to the language in the course of using it; using the language in ways that reveal its structure; providing explicit discussion of vocabulary and structure; explaining and in some cases demonstrating what students will be doing or experiencing; providing students with appropriate background knowledge; building on students' previous knowledge and understanding to establish a connection between personal experience and the subject matter they are learning; and using manipulatives, pictures, objects, and film related to the subject matter (Wong Fillmore et al., 1985; Gersten, 1996; Mace-Matluck et al., 1989; Saunders et al., 1996; Short, 1994).

Opportunities for Practice

This attribute entails building redundancy into activities, giving English-language learners opportunities to interact with fluent English-speaking peers, and providing opportunities for extended dialogue. Saunders et al. (1996:15) help students "work the text," which means studying it carefully—reading it, rereading it, discussing it, writing about it, and listening to what others have written about it. CIRC (Calderon et al., 1996) uses a set of activities that take place before, during, and after reading to ensure that students understand the text profoundly. These activities include, for example, the building of background knowledge and vocabulary, the making of predictions, teacher and then student reading of the same selection, discussion of answers to key questions, story mapping, story retelling, and story-related writing.

Through interactions with native speakers, second-language learners gain access to language that is unavailable in traditional teacher-directed classroom settings. Berman et al. (1995) report that exemplary schools provided opportunities for contact between monolingual English speakers and English-language learners during instruction in core content, in electives, or in alternative activities such as projects. Wong Fillmore et al. (1985) note that all learners profit from opportunities to interact with peers who speak the target languages, but Hispanic (rather than Chinese) students profit in particular; Chinese learners profit from opportunities for interaction with peers after they have reached intermediate levels of English proficiency. CIRC (Calderon et al., 1996) provides opportunities for English-language learners to interact with peers, which helps students develop fluency in and comfort with English.

Effective teachers create opportunities for extended dialogue to enhance English acquisition and learning.[11] In the Special Alternative Instructional Programs reviewed by Tikunoff et al. (1991), teachers structured activities that provided English-language learners with opportunities for frequent, meaningful interactions among themselves and the teacher. In addition, they encouraged contributions by these students by focusing on the content of their responses, rather than on grammatical correctness, during content area instruction. Garcia (1990a) observes that in effective kindergarten and third and fifth grade classrooms, teachers allowed for a great deal of student-to-student interaction in the child reply component of instructional discourse segments. Gersten (1996) notes that effective teachers use questions that press students to clarify or expand on initial statements, as well as encourage students to participate in conversations.

Recently, a good deal of attention has been paid to instructional conversations—discussion-based lessons that focus on an idea or concept that has both educational value and meaning and relevance for students (see Chapter 4). The teacher encourages students to express their ideas either orally or in writing and guides them to increasingly sophisticated levels of understanding. This is a particular instance of the opportunity for extended dialogue proposed as a feature of effective instruction. Saunders et al. (1996) found that students who have opportunities for using language to elaborate and develop ideas in writing and discussion outperform their peers who do not. In a forthcoming study (Saunders and Goldenberg, in press), the authors report that fourth grade English-language learners who participated in an instructional conversation outperformed comparable students who participated in a more conventional recitation or basal-like recitation lesson.

Systematic Student Assessment

Many studies have found that effective schools use systematic student assessment—a feature identified in the effective and nominated schools research—to inform ongoing efforts to improve achievement (see also Chapter 5). For example, Carter and Chatfield (1986) report ongoing assessment of student outcomes to monitor program effectiveness. Four studies that report actual student achievement (Carter and Chatfield's [1986] effective schools study, and

---

[11]Much of the discussion here is based on research by Tharp and Gallimore (1991), Goldenberg (1992), and Rueda et al. (1992).

Goldenberg and Sullivan's [1994], Slavin and Yampolsky's [1992], and Slavin and Madden's [1994] quasi-experiments) note the systematic assessment of student achievement by their study sites. In the Success for All programs, students are assessed every 8 weeks to determine who needs tutoring and whether groups should be changed, and to identify students who might need some other type of assistance. In the study documented by Goldenberg and Sullivan (1994), the school had developed a mechanism for assessing and discussing student progress, at least in the aggregate, on a regular basis. Although systematic student assessment is not identified as a feature in a fifth study that reports student achievement (Goldenberg and Gallimore, 1991), the principal and instructional specialist met with teachers quarterly for individual "pacing conferences," where they reviewed the progress and achievement of students in each teacher's classroom.

Staff Development

Staff training and development are important components of effective schools for English-language learners not identified in the original effective schools research. As previously mentioned, one important way to raise teacher expectations is to raise student achievement by helping teachers acquire skills and knowledge needed to be more successful with students, rather than exhorting teachers to raise their expectations. Often the training identified in the studies reviewed here is specific to teachers of these students, such as English-language development and use of sheltered instruction (Lucas et al., 1990). In other instances (e.g., Slavin and Yampolsky, 1992; Slavin and Madden, 1994), the training is in instructional strategies that are specific to the implemented program, such as use of thematic units, vocabulary development, classroom management, instructional pace, and cooperative learning, but not targeted at English-language learners per se.

Staff development for all teachers in the school, not just language specialists, was an important component of many of these programs. Although the programs provided ongoing staff development directly related to resolving new instructional issues for ESL and bilingual education teachers, they also recruited excellent content area teachers and trained them in English-language development strategies. Carter and Chatfield (1986), Lucas et al. (1990), Minicucci and Olsen (1992), and Berman et al. (1995) also document staff development explicitly designed to prepare all teachers to work with English-language learners. This contrasts with prior policies whereby ESL teachers were expected to teach content matter to these students, and mainstream teachers had no training in how to instruct them.

In preparing teachers, Moll and his colleagues (Moll et al., 1992) have avoided one pitfall often associated with culturally responsive pedagogy (defined as teaching practices attuned to the cultural background of students)—the tendency to base instructional practices on teachers' assumptions and stereotypical beliefs about groups of students. Drawing on the principle that "the students' community represents a resource of enormous importance for educational change and improvement," teachers and researchers involved in this work interview parents and other community members to identify the information and skills or "funds of knowledge" that are available to Mexican households through their social networks (see also Chapter 4). Teacher-researchers participating in the project then organize their curriculum accordingly. In addition, they call upon the expertise of community members and incorporate community-based knowledge sources into their curriculum. As a result, their culturally responsive curriculum is based on empirical findings about the community, rather than stereotypes.

Ongoing professional staff development is not prominently featured—if it is mentioned at all—in the original effective schools literature. Yet it is now a universally agreed-upon component of any effective school and certainly of any effort to change and improve a school. A real question that remains is what sort of training is most relevant for improving school processes, as well as teacher knowledge and skills. It is also important to validate the effectiveness of this training through assessments of student outcomes (see also Chapter 8).

Home and Parent Involvement

Home and parent involvement—an attribute that, like staff development, was not a part of the original effective schools conceptualization—plays an important role in enhancing outcomes for English-language learners. Moll (1988), Garcia (1990b), and Carter and Chatfield (1986) all note that in the effective schools they document, an ongoing community/school process is an important contributor to the school's success. Garcia observes that in effective schools, teachers have a strong commitment to school-home communication, and parents are involved in formal parent support activities. In the school documented by Carter and Chatfield, volunteers from the community worked in the school, both directly with children and in helping teachers prepare classroom materials. The school's staff also tried to enhance home-school connections even further by improving the quality of homework teachers assigned.

Lucas et al.'s (1990) effective high schools encouraged parents to become involved in their children's education. This was accomplished in different ways at the various schools, through means such as parent advisory committees, newsletters, monthly parent nights, evening student performances, teacher-parent meetings, student-of-the-month breakfasts, honors assemblies, and community liaisons. It is important to note that home-school connections apparently played a role even in high school, despite the fact that parents' direct involvement in children's schooling declines as children get older (Stevenson and Baker, 1987). Lucas et al. do report, however, that parent participation was the "least developed component" in the high schools they visited (p. 334).

Different types of home-school connections probably have different types of effects (Epstein, 1992). For example, newsletters can make parents knowledgeable about what is happening at school, but we should not expect them to improve student achievement unless they contain information parents can actually use to influence, for example, TV viewing, time spent reading or doing homework, or trips to the library or museums. Similarly, parent participation in school governance is likely to help parents feel empowered, but we should not expect it to make parents more knowledgeable about disciplining or motivating children or helping them achieve more academic success unless parents are provided with pertinent information or training in the course of their governance activities.

Neither the studies reviewed here nor any other existing studies can answer the question of what type of home or parent involvement is most effective. Extrapolating from the observations in these studies, however, two hypotheses seem reasonable. First, cognitive or academic effects are most likely to be the result of home-school connections that focus specifically on cognitive or academic learning at home, that is, increasing and improving home learning opportunities through the use of homework or other organized activities designed to promote learning. Second, schools with comprehensive home involvement programs encompassing various types of home-school connections probably help families and children in a number of important ways. The more types of productive connections homes and schools can forge, the more positive and powerful the effects on children, families, and schools will be. At least in U.S. settings, these hypotheses are probably valid regardless of students' cultural or language background (Goldenberg, 1993). (See Chapter 4 for further elaboration on this theme.)

Methodological Strengths and Limitations of the Studies

Each of the major types of studies reviewed here has its methodological strengths and limitations. These are examined in the subsections that follow.

Effective and Nominated Schools and Classroom Designs

The nominated schools and classroom designs have introduced a valuable element to the literature—rich and highly detailed descriptions, some quantitative and some qualitative, of schools and classrooms. School and community contexts, relevant histories with specific populations of students, and the perceptions of key players—students, teachers, administrators, and parents—are prominently featured in articles and technical reports, as are detailed and sophisticated studies of classroom learning and discourse environments. Although detailed accounts of effective schools are not completely absent from the earlier effective schools literature (e.g., Weber, 1971), researchers have become increasingly sophisticated in the range and depth of data they collect. The resulting rich portraits of supposedly effective programs and practices are especially welcome given the growing diversity of the U.S. school population.

As exploratory strategies, both the effective and nominated schools designs make a great deal of intuitive and logical sense. But there are also limitations to what they can tell us. First, and most fundamental, neither design directly or empirically addresses the issue of how a school or classroom came to be effective, except for possible retrospective accounts and inferences. Carter and Chatfield (1986:204), who provide one example of the effective schools paradigm applied to English-language learner schooling issues, explicitly recognize this limitation: "This paper makes no claim of providing solutions to the profound problems associated with educational change, knowledge utilization, and innovation acceptance." Carter and Chatfield also recognize the danger inherent in attempting to implement willy-nilly the results of effective schools research. Such attempts almost certainly lead to what they call an "implementation of attributes" approach, involving the issuance of top-down mandates requiring local schools to "implement" strong leadership, high expectations, a safe and businesslike school climate, and so on. "Serious, objective research is required to analyze school-improvement strategies and ultimately to develop strategies appropriate to the complexity of effective schools" (p. 203).

A second limitation of these designs, related to the first, is the difficulty of separating cause from effect: Do the characteristics of schools cause them to be effective, or does effectiveness lead to these characteristics? This is a particular problem with effective and nominated schools designs, both of which make strong claims about causes (e.g., high expectations, positive school climate) and effects (e.g., high student achievement). However, since the conditions that presumably make a school effective are gauged at the same time as (or even after) achievement data are collected, such claims are problematic. For example, in the effective schools studies, we do not know whether high expectations preceded or followed increased effectiveness. The cause-effect problem is particularly acute in the effective and nominated schools studies reviewed here since these studies do not include comparison sites, which would at least permit the studies to claim (empirically) a correlation between school factors that contribute to effectiveness on the one hand and desirable outcomes for students on the other.

A third limitation is that the nominated schools design now in favor reports no data whatsoever on student outcomes, although some gauge of student outcomes may have been used in the selection process. Exemplary schools are selected because they satisfy criteria shared by nominators and investigators regarding what effective schooling for English-language learners should look like. In many cases these schools are chosen regardless of whether it can be shown that the characteristics they display lead to desired outcomes (social, cognitive, or affective), gauged independently of the processes considered "effective," "exemplary," or "desirable." Thus, these studies by definition remain inconclusive on the question of effectiveness. Moreover, there is a major risk of circularity: the exemplary schools do things that are "exemplary" or, as some authors note, are consistent with what researchers and leading practitioners say should be done. Berman et al. (1992:Vol.1, 26) readily acknowledge the issue:

> It is impossible to know how many programs were included or excluded [in their study of well-implemented programs for English-language learners] by nominators on the basis of their own philosophies about what constitutes a good LEP program . . . .

Problems with the methods used to investigate instructional processes and environments compound the issue. Some studies describe only one school, which makes it difficult to determine which factors are important. In some cases, very little information is provided on data collection methods. For those studies that report information, other problems are apparent, including poor or absent reporting of interrater reliability, limited depth and duration of observations, lack of systematic methods for observing classroom events, or combining of information across sites.

Prospective Case Studies

Prospective case studies have the advantage, in principle, of collecting data contemporaneously with change efforts, permitting observation and analysis of the actual change process, participants' views and perspectives, and the apparent ongoing results of the changes undertaken. Under ideal circumstances, they would be true cases of the implementation of theories regarding effective schooling.

Our systematic review uncovered very few studies beyond those described in the previous section. Even in the California Case Studies project, funding was terminated prematurely before important issues, such as the processes and dynamics of change and school-level factors related to change and improvement, could be documented, analyzed, and reported (N. Gold, personal communication, December 1995; Crawford, 1995).

An inherent characteristic of prospective studies in schools is the close relationship between the educator who implements the program and the researcher. In the studies reviewed here, the school changes that were made and studied were instigated by the researcher/author of the report in collaboration with educators at their respective sites. Thus, this set of studies constitutes "action research," where the line separating efforts to improve schooling for English-language learners and the conduct of academic research has been blurred or removed. An advantage of these studies, from a purely pragmatic standpoint, is that if the changes are effective and actually work, the students and teachers at the intervention site will have benefited. However, methodological problems, possibly related to the close collaboration of researchers and educators, can compromise study findings. For example, in one study, investigators who analyzed the interview protocols for changes in student knowledge knew which protocols were pre-test and which were post-test.

Many of the issues noted above regarding effective and nominated schools research are classic threats to validity. How do we separate cause from effect? How do we establish causality at all? How do we know whether something has an "effect"? How do we gauge that effect? Similar questions can be asked about the prospective case study design that focuses exclusively on the intervention site: How do we know that shifts in achievement patterns following implementation of the changes are due to those changes? What about extraneous factors, general upward drift in scores, or regression effects?

Quasi-Experiments

Traditionally, threats to validity have been addressed within an experimental framework or, when dealing with social phenomena where random assignment is impossible, a quasi-experimental framework. From a design standpoint, the quasi-experimental design obviously offers a stronger basis for claiming that changes in student achievement resulted from something that happened at a target site. In the absence of a comparison site with students who are comparable in features such as demographics and transience, changes in student outcomes at a particular school can be due to any number of extraneous factors or artifacts. Quasi-experiments also permit stronger causal inferences about school processes, dynamics, and structures on the one hand and improvements in student outcomes on the other.

However, school changes are so complex and involve so many dimensions that it is usually very difficult to draw tight linkages between specific processes or program components and student outcomes. For example, although one study (Henderson and Landesman, 1992) indicated that students in thematic math instruction outperformed those in a regular math program, the cause of this effect is unclear. The experience of the treatment group differed from that of the control group on more dimensions than thematic instruction, including student access to bilingual instruction, extended periods of time with the same teacher and classmates, and instruction in omitted content between themes and at the conclusion of the school year. Many of the quasi-experimental studies also have the limitation of providing very little information about the intervention received by the control group, thus making it difficult to gauge the actual merits of the intervention.

Quasi-experimental designs are really just parallel case studies and do not preclude in-depth study and subtle analysis of school and instructional organization features. On the contrary, richer descriptions of the processes and dynamics of school change would permit clearer interpretations or hypotheses about what explains changes in student outcomes—or the failure to effect such changes. Quasi-experimental designs do require that investigators either take an active hand in helping to bring about changes at a school or be present when a school, on its own, decides to try to instigate changes, so that appropriate measures in the "before" state can be taken. In either case, investigators must then gauge the effects of those changes on student outcomes, using appropriate measures and comparable schools as controls.

Some of the studies reviewed here—particularly those that examine student outcomes and relate them to changes in school-wide and classroom functioning and organization—suggest processes by which schools and classrooms can reorganize themselves to promote higher levels of achievement for students. One framing of this complex issue has been articulated by Slavin and Madden (1995) in their most recent summary of the research on Success for All: Can a school become effective by successfully adopting an effective, externally developed program, or is a certain amount of "reinventing the wheel" required, school by school? Although Slavin and Madden's results provide a strong basis for concluding that some well-defined effective programs can be exported successfully to other schools in other communities with different students and staffs, their position (and, apparently, their data) runs counter not only to much of the accepted wisdom in the school reform literature, but also to previous efforts to disseminate and replicate effective programs (e.g., Anderson et al., 1978).

A Note About Process

In the conduct of the research recommended below, collaborative efforts between practitioners and other groups (e.g., state departments of education, universities, research laboratories) are especially important, given the inordinate difficulty of simultaneously bringing about substantive school change and conducting research on it. The California Case Studies in bilingual education, a partnership between the California State Department of Education and five public elementary schools, provides a model for such collaboration between a public agency and the schools (Gold and Tempes, 1987). School-university partnerships (e.g., the early Success for All studies; see Goldenberg and Sullivan, 1994) are also recommended, complex and fraught with difficulties though they may be (Trubowitz et al., 1984).

RESEARCH NEEDS

Identification of Effective Classrooms and Schools

7-1. Researchers should make explicit their principles for selecting effective schools and classrooms. These principles should be based on some combination of indicators of process (e.g., curriculum, leadership, school climate, instructional strategies) and outcomes (e.g., standardized and performance-based achievement measures). The definition should be influenced by local priorities and contexts.

Given the variation in the way effectiveness is defined across studies, research needs to address what we mean by "effective." Research on effective schools could benefit greatly from the development of some principles of effectiveness for English-language learners that would still leave room for variations based on local priorities and contexts. These principles might incorporate issues of equity and access for all students (which would address the issue of separation of English-language learners from native-English speakers), theoretical foundations for programs and practices, evidence from student achievement, and evidence from student behavior and engagement in school (e.g., attendance, suspensions, graduation rates). The development of principles of effectiveness is especially important in the field of education research, a methodologically pluralistic field in which interpretive and postmoderist approaches thrive alongside traditional approaches that pursue objectivity and positivism. In some cases, effectiveness appears to be tied to a particular theory of teaching and learning. Other studies take a different approach and define effectiveness in terms of measurable student achievement outcomes: a school or teachers are relatively effective if students are achieving at some criterion level, or at least significantly better than students in comparable schools.

Research on effectiveness should clearly state how effective schools and classrooms are recognized. Nominated schools studies are useful in the provision of exploratory data and in their ability to integrate a wide array of complex information, some of which is difficult to capture through objective methods. However, we urge researchers to identify the nature of the complex decisions made by nominators. In addition, we must look for concrete and documented evidence that programs and practices claiming to be "exemplary" also help produce desirable student outcomes.

Extent of Variability in the Definition of Effective Schools and Classrooms for English-Language Learners

7-2. Research should investigate how definitions of effectiveness interact with local site characteristics and student characteristics.

The following sorts of questions might be pursued. Does effective leadership have one set of attributes in a school with certain cultural and demographic characteristics and a different (perhaps related) set of attributes in a school with a different cultural make-up? Do effective home-school connections have different characteristics depending on the cultural group involved? In general, do attributes of effective schooling for language-minority students vary by students' linguistic, cultural, or national-origin group; socioeconomic level (including transiency); degree of exposure to English outside of school; generational status (immigrant, first or second generation); and/or schooling level (early or late elementary, middle, or high school)? The hypotheses and possible interactions are nearly limitless. But if we are to advocate differentiated programming for students, this should be done on the basis of evidence that such programming has practical and meaningful benefits to students, their families, and their communities.

A key issue is whether effective teacher practices for students generally are sufficient to help English-language learners succeed in school, or whether knowledge and skills specific to the latter are needed. Lucas et al. (1990:329) take an unequivocal stand: "Teachers who are expert in the instruction of mainstream students are not necessarily effective instructors of language-minority students." They cite examples from their nominated high schools of policies that encourage teachers to get ESL and bilingual certification and training. Carter and Chatfield (1986:228), in contrast, are more cautious, suggesting the question is an empirical one:

> The present popularity of the immersion approach for LEP children implies that bilingual education is unnecessary and that LEP children can achieve without it....[S]uch situations should be carefully studied; the independent influence of school effectiveness with minority-language children can only be isolated by the careful analysis of any such situations.

7-3. Research should examine the extent to which "generic" reform efforts incorporate English-language learners. Moreover, this research should explore whether these reform efforts are beneficial, and if not how they can be adapted to this group of students.

Several questions in this area need further study: To what extent do school reform efforts include English-language learners? Are the reforms in curriculum, instruction, assessment, school organization and governance, and community engagement beneficial for English-language learners? Are some more beneficial than others? Are adaptations needed to make them beneficial, or are they effective for all students without major adaptations? If adaptations are needed, what might they be?

This is a variation on recommendation 7-2, addressing whether teachers need special skills and knowledge to teach English-language learners effectively. There are those who believe that good teaching is good teaching, no matter who the students are. Research on how current reforms in curriculum, assessment, and school organization and the particulars of classroom instruction are and are not appropriate for and effective with English-language learners would provide empirical evidence to support or refute such beliefs.

Developmental Issues

7-4. There is a clear need for research to examine the effects of instructional interventions and social environments on the linguistic, social, and cognitive development of young children.

At all grade levels, special challenges exist for English-language learners and their educators. As a result, findings based on elementary school studies may not be fully appropriate for early education or secondary contexts, and some questions may not have been dealt with at all. At the primary level, such challenges include the fact that young children have not yet developed many concepts in their native language. The few studies at the early childhood level focus on program effects on the English-language development of young children (see Chapter 2). Given the increasing numbers of children who attend school earlier, this is an especially important area of research. Other research areas that merit attention include the effects of various kinds of programming on students' first-language development, as well as their social and cognitive development. An important aspect of this research is the need for appropriate assessment (see Chapter 5).

7-5. More studies are needed to identify attributes of effective middle and secondary schools and classrooms serving English-language learners.

Although there are more studies that focus on middle and secondary school than on very young English-language learners, more prospective and quasi-experimental research is needed at these levels, as is research examining issues that adversely affect students at these levels. Issues related to sheltered instruction are particularly important for secondary school students, who are expected to master more complex content through their second language. Other challenges include the relative lack of time to master language and content needed for graduation and post-secondary opportunities, great variability among students in prior preparation for this level of schooling, and noninstructional features such as transiency and family/work responsibilities. Specific research questions include the following: How is such content best made accessible? What practices are effective for students with limited prior formal schooling? What factors contribute to students' persistent classification as English-language learners after a number of years in U.S. schools, and how can their needs be met? How can secondary schools integrate English-language learners into the life of the school while meeting their specific needs? What programs and practices lead to best access to post-secondary opportunities? Assessment issues are also extremely important and difficult in connection with these questions (see Chapter 5).

7-6. Research is needed to assess the effectiveness of newcomer programs, either in relationship to each other or compared with doing nothing at all. Further research is needed to determine whether there is a well-realized and -packaged program that could be readily exported.

Late enrollment, especially of non-English-speaking students entering the upper grades, presents a challenge; the constant influx of new students is clearly disruptive to teachers, support staff, and students themselves. A program that is effective under fairly stable conditions might be taxed to the breaking point with a continual stream of new enrollments. Many new enrollments, particularly among English-language learners, are also new to schooling in the United States. Some schools and districts have opted for "newcomer centers" where late-enrolling students, particularly those who come from other countries, attend school for some transition period (Friedlander, 1991). The curriculum and services offered address the needs of newcomers specifically by providing intensive language and cultural orientation, as well as basic skills and content remediation as appropriate. A number of models and programs are currently in operation, and anecdotal data suggest that newcomer programs are very successful and popular with students (Chang, 1990; Friedlander, 1991; Mace-Matluck et al., in press). Studies have described some of the programs (Chang, 1990; Friedlander, 1991; McDonnell and Hill, 1993; Olsen and Dowell, 1989) or included such programs in their reviews of promising school practices (Mace-Matluck et al., in press; Romo, 1993), but no comprehensive research has been conducted to compare student achievement in newcomer programs with that in other program options (e.g., transitional bilingual education, sheltered instruction).

Special Issues

7-7. Once learning goals have been set by the community, research is needed to determine the linguistic and cultural adaptations that will help English-language learners meet these goals. What methods work best to give English-language learners access to the academic and social opportunities that native English speakers have while they are learning English? Such methods include both school-wide adaptations, such as the way sequences of classes are organized to give English-language learners optimal access to subject matter knowledge and English proficiency, and classroom adaptations, such the use of particular teaching strategies and classroom composition.

An obvious characteristic that distinguishes English-language learners from others with regard to effective schooling is that their native language is not English, the primary medium of instruction in the United States. This fact raises two major issues that remain unresolved in the research literature: How should language of instruction (native language and English) be arranged, and when instruction is in the second language, what adjustments, if any, are needed?

The need to determine the appropriate instructional role for the native language and English is a recurring theme in our review. Because of the complexity involved (e.g., the need to consider demographic and contextual factors) and the dearth of rigorous studies addressing the question, the evidence in the literature is contradictory. For example, there is conflicting evidence regarding whether the native language and English should be used concurrently or kept separate. Wong Fillmore et al. (1985) found that when two languages are used concurrently, students listen only to their native language and ignore the second, thus hampering English learning. However, other investigators have found otherwise (Tikunoff, 1983; Gersten, 1996). For example, Tikunoff (1983) found that in successful classrooms, the students' native languages were used substantially by instructors to develop the lesson content. When a student was not comprehending what was required or needed feedback to complete a task, teachers frequently switched to the student's native language and used it to clarify the instruction.

There are also many open questions related to how to adapt English-language materials and instruction so they are both comprehensible and conceptually appropriate for English-language learners. For example, some experts recommend reducing nonessential details and simplifying grammatical structures in text (Short, 1994). Others, however, maintain that simplifying "surface linguistic features" will not necessarily make the text easier to comprehend, and that reducing nonessential details may delete important background information crucial to the interpretation of meaning when knowledge of language forms is limited (Saville-Troike, 1991). Moreover, Berman et al. (1992:5) found that sheltered English classes (in which both content instruction and ESL instruction are provided in a self-contained classroom, and teachers use a simplified form of English and modify their teaching techniques to make instruction comprehensible to English-language learners) result in instruction "prone to low-expectations and overly simplified curriculum."

Concerns about effectiveness must go beyond language as well. As noted elsewhere in this report, not only are English-language learners language-minority students; they are also usually from cultural or ethnic groups whose sociolinguistic, cognitive, or motivational attributes may not coincide or be congruent with attributes conducive to success in U.S. schools. There is a wealth of writing and research bearing on precisely this issue (e.g., Tharp, 1989). However, there is surprisingly little direct empirical confirmation that culturally accommodated instruction (or school-wide organization) actually produces higher levels of academic achievement. We need research that will examine in depth and in detail how instruction, assessment, curriculum, school organization, school leadership, and professional development can be designed and adapted to be "effective" with students of widely varying backgrounds and experiences—including English-language learners of different backgrounds.

7-8. Involving families of English-language learners and engaging community resources on their behalf poses special challenges for schools. More focused research is needed to provide information about the challenges to such involvement and engagement, the potential benefits, and successful approaches.

Several important questions need to be addressed in this area: What approaches are most effective in getting families of English-language learners of different backgrounds involved in school activities? How can school involvement be made more inviting to parents? How can school staff be made more receptive to parent and community involvement? What types of family involvement are most effective in influencing the academic achievement of English-language learners? Other entities besides schools and families play a significant role in the lives of many English-language learners. Research needs to reach beyond the classroom and school to examine how external agencies can work with schools to increase educational effectiveness for English-language learners.

7-9. Research is needed to determine the resources required for effective instruction of English-language learners in different contexts.

Many authors attribute poor implementation of program models to lack of sufficient resources. Berman et al. (1992) found, for example, that schools face severe resource limitations, and thus have problems implementing their programs, regardless of the model they adopt. Thus outcomes for most schools may be due to implementation factors that have nothing to do with the validity of the approach underlying a program.

Prospective Research

7-10. Prospective research that examines the school change process is needed, beginning from the point before a school undertakes change, to document the processes and outcomes on a sound theoretical and programmatic basis. Prospective studies should document the problems, possibilities, dynamics, difficulties, successes, and outcomes of school and program change. An important focus would be on how schools and teachers maintain effective components once in place. Research should also determine which kinds of improvement strategies are exportable and which aspects may be influenced by local context.

In addition, future research should examine the benefits and shortcomings of different improvement strategies, again using models and programs already in existence. A component of this research would be to examine whether educators and policymakers find empirical research or rich cases more compelling in prompting them to change their current practices. Some prospective case studies of sites on the verge of reform could help answer these important policy implementation questions.

To what extent and under what conditions are successful models transportable? How much adaptation, even reinvention, is needed? Clearly, such research should build on lessons learned from previous studies of implementation. For example, a 4-year two-phase study conducted in the 1970s (Berman and McLaughlin, 1978) examined the initiation and implementation of federally funded local projects, including Title VII. The study findings indicate the importance of "mutual adaptation, the process by which a project is adapted to the reality of its institutional setting, while at the same time, teachers and school officials adapt their practices in response to the project. Effective strategies provide each teacher with necessary and timely feedback, allow project-level choices to be made to correct errors, and encourage commitment to the project" (p.viii). In their evaluation of Academic Excellence Program dissemination efforts, Wilson et al. (1994:85) conclude that more attention should be paid to finding out and communicating what works best to disseminate effective bilingual education practice....[There need to be] on-site case studies of various projects followed by larger scale surveys." For example, are generalizable findings more or less convincing than a well-told story of a school that worked? Does evidential preference interact with one's stance toward the innovation; that is, are advocates more likely to rely on the compelling case, whereas opponents are more likely to cite quantitative findings? Here again, we are likely to learn more about how to help English-language learners, indeed all children, if we have an understanding of the processes leading to successful change at particular sites, including the successful implementation and adaptation of effective models.

The effect of very locally specific factors is an important issue. The integration of various research-based responses in a single site may be impossible, or some responses may be incompatible with local factors. Samaniego and Eubanks' (1991) secondary analysis of the California Case Studies data suggests that the language characteristics of the community in which a bilingual program exists have a strong "effect on the development of second language proficiency [suggesting] that no bilingual education approach, however sensible and theoretically well-supported, can be applied in a uniform way with equal success in substantially different learning environments." Slavin and Madden (1994) are undoubtedly correct when they warn of the dangers of reinventing the wheel, school by school. Yet local and school realities also seem to suggest the need to consider site- and community-specific dimensions in the creation and evolution of effective schools for English-language learners. A certain amount of invention, perhaps even reinvention, may always be necessary. It is undoubtedly also true, however, that schools and students clearly stand to gain by learning about and even importing successful practices, even if not entire programs, developed elsewhere.

ANNEX: TABLE 7-1
STUDIES OF SCHOOL AND CLASSROOM EFFECTIVENESS

TABLE 7-1   Studies of School and Classroom Effectiveness

1 **Carter and Chatfield (1986),** *Effective Bilingual Schools: Implications for Policy and Practice*

2 School(s) and Level(s) Studied	3 Language-Minority Group(s)/ School Mix	4 Study Design[1]	5 Method for Selecting Target School(s)/Classrooms
One elementary school	50% Latino; 20% African American, Asian	Effective schools	One of three bilingual elementary schools identified as effective in earlier report to California State Dept. of Education

6	7	8
Student Outcome Data Reported	School-level Attributes	Classroom-level Attributes
Academic achievement in English: state (California Assessment Program), national (Stanford Achievement Test), and local (district proficiency tests).	Bilingual education + effective schools dimensions, e.g., safe and orderly environment; opportunities to learn (OTL), defined as ample time allocated to basic subjects and high task engagement; expectations and demand for student performance; high staff morale; instructional leadership provided by principal; active involvement of teachers in school organization and management; community support and active participation.	Organized and coherent instructional program; direct instruction; maintenance of task engagement; monitoring of students; use of bilingual instruction.

TABLE 7-1   Continued

1 **Edelsky et al. (1983), *Hookin' 'Em in at the Start of School in a "Whole Language Classroom"***

2 School(s) and Level(s) Studied	3 Language-Minority Group(s)/ School Mix	4 Study Design[1]	5 Method for Selecting Target School(s)/Classrooms
One inner city grade 6 classroom	Approximately 75% Mexican-American, 10% African American, and 15% Caucasian	Effective classrooms	Effective classrooms based on teachers' reputation, researchers' knowledge of student performance and actual work in classroom in previous years, and spontaneous reports from parents; use of whole-language approach

1 **Wong Fillmore et al. (1985), *Learning English Through Bilingual Instruction***

Thirteen grade 3 bilingual and English-only classes; four grade 5 bilingual and English-only classes	157 Chinese or Spanish first-language students in these classes, with 2-3 years of exposure to English	Effective classrooms	Testing, observation of learners and teachers, audio and video recordings of lessons

6	7	8
Student Outcome Data Reported	School-level Attributes	Classroom-level Attributes
No	No	In attaining teacher's goals of helping students build a relationship with her, get along with each other, and implement a whole-language writing program, teacher played various roles (consultant/coach; scout leader), emphasized certain values (respect, interdependence, the idea that people are good), and provided common cues (i.e., used work of others as examples, modeled desired outcomes, reminded and checked up, held high expectations).
No	No	Different aspects of instructional practices and classroom experiences influence development of comprehension vs. production skills; instructional practices found to influence language development have differential effects on learners depending on their initial level of proficiency in English and on their cultural background; role played by the teacher depends on the concentration of English-language learners.

TABLE 7-1   Continued

1 **Mace-Matluck et al. (1989),** *Teaching Reading to Bilingual Children: A Longitudinal Study of Teaching and Learning in the Early Grades*

2 School(s) and Level(s) Studied	3 Language- Minority Group(s)/ School Mix	4 Study Design[1]	5 Method for Selecting Target School(s)/Classrooms
250 bilingual students in grades K-4 in 20 schools	Bilingual students (English/Spanish); students selected within a classroom based on sex, language status, and index of cognitive style	Effective classrooms, longitudinal study examining relationships among student characteristics, instruction, and outcomes in reading in English and Spanish	Predetermined variables used to determine regions, select 6 school districts from 4 regions (3 in Texas and 1 in northern Mexico), 20 schools from these districts, 37 teachers (initially) from these districts, and 10 students from each class

6	7	8
Student Outcome Data Reported	School-level Attributes	Classroom-level Attributes
Multiple measures used to assess each of major components of skilled reading (vocabulary knowledge, decoding, and text comprehension); for bilingual sample, growth monitored in English and Spanish (see classroom domains for correlations).	Spanish literacy more advanced at U.S.-Mexico border sites that provided the greatest nonschool support for Spanish.	Literacy skills in general advanced by instruction that made strong formal language demands on students, employed primary materials, and engaged students in work with text materials. Comprehension and vocabulary skills advanced by increased amounts of instructional time devoted to such skill development, but decoding skills showed the opposite relationship, perhaps because of the relatively low quality of such instruction in this data set. Literacy skill showed greater improvement with increased exposure to instruction. In Spanish, literacy advanced by instruction that engaged students in work with text materials, increased the quantity and quality of decoding instruction, and decreased the number of students in the instructional group.

TABLE 7-1   Continued

1 **Garcia (1990a),** *Instructional Discourse in 'Effective' Hispanic Classrooms*

2 School(s) and Level(s) Studied	3 Language- Minority Group(s)/ School Mix	4 Study Design[1]	5 Method for Selecting Target School(s)/Classrooms
Grade K, 3, and 5 classrooms	Hispanic	Effective and nominated classrooms	Classrooms selected from K, 3, and 5 classrooms nominated by school district and teaching personnel in 12 metropolihn Phoenix school districts, based on high ratings by nominators and students at or above grade level

1 **Moll (1988),** *Some Key Issues in Teaching Latino Students*

| Two grade 5 teachers—one bilingual, one monolingual (English) | Latino children in a major metropolitan area in the Southwest | Effective and nominated classrooms | Teachers judged to be outstanding or effective teachers of Latino children by their peers and administrators; students achieving at or above grade level |

6	7	8
Student Outcome Data Reported	School-level Attributes	Classroom-level Attributes
"Reported to be" at or above grade level on standardized achievement measures.	No	Teachers elicited student responses at relatively lower-order cognitive and linguistic levels. Once elicitation had occurred students allowed to take control of topic and interact with fellow students. Shift from emphasis on Spanish in K, to mixed use in 3, to total use of English by 5.
Students reported to be achieving at or above grade level.	No	Teachers offer flexibility, higher-level reading and writing, and lessons with purpose and meaning and give students options and autonomy.

TABLE 7-1   Continued

1 **Berman et al. (1995),** *School Reform and Student Diversity*

2 School(s) and Level(s) Studied	3 Language- Minority Group(s)/ School Mix	4 Study Design[1]	5 Method for Selecting Target School(s)/Classrooms
Eight schools, grades 4-8	Seven schools with sizable Latino populations— 38 89%, with 20-67% English-language learners; three schools with 20-43% Asian, with some portion English-language learners; one school 25% Haitian	Nominated schools	Peer nomination, followed by staff phone interviews and on-site visits to selected schools that "follow practices . . . considered . . . to provide outstanding learning opportunities for LEP—and all—students"

6	7	8
Student Outcome Data Reported	School-level Attributes	Classroom-level Attributes
No	School-wide vision of excellence embracing English-language learners' native language and culture; school-wide restructuring; presence of external partners; active support of school district; qualified and trained staff; transition from special classes to mainstream carefully executed.	Use of effective language development strategies to give students access to core curriculum and develop language skills; curricula and instructional strategies that engaged students in meaningful, in-depth learning.

TABLE 7-1 Continued

1 **Berman et al. (1992),** *Meeting the Challenge of Language Diversity*

2 School(s) and Level(s) Studied	3 Language-Minority Group(s)/ School Mix	4 Study Design[1]	5 Method for Selecting Target School(s)/Classrooms
Fifteen elementary schools	Mostly Latino, with schools ranging from 15-67% English-language learners; in 14 schools, Latinos 25-100% of total English-language learner population; in seven schools, unknown percentages of non-Spanish-speaking language minority students (e.g., Asian, Persian, Armenian)	Nominated schools	Elaborate nomination process to identify schools that had "well-implemented" programs for English-language learners— late-exit bilingual, early-exit bilingual, double immersion, sheltered English, or ESL pull-out

6	7	8
Student Outcome Data Reported	School-level Attributes	Classroom-level Attributes
No	Varied slightly by program model, but some combination of the following: schools developed models in response to demographic conditions and resources; effective implementation depended on shared vision and cultural validation, suitable staff, ongoing training, supportive resource allocation, and collaborative coordination and articulation.	Childrens' home language not used extensively in sheltered English or ESL pull-out programs. In most bilingual programs, native language used extensively in lower grades, with decreases as grade level increased; teachers relied on recitation script (teachers present information, ask questions, have students respond, and evaluate responses); most discourse initiated by teachers; teachers skilled at managing classrooms and involving students; ESL and sheltered English programs poorly coordinated with other classes; wide variation in validation of cultural heritage.

TABLE 7-1   Continued

1 **Gersten (1966),** *Literacy Instruction for Language-Minority Students:*
   The Transition Years

2 School(s) and Level(s) Studied	3 Language- Minority Group(s)/ School Mix	4 Study Design[1]	5 Method for Selecting Target School(s)/Classrooms
Twenty-four classrooms in three schools in grades 3-6; two additional classrooms in El Paso schools added in year 2; students making transition from Spanish-language to all-English classrooms	Language-minority populations were 60-85%; in two schools, preponderant native language was Spanish; in one, there was a wide range of southeast Asian languages and cultures	Nominated classrooms (for two El Paso classrooms), exploratory for others	Teachers in El Paso deemed exemplary by district's bilingual education department; other students selected because transitioning from native-language instruction to English (not necessarily in exemplary classroom)

1 **Lucas et al. (1990),** *Promoting the Success of Latino Language-Minority Students:*
   An Exploratory Study of Six High Schools

Six high schools	Schools ranging from 27.5 to 89.0% Latino (from Lucas and Henze, 1992)	Nominated schools	Nominations by knowledgeable sources + "some quantitative evidence" of school's success, e.g., drop-out rates, average daily attendance, language-minority students going on to post-secondary education, standard test scores; criteria not specified

6	7	8
Student Outcome Data Reported	School-level Attributes	Classroom-level Attributes
No	No	Monolingual English-speaking teachers work with language-minority students by selecting key vocabulary to enhance understanding, providing a range of activities using key vocabulary, providing feedback related to meaning, and actively encouraging students to practice expressing ideas and concepts in English; instruction builds on effective instruction for at-risk English speakers.
No	For language-minority students: native language and culture valued; high expectations; leaders make education a priority; staff development geared to needs; variety of courses/programs available; counseling program; parent involvement encouraged; school staff committed to empower through education.	No

TABLE 7-1   Continued

1 **Pease-Alvarez et al. (1991),** *Effective Instruction for Language-Minority Students: An Early Childhood Case Study*			
2	3	4	5
School(s) and Level(s) Studied	Language-Minority Group(s)/ School Mix	Study Design[1]	Method for Selecting Target School(s)/Classrooms
Two bilingual early childhood education teachers	70% of students Chicano/ Latino, mixed socioeconomic status	Nominated classrooms	Teachers have features deemed effective (bilingual, biliterate, mentor teachers, involved in ongoing staff development)

6	7	8
Student Outcome Data Reported	School-level Attributes	Classroom-level Attributes
No	No	Classroom practices reflect cultural and linguistic background of students; teachers take a holistic, experiential stance toward instruction, provide opportunities for active learning, encourage collaborative/cooperative interactions among students; classroom is a community with trusting, caring relationships.

TABLE 7-1   Continued

1   **Tikunoff et al. (1991),** *A Descriptive Study of Significant Features of Exemplary Special Alternative Instructional Programs*

2 School(s) and Level(s) Studied	3 Language-Minority Group(s)/ School Mix	4 Study Design[1]	5 Method for Selecting Target School(s)/Classrooms
Thirty-nine grade K-12 schools (exemplary Special Alternative Instructional Programs in nine different districts)	Spanish-speaking most prevalent; also Vietnamese, Laotian, Khmer, Chinese, Japanese, Korean, Filipino, Eastern European, Middle Eastern languages	Nominated schools	Programs nominated nationally; selected sites provided evidence (verified by researchers) of "exceptional student performance" for at least 2 consecutive years (some combination of English and academic gains, time to mainstream, grade promotions); "exceptional" not defined.

6	7	8
Student Outcome Data Reported	School-level Attributes	Classroom-level Attributes
No	Context-sensitive programs, many built on prior English-language learner programs; instructional leadership; intensive staff development; availability of expert teachers; reallocation of administrative resources; Special Alternative Instructional Program fully integrated into overall instructional program; housing arrangement for program based on configuration of English-language learners in district and program goals; excellent content area teachers recruited and trained in English-language development strategies.	Built on generic effective practice; facilitated English-language learners' comprehension of and participation in academic learning; structured activities that prompted English-language learners' active use of language and concept development; integrated English-language development with academic instruction.

TABLE 7-1   Continued

1 **Tikunoff (1983), *Significant Bilingual Instructional Feature Study***

2 School(s) and Level(s) Studied	3 Language-Minority Group(s)/ School Mix	4 Study Design[1]	5 Method for Selecting Target School(s)/Classrooms
Fifty-eight classrooms in grades K-12 at six diverse sites	Each of five sites represented a different ethnolinguistic group (Mexican, Puerto Rican, Cuban,Cantonese, and Navajo), and one site was multilingual	Nominated classrooms	Classrooms nominated as successful by local constituents (administrators, teachers, parents, former students); four target students selected in each classroom.

6	7	8
Student Outcome Data Reported	School-level Attributes	Classroom-level Attributes
No	No	Congruence of instructional intent, organization and delivery of instruction, and student consequences; use of active teaching behaviors; use of students' native language and English for instruction; integration of English-language development with basic skills instruction; use of information from English-language learners' home culture.

TABLE 7-1   Continued

1   **Cohen (1984),** *Talking and Working Together: Status, Interaction, and Learning*

2 School(s) and Level(s) Studied	3 Language-Minority Group(s)/ School Mix	4 Study Design[1]	5 Method for Selecting Target School(s)/Classrooms
Nine bilingual classrooms, grades 2-4; 304 students and nine teacher aide teams; schools located in five districts in San Jose, CA, area	Largely children of Hispanic background, with a small proportion of Caucasians, African Americans, and Asians	Prospective case study	None given

6	7	8
Student Outcome Data Reported	School-level Attributes	Classroom-level Attributes
Content-referenced test especially constructed to measure learning outcomes of the curriculum; standardized achievement test, Language Assessment Scales as a measure of English language proficiency; also measures of status (sociometric instrument consisting of eight questions); timed observations of task-related behavior. Findings indicate that children of higher social status are more likely to talk and work together than children of lower social status, holding constant a measure of knowledge relevant to the curriculum in question. The more children talked and worked together, the more they learned from the curriculum.	No	Intervention consisted of a curriculum entitled Finding Out/Descubrimiento, which features multiple learning centers, each with different materials and activities to teach math and science concepts. Over a period of 15 weeks, for 1 hour per day, children are required to complete each learning center and fill out the worksheet that accompanies the task for that learning center. Worksheets are printed in English, Spanish, and pictographs.

TABLE 7-1   Continued

1 **Gold and Tempes (1987),** *California Case Studies;* **secondary analysis by Samaniego and Eubank (1991)**

2 School(s) and Level(s) Studied	3 Language-Minority Group(s)/ School Mix	4 Study Design[1]	5 Method for Selecting Target School(s)/Classrooms
Four elementary schools and one "newcomer school" (grades K-6)	Heavy Latino populations (percentages not reported)	Prospective case study	California elementary schools serving large numbers of Spanish-speaking English-language learners and already operating some sort of bilingual program invited to participate; five selected from thirty responding.

1 **Hernandez (1991),** *Assisted Performance in Reading Comprehension Strategies with Non-English Proficient Students*

Spanish-speaking, non-English-proficient students attending summer school prior to grade 7	Latino	Prospective case study	No information available on school; students selected based on low scores on the Language Assessment Scales and teacher nomination as poor English readers; all literate in Spanish

6	7	8
Student Outcome Data Reported	School-level Attributes	Classroom-level Attributes
Academic achievement in English: state (California Assessment Project) and national (Comprehensive Test of Basic Skills).	"Contextual interaction model" used as basis for school-level change. (Samaniego and Eubank conclude that study results are mixed and depend upon students' language environment outside school.)	California State Dept. of Education's "theoretical framework" for the education of English-language learners, which includes development of proficiencies in both languages, comprehensible second-language instruction, and student status equalization.
Story comprehension in Spanish and strategy use in English. Results indicate students increased average Spanish comprehension scores over six sessions by 25%. Students used comprehension strategies when trying to read in English.	No	Six sessions of a schema-activated approach used to teach various comprehension strategies in which the reciprocal-teaching form of assisted performance was modified to include discussion.

TABLE 7-1   Continued

1 **Rosebery et al. (1992),** *Appropriating Scientific Discourse: Findings from Language Minority Classrooms*

2 School(s) and Level(s) Studied	3 Language-Minority Group(s)/ School Mix	4 Study Design[1]	5 Method for Selecting Target School(s)/Classrooms
Creole bilingual program (16 Haitian Creole grade 7 and 8 students); one high school basic skills class (4 Haitian Creole high school students)	Native speakers of Haitian Creole	Prospective case study	No information available

6	7	8
Student Outcome Data Reported	School-level Attributes	Classroom-level Attributes
Assessments of student content knowledge and use of knowledge to reason scientifically in terms of hypotheses and experiments (given in Haitian Creole). Significant increase found in students' conceptual knowledge and use of hypotheses, experiments, and explanations to organize their reasoning in the context of two think-aloud problems about aquatic ecosystems.	No	Students in both classes planned and carried out investigations into local aquatic ecosystems using a collaborative inquiry approach.

TABLE 7-1 Continued

1 **Short (1994),** *Expanding Middle School Horizons: Integrating Language, Culture, and Social Studies*

2 School(s) and Level(s) Studied	3 Language-Minority Group(s)/ School Mix	4 Study Design[1]	5 Method for Selecting Target School(s)/Classrooms
Sheltered and mainstream middle school (grades 6-9) social studies classes	English-language learners from a variety of backgrounds	Prospective case study	Observations of teachers trained to teach integrated English and content curriculum (social studies) to English-language learners during a training institute conducted by the author; use of social studies materials designed for English-language learners (language development an integral component of lesson, inclusion of information about cultural diversity and balanced viewpoints, combination of adapted and authentic reading passages).

6	7	8
Student Outcome Data Reported	School-level Attributes	Classroom-level Attributes
No	No	Teachers carefully prepared unit lessons to accommodate the particular needs of their students: vocabulary building through explicit instruction, demonstrations, and illustrations, use of examples from students' personal experiences and current events to teach concepts; modeling of assignment to bolster comprehension; use of English-speaking students as tutors and partners; engagement in critical thinking activities; extensive use of graphic organizers to assist learning; hands-on and cooperative learning activities to provide frequent opportunities to engage in communicative skills practice; teaching and reinforcement of use of signal words that cue relationships; concentration on traditional social studies skills.

TABLE 7-1   Continued

1 **Chamot et al. (1992),** *Learning and Problem Solving Strategies of ESL Students*

2 School(s) and Level(s) Studied	3 Language-Minority Group(s)/ School Mix	4 Study Design[1]	5 Method for Selecting Target School(s)/Classrooms
Elementary and secondary	32 students with low or intermediate English proficiency in elementary, middle, and high school ESL-math classrooms; 25 students Hispanic, 7 from a variety of other language backgrounds	Quasi-experimental study in which students of teachers deemed high implementers of the Cognitive Academic Learning Approach (CALLA) were compared with students deemed low implementers based on predetermined set of criteria	No information available

6	7	8
Student Outcome Data Reported	School-level Attributes	Classroom-level Attributes
Think-aloud interview used to assess correct answer on math word problem, number and sequence of problem-solving steps, metacognitive strategies. Students in high CALLA-implementation classrooms correctly solved the math problem significantly more often than those in low-implementation classrooms; they also correctly mentioned the sequence of problem steps and mentioned metacognitive strategies significantly more often.	No	Staff development activities for CALLA math project emphasize importance of providing direct instruction in learning strategies and teaching problem-solving procedures. Learning strategies emphasized were metacognitive strategies such as planning and self-evaluation, cognitive strategies such as elaboration of prior knowledge, and social/affective strategies such as cooperation. Specific techniques for teaching problem solving included modeling and explaining a problem-solving procedure, asking students to work in cooperative groups to implement procedures, and explaining orally or in writing how a solution was achieved.

TABLE 7-1   Continued

1 **Dianda and Flaherty (1994),** *Effects of Success for All on the Reading Achievement of First Graders in California Bilingual Programs*

2 School(s) and Level(s) Studied	3 Language-Minority Group(s)/ School Mix	4 Study Design[1]	5 Method for Selecting Target School(s)/Classrooms
Three elementary schools (grade l)	24-65% Latino; 3-21% Asian; 0-12% African American; 20-55% English-language learners	Quasi-experimental study	Information not available

1 **Goldenberg and Sullivan (1994),** *Making Change Happen in a Language-Minority School: A Search for Coherence*

| One elementary school | 95% Latino, of whom 85% were English-language learners, 75% Mexican origin, 24% Central American; most students U.S. born | Quasi-experimental study | School/university collaboration; authors had worked together for several years previously before starting school-improvement project. |

6	7	8
Student Outcome Data Reported	School-level Attributes	Classroom-level Attributes
Students assessed in reading in English or Spanish, depending on language of instruction (Woodcock Language Proficiency Battery; Bateria de Woodcock). Success for All students performed significantly better than controls on all post-tests.	Same as Slavin and Yampolsky (1992) and Slavin and Madden (1994); implemented in two bilingual settings and one sheltered setting.	Same as Success for All model (Slavin and Yampolsky, 1992; Slavin and Madden, 1994).
Students assessed in reading and writing achievement in English (California Assessment Program/California Learning Assessment System) and reading achievement in Spanish (Spanish Assessment of Basic Education). Student achievement now exceeds that in other school districts.	School change model within a bilingual education context: school-wide academic goals and expectations set by faculty; use of indicators of student achievement; assistance (including training) by capable others; leadership that supports and pressures.	Staff development in various subject areas; grade-level meetings to help teachers deal with changes necessary for student improvement; use of bilingual aide for homework liaison.

TABLE 7-1   Continued

1 **Goldenberg and Gallimore (1991),** *Local Knowledge, Research Knowledge, and Educational Change: A Case Study of First-Grade Spanish Reading Improvement*

2 School(s) and Level(s) Studied	3 Language-Minority Group(s)/ School Mix	4 Study Design[1]	5 Method for Selecting Target School(s)/Classrooms
One elementary school, grades K-1	90% Latino	Quasi-experimental study	School where first author did thesis research and taught first grade

1 **Henderson and Landesman (1992),** *Mathematics and Middle School Students of Mexican Descent: The Effects of Thematically Integrated Instruction*

| 102 grade 7 students in a middle school, divided into treatment and control groups | 90% Hispanic (60% of whom were English-language learners) | Quasi-experimental study | No information available |

6	7	8
Student Outcome Data Reported	School-level Attributes	Classroom-level Attributes
Achievement data come from the Comprehensive Test of Basic Skills (CTBS), the Spanish Assessment of Basic Education, and the California Assessment Project. Level of student achievement rose relative to local and national norms, particularly among lowest-achieving students; "treatment" students outperformed students in other schools in Spanish reading achievement on the CTBS.	In primary-language program: home/parent involvement.	Increased emphasis on literacy in kindergarten; "balance" between phonics and meaning in first grade reading; improved pacing of instruction; children provided with literacy opportunities in kindergarten; balance between phonics and meaning in grade 1 reading; improved pacing of instruction; books, reading materials, and literacy-related assignments sent home to reinforce classwork.
Parallel forms (English and Spanish) of an assessment of math computation, concepts, and applications; attitudinal measure; assessment of motivational self-perception. Findings indicate nonsignificant effects for computation, but significant effects for concepts and applications; no differences on self-perception and attitudinal subscales.	No	Treatment consisted of heterogeneous classes—one bilingual, one English only—that stayed together most of the day using thematic instruction. Control group participated in nonintegrated content classes.

TABLE 7-1   Continued

1 **Muniz-Swicegood (1994),** *The Effects of Metacognitive Reading Strategy Training on the Reading Performance and Student Reading Analysis Strategies of Third Grade Bilingual Students*

2 School(s) and Level(s) Studied	3 Language-Minority Group(s)/ School Mix	4 Study Design[1]	5 Method for Selecting Target School(s)/Classrooms
95 grade 3 bilingual students aged 8-9, divided into treatment and control groups	Spanish dominant, with English as the second language	Quasi-experimental study	No information available

1 **Saunders et al. (1996),** *Making the Transition to English Literacy Successful: Effective Strategies for Studying Literature with Transition Students*

| 18 grade 5 project students and 18 matched comparison students | Latino elementary schools in Los Angeles where on average 84% of the students are English-language learners upon enrollment | Quasi-experimental study; two groups matched on grade 1 standardized measures of Spanish reading and language achievement; control students selected from comparable, neighboring schools in the district; all children in Spanish bilingual programs following district guidelines | Part of authors' research and development effort |

6	7	8
Student Outcome Data Reported	School-level Attributes	Classroom-level Attributes
No significant group differences on La Prueba Spanish reading test, Iowa Test of Basic Skills (ITBS) English reading test; Burke Reading Inventories (qualitative measures) yielded more positive results; more improvements in types and frequency of metacognitive strategy use by experimental than control group.	No	Metacognitive reading strategy training in Spanish for treatment group for 90 minutes a day for 6 weeks; control group instructed in grade 3 basal readers.
Project students made significantly higher gains in Spanish reading and language and in English reading and language arts on standardized achievement tests; scored significantly higher than nonproject students on project-developed performance-based measures of English reading and writing.	No	Four strategies used with the study of literature: building on students' background knowledge, drawing on students' personal experiences, assisting students in rereading pivotal portions of the text, and promoting extended discourse through writing and discussion.

TABLE 7-1   Continued

1 **Slavin and Madden (1994),** *Lee Conmigo: Effects of Success for All in Bilingual First Grades, and (1995) Effect of Success for All on the Achievement of English Language Learners*

2 School(s) and Level(s) Studied	3 Language- Minority Group(s)/ School Mix	4 Study Design[1]	5 Method for Selecting Target School(s)/Classrooms
One elementary school, grades I and 2	78% Latino (mostly Puerto Rican); 22% African American; approximately half of first graders in bilingual program	Quasi-experimental study	Information not available; presumably same as Slavin and Yampolsky (1992)

1 **Slavin and Yampolsky (1992),** *Success For All*

One elementary school, grades K-5	62% Asian, mostly Cambodian; rest Caucasian and African American	Quasi-experimental study	School/university collaboration; Johns Hopkins researchers worked with school staff to implement Success for All in a language-minority school

6	7	8
Student Outcome Data Reported	School-level Attributes	Classroom-level Attributes
Reading and comprehension in Spanish. Success for All students scored substantially higher than controls on all measures (Spanish Woodcock).	Same as Slavin and Yampolsky (1992), but implemented in a bilingual, rather than ESL, context.	Same as Success for All (Slavin and Yampolsky, 1992) model.
For kindergarten students, measures included four scales assessing language development and pre-reading skills; for grades 1-3, the Woodcock Language Proficiency Battery, the Durrell Oral Reading Scale, and the IDEA Proficiency Test. Asian Success for All students outperformed control students at all grade levels in reading and in grades K-2 in English proficiency. For non-Asian students, results were positive for grades 1 and 2.	Success for All model within an "ESL approach": full-time program facilitator; ongoing staff develop-ment; advisory committee family support team that provides parenting education, helps parents support their childrens' education and solve problems that hinder student achievement.	School-wide reading program: reading tutors, direct instruction in skills beginning in K, literature, grouping by reading level, cooperative learning, 8-week assessments. Peer tutoring, use of story telling and retelling materials; separate ESL instruction focused on supporting regular reading program.

TABLE 7-1   Continued

1 **Escamilla (1994),** *Descubriendo La Lectura: An Early Intervention Literacy Program in Spanish*

2 School(s) and Level(s) Studied	3 Language-Minority Group(s)/ School Mix	4 Study Design[1]	5 Method for Selecting Target School(s)/Classrooms
180 grade 1 students from six elementary schools in an urban southern Arizona school district	Spanish-dominant students	Quasi-experimental study; 23 treatment group students from the four schools with Descubriendo La Lectura (DLL) who were in the bottom 20% of grade 1 students from six elementary grades based on Spanish Observation Survey and teacher ratings; 23 control group students selected from schools without DLL who were in the bottom 20% on similar criteria; all other students assigned to a comparison group	

6	7	8
Student Outcome Data Reported	School-level Attributes	Classroom-level Attributes
Assessments used include the Spanish Observation Survey (six observational tasks that provide a profile of a student's reading repertoire) and Aprenda Spanish Achievement Test (standardized assessment of reading achievement). Statistically significant differences found in favor of treatment group (compared with both control and comparison group students) on all measures of Spanish Observation Survey. On standardized reading test, only treatment and control groups made gains in percentile scores, but 13 points for treatment and 2 for control. Comparison group declined by 4 percentile points.		Supplemental pull-out program consisting of individualized instruction from 12 to 16 weeks; consists of reading familiar as well as new stories (with teacher recording and analyzing students' reading), working with letters, writing a message or story.

TABLE 7-1   Continued

1 **Calderon et al. (1996), *Effects of Bilingual Cooperative Integrated Reading and Composition on Students Transitioning from Spanish to English Reading***

2 School(s) and Level(s) Studied	3 Language-Minority Group(s)/ School Mix	4 Study Design[1]	5 Method for Selecting Target School(s)/Classrooms
Bilingual programs in three experimental and four comparison schools in Ysleta Independent School District, a large district within El Paso, Texas	Schools almost entirely Hispanic, with high percentages of English-language learners	Quasi-experimental study: teachers in comparison group used traditional reading methods that emphasized round-robin reading and independent workbook activities and received training in cooperative learning, but not Cooperative Integrated Reading and Composition (CIRC) or BCIRC (a bilingual adaptation of CIRC); comparison group students received 1-1/2 hrs. of reading/language instruction daily, plus 30 min. of ESL; teachers in treatment group used BCIRC.	Information not available

6	7	8
Student Outcome Data Reported	School-level Attributes	Classroom-level Attributes
The more years students were in the program, the better their English reading performance. Students who experienced a full 2 years of BCIRC in grades 2 and 3 scored almost a full standard deviation higher than comparison students in reading. Third graders who had been in BCIRC were significantly more likely than comparison group students to meet criteria for exit from bilingual education in reading and language. Second graders taught primarily in Spanish also scored significantly better than comparison students on a Spanish writing scale and marginally better on a Spanish reading scale ($p<.06$).	No	BCIRC consists of three principal elements: direct instruction in reading comprehension, worksheets (which include comprehension questions, prediction guidelines, new vocabulary to be learned, story retell, and story-related writing suggestions), and integrated language arts and writing. In all activities, students work in heterogeneous learning teams of four. All activities follow a series of steps that involve teacher presentation, team practice, independent practice, peer preassessment, additional practice, and testing. Also included is extensive teacher development whereby teachers become researchers/collaborators in all phases.

TABLE 7-1   Continued

1 **Tharp (1982),** *The Effective Instruction of Comprehension: Results and Description of the Kamehameha Early Education Program*

2 School(s) and Level(s) Studied	3 Language-Minority Group(s)/ School Mix	4 Study Design[1]	5 Method for Selecting Target School(s)/Classrooms
One laboratory school and two export schools (grades 1-3)	Hawaiian or part-Hawaiian; Hawaiian Creole English ("pidgin") speakers	Experiment (students randomly assigned to treatment within school)	Privately funded laboratory school; unspecified how public schools selected

1 **Fisher et al. (1983),** *Verification of Bilingual Instructional Features*

| Eighty-nine classrooms at eight sites | Filipino, Vietnamese, and other Hispanic groups added to original Significant Bilingual Instructional Features (SBIF) study | Replicability, stability, utility, and compatibility of features identified in Part I of SBIF | Replication study included some of same classrooms nominated as successful, as well as other, non-nominated classrooms; stability study examined a subset of nominated teachers and students a second year in different settings |

6	7	8
Student Outcome Data Reported	School-level Attributes	Classroom-level Attributes
Reading achievement in English (Gates-MacCintie Reading Test).	No	Reading program organized to emphasize direct instruction of comprehension (two-thirds allocated time); small group classroom organization permitted culturally accommodated instruction; monitoring and feedback of student achievement; some degree of individualization; quality control—monitoring of "instructional inputs."
No	No	Five features of effective instruction replicated only to varying degrees at two new sites and in non-nominated classrooms; teachers and students behaved differently during the second year in different contexts.

TABLE 7-1   Continued

1 **Minicucci and Olsen (1992)**, *An Exploratory Study of Secondary LEP Programs*

2	3	4	5
School(s) and Level(s) Studied	Language-Minority Group(s)/ School Mix	Study Design[1]	Method for Selecting Target School(s)/Classrooms
Twenty-seven secondary schools (intermediate and high school); site visits to five schools (two intermediate, three high school)	Spanish most prevalent; also Asian; visited schools approximately 50% English-language learners	Not applicable— exploratory only	Unknown; regionally and demographically representative schools selected

[1]Study design is "effective schools," "nominated schools," "prospective case study," or "quasi-experimental." An effective schools design is one in which one or more effective schools are selected on the basis of test data showing that students at the school(s) achieve either at grade level or at least at higher levels than the school's sociodemographic characteristics would predict. A nominated schools design is one in which schools are chosen on the basis of nominations from professionals who consider the school "good," "effective," "exemplary," etc. In both effective schools and nominated schools designs, researchers work essentially retrospectively, attempting to determine features of the school's organization or operation that help explain its effectiveness. Neither design directly or empirically addresses the issue of how a school came to be effective, except for retrospective accounts or inferences. A prospective case study begins with a school that is no better or perhaps even worse (in terms of effectiveness) than other comparable schools. It then examines changes in the

6	7	8
Student Outcome Data Reported	School-level Attributes	Classroom-level Attributes
No	Exploratory only; study designed to describe programs and identify issues. However, English-language learner programming dependent upon site leadership; availability of trained staff; and staff willingness, organization, and departmentalization.	No

school over time and tries to explain how the school(s) went from less to more effective and what the effects of these changes have been. There is no direct, concurrent comparison with other comparable schools. A quasi-experimental study is also a prospective study and begins with a school (or schools) that is no more effective and perhaps less effective than other comparable schools. However, it examines the effects of specific interventions on student outcomes and, most critically, concurrently in comparison with student outcomes at a comparable school (or groups of schools) not participating in the intervention. The quasi-experimental design offers the strongest basis for making causal inferences about school processes, dynamics, and structures on the one hand and improvements in student outcomes on the other.

REFERENCES

Anderson, R., R. St. Pierre, E. Proper, and L. Stebbins
  1978   Pardon us, but what was the question again? A response to the critique of the follow-
          through evaluation. *Harvard Educational Review* 48:161-170.
Berman, P., and M.W. McLaughlin
  1978   *Federal Programs Supporting Educational Change, Vol. VII: Implementing and Sustain-
          ing Innovations.* R-1589/8-HEW. Santa Monica, CA: Rand.
Berman, P., J. Chambers, P. Gandara, B. McLaughlin, C. Minicucci, B. Nelson, L. Olsen, and T.
Parrish
  1992   *Meeting the challenge of language diversity: An evaluation of programs for pupils with
          limited proficiency in English.* Vol. 1 [R-119/1: Executive Summary; Vol. 2 [R-119/2]:
          Findings and Conclusions; Vol. 3 [R-119/3]: Case Study Appendix. Berkeley, CA: BW
          Associates.
Berman, P., B. McLaughlin, B. McLeod, C. Minicucci, B. Nelson, and K. Woodworth
  1995   School Reform and Student Diversity: Case Studies of Exemplary Practices for LEP
          Students (Draft Report). National Center for Research on Cultural Diversity and Second
          Language Learning and BW Associates. Berkeley, CA.
Bliss, J., W. Firestone, and C. Richards, eds.
  1991   *Rethinking Effective Schools: Research and Practice.* Englewood Cliffs, NJ: Prentice
          Hall.
Calderon, M., R. Hertz-Lazarowitz, and R. Slavin
  1996   Effects of Bilingual Cooperative Integrated Reading and Composition on Students
          Transitioning from Spanish to English Reading. Unpublished paper for the Office of
          Educational Research and Improvement, U.S. Department of Education, Washington,
          DC.
Carter, T., and M. Chatfield
  1986   Effective bilingual schools: Implications for policy and practice. *American Journal of
          Education* 95:200-232.
Chamot, A.U., M. Dale, J.M. O'Malley, and G. Spanos.
  1992   Learning and problem solving strategies of ESL students. *Bilingual Research Journal*
          16(3-4):1-33.
Chang, H.
  1990   *Newcomer Programs: Innovative Efforts to Meet the Educational Challenges of Immi-
          grant Students.* San Francisco, CA: California Tomorrow.
Chasin, G., and H. Levin
  1995   Thomas Edison accelerated elementary school. In J. Oakes and K. H. Quartz, eds.,
          Creating New Educational Communities. 94th Yearbook of the National Society for the
          Study of Education, Part 1. Chicago, IL: University of Chicago Press.
Cohen, E.
  1984   Talking and working together: Status, interaction, and learning. Pp. 171-187, Chapter 10
          in P.L. Peterson et al., eds., *The Social Context of Instruction: Group Organization and
          Group Processes.* Orlando, FL: Academic Press.
Coleman, J., E.Q. Campbell, C.J. Hobson, J. McPartland, A.M. Mood, F.D. Weinfeld, and R.L. York
  1966   *Equality of Educational Opportunity.* Office of Education, U.S. Department of Health,
          Education, and Welfare. Washington, DC: U.S. Government Printing Office.
Comer, J.
  1980   *School Power: Implications of an Intervention Project.* New York: Free Press.
Cook, T.D., and D.T. Campbell
  1979   *Quasi-experimentation.* Chicago, IL: Rand McNally.

Crawford, J.
   1995   *Bilingual Education: History Politics Theory and Practice.* Los Angeles: Bilingual Educational Services.
Dianda, M., and J. Flaherty
   1995   *Effects of Success for All on the Reading Achievement of First Graders in California Bilingual Programs.* Los Alamitos, CA: The Southwest Regional Educational Laboratory.
Edelsky, C., K. Draper, and K. Smith
   1983   Hookin' 'em in at the start of school in a 'whole language' classroom. *Anthropology & Education Quarterly* 14:257-281.
Edmonds, R.
   1979   Effective schools for the urban poor. *Educational Leadership* 37(1):15-24.
Education Week
   1995   Next generation of effective schools looks to districts for lasting change. *Education Week* (April 12):8-9.
Epstein, J.
   1992   School and family partnerships. Pp. 1139-1152 in M. Alkin, ed., *Encyclopedia of Educational Research.* 6th ed. New York: MacMillan.
Escamilla, K.
   1994   Descubriendo la lectura: An early intervention literacy program in Spanish. *Literacy, Teaching and Learning* 1(1):57-70.
Fisher, C.W., L.F. Guthrie, and E.B. Mandinach
   1983   *Verification of Bilingual Instructional Features.* San Francisco, CA: Far West Laboratory for Educational Research and Development.
Friedlander, M.
   1991   *The Newcomer Program: Helping Immigrant Students Succeed in U.S. Schools.* Program information guide series, No. 8. Washington, DC: National Clearinghouse for Bilingual Education.
Garcia, E.E.
   1990a   Instructional discourse in 'effective' Hispanic classrooms. Pp. 104-117 in Rodolfo Jacobson and Christian Faltis, eds., *Language Distribution Issues in Bilingual Schooling.* Bristol, PA: Multilingual Matters.
   1990b   Education of Linguistically and Culturally Diverse Students: Effective Instructional Practices. The National Center for Research on Cultural Diversity and Second Language Learning. Educational Practice Report, No. 1. Center for Applied Linguistics, Washington, D.C.
Gersten, Russell
   1996   Literacy instruction for language-minority students: The transition years. *The Elementary School Journal* 96(3):228-244.
Gold, N., and F. Tempes
   1987   A State Agency Partnership with Schools to Improve Bilingual Education. Paper presented at the annual meeting of the American Educational Research Association, Washington, DC. California State Department of Education.
Goldenberg, C.
   1992   Instructional Conversations and Their Classroom Application. The National Center for Research on Cultural Diversity and Second Language Learning. Educational Practice Report, No. 2. Center for Applied Linguistics, Washington, D.C.
   1993   The home-school connection in bilingual education. Pp. 225-250 in B. Arias and U. Casanova, eds., *Ninety-second Yearbook of the National Society for the Study of Education. Bilingual education: Politics, Research, and Practice.* Chicago, IL: University of Chicago Press.

Goldenberg, C., and R. Gallimore
    1991   Local knowledge, research knowledge, and educational change: A case study of first-grade Spanish reading improvement. *Educational Researcher* 20(8):2-14.
Goldenberg, C., and J. Sullivan
    1994   *Making Change Happen in a Language-minority School: A Search for Coherence.* EPR #13. Washington, DC: Center for Applied Linguistics.
Henderson, R.W., and E.M. Landesman
    1992   *Mathematics and Middle School Students of Mexican Descent: The Effects of Thematically Integrated Instruction.* Research Report: 5. National Center for Research on Cultural Diversity and Second Language Learning, Santa Cruz: University of California.
Hernandez, J.S.
    1991   Assisted performance in reading comprehension strategies with non-English proficient students. *The Journal of Educational Issues of Language Minority Students* 8:91-112.
Jencks, C., M. Smith, H. Acland, M.J. Bane, D. Cohen, H. Gintis, B. Heyns, and S. Michelson
    1972   *Inequality: A Reassessment of the Effect of Family and Schooling in America.* New York: Harper.
Jussim, L.
    1986   Self-fulfilling prophecies: A theoretical and integrative review. *Psychological Review* 93:429-445.
Krashen, S., and D. Biber
    1988   *On Course: Bilingual Education's Success in California.* Sacramento, CA: California Association for Bilingual Education.
Lucas, T., and A. Katz
    1994   Reframing the debate: The roles of native languages in English-only programs for language minority students. *TESOL Quarterly* 28(3):537-561.
Lucas, T., R. Henze, and R. Donato
    1990   Promoting the success of Latino language-minority students: An exploratory study of six high schools. *Harvard Educational Review* 60:315-340.
Mace-Matluck, B. J., R. Alexander-Kasparik, and R. Queen
    in   *Toward an Effective Educational Delivery System for Low-schooled Immigrant Adoles-*
    press   *cents.* Washington, DC: Center for Applied Linguistics.
Mace-Matluck, B.J., W.A. Hoover, and R.C. Calfee
    1989   Teaching reading to bilingual children: A longitudinal study of teaching and learning in the early grades. *NABE Journal* 13:3.
McDonnell, L., and P. Hill
    1993   *Newcomers in American Schools: Meeting the Educational Needs of Immigrant Youth.* Santa Monica, CA: Rand.
Minicucci, C., and L. Olsen
    1992   An exploratory study of secondary LEP programs. R-119/5; Vol. V of *Meeting the Challenge of Language Diversity: An Evaluation of Programs for Pupils with Limited Proficiency in English.* Berkeley, CA: BW Associates.
Moll, Luis C.
    1988   Some key issues in teaching Latino students. *Language Arts* 65(5):465-472.
Moll, L.C., C. Amanti, D. Neff, and N. Gonzalez
    1992   Funds of knowledge for teaching: Using a qualitative approach to connect homes and classrooms. *Theory into Practice* 31(2):132-141.
Moll, L., E. Diaz, E. Estrada, and L. Lopes
    1981   *The Construction of Learning Environments in Two Languages.* San Diego, CA: Laboratory of Comparative Human Cognition.

Muniz-Swicegood, M.
    1994   The effects of metacognitive reading strategy training on the reading performance and student reading analysis strategies of third-grade bilingual students. *Bilingual Research Journal* 18(1&2):83-97.
Olsen, L., and C. Dowell
    1989   *Bridges: Promising Programs for the Education of Immigrant Children.* San Francisco, CA: California Tomorrow.
Pease-Alvarez, L., E. E. Garcia, and P. Espinosa
    1991   Effective instruction for language-minority students: An early childhood case study. *Early Childhood Research Quarterly* 6:347-361.
Purkey, S., and M. Smith
    1983   Research on effective schools: A review. *Elementary School Journal* 83:427-452.
Romo, H.
    1993   *Mexican Immigrants in High Schools: Meeting Their Needs.* ERIC Digest. Charleston, WV: ERIC Clearinghouse on Rural Education and Small Schools.
Rosebery, A. S., B. Warren, and F. R. Conant
    1992   Appropriating scientific discourse: Findings from language minority classrooms. *The Journal of the Learning Sciences* 2(1):61-94.
Rosenshine, B., and R. Stevens
    1986   Teaching Functions. Pp. 376-391 in M. Wittrock. ed., *Handbook of Research on Teaching.* 3rd ed. New York: Macmillan.
Rueda, R., C. Goldenberg, and P. Gallimore
    1992   *Rating Instructional Conversations: A Guide.* Educational Practice Report, No 4. Santa Cruz, CA: National Center for Research on Cultural Diversity and Second Language Acquisition.
Rutter, M., B. Maughan, P. Mortimore, and J. Ouston
    1979   *Fifteen Thousand Hours: Secondary Schools and Their Effects on Children.* Cambridge, MA: Harvard University Press.
Samaniego, F., and L. Eubank
    1991   *A Statistical Analysis of California's Case Study Project in Bilingual Education* (TR#208). Davis, CA: Intercollegiate Division of Statistics, University of California, Davis.
Saunders, W., and C. Goldenberg
    in   Can you engage students in high-level talk about text and support literal comprehension
    press   too? The effects of instructional conversation on transition students' concepts of friendship and story comprehension. In R. Horowitz, ed., *Talk About Text: Developing Understanding of the World Through Talk and Text.* Newark, DE: International Reading Association.
Saunders, W., G. O'Brien, D. Lennon, and J. McLean
    1996   Making the transition to English literacy successful: Effective strategies for studying literature with transition students. In R. Gersten and R. Jimenez, eds, *Effective Strategies for Teaching Language Minority Students.* Monterey, CA: Brooks Cole.
Saville-Troike, M.
    1991   *Teaching and Testing for Academic Achievement: The Role of Language Development.* Focus, Occasional Papers in Bilingual Education, No. 4. Washington, DC: National Clearinghouse for Bilingual Education.
Scott, R., and H. Walberg
    1979   Schools alone are insufficient: A response to Edmonds. *Educational Leadership* 37(1):24-27.
Short, D.J.
    1994   Expanding middle school horizons: Integrating language, culture, and social studies. *TESOL Quarterly* 28(3):581-608.

Slavin, R., and N. Madden
    1994   Lee Conmigo: Effects of Success for All in Bilingual First Grades. Paper presented at the annual meeting of the American Educational Research Association, New Orleans, April. Center for Children Placed at Risk of School Failure, Johns Hopkins University, Baltimore, Maryland.
    1995   Effects of Success for All on the Achievement of English Language Learners. Paper presented at the annual meeting of the American Educational Research Association, San Francisco, April. Center for Children Placed at Risk of School Failure, Johns Hopkins University, Baltimore, Maryland.
Slavin, R., and R. Yampolsky
    1992   *Success for All. Effects on Students with Limited English Proficiency: A Three-year Evaluation.* Report No. 29. Baltimore, MD: Center for Research on Effective Schooling for Disadvantaged Students, The Johns Hopkins University.
Slavin, R., N. Madden, L. Dolan, and B. Wasik
    1995   Success for All: A Summary of the Research. Paper presented at the annual meeting of the American Educational Research Association, San Francisco, April. Center for Children Placed at Risk of School Failure, Johns Hopkins University, Baltimore, Maryland.
Slavin, R., N. Madden, L. Dolan, and B. Wasik
    in   *Every Child, Every School: Success for All.* Thousand Oaks, CA: Corwin Press.
    press
Stedman, L.
    1985   A new look at the effective schools literature. *Urban Education* 20:295-326.
    1987   It's time we changed the effective schools formula. *Phi Delta Kappan* 69: 215-224.
Sternberg, R.J.
    1986   Cognition and instruction: Why the marriage sometimes ends in divorce. Pp 375-382 in R.F. Dillon and R.J. Sternberg, eds., *Cognition and Instruction.* Orlando, FL: Academic Press.
Stevenson, D., and D. Baker
    1987   The family-school relation and the child's school performance. *Child Development* 58:1348-1357.
Tharp, R.
    1989   Psychocultural variables and constants: Effects on teaching and learning in schools. *American Psychologist* 44:349-359.
Tharp, R., and R. Gallimore
    1991   *The Instructional Conversation: Teaching and Learning in Social Activity.* The National Center for Research on Cultural Diversity and Second Language Learning. Research Report No. 2. Washington, DC: The Center for Applied Linguistics.
Tharp, R.G.
    1982   The effective instruction of comprehension: Results and description of the Kamehameha Early Education Program. *Reading Research Quarterly* 17(4):503-527.
Tikunoff, W.J.
    1983   *An Emerging Description of Successful Bilingual Instruction: Executive Summary of Part I of the SBIF Study.* San Francisco, CA: Far West Laboratory for Educational Research and Development.
Tikunoff, W.J., B.A. Ward, L.D. van Broekhuizen, M. Romero, L.V. Castaneda, T. Lucas, and A. Katz
    1991   *A Descriptive Study of Significant Features of Exemplary Special Alternative Instructional Programs.* Final Report and Vol. 2: Report for Practitioners. Los Alamitos, CA: The Southwest Regional Educational Laboratory.
Trubowitz, S., J. Duncan, P. Longo, and S. Sarason
    1984   *When a College Works With a Public School: A Case Study of School-College Collaboration.* Boston: Institute for Responsive Education.

Weber, G.
   1971   *Inner-City Children Can be Taught to Read: Four Successful Schools.* Washington, DC: Council for Basic Education.
Wilson, C.L., P.M. Shields, and C. Marder
   1994   *The Title VII Academic Excellence Program: Disseminating Effective Programs and Practices in Bilingual Education.* Menlo Park, CA: SRI International.
Wong Fillmore, L., P. Ammon, B. McLaughlin, and M. Ammon
   1985   *Learning English Through Bilingual Instruction.* Final Report. Berkeley: University of California.

PREPARATION AND DEVELOPMENT OF TEACHERS SERVING ENGLISH-LANGUAGE LEARNERS: SUMMARY OF THE STATE OF KNOWLEDGE

The literature on preparation and development of teachers of English-language learners offers the following key findings:

• In the view of many individuals and organizations, the nation does not have enough teachers with the skills needed to serve a linguistically diverse population.

• Most teacher preparation and professional development programs are based on a growing body of knowledge regarding attributes of effective teaching for English-language learners. However, more empirical research and evidence on the effectiveness of these programs are needed.

• Over the years, several organizations have developed guidelines and certification standards for teachers who work in English as a second language (ESL) and bilingual programs. These standards build on basic program standards and also include proficiency in written and oral forms of two languages, as well as skills in developing students' language abilities.

• Recently, programs for teacher preparation and development have expanded their focus beyond skills-based, competency-driven curriculum to incorporate innovative methods for enhancing teacher learning. These efforts stress an inquiry-based approach to teacher learning whereby teacher reflection on practice is emphasized, along with collaboration with colleagues in "learning communities" and methods that involve ongoing teacher learning.

• Current trends also include requiring that those entering or already in the profession—including mainstream, bilingual, and ESL teachers—be prepared to serve English-language learners and targeting minority populations to increase the pool of bilingual teachers.

• Recent and ongoing innovative programs for professional development of teachers of English-language learners include the following:

—The Cooperative Learning in Bilingual Settings program of the Johns Hopkins University Center for Research in Educating Students Placed at Risk (CRESPAR)
—The Latino Teacher Project of the University of Southern California
—The English for Speakers of Other Languages Inservice Project of Dade County Public Schools in Miami, Florida
— The California Cross-cultural, Language, and Academic Development Program

8

Preparation and Development of Teachers Serving English-Language Learners

This chapter reviews the current knowledge base regarding the preparation and professional development of teachers of English-language learners.

STATE OF KNOWLEDGE

We begin our review of the state of knowledge in this area with a brief overview of studies investigating the preparation and development of teachers serving English-language learners. We then summarize the evolution of programs designed to develop teachers of these students. This is followed by a description of four innovative programs for professional development of teachers of English-language learners, highlighting recent trends in teacher preparation and development and some emerging efforts to examine the effects on teacher participants. These initiatives exemplify the current state of professional development in this field and suggest research directions outlined at the end of the chapter.

Overview

In the view of many individuals and organizations, the nation does not have enough teachers with the skills needed to serve a linguistically diverse student population. Although estimates vary on the demand and supply of teachers for English-language learners, experts state that a severe shortage exists and that institutions are not graduating bilingual and English as a second language (ESL) teachers quickly enough to overcome this shortage (Boe, 1990). Based on a review of teacher supply and demand studies, Macias (1989, cited in Leighton et al., 1993) estimates a need for approximately 170,000 additional teachers to serve English-language learners by the year 2000. In its 1994 report on limited English proficiency, the General Accounting Office (U.S. GAO, 1994) cites the National Education Association's estimate that 175,000 additional bilingual teachers are needed. The National Center for Education Statistics (1993:125) Schools and Staffing Survey reveals that during the 1990-91 school year, 37 percent of school administrators who had vacancies in ESL or bilingual education found them "very difficult or impossible to fill." A 1990 California State Department of Education report cited the need for approximately 20,000 ESL and bilingual teachers; the state also reported that more than half of its existing bilingual staff was teaching under waivers (National Forum, 1990). A national survey of teacher placement officers ranked bilingual education as the field with the highest degree of teacher shortage and with the highest demand (Association for School, College, and University Staffing, 1990, cited in Milk et al., 1992).

There are large and increasing numbers of English-language learners and few teachers specially trained to work with them. A widely held assumption is that minority individuals may be especially effective as teachers for these students given similarities in linguistic and cultural background. However, supply and demand studies reveal that as "the student population becomes more culturally heterogeneous, the teaching force is expected to become increasingly homogeneous" (Villegas et al., 1995:6). The American Association of Colleges for Teacher Education 1994 report on the multicultural status of today's teaching workforce, *Teacher Education Pipeline III* (AACTE, 1994), states that while teacher education enrollment has increased by approximately 10 percent since 1989, the racial/ethnic balance of the workforce has not been significantly affected. Only about 14 percent of current public and private school teachers are members of a non-Caucasian racial/ethnic group. Conversely, K-12 minority enrollment has exceeded 31 percent and continues to climb steadily. In teacher education, 85 percent of enrolled students are white, while only about 12 percent are members of a minority group. Pipeline studies reveal that the number of minority teachers is expected to fall to 6 percent by the year 2000 (Spellman, 1988, cited in Hill et al., 1993).

Student demographic projections, supply and demand studies, and analyses of the type of preparation received by teachers serving English-language learners (see Chapter 1) lead to several conclusions. Researchers cite a need to recruit more teachers and provide high-quality development experiences to both preservice and inservice teachers serving these students, particularly given the continuing rapid increase in the number of such students. Many educators and advocates further conclude that the shortage of minority teachers signals a need to increase the pool of professionally trained minority teachers who can serve as role models and cultural brokers for a student population that is growing more and more linguistically and culturally diverse (Villegas et al., 1995; Irvine, 1992).

Those same researchers and advocates who stress the need for more teachers of color, however, also emphasize the need to prepare *all* those entering, and already working in, the teaching profession—regardless of background—to meet the linguistic and subject matter needs of students of limited English proficiency (Villegas et al., 1995; Milk et al., 1992; National Forum, 1990).

While various studies indicate the need for a "well-trained" teaching workforce for English-language learners, we know less about how best to train these teachers. The field of teacher preparation and professional development for those serving English-language learners is relatively new (Garcia, 1990), and research in this area is rather sparse (Garcia, 1991; Grant and Secada, 1990; Grant, 1991; Irvine, 1992; National Clearinghouse for Bilingual Education, 1987/88; Romero, 1990; Villegas et al., 1995; Zeichner, 1992; Zeicher and Hoeft, 1996). However, most teacher preparation (preservice) and professional development (inservice) programs are based on a growing body of knowledge regarding attributes of effective teaching for English-language learners (Milk et al., 1992; Collier, 1985; Garcia, 1990; Grant, 1991). This knowledge, much of it reviewed in earlier chapters, comes from various sources, including basic, theoretical, and school-based research and professional judgments about effective practice. However, empirical research and evidence of the effectiveness of staff preparation and development programs based on these principles is needed (Minaya-Rowe, 1990). Empirical research and evidence of the relationship between proposed attributes of effective teaching and student learning is only slowly emerging, and this also is an area in need of further research (Grant and Secada, 1990).

The Evolution of Programs to Develop Teachers of English-Language Learners Certification Standards and Guidelines

Over the years, several organizations, such as the Center for Applied Linguistics (1974), Teachers of English to Speakers of Other Languages (1975), the National Association for Bilingual Education (1992), and the National Board for Professional Teaching Standards (1996) have developed guidelines and certification standards for teachers who work in ESL and bilingual programs. These standards build on basic program standards, such as those outlined by the National Board for Professional Teaching Standards (1989) and the National Council for Accreditation of Teacher Education. In 1984, the National Association of State Directors of Teacher Education and Certification developed standards for bilingual and ESL teachers based on the guidelines of the Center for Applied Linguistics and Teachers of English for Speakers of Other Languages. These standards have been the most widely distributed and have served as the cornerstone of many teacher-preparation programs in the United States (Garcia, 1990). They have also served as a general guide for state certification. In general, the various guidelines and standards include proficiency in written and oral forms of two languages and skills in developing students' language abilities. Proposed

English as a New Language Standards (National Board for Professional Teaching Standards, 1996:13-14) also call for "preparing for student learning through knowledge of students, language development, culture, and subject matter; advancing student learning through the use of approaches that allow for meaningful learning, the provision of multiple paths to knowledge, the selection, adaptation and use of rich instructional resources, creation of rich community of learning; use of a variety of assessment methods to obtain useful information; and supporting student learning through reflective practice, linkages with families, and professional leadership."

Inservice Staff Development

Traditional approaches to staff development for teachers of English-language learners, described by Arawak (1986), followed a typical pattern (cited in Romero, 1990). Staff development often began with an assessment of needs done by either an outsider or the project director. In some cases, needs were determined without input from teachers. A second step involved the development of incentives to encourage teacher attendance at a workshop or symposium. Follow-up staff development was rare, leaving application of the newly learned information to the teachers who had participated in the workshop or symposium. At times, evaluation was built into the staff development program, but rarely was it used to improve the training process. The traditional development programs often centered on transmitting knowledge about attributes and competencies and focused less on the "process by which teachers develop competence" (Romero, 1990:487).

Evolution of Programs

In his review of the evolution of professional development for bilingual and ESL teachers, Milk (1991:275) contends that the initial stage in the development of bilingual teacher preparation—identifying competencies—was an "important first step toward development of state teacher certification in bilingual education as well as institutionalization of bilingual teacher preparation programs within universities." Milk and others state, however, that in recent years, programs for teacher preparation and development have expanded their focus beyond skills-based, competency-driven curriculum to incorporate innovative methods for enhancing teacher learning. These recent trends in the preparation and ongoing professional development of teachers of English-language learners draw on the growing research on effective staff development in general (e.g., Joyce and Showers, 1982, cited in Calderon, 1994; Little, 1993; Lieberman, 1995; McLaughlin and Oberman, 1996). Contemporary teacher preparation and development efforts stress an inquiry-based approach to teacher learning, which places the teacher in a more active role in the professional development process. Teacher reflection on practice is emphasized, along with collaboration with colleagues in "learning communities." Teacher learning communities give teachers opportunities to learn from one another—to share ideas, consult one another, and critically analyze assumptions about teaching and student learning (Little, 1993). This type of "teacher-as-learner" approach frequently involves teachers working together as peer coaches or in collaborative teams to observe one another and offer insights and feedback (Romero, 1990; Milk, 1991; Milk et al., 1992; Calderon, 1994). In addition, teachers are often placed in the role of action researchers to investigate issues affecting their students within the classroom and school contexts. More contemporary professional development methods also underscore ongoing teacher learning, which involves follow-up and continuous feedback from trainers and colleagues (i.e., peer coaches) (Darling-Hammond and McLaughlin, 1995).

Other recent trends include requirements that all those entering or already in the profession, including mainstream, bilingual, and ESL teachers, receive preparation to serve English-language learners (Milk, 1991; Milk et al., 1992). In addition, a growing number of professional development initiatives are targeting minority populations to increase the pool of bilingual teachers. These and other innovative programs focus on recruiting paraprofessionals and providing them with career ladders to receive their credentials.

However, despite advances in some programs, the research on staff development and preservice programs concludes that there is a marked mismatch between what we know about effective professional development and what is actually available to most teachers. Although there has been a paradigm shift in theoretical approaches to professional development, these approaches are not well established in practice. For example, most inservice professional development continues to take the form of short-term, superficial workshops that expose teachers to various concepts without providing the depth of treatment or connection to practice necessary for lasting effects.

Professional Development for Teachers of English-Language Learners: A Description of Four Programs

This section describes a sample of four professional development programs that exemplify the recent trends in professional development and teacher preparation discussed above. Like many teacher development programs across the country, the programs are based on theories of effective instruction from basic, school-based, and program-based research and expert judgment (e.g., Carter and Chatfield, 1986; Pease-Alvarez et al., 1991; Tikunoff, 1983; Villegas, 1991) that have contributed to the enumeration of competencies and attributes characterizing effective teachers of English-language learners (Collier, 1985). Three of the programs are described at length in Leighton et al. (1995) and were selected on the basis of attributes of best practice, nomination by experts, telephone interviews, document reviews, and site visits. A fourth—the California Cross-Cultural Language and Academic Development Program—was selected because of its state sponsorship and its extensive use in a state with the largest number of English-language learners in the nation.

Cooperative Learning in Bilingual Settings: Johns Hopkins University's Center for Research in Educating Students Placed at Risk (CRESPAR)

Cooperative Learning in Bilingual Settings is a CRESPAR-sponsored inservice program operating in schools across the Ysleta and El Paso, Texas, school districts. From 1988 to 1993, the program operated as a 5-year experimental project for seven elementary schools in the Ysleta School District. In 1992, it was incorporated into a two-way bilingual project in the El Paso school district. This joint venture is the focus of a new research project that will run from 1994 to 1999 (Calderon, 1994). Coordinated with the University of Texas at El Paso for the first 5 years, the program is now solely sponsored by CRESPAR under the direction of Margarita Calderon, one of the program's founders, in collaboration with Robert Slavin and other researchers at The Johns Hopkins University.

Teachers participating in the Cooperative Learning in Bilingual Settings program receive intensive professional development in the Cooperative Integrated Reading and Composition (CIRC) instructional model, an approach developed by researchers at Johns Hopkins to promote students' acquisition of literacy in English and Spanish.[1] The model focuses on effective practices in reading, writing, and language arts. Through structured lessons with a basal reader, students actively discuss the content of stories, learn new vocabulary, analyze the story's literary aspects, and develop word recognition and spelling skills. The model consists of a sequence of cooperative, independent, teacher-directed, and partner learning strategies that can take 2 to 6 weeks to implement. Bilingual CIRC (BCIRC), based on the original model, integrates the principles of first- and second- language acquisition and literacy and cognitive development (Calderon, 1994:3) Students in BCIRC participate in activities similar to those of monolingual CIRC students; however, more time is spent on interactive language development and writing (Leighton et al., 1995).

In primary-language classrooms in Ysleta, 15 teachers with a wide range of experience participated in the first 5-year project. This was designed as an experimental project, and novice and veteran skilled and struggling teachers were recruited to test the rigor of the training approach. Teachers used CIRC in a transitional bilingual program with a goal of facilitating English-language acquisition while supporting the development of Spanish literacy. In the newer El

---

[1]For more extensive descriptions of this and the next two programs discussed in this section, see Leighton et al. (1995).

Paso two-way bilingual project, 24 teachers (mainstream and bilingual) in two elementary schools (12 from each school) volunteered to participate. Classes at each grade level include approximately 15 Spanish-speaking and 15 English-speaking students. Each class is staffed by two teachers, one bilingual and the other monolingual.

Teachers in the two school districts received slightly different professional development. Ysleta teachers attended weekly after-school staff development sessions with project leaders during the project's first year. Sessions involved project staff modeling the CIRC instructional techniques and teachers practicing these methods. El Paso school district teachers participated in 45 hours of weekly professional development activities on a variety of topics, such as team teaching, cooperative learning, multiple intelligences, and alternative assessments. About one-third of this training focused on CIRC (Leighton et al., 1995).

Comprehensive staff development for both groups centered on providing theoretical content knowledge "needed for effective transfer of [teacher] knowledge into the classroom" (Calderon, 1994:27). Teachers also worked in peer coaching teams to observe each other and share ideas. A key feature of the professional development process was teacher learning communities, in which teachers met regularly (weekly or monthly) to identify areas of interest, problems, and solutions; to coach each other; and to share knowledge and skills. Often these meetings included the presentation of research and discussions of how, if at all, new ideas from research connected to the teachers' experience could be applied to their particular needs (Leighton et al., 1995). Another essential element of staff development was project staff follow-up. Staff visited teachers' classrooms to observe, offer feedback, make videotapes for joint analysis, and offer guidance with peer coaching and the teacher learning communities process. This approach to staff development—providing teachers with a theoretical rationale, follow-up and feedback by trainers, structured time for teacher reflection and practice, and collaborative teacher learning teams and peer coaching to facilitate use of the newly learned skills—is based on the literature on effective staff development (e.g., Joyce et al., 1987, cited in Calderon, 1994).[2]

The 5-year research study of BCIRC in the Ysleta schools involved approxi-

---

[2]In 1980, Calderon incorporated the Joyce et al. professional development model into a California district training project she developed for bilingual and ESL teachers, called Multi-District Trainers of Trainers. Her earlier research on this approach had examined the effects on teacher skills and the continuous use of these skills in the classroom. Her findings revealed that providing teachers with theory, practice, feedback, and peer coaching increased classroom use from 5 percent to the range of 75 to 90 percent of the time (Grant and Secada, 1990). Grant and Secada note, however, that it is unclear whether these data were drawn from the same teachers progressing through the program, or four groups of teachers were given different treatments. Grant and Secada contend that if the former is the case, it would be important to disentangle the effects of increased familiarity with the materials from those of the actual delivery model.

mately 500 students from 12 experimental and 12 control classrooms and the 24 teachers who participated in the study. The study consisted of quantitative and qualitative approaches that examined both teacher and student effects: (1) student academic, linguistic, and social development; (2) teacher development of new teaching and collaborative skills, fidelity to the model, and creativity; (3) effective staff development processes for teachers and how these teachers constructed collegial work settings; and (4) implementation of the innovation in different school settings (Calderon, 1994). Students were matched by grade level, socioeconomic status, and academic and linguistic levels. Student effects were measured by project-developed pre-post tests. These tests, along with state standardized tests, were triangulated with attitude surveys, student portfolios, and ethnographic analyses of video recordings of students involved in cooperative groupwork. Teacher development was measured on a yearly basis through video recordings of teacher practice in the classroom and staff development sessions with colleagues. Interviews and classroom observation using systematic instruments and ethnographic guides were also used, in conjunction with teacher narratives of their professional growth and their students' achievement.

With respect to teacher development effects, the study focused on the content teachers needed to adopt, a cooperative learning philosophy, and use of the CIRC model appropriately in the classroom. It also examined the processes of teacher development and the creation of a support system for teachers adopting and implementing a new instructional philosophy and teaching system. In general, the study demonstrated gains for experimental teachers in terms of personal growth and implementation of innovative practices. The study findings confirmed that "although the comprehensive coverage of content at the teacher inservice session is vitally important, the process for renewal and follow-up support systems for collegial learning are critical. Without certain processes for preparing teachers, content rarely transfers into teachers' active teaching repertoire" (Calderon, 1994:18).

Calderon states that perhaps the greatest contribution of the study was the empirical testing of the effects of various theories of cooperative learning on students' second-language acquisition (e.g., Cummins, 1981; Cohen, 1986). Calderon (1994:7) found that cooperative learning increases the "variety of and frequency of second-language practice" and that the structured curriculum becomes a way of facilitating the processing of new information that helps students develop the native language en route to second-language development. The study further revealed that BCIRC students made greater academic gains in standardized tests during their involvement in the project than did students in the control classrooms. BCIRC students were also ready to transition into regular classrooms sooner and sustained academic success.

In the two-way CIRC project in El Paso schools, the staff development process described above has continued. In the 5-year study, research on the transfer of teacher preparation to the classroom is a major focus. The general research questions include the following: "How do teachers construct common knowledge of what a two-way bilingual program should be?" and "How do mainstream teachers and minority teachers collaborate to share one another's talents on the construction of knowledge about their students' instructional needs?" (Calderon, 1996:6). Quantitative and qualitative data will be collected from teachers and students. Preliminary research findings reveal positive effects on student attitudes toward each other and the language they are learning (Calderon, 1994).

In addition, preliminary studies have been conducted on a "peer ethnography" segment of the teacher development process. Peer ethnography involves teachers taking the roles of peer coaches, classroom ethnographers, teacher trainers, and curriculum writers. Teachers are trained in the use of ethnographic techniques to observe and analyze their teaching practice and students' learning processes. One teacher conducts a mini-ethnography, while the other teaches and "scripts" segments of the instructional activities that occur within a 30- to 90-minute time period. Teachers then use these scripts as a tool to "step back and generate a set of questions that serve for general analysis, reflection and reorganization of time, and analysis of language status and implicit power issues in [student] participation structures" (p. 17). Preliminary evidence from the classroom ethnographies indicates that the approach draws monolingual and bilingual teachers closer together and provides "texts and contexts for teachers for self-analysis, negotiation, and problem solving" (p. 18).

The Latino Teacher Project: University of Southern California

The Latino Teacher Project was developed in 1991 in response to a shortage of bilingual Latino teachers available to teach California's growing number of language-minority students. The project taps into the underutilized paraprofessional or teaching assistant workforce in the state and structures a career ladder by which they can receive their bilingual teaching credentials (Genzuk and Hentschke, 1992). The project provides financial, social, and academic support to aspiring teachers.

The Latino Teacher Project was developed at the University of Southern California and is part of a consortium that includes the Los Angeles Unified School District, the Little Lake City School District, the Lennox School District, local teacher and teacher assistant union representatives, California State University at Dominguez Hills, California State University at Los Angeles, and Loyola Marymount University. Consortium members are part of an advisory group that shares in decision making and provides support (e.g., workshops) for participants.

Paraeducators, as they are called in this project, are recruited from three groups of applicants: (1) teaching assistants who are enrolled in undergraduate programs, (2) teaching assistants who are currently enrolled in teacher education programs and pursuing their post-baccalaureate teaching credentials, and (3) teaching assistants in community colleges who intend to transfer to a 4-year institution. Applicants who live and work in the South Central area of Los Angeles and are fluently bilingual receive priority; participants living and working in other Los Angeles area schools are also involved. There are 50 slots currently available in the project, with another 25 slots at the intermediate and secondary school levels.

Participants in the program are involved in various staff development activities that are based on a "sociocultural, assisted performance model of professional development and create a community of learners to provide professional socialization to students enrolled" (M. Genzuk, personal communication). These activities include workshops to help participants prepare for benchmark tests and develop strategies for progressing smoothly through teacher education programs. Each university in the consortium offers workshops on varying topics, depending on the participants' needs.

Initial research on the obstacles to program completion led to measures to assist the participants in a variety of areas. For example, monetary stipends are provided to students twice a year, depending on student need, to help offset the costs of enrollment. Participant cohorts are developed to provide a support network; these cohorts often form study groups and work in the same school. The project also sponsors social gatherings for participants and their families. Finally, the project creates a network of professional support that provides academic guidance, as well as professional modeling. Each participant is assigned a mentor trained by the Los Angeles County Office of Education. At project expense, mentors, participants, and principals attend conferences together to make presentations and network with other professional educators (Leighton et al., 1995). The project director notes that to date, 100 participants have successfully attained their credentials, and that the completion rate is approximately 99 percent (M. Genzuk, personal communication).

Research thus far on the project has focused primarily on retention and participants' rates of completion of credentialing programs. One significant finding is that the participant attrition rate is extremely low—2.7 percent. The project's principal investigator has also examined "departure and persistence" factors for participating teachers (M. Genzuk, personal communication). An important finding is that working as paraeducators bolsters students' persistence in completing university programs, rather than detracting from it. In addition, external studies of the project have been conducted to identify the elements and factors that have contributed to the project's success, such as district/school collaboration and community building (Joy and Bruschi, 1995, cited in Villegas et al., 1995).

In the near future, through the new Center on Meeting the Educational Needs of a Diverse Student Population, Robert Rueda plans to conduct a formal research study to investigate the nature and use of bilingual Latino paraeducators' "funds of knowledge" in classroom settings, with focus on reading and language arts instruction. Funds of knowledge refers to the language, social norms, and other cultural and linguistic community and family resources that individuals possess (Moll et al., 1992) (see also Chapter 4). Candidates entering the Latino Teacher Project and those who have been out of school for 2 to 3 years will be the focus of the study. The major research questions are as follows (M. Genzuk, personal communication): Do Latino paraeducators have existing funds of knowledge that can serve as special resources to at-risk English-language learners in urban schools? Are the instructional interactions and activity settings they create for their students different from those created by their peers without the same background? How are these affected by the formal preparation involved in acquiring a teaching credential? The goal of the study is to address the gap in research regarding "ethnic and linguistic matching" of teachers and students. To date, Genzuk notes, there is no strong evidence that ethnic or linguistic matching is effective; questions still remain unanswered regarding how teachers' funds of knowledge can be used to improve instruction.

English for Speakers of Other Languages (ESOL) Inservice Project: Dade County Public Schools

Of the 225,000 students in the Dade County Public Schools, 51,000 have limited English proficiency. Although a variety of languages are spoken in the Miami area, the large majority of students are Spanish speaking. In the summer of 1989, Multicultural Education Training and Advocacy informed the state education agency of its intent to sue on behalf of the language-minority students who were receiving inadequate educational services. The suit alleged that the state had failed to develop standards and guidelines for the provision of services to these students. Multicultural Education Training and Advocacy and the state reached an agreement (called the consent decree) requiring that all teachers and support personnel (e.g., counselors) who come into contact with English-language learners will be prepared to meet those students' academic needs. The consent decree has four parts: (1) identifying, assessing, and monitoring the progress of language-minority students; (2) providing these students with equal access to appropriate programming; (3) requiring teachers to obtain appropriate preparation and certification; and (4) evaluating program effectiveness (Leighton et al., 1995). To comply with the consent decree, Dade County Public Schools and other districts across the state were faced with the task of training more than 15,000 teachers.

English for Speakers of Other Languages (ESOL) training is now required of all teachers serving English-language learners. "All" teachers include basic ESL teachers with or without experience, primary-language (other than English) teachers, and teachers of basic and nonbasic subject areas whose classrooms include English-language learners. Teachers are required to take specified courses, each of which is assigned a certain number of "master plan points." They must acquire a certain number of points within a particular time frame according to their teaching assignment (for example, ESOL teachers have 6 years to accumulate their points). Courses are provided to teachers throughout the year to accommodate their schedules, and include Methods of Teaching ESOL, Cross-Cultural Communication and Understanding, and Testing and Evaluation of ESOL. An additional professional development opportunity—attaining a masters degree in urban education with a concentration in ESOL—is offered in collaboration with Florida International University.

Funded by a Title VII grant, the program accepted 33 Dade County elementary teachers and provided full tuition scholarships. Upon completion of the program, participating teachers will receive a permanent $3,000 salary increase. Project outcome data indicate that by May 1993, more than 9,000 teachers had completed the course in ESOL Issues and Strategies, and 3,000 had completed the course in Issues and Strategies for LEP Students.

In a descriptive review of the ESOL inservice project in Dade County Public Schools, Leighton et al. (1995) note that thus far, the district staff operating the professional development initiative have learned several lessons. They quickly learned that because the consent decree is a top-down mandate, teachers are often reluctant to participate in the professional development program. The staff have tried to address this lack of interest by informing teachers about the decree and the pedagogical rationale that underlies the program. In addition, teachers and district staff are concerned that the program targets too many teachers with a wide range of experiences and classroom needs. Project staff are therefore constantly trying to find ways to tailor the courses to meet the diverse needs of a large, heterogeneous group of teachers.

The University of Florida recently completed a state-wide technical assistance report evaluating Florida's ESOL staff development initiative (Harper, 1995), funded in part by a Title VII personnel development grant. For the evaluation, 126 trainers and 237 teachers were surveyed to examine their attitudes and perceptions regarding their professional development experience; 36 trainers and teachers were also interviewed. Among other questions, teachers were asked what they found most and least useful in the program, what they are now doing differently in their classrooms as a result of their participation, and how their expectations of language-minority students may have changed. The trainers' survey addressed a variety of issues, including their attitudes toward the ESOL staff development and its usefulness.

Survey results revealed that the majority of teachers (82 percent) found the professional development in the program useful; however, teachers reported that it did not provide enough subject-specific information to meet their needs. Moreover, 70 percent of the teachers reported having developed new skills as a result of the program; for example, 66 teachers reported developing alternative materials (oral, visual, and experiential) to suit varying student learning styles, and 47 said they were incorporating students' home culture into the curriculum. In addition, 68 percent of teachers indicated that their expectations of English-language learners had changed as a result of the ESOL staff development, with 81 reporting changes in expectations for language development. The most frequently cited result was the realization that second-language acquisition is a developmental process. In general, the trainer survey results indicated that a large number of trainers believed the teachers found the information presented in the workshops useful.

As a result of the survey, researchers at the University of Florida who conducted the study plan to work with the Center for Applied Linguistics to revise segments of the ESOL inservice staff development program to make them more subject-specific and practicum-oriented. A practicum approach would involve teachers alternating between staff development sessions and classroom practice to receive feedback and work cooperatively with their peers to improve their teaching practice (C. Harper, personal communication).

The California Cross-Cultural, Language and Academic Development (CLAD) Program

California's CLAD program is another recent effort to reform state staff development programs and credentialing procedures for teachers of English-language learners (California Commission on Teacher Credentialing, 1992, cited in Leighton et al., 1993). The large and growing population of English-language learners across the state prompted the development of this new certification system, which combines cross-cultural, language, and academic development emphases into regular preservice and inservice teacher staff development programs. To add the CLAD endorsement to their license, already-credentialed monolingual teachers must pass examinations in (1) language structure and first- and second-language development; (2) special methods of instruction for English-language learners; and (3) cultural diversity. With the CLAD credential, teachers are allowed to teach in a classroom with English-language learners. To earn the bilingual credential (BCLAD), already-credentialed teachers must also pass examinations on (1) the target language, (2) the target culture, and (3) methodology for target language instruction. Preservice teachers are expected to meet the competency requirements for these credentials through their preparation programs. In addition, specialists who will train or supervise teachers in programs for English-language learners must complete professional development programs that address student assessment, curriculum development, staff development, community/parent relations, and research (Leighton et al., 1993).

Research on the implementation and effects of the CLAD/BCLAD credentialing system is sparse. Ross (1993) reports on a study of two preservice teacher education programs at San Diego State University and the University of California at Santa Barbara that prepare teachers for the CLAD/BCLAD certificate. The San Diego State University program prepares teachers to work with English-language learners where bilingual programs are not available or to work in the English component of a bilingual program using English-language development methods (i.e., sheltered instruction). Preservice students can move from the monolingual CLAD program to the BCLAD program as they become proficient in a second language. The CLAD emphasis is offered within specified blocks of existing credential programs and requires that students complete both additional courses and field experience supervised by master teachers and university faculty. The required courses include Child Language Acquisition and Multicultural Education and Bilingual Teaching Strategies. The CLAD courses are based on the competency areas identified above.

In 1992, nine university faculty members representing different disciplines (language arts, mathematics, educational psychology, science, and social studies) participated in a year-long pilot program to prepare for teaching prospective teachers to receive the new credential. The faculty's main goal was to increase their knowledge in the areas of language and culture and to develop strategies for infusing relevant content into teacher preparation courses. Researchers at San Diego State University designed a study to assess the results of the faculty preparation program and its impact on student teacher preparation. This study included analysis of syllabi before and after staff development, interviews with faculty, and surveys of a pilot group and a comparison group of students. Ross (1993) states that the study's results were positive. The year-long process helped faculty focus on a wide array of cross-curricular goals to be pursued in the future. The majority of students in the CLAD program found it effective and perceived themselves as better prepared to meet the needs of English-language learners. For example, students in the program (as opposed to those in the comparison group) rated their program as more effective in dealing with the nature of culture (72 vs. 46 percent) and all areas of language structure and acquisition (71 vs. 27 percent).

Beginning in 1992, the California State Commission for Teacher Credentialing initiated a collaborative review of the CLAD/BCLAD programs at four University of California campuses—Santa Cruz, Berkeley, San Diego, and Los Angeles Representatives from each campus provided input for the process, including the decision to conduct a formative review followed by a summative phase that would ascertain whether the CLAD/BCLAD standards developed by the commission were addressed at each campus.

The formative components of the evaluation have been used to assist each campus in its development of CLAD/BCLAD programs that meet the set of standards set by the commission. Relying primarily on interview data collected from participants in each program (i.e., students, instructors, local teachers, and administrators) over a 2-day period, the formative review uncovered important information about the variations in the programs' contexts and structures and the effect on program implementation. Some of these variations included the development of a more cohesive curriculum at campuses that involved all program faculty in the design of their CLAD/BCLAD programs, strong collaboration among program faculty at campuses where teacher education was part of divisions of social science, and low levels of commitment and involvement from faculty in schools of education. Findings focusing on the quality of curriculum and instruction available to students across the four campuses indicated a need for additional curriculum preparation of CLAD/BCLAD candidates in the areas of English-language development and Specially Designed Academic Instruction in English (SDAIE). Students at all four campuses requested greater integration between theory and practice in methods courses and more modeling of English-language development and SDAIE strategies by instructors in the content areas. In addition, BCLAD students at each campus expressed a need for more opportunities to develop their ability to teach in languages other than English, especially in the content areas. The lack of master teachers with knowledge of CLAD/BCLAD methods was also an issue at all four campuses.

At this stage of the process, the formative phase of the review has been completed. The summative component is currently under way and is scheduled to be finalized in early 1997.

Summary and Conclusion

The four programs just described represent a variety of staff development efforts including continuing education (Cooperative Learning in Bilingual Settings, ESOL inservice project) recruitment (Latino Teacher Project), preservice education (Latino Teacher Project), and credentialing (CLAD program). All are informed by various sources (e.g., theoretical, basic, or school-based research) or professional judgment. Findings from the studies exemplify current thinking about what teachers of English-language learners should know and be able to do, effective methods for accomplishing this, and strategies for increasing the numbers of qualified instructors.

The Cooperative Learning in Bilingual Settings programs trains teachers to use an empirically validated method of teaching (BCIRC). The staff development effort stresses a comprehensive approach in which teachers are provided with theoretical content knowledge, as well as practice through supervision. A key emphasis of the project is on inquiry-based learning, in which teachers engage in peer coaching and collaboration with colleagues. The project highlights the importance of follow-up support systems.

The Latino Teacher Project is an effort to target minority populations to increase the pool of bilingual teachers in Central Los Angeles by creating a career ladder for Latino teaching assistants. Staff development efforts are based on a "community of learners" model in which participants are assisted and assist each other in progressing through teacher education programs.

The ESOL inservice project, designed to assist all teachers serving English-language learners in Florida, provides teachers with courses to help them better educate these students. Coursework includes methods of teaching ESL, cross-cultural communication and understanding, and testing and evaluation of English-language learners. Program staff are engaged in ongoing efforts to tailor the courses to meet the diverse needs of a heterogeneous group of teachers.

The CLAD Program, an effort to reform state staff development and credentialing programs, is geared to giving all teachers who work with English-language learners the skills and knowledge necessary to be effective. Teachers need the CLAD endorsement to instruct English-language learners.

RESEARCH NEEDS

All four of the teacher development programs described above have conducted or plan to conduct empirical research. This research consists of descriptive studies, surveys, and experiments examining the training process and its effects on teachers and/or students (e.g., Cohen, 1990; Cohen et al., 1996; De Avila, 1981, cited in Cohen, 1990). However, educators agree that more solid, empirical research on the development, implementation, and effects of professional development is greatly needed (Milk, 1991; Grant, 1991; Grant and Secada, 1990; Irvine, 1992; Lara-Alecio and Parker, 1994). The following recommendations address these research needs.

Origin of and Basis for Teacher Competencies

8-1. Research is needed to identify the origins of the components/attributes of teacher certification and professional development programs and assess the strength of the evidence that supports them. For example, what are the origins of the attributes and required qualifications included in the new California credentialing systems (California Cross-Cultural, Language and Academic Development [CLAD] and bilingual CLAD [BCLAD]) and Florida English for Speakers of Other Languages (ESOL) inservice staff development efforts. Are they based on theory, empirical evidence, or expert judgment? Attributes that are missing according to our current knowledge base should be incorporated.

As noted in this and earlier chapters, most certification and professional development programs—preservice and inservice—are based on lists of teacher competencies and attributes informed by various sources (e.g., theoretical, basic, or school-based research) or professional judgment. As Grant and Secada (1990:419) argue, teacher certification programs and requirements have not been empirically validated: "Though there are some things that we all agree are desirable to know and to do, it is far from clear that we have enough information to specify such domains on the basis of empirical evidence." Clearly research recommended in Chapter 7 will help elucidate what these attributes and components, including subject matter knowledge, should be. Attributes that are justified by empirical evidence should be incorporated into professional development efforts.

8-2. Research is needed to examine the effects of matching teachers and students on cultural and linguistic characteristics.

As described earlier, the Latino Teacher Project is planning to conduct such a study. However, these studies are rare. Reviewing the literature on preparing teachers for diversity, Grant and Secada (1990:406) could not find research that investigated different recruitment and retention models for a diverse teaching force. They agree that the homogenization of the teaching workforce is "undesirable," but believe that "agreement should not preclude empirical inquiry." "The hypothesis [is] that teachers of color understand the cultural backgrounds of diverse learners better than whites; hence they can adapt instruction to meet those differences. What the source of such understanding is...and how that understanding actually translates into practice and student outcomes are all empirical questions."

The Development of Effective Strategies for Teacher Education

8-3. Research is needed to develop effective methods for use in preparing teachers of English-language learners.

As Milk et al. (1992:10) state, "there is a need to examine instructional practice in university-based teacher training programs, much the way that instructional practices have been examined in school settings." For example, what benefit do teachers gain from supervised internships, readings, and classroom discussion. How should these forms of teacher development be aligned? Further, more research is needed to identify factors, including theoretical knowledge, needed to support teacher learning once in the classroom and ensure that what is learned in professional development is applied in the classroom (e.g., feedback and peer coaching, organizational/school-based support, and opportunities to work in students' communities). Should preparation differ for different levels of teachers (i.e., early education, primary, secondary), as well as for teachers with different training and experience (e.g., ESL, mainstream), and if so, how? How are the needs of novice and veteran teachers different, and how does staff development accommodate these differences?

Effectiveness of Teacher Education Programs

8-4. Research is needed to evaluate current teacher education programs and staff development efforts to determine how well they have incorporated theory-based conceptions of effective teaching, as well as how well they have helped teachers acquire the skills and knowledge they need.

There are a number of important questions to be addressed in this area. First, is the curriculum consonant with the knowledge and skills teachers need to be effective (i.e., is the course content valid)? Second, are these programs using methods that are effective in helping teachers acquire the needed knowledge and skills (Romero, 1990; Calderon and Marsh, 1988; Calderon, 1994)? Third, have programs established learning goals and short- and long-term indicators, and are they using them to monitor teacher progress? If not, how is the acquisition of skills and knowledge assessed? Fourth, how are integrated teacher education programs structured and delivered in university settings? Are they adjunct courses, or are courses integrated and content infused throughout the teacher education curriculum? Finally, how well have teachers acquired the needed knowledge and skills? Appropriate models must be developed for evaluating the effectiveness of these initiatives.

Improving Assessments of Teacher Knowledge and Skills

8-5. Descriptive research on current teacher exams is needed to determine how well they assess teacher skills and knowledge characteristic of effective teaching for English-language learners. If these exams fall short, research is needed to inform the development of reliable and valid assessments of teacher knowledge and skills.

Currently, a variety of methods are used to assess teacher competencies within the context of teacher education and staff development. They include portfolios, as well as more traditional paper-and-pencil tasks. What is the best way to assess teacher competencies, taking into consideration variables such as whether the teacher is a novice or experienced?

8-6. The relationship between knowledge gained in professional develop-ment and its implementation in the classroom requires empirical investigation.

Few professional development programs include a follow-up component that assesses the correspondence between teacher learning and doing. The Center for Research in Educating Students Placed at Risk (CRESPAR) program profiled in this chapter is an example of this type of comprehensive staff development effort. An additional research step that would help validate the effectiveness of professional development would be to examine its effects on student learning and behavior. Do the attributes and competencies gained in professional develop-ment have a positive effect on student academic gains?

8-7. Studies need to go beyond fidelity assessments (Are teachers doing what we taught them?) to analysis of what the professional development field can learn from teachers in school and classroom contexts.

Grant and Secada (1990:420) contend that "we need to inquire about the sense in which teachers who fail to use content from their courses are making valid responses to their situations." They suggest models need to be created to examine "why teachers use, or fail to use, what we think they know." Research at the classroom level is needed to investigate more closely the factors that might affect how teachers implement new methods learned in the classroom. What role do teacher attitudes play? To what extent do organizational factors (the provision of structured time to collaborate with colleagues, principal support) affect implementation of new knowledge and practices learned in the classroom?

Strategies to Increase the Pool of Teachers Serving English-Language Learners

8-8. Research is needed to learn how to increase the number of teachers skilled in working with English-language learners.

More studies are needed to examine existing programs geared toward recruiting teachers to work with such students. How successful are projects designed to encourage and assist bilingual individuals, such as secondary school students, community college students, and paraprofessionals, in becoming educators of English-language learners? How does the support such projects provide to applicants (e.g., support for preprofessional coursework, credentialing programs) improve the number of teachers available to teach these students?

8-9. More research is needed to examine new teacher credentialing systems (e.g., CLAD/BCLAD) and professional development efforts (e.g., the Florida ESOL program) that attempt to serve all teachers who come into contact with English-language learners.

Recent efforts to prepare all future and existing teachers to meet the academic needs of language-minority students provide important research opportunities to examine more closely how best to structure such programs and assess their effects. A few studies have documented the development of teacher education programs for bilingual, ESL, and mainstream teachers (Milk, 1990, 1991; Calderon, 1994; Collier, 1985). For example, Calderon's work, which focuses on collaborative staff development, documents how this method facilitates professional growth and knowledge development among all teachers serving English-language learners. Her research highlights the different areas of professional change needed by mainstream and bilingual teachers to implement the BCIRC model. Many questions remain to be answered, however.

Preparation and Development of Teachers for English-Language Learners with Disabilities

8-10. Research on how to prepare teachers to work with culturally and linguistically diverse students with disabilities is much needed. Research on professional development activities for these teachers is also needed.

Ortiz (1995) contends that given the large amount of time linguistically diverse students with disabilities spend in the regular classroom, regular-education personnel need to be prepared to distinguish learning disabilities from the normal development of second-language proficiency and to work collaboratively with specialists on meeting the needs of these students. ESL specialists also need training to be able to identify disabilities in English-language learners and coordinate with children's classroom teachers and learning disability specialists. Ortiz adds that once models are developed, their effectiveness requires empirical testing.

One promising model that should be investigated is the Optimal Learning Environment Project, developed by Ruiz and Figueroa (1995) to change the way teachers work with English-language learners with disabilities, as well as improve educational outcomes for these children.[3]

REFERENCES

American Association of Colleges for Teacher Education
    1994   *Teacher Education Pipeline III: Schools, Colleges, and Departments of Education Enrollments by Race, Ethnicity, and Gender.* Washington, DC: American Association of Colleges for Teacher Education.
Arawak Consulting Corporation
    1986   A Study of Alternative Inservice Staff Development Approaches for Local Education Agencies Serving Minority Language Limited-English Proficient Students. Final synthesis report. The Arawak Consulting Corporation, New York.
Boe, E.E.
    1990   Demand, supply, and shortage of bilingual and ESL teachers: Models, data, and policy issues. Pp. 23-63 *in Proceedings of the First Research Symposium on Limited English Proficient Students' Issues.* Office of Bilingual Education and Minority Languages Affairs. Washington, DC: U.S. Department of Education.
Calderon, M.
    1994   *Cumulative Reports: 1. Bilingual Teacher Development Within School Learning Communities: A Synthesis of the Staff Development Model. 2. The Impact of the Bilingual Cooperative Integrated Reading and Composition Model on Bilingual Programs.* El Paso, TX: Department of Educational Leadership.
    1996   Talent Development of Language Minority Students and their Teachers. Paper presented at the annual meeting of the American Educational Research Association, New York. Center for Research on the Education of Students Placed at Risk, The Johns Hopkins University, Baltimore, MD.
Calderon, M., and D. Marsh
    1988   Applying research on effective bilingual instruction in a multi-district inservice teacher training program. *Journal of the National Association for Bilingual Education* 12(2):133-152.

---

[3]The Optimal Learning Environment Project used instructional strategies consistent with a holistic-constructivist paradigm, focusing on interactive journals, a writer's workshop, patterned writing, shared reading, literature conversations, literature study with response journals, creation of text for wordless books, and ample reading time, as well as collaboration with teachers in the design of inservice education and implementation of program change.

Carter, T., and M. Chatfield
  1986   Effective bilingual schools: Implications for policy and practice. *American Journal of Education* 95(1):200-234.
Center for Applied Linguistics
  1974   *Guidelines for the Preparation and Certification of Teachers of Bilingual/Bicultural Education.* Arlington, VA: Center for Applied Linguistics.
Cohen, E.G.
  1986   *Designing Groupwork: Strategies for Heterogeneous Classrooms.* New York: Teachers College Press.
  1990   Teaching in multiculturally heterogeneous classrooms: Findings from a model program. *McGill Journal of Education* 26(1):7-23.
Cohen, E.G., R.A. Lotan, and C.C. Morphew
  1996   Beyond the workshop: Evidence from complex instruction. Unpublished manuscript. School of Education, Stanford University.
Collier, V.
  1985   University models for ESL and bilingual teacher training. Pp. 81-90 in *Issues in English Language Development.* Washington, DC: National Clearinghouse for Bilingual Education.
Cummins, J.
  1981   The role of primary language minority students. Pp. 3-49 in California State Department of Education, ed., *Schooling and Language Minority Students: A Theoretical Framework.* Los Angeles: California State University Evaluation, Dissemination, and Assessment Center.
Darling-Hammond, L., and M.W. McLaughlin
  1995   Policies that support professional development in an era of reform. *Phi Delta Kappan* 76(8):597-604.
Garcia, E.
  1990   Educating teachers for language minority students. Pp. 717-729 in W.R. Houston, ed., *Handbook of Research on Teacher Education.* New York: Macmillan.
  1991   Teachers for language minority students: Evaluating professional standards. Pp. 383-424 in *Proceedings of the Second National Research Symposium on LEP Student Issues: Focus on Evaluation and Measurement.* Vol. 1. Office of Bilingual Education and Minority Languages Affairs. Washington, DC: U.S. Department of Education.
Genzuk, M., and G. Hentschke
  1992   *Career Pathways for Practitioners: Progress Report.* USC Latino Teacher Project. Los Angeles: University of California at Los Angeles.
Grant, C.A.
  1991   Educational research and teacher training for successfully teaching limited English proficient students. Pp. 431-456 in *Proceedings of the Second National Research Symposium on LEP Student Issues: Focus on Evaluation and Measurement.* Vol. 1. Washington, DC: U.S. Department of Education.
Grant, C.A., and W.G. Secada
  1990   Preparing teachers for diversity. Pp. 403-422 in W.R. Houston, ed., *Handbook of Research on Teacher Education.* New York: Macmillan.
Harper, C.
  1995   *An Evaluation of ESOL Inservice Training in Florida: Technical Report.* Leadership in Education (LEADS). Gainesville, FL: University of Florida.
Hill, R., J. Carjuzaa, D. Aramburo, and L. Baca
  1993   Culturally and linguistically diverse teachers in special education: Repairing or redesigning the leaky pipeline. *Teacher Education and Special Education* 16:258-269.

Irvine, J.J.
  1992   Making teacher education culturally responsive. Pp. 79-92, Chapter 5, in M.E. Dilworth, ed., *Diversity in Teacher Education: New Expectations.* San Francisco: Jossey-Bass.
Lara-Alecio, R., and R.I. Parker
  1994   A pedagogical model for transitional English bilingual classrooms. *Bilingual Research Journal* 18(3-4):119-133.
Leighton, M.S., A.W. Russo, and A.M. Hightower
  1993   Improving education for language minority students: Promising practices in professional development. Unpublished manuscript. Policy Studies Associates, Washington, D.C.
Leighton, M.S., A.M. Hightower, and A.M. Wrigley
  1995   *Model Strategies in Bilingual Education: Professional Development.* Washington, DC: U.S. Department of Education.
Lieberman, A.
  1995   Practices that support teacher development. *Phi Delta Kappan* (April):591-604.
Little, J.
  1993   Teachers' professional development in a climate of education reform. *Educational Evaluation and Policy Analysis* 15(2):129-151.
McLaughlin, M.W., and I. Oberman, eds.
  1996   *Teacher Learning: New Policies, New Practices.* New York: Teachers College Press.
Milk, R.
  1990   Preparing ESL and bilingual teachers for changing roles: Immersion for teachers of LEP children. *TESOL Quarterly* 24(3):407-426.
Milk, R.
  1991   Preparing teachers for effective bilingual instruction. Pp. 267-280 in M. McGroarty and C. Faltis, eds., *Languages in School and Society.* New York: Mouton de Gruyter.
Milk, R., C. Mercado, and A. Sapiens
  1992   *Re-thinking the Education of Teachers of Language Minority Children: Developing Reflective Teachers for Changing Schools.* Occasional Papers in Bilingual Education, Number 6. Washington, DC: National Clearinghouse for Bilingual Education.
Minaya-Rowe, L.
  1990   Teacher training in bilingual education and English as a second language: Recent research developments. Pp. 259-297 in A.N. Ambert, ed., *Bilingual Education as a Second Language: A Research Handbook.* New York: Garland Publishing, Inc.
Moll, L.C., C. Amanti, D. Neff, and N. Gonzalez
  1992   Funds of knowledge for teaching: Using a qualitative approach to connect homes and classrooms. *Theory into Practice* 31(2):132-141.
National Association for Bilingual Education
  1992   *Professional Standards for the Preparation of Bilingual/Multicultural Teachers.* Washington, DC: National Association for Bilingual Education.
National Board for Professional Teaching Standards
  1989   *Toward High and Rigorous Standards for the Teaching Profession.* Washington, DC: National Board for Professional Teaching Standards.
  1996   *Proposed English as a New Language Standards.* Washington, DC: National Board for Professional Teaching Standards.
National Center for Education Statistics
  1993   *Schools and Staffing in the United States: A Statistical Profile.* NCES 93-146. Washington, DC: U.S. Department of Education.
National Clearinghouse for Bilingual Education
  1987-   *Innovative Staff Development Approaches.* Occasional Papers in Bilingual
  1988   *Education* 4:1-8. Washington, DC: National Clearinghouse for Bilingual Education.

National Forum on Personnel Needs for Districts with Changing Demographics
    1990   *Staffing the Multilingually Impacted Schools of the 1990s.* Office of Bilingual Education
            and Minority Language Affairs. Washington, DC: U.S. Department of Education.
Ortiz, A.A.
    1995   Special Education and English Language Learners. Unpublished paper prepared for the
            Committee on Developing a Research Agenda on the Education of Limited English Profi-
            cient and Bilingual Students. College of Education, The University of Texas at Austin.
Pease-Alvarez, L., E.E. Garcia, and P. Espinosa
    1991   Effective instruction for language-minority students: An early childhood case study.
            Early Childhood Research Quarterly 6:347-361.
Romero, M.
    1990   Discussant response to E. Rojas Clark, "The state of the art in research on teacher training
            models with special reference to bilingual education teachers." Pp. 487-502 in *Proceed-
            ings of the First Research Symposium on LEP Students' Issues.* Office of Bilingual
            Education and Minority Languages Affairs. Washington, DC: U.S. Department of Edu-
            cation.
Ross, P.
    1993   Preparing Teacher Educators and Prospective Teachers to Meet the Challenge of Diver-
            sity. Paper presented at the 43rd annual meeting of the National Reading Conference,
            December 1993.
Ruiz, N.T., and R.A. Figueroa
    1995   Learning-handicapped classrooms with Latino students: The optimal learning environ-
            ment (OLE) Project. *Education and Urban Society* 27(4):463-483.
Teachers of English to Speakers of Other Languages
    1975   *Statement of Qualifications and Guidelines for the Preparation and Certification of Teach-
            ers of English to Speakers of Other Languages in the United States.* Washington, DC:
            Teachers of English to Speakers of Other Languages.
Tikunoff, W.
    1983   *An Emerging Description of Successful Bilingual Instruction: Executive Summary of
            Part I of the SBIF Study.* San Francisco, CA: Far West Laboratory for Educational
            Research and Development.
U.S. General Accounting Office
    1994   *Limited English Proficiency: A Growing and Costly Educational Challenge Facing Many
            School Districts.* GAO/HEHS-94-38. Washington, DC: U.S. General Accounting Of-
            fice.
Villegas, A.M.
    1991   *Culturally Responsive Pedagogy for the 1990s and Beyond.* Princeton, NJ: Educational
            Testing Service.
Villegas, A.M., B.C. Clewell, B.T. Anderson, M.E. Goertz, M.F. Joy, B.A. Bruschi, and J.J. Irvine
    1995   *Teaching for Diversity: Models for Expanding the Supply of Minority Teachers.*
            Princeton, NJ: Educational Testing Service.
Zeichner, K.
    1992   *Educating Teachers for Cultural Diversity.* NCRTL Special Report. East Lansing, MI:
            National Center for Research on Teacher Learning, Michigan State University.
Zeichner, K., and K. Hoeft
    1996   Teacher socialization for cultural diversity. In J.S. Kula, ed., *Handbook of Research on
            Teacher Education.* Second Edition. New York: Macmillan.

ESTIMATING POPULATION PARAMETERS: SUMMARY OF THE STATE OF KNOWLEDGE

A review of the state of knowledge in estimating population parameters—or the work generally referred to as education statistics—reveals the following key points:

• Over the last 10 years, the National Center for Education Statistics (NCES) within the U.S. Department of Education has taken several steps to improve its collection and reporting of education statistics.

• Eligibility rules for the participation of English-language learners in the National Assessment of Educational Progress have become more standardized to ensure greater consistency in student inclusion. A number of studies are under way to help ascertain the validity of using current or other criteria for exclusion, as well as to investigate other issues related to the inclusion of English-language learners.

• Weaknesses in the collection and reporting of education statistics persist in a number of areas, particularly with regard to certain subpopulations, including English-language learners. Among these weaknesses are the following:

—Insufficient coverage of subpopulations, which biases the results; results often cannot be generalized to the excluded groups.
—Inconsistent data definitions across the various surveys and studies, limiting comparability.
—Similar variation in identification procedures, data collection methods, data collection levels (degree of aggregation of numbers), and data collection purposes.
—Gaps in the data on important variables of interest.

• The central problem in assessing English-language learners is their limited ability to perform on a test administered in English. Assessments based on translations into a second language have questionable validity.

• To address this problem, various testing modifications have been introduced, including flexible scheduling, small-group test administration, use of dictionaries, simplification of directions, reading of questions aloud, and extra time. The validity of such modifications has not been adequately researched to date.

9

Estimating Population Parameters

This chapter reviews the work generally referred to as education statistics. Unlike the basic and applied research reviewed in earlier chapters, this work places less emphasis on the testing, elucidation, or elaboration of scientific or practical theories. Theories in education statistics are often implicit, and assume broad agreement among the community of researchers and consumers such that data collection and reporting of their population parameter estimates is publicly defensible. Collection of education statistics is also governed by relatively established professional norms about sound sampling and measurement. In this sense, education statistics are bound by a conservatism about the object and means of measurement similar to that found for program evaluation research (see Chapter 6). Since both education statistics and program evaluation are exposed to much more public scrutiny and accountability than basic or program development research, they tend toward a broadly shared set of common-denominator variables, such as student dropout rates, grade promotion, and achievement test scores.

STATE OF KNOWLEDGE

Several agencies within the Department of Education collect information on English-language learners. They include the National Center for Education Statistics (NCES), the Office of Bilingual Education and Minority Languages Affairs (OBEMLA), the Office for Civil Rights (OCR), and the Office of the Under Secretary (OUS) through its Planning and Evaluation Service. In addition, the Bureau of the Census collects decennial and annual data about the English proficiency level of individuals through self-report. The Department of Education collects counts of students with limited English proficiency status at the state and district levels, but these figures are not generally considered to be accurate as varying definitions and methods of aggregation are used. Because the data collected by OBEMLA, OCR, and OUS are generally counts of students for purposes of project accountability, technical assistance, or compliance, this chapter focuses primarily on the data collection efforts of NCES and the Bureau of the Census, although it also reviews some relevant efforts by other offices.

One of the major charges to NCES is to report on the condition of education in the United States. To address that charge, NCES conducts many sample surveys and some censuses. Although data collected from samples are considered statistics, the agency aims to generalize to the nation—to estimate the true population parameters in order to report on the condition of education nationwide. This is possible through the use of well-designed, large samples and the application of sample weights to allow extrapolation to the entire population (for example, to all K-12 English-language learners in the United States).

Education statistics address a major issue facing national policymakers: the need for reliable and valid information on language-minority and limited-English-proficient students to assess the effectiveness of policies and services at the broadest national level. Yet currently, there are various obstacles to the collection and reporting of good data to address this need, resulting in inadequate data at the local, state, and national levels. Obstacles frequently mentioned include the following:

• Inconsistent definitions and decision rules across surveys, resulting in differences in the comparison of results or the aggregation of data
• Lack of definition of and agreement on common indicators for measuring student status and outcomes for English-language learners
• Lack of data on and inability to monitor English-language learner achievement and other outcomes
• Lack of consensus on how (and by whom) data on the education of English-language learners should be collected and/or funded

This review of the state of knowledge in education statistics begins with a description of efforts to improve NCES data collection efforts, with particular focus on issues of interest to the education of English-language learners. This is followed by three sections providing a review of the major data collection efforts: the first summarizes the various national and state surveys and data collection efforts, the second examines limitations of current surveys and population estimate studies, and the third reviews assessment issues.

Efforts to Improve NCES Data Collection

General Improvement Efforts

NCES was created in 1965 and became part of the Office of Educational Research and Improvement (OERI) in 1980 as the new Department of Education was created. The education reform movement of the early 1980s brought education statistics into the limelight. In 1985, OERI asked the National Research Council (NRC) to evaluate NCES' overall program and data quality. A committee was established, and in 1986 the NRC published *Creating a Center for Education Statistics: A Time for Action.* The major problems identified were poor data quality, lack of credibility, lack of understanding of user needs, lack of statistical standards, lack of timeliness, lack of resources, and lack of a publication policy. The NRC report made several recommendations in these areas. In the following year, NCES published its first *Statistical Standards* (1987) in response to the NRC report. Over the ensuing years, NCES made many positive strides in responding to the criticisms of the NRC report.

At the same time, and on a parallel track, critical events in the area of indicator systems and education models occurred. In 1987, Rand Corporation published Shavelson et al.'s *Indicator Systems for Monitoring Math and Science Education.* Funded by the National Science Foundation (NSF), the report identified a set of critical indicators and various indicator systems for monitoring math and science education at a national level. It also recommended the use of an input-process-output model. This report was an important milestone in the use of indicators for monitoring education systems.

In 1990, the National Forum on Education Statistics published *A Guide to Improving the National Education Data System.* This report made numerous recommendations for improving the collection of education data. The four domains addressed were background/demographics, educational resources, school processes, and student outcomes. That same year, the historic meeting of President George Bush and the nation's governors at the Education Summit in Charlottesville, Virginia, established the National Education Goals Panel to assess and report on six national education goals, giving further momentum to the interest in quality indicators.

In 1991, NCES published *Education Counts: An Indicator System to Monitor the Nation's Educational Health* (NCES, 1991a), written by a Special Panel on Education Indicators. The report focuses strongly on equity issues and proposes five issue areas: learning outcomes, quality of educational institutions, readiness for school, societal support for learning, and education and economic productivity. Also in 1991, the National Education Goals Panel published *Potential Strategies for Long Term Indicator Development: Reports by Six Technical Planning Subgroups.* Among the recommendations made are the development of an early childhood assessment system to measure five dimensions of readiness (including language use) and development of a national/state/local student record system. Although these developments do not in most cases deal directly with English-language learners, they have some significance for current efforts to improve the capacity of the education data system to address the needs of these students.

Improvement Efforts Related to English-Language Learners

Several related developments in the area of federal monitoring of English-language learner status also occurred at around this time. In 1991, as part of a project funded by NCES and run by the Council of Chief State School Officers (CCSSO)—the Education Data Improvement Project—NCES published *A Study of the Availability and Overlap of Education Data in Federal Collections* (NCES, 1991b). This report focused on the amount of overlap in various education data collections and on differences in definitions of English-language learner status and similar concepts.

In 1994, the CCSSO published a report under contract to NCES entitled *The Feasibility of Collecting Comparable National Statistics About Students with Limited English Proficiency* (Council of Chief State School Officers, 1994a). As part of a larger Educational Data System Implementation Program, the CCSSO conducted an LEP Student Count Study. The goal of this study was to determine the feasibility of making accurate counts of English-language learners from NCES surveys by using standardized definitions and procedures, and of obtaining consistent data on these students across several agencies within the Department of Education. The report is a descriptive study of current practices that provides an overall picture of what data are available. In addition, it gives recommendations on which statistics should be collected and on who should collect them.

In 1995, NCES and the National Forum published *Improving the Capacity of the National Education Data System to Address Equity Issues* (National Center for Education Statistics, 1995a). This report examines how most data collection efforts at the federal level are organized from the point of view of equal access to resources and processes for at-risk children. The Office of Compensatory Education (Title I) collects state-level English-language learner counts. OCR collects school-level data on the status of these students by race and sex. The Migrant Education Office collects state-level data on these students by grade, and the Bureau of Indian Affairs (BIA) collects school-level data. Although the OCR data are seen as the most comprehensive, sample coverage is not representative of all districts and schools in the United States. With regard to coverage of English-language learner issues in NCES' cross-sectional and longitudinal surveys, the Schools and Staffing Survey collects school-level data on these students, and the National Assessment of Educational Progress (NAEP) collects student-level data. The National Educational Longitudinal Study (NELS) collects data on English-language learners, their parents, and their teachers, with significant sections in the questionnaires addressing home language use and English-language ability.[1] Prospects reports on these students' English proficiency status (self-, teacher, and parent reports).

The NCES/Forum report notes limitations in the following areas: inconsistent definitions across surveys, resulting in difficulties in comparing results; incomplete coverage of background processes, resources, and outcome issues, as well as English-language learner issues; and gaps in data at the national level that result in undercoverage of important student populations (e.g., English-language learners). The report points out that it is difficult to improve coverage of English-language learners because information about this population is not available on the Common Core of Data (CCD) sampling frame. Its main recommendations that are relevant to English-language learners are creating a student-based record system with common definitions and reporting metrics; linking current and future surveys; using the CCD as the basic NCES sampling frame; developing new measures of indicators and surveys for research on equity; and reporting state- and national-level data broken out by various school- and student-level characteristics, including English-language learner status.

The most visible and forceful impetus for the Department of Education to consider fully the issue of English-language learner inclusion in education data collection efforts came through legislation. The Improving America's Schools Act of 1994 (P.L. 103-382) states in the Title VII section (Section 7404 (b)):

> The Secretary shall, to the extent feasible, ensure that all data collected by the Department shall include the collection and reporting of data on limited English proficient students.

The passage of the Perkins Act (vocational-technical education) (P.L. 98-524) also gave some impetus to NCES efforts to monitor the educational progress of English-language learners and bilingual students. The Perkins Act requires that the Department of Education use "appropriate methodologies" in testing students with disabilities and English-language learners. It requires (Section 421 (c)(3)) that the Secretary of Education

> ensure that appropriate methodologies are used in assessments of students with limited English proficiency, and students with handicaps, to ensure valid and reliable comparisons with the general student population and across program areas.

Thus, NCES feels an obligation to provide information that is comparable and generalizable so it is representative of the U.S. population. If data are not representative and comparisons cannot be made between English-language learners and the general student population, NCES is obliged to acknowledge this to its users.

---

[1]The National Educational Longitudinal Study began with a cohort of students who were eighth graders in 1988. There have been follow-ups in 1990, 1992, and 1994.

Inclusion of English-Language Learners in the
National Assessment of Educational Progress

Because states have different definitions and criteria for limited English proficiency, and the determination of exclusion has been left to school officials, there are large variations in the proportion of English-language learners included in NAEP. State-by-state comparisons of the inclusion of these students in the Trial State Assessment show large variations (McLaughlin et al., 1995). However, since the Perkins Act requires the Department of Education to ensure that appropriate methodologies are used in assessing English-language learners to allow valid comparisons with the general student population, NCES must develop adequate guidelines for inclusion.

Eligibility rules for English-language learners and students with disabilities in the NAEP program were standardized to ensure greater consistency.[2] Beginning with the 1995 NAEP field test, the criteria were revised to be more inclusive. English-language learners are now included in NAEP if they meet any of the following criteria:

- They have received academic instruction primarily in English for at least 3 years.
- They have received academic instruction in English for less than 3 years, if school staff determine that they are capable of participating in the assessment in English.
- Students whose native language is Spanish have received academic instruction in English for less than 3 years, if school staff determine that they are capable of participating in the assessment in Spanish[3] (Olson and Goldstein, 1996).

Current NAEP experiments help ascertain the validity of using current or other criteria for exclusion. NCES recently funded studies to investigate the incorporation of English-language learners in NAEP and the effects of exclusions and modifications. One of these studies was conducted by the Educational Test-

---

[2]Note that these criteria are still experimental. Prior to 1990, NAEP procedures allowed schools to exclude sampled students if they were limited-English-proficient and if local school personnel judged them incapable of meaningful participation in the assessment (Strang and Carlson, 1991). Between 1990 and 1994, NCES instructed schools to exclude students with limited English proficiency from its assessments only if all the following conditions applied: the student was a native speaker of a language other than English, the student had been enrolled in an English-speaking school for less than 2 years (not including bilingual education programs), and school officials judged the student to be incapable of taking the assessment (Olson and Goldstein, 1996:3).

[3]The Spanish-language assessment in mathematics is still considered experimental. By examining the results of the 1996 NAEP, NCES staff will determine whether the assessment results for students tested in Spanish are scalable to the English-language assessment.

ing Service for the NAEP 1995 field tests. The LEP Special Study explored the feasibility and validity of providing NAEP assessments in Spanish and Spanish-English bilingual versions in grades 4 and 8 in preparation for the 1996 NAEP in mathematics. The findings indicated that "in general, the 1995 field test results appear to be encouraging. Some LEP students who would not have participated under previous assessment conditions were able to participate in the field test. However, a preliminary analysis of the test items and student performance indicated that for the LEP samples of students included and assessed under nonstandard conditions (i.e., with accommodations or adaptations) in the field test, the results may not be comparable to those from other students. Further study of the statistical and measurement issues was indicated for 1996" (Olson and Goldstein, 1996). To address the need for further study, a special sample design was developed to examine the effects of inclusion criteria and accommodations for the 1996 NAEP in mathematics.

A number of studies are under way to investigate further issues related to the inclusion of English-language learners. These studies are investigating scaling issues, reporting issues, the appropriateness of inclusion criteria, the construct validity of the assessment for English-language learners, language complexity issues, and inclusion procedures.

The National Center for Research on Evaluation, Standards, and Student Testing at the University of California, Los Angeles, conducted a study for NCES on linguistic modification of NAEP math items. Researchers examined the role of linguistic complexity in students' performance on original and revised NAEP math items (Abedi et al., 1995). The study found no significant improvement in performance for students taking assessments whose linguistic complexity, defined syntactically, had been modified. Students in English as a second language (ESL) math classes scored the lowest and showed only a slight improvement on the simplified items; those students in remedial/basic or average classes showed the largest improvement. It should be noted that the study examined only one aspect of linguistic complexity—complex syntax—and did not address other aspects of linguistic organization, such as semantic or lexical complexity.

The American Institutes for Research is currently conducting a follow-up study of fourth grade students who were excluded from the 1994 NAEP Trial State Assessment in reading. The purpose of the study is to determine the assessibility of the excluded students and the types of adaptations that would be needed to include them, as well as to obtain more detail on the exclusion decision process. The ultimate aim of the study is to suggest improvements in the directions provided to local sites. The study procedures include analysis of questionnaire data, visits to schools in states that have high percentages of English-language learners, and collection of data from assessments and interviews.

The 1995 field test of NAEP included several feasibility studies aimed at increasing the participation of students with disabilities and those with limited English proficiency. The approaches to be studied included administering tests in Braille, in large print, or in Spanish and varying the testing time and methods.

NCES contracted with Hakuta and Valdes in 1994 to prepare a study design for evaluating strategies for including English-language learners in NAEP. Hakuta and Valdez suggested using two basic principles: a continuum-of-strategies principle (trying out a number of options, with ongoing attempts to maximize the number of students offered options) and a reality principle (considering only options that are realistic in the context of policy and NAEP). In addition, Hakuta and Valdes designed a student questionnaire and a study that randomly assigns various test conditions to students.

NCES convened a study group in late 1994 for a conference on Inclusion Guidelines and Accommodations for LEP Students in NAEP and published the proceedings (August and McArthur, 1996). The study group recommended research in all areas surrounding testing, translation of materials, and various types of accommodation. However, they cautioned that such research is complex given individual differences in native-language and English literacy and proficiency. Participants stressed the importance of developing a set of consistent guidelines for determining whether to include and how to assess English-language learners using NAEP.

The equitable inclusion of minority students has been a critical policy issue for NCES in the development of its surveys and databases for some time. However, for some advocates, "equity" per se is presently too broadly conceived, and there is a perceived need for a more detailed description of the needs of English-language learners.

Surveys and Data Collection Efforts

National Efforts

NCES administers a large number of surveys and data collection efforts. The major ones are described in Annex 9-1, along with a Census Bureau survey, the Current Population Survey, and two OUS-sponsored surveys (Prospects and the Descriptive Study of Services to LEP Students).

State Efforts

States actively collect data on their English-language learner populations, both through their assessment programs and through their bilingual education programs (including those funded by state education agencies through Title VII). This section provides a brief review of these efforts.

A major effort to improve the quality of education data available at both the state and federal levels since the mid-1980s is the CCSSO Education Data Improvement Project. The project has published several reports on the availability and overlap of education data in federal collections. In addition, it published a report in 1991 entitled *Summary of State Practices Concerning the Assessment of and the Data Collection About LEP Students* (Council of Chief State School Officers, 1991). Areas of focus in the report include identification of English-language learners, state-level data collection, reporting, and utilization. Almost all state education agencies reported collecting data about English-language learners, and about half said they had laws or policies regarding the identification of these students and the provision of language assistance programs to meet their needs. Major data collected by state instruments are number of English-language learners identified and served, language background, and grade retention rate.

CCSSO (1995) recently published an implementation guide for a new system for a standardized data format, called Speedee Xpress. This guide represents an attempt to develop a national standard for state and local data collection efforts and to define commonly used data elements. In addition, use of Speedee Xpress allows states and localities to exchange data electronically. Although most states have accepted the Speedee Xpress standards, only a handful are actively using the system (Utah, Colorado, Nevada, and Delaware).

To document assessment policies and practices and develop policy recommendations for English-language learners, the Evaluation Assistance Center East at The George Washington University[4] surveyed all 50 state assessment directors in 1994 (Hafner et al., 1995). The survey findings provide baseline information on state assessment policies and practices and identify key issues affecting our ability to measure the academic progress of these students. Key findings include the following: (1) there is no common operational definition used by states to identify English-language learners; (2) about 80 percent of states have an assessment policy pertaining to these students; (3) most states allow exemptions for English-language learners (they are not required to take the same assessments as their fluent English-speaking peers), and 33 percent report the actual number of these students assessed in their state; (4) a majority of states allow test modifications for English-language learners, but only 4 states provide assessments for these students in languages other than English; and (5) only 4 states report disaggregated scores of English-language learners, while 24 states report that they do not usually but could report disaggregated scores.

Although most states collect some data on English-language learners, we currently cannot make state-to-state or state-to-nation comparisons. Speedee/Xpress and the *Student Data Handbook* are steps toward these ends.

Limitations of Surveys and Population Estimate Studies

This section examines further the issue of limited coverage of surveys and population estimate studies and the various other limitations of these efforts,

---

[4]The Evaluation Assistance Center East was a Title VII-funded center that provided technical assistance in the area of assessment to Title VII-funded schools.

including issues of data definition, data collection, and coverage of the variables of interest.

Population Coverage

Population coverage refers to whether a survey includes in its sampling frame all the possible attributes of interest of its intended population. This issue has arisen perhaps most prominently with respect to the 1990 Bureau of the Census decennial count of the U.S. population. There have been many criticisms of that census, including a lawsuit claiming that the true population was undercounted, especially minority persons in central cities. It is claimed that many homeless and transient persons were not counted and that the Census Bureau should adjust its estimates accordingly. Although most people agree that there was an undercount, there is disagreement over its extent and whether and how the Bureau should adjust the estimates.

NCES' *Statistical Standards* (National Center for Education Statistics, 1992) sets forth department and agency policies on sample and data quality, data collection, and reporting. In its standard for the design of a survey, response rates are set at a minimum of 90 percent for longitudinal surveys and 85 percent for cross-sectional sample surveys. The target response rate for each critical variable is at least 90 percent.

The exclusion of English-language learners and students with disabilities in NCES' censuses and surveys has come to be seen as an undercoverage problem. In recent years, it has become evident that NCES (as well as other agencies) has gaps in its coverage of these students, as well as incarcerated students, American Indian students, preschool children, and migrant children.

According to Houser (1994), the exclusion of a subpopulation potentially biases the results of a study, and the data collected may not be generalizable to the excluded students. For this reason, NCES carried out the NELS base year followback study of students who had initially been deemed ineligible and recalculated the grade 8-10 dropout rate. In addition, the exclusion of students with disabilities and limited English proficiency from NCES' surveys and assessments may bias data on racial and ethnic groups since minority students are overrepresented among these two subgroups.

In general, students who are excluded from NCES' assessments have also been excluded from background questionnaires linked to the assessments. About 2 percent of all eighth grade students were excluded from the NELS tests and surveys in the base year because of language barriers (Spencer, 1994). NELS did provide Spanish-language questionnaires for students in the first and second follow-ups, as well as Spanish-language surveys for students' parents. However, not many students chose to use those surveys. The Early Childhood Longitudinal Study (National Center for Education Statistics, 1995b) also plans to gather background data from English-language learners, even though all of them may not be included in direct assessments during their first few years in the study. Moreover, as mentioned previously, NCES has initiated several efforts, primarily with the NAEP program, to improve its estimates and coverage, including the use of alternative assessments and accommodations for English-language learners and students with disabilities. These activities are intended to have broader applicability to other national and subnational survey and assessment activities.

One way to ensure that a survey will cover groups of policy interest adequately is to oversample those groups. For example, in NELS, Hispanic and Asian students were oversampled to provide a sufficient number for subgroup analysis. Although English-language learners were not oversampled, NELS did include some students with low levels of English proficiency (about 300 were identified as such by their teachers). Of the Asian and Hispanic eighth graders included in the study, three-quarters came from language-minority families. About 4 percent of these students showed low English proficiency, 32 percent moderate proficiency, and 66 percent high proficiency (Bradby, 1992). However, no additional money was obtained to oversample American Indian students, so the sample included only a small number of those students—about 200, a number that does not allow extensive analyses of this subgroup.

The Prospects (Office of Policy and Planning, 1995) study included a supplemental sample of language-minority students from schools with high concentrations of English-language learners. This sample included 2,036 first grade English-language learners, 1,691 third grade English-language learners, 1,380 first grade language-minority students, and 1,837 third grade language-minority students. It was included to maximize the policy relevance of the study for the first and third grade cohorts. Although English-language learners were oversampled, about 25 percent of them were not tested in Spanish or English, which is a highly unacceptable response rate (according to NCES' *Statistical Standards*). No oversampling was done for the seventh grade cohort, since that grade contains fewer English-language learners in need of services.

Data Definitions

Another problem with surveys and population estimate studies is that they use inconsistent definitions of limited English proficiency. The following examples show the wide variation in the definitions used.

Prospects Study (1995:i-2):
Children whose native language is other than English and whose skills in speaking, reading, or writing English are such that they can derive limited benefit from school instruction in English.

Bilingual Education Act (1988) (P.L. 100-297)
> An LEP Student is one who:
> a. meets one or more of the following conditions:
> —the student was born outside of US or whose native language is not English;
> —the student comes from an environment where a language other than English is dominant; or
> —the student is American Indian or Alaskan Native and comes from an environment where a language other than English has a significant impact on his/her English language proficiency; and
> b. has sufficient difficulty speaking, reading, writing, or understanding the English language to deny him or her the opportunity to learn successfully in English only classrooms.

Council of Chief State School Officers (CCSSO) Report (1994a:8-9)
> A limited-English proficient student is one who has a language background other than English and his or her proficiency in English is such that the probability of the student's academic success in an English only classroom is below that of an academically successful peer with an English language background.

Student Data Handbook for Early Childhood, Elementary and Secondary Education (National Center for Education Statistics, 1994:33) (developed by CCSSO)
> LEP: An individual with a language background other than English, and whose proficiency in English is such that the probability of the individual's success in an English only environment is below that of a successful peer with an English language background.

CCSSO's two definitions are very similar; they are closest among the definitions to the intent of the Supreme Court *Lau* decision (see Appendix A), and therefore perhaps the most meaningful. However, operationalization of such a definition could be problematic.

A CCSSO (1991) report notes that operational definitions of an English-language learner also vary across and within states. Some states use the definition provided in the Bilingual Education Act, while others use various other definitions. One that is used commonly defines proficiency by setting a performance standard level (e.g., reaching the 40th percentile on standard English proficiency tests).

The *Student Data Handbook for Early Childhood, Elementary and Secondary Education* developed by CCSSO (National Center for Education Statistics, 1994) is a large-scale attempt to bring states, districts, and the federal government to agreement on common definitions. It is quite comprehensive, but not widely used as yet.

Data Collection Issues

According to CCSSO (1994a), current English-language learner data collection efforts at the federal and state levels are complicated not only by variation in definitions, but also by variations in identification procedures, data collection methods, and data collection levels and purposes.

There is great variation in the procedures used to identify students as being of limited English proficiency (see Chapter 5). A majority of schools and districts (77 percent) use a home-language survey to identify students who should be tested for this purpose, and many (83 percent) use oral proficiency tests or interviews or scores on standardized tests. A majority use two or three methods to identify such students. It is generally assumed that identification procedures are used judiciously in most cases and that most students who have limited English proficiency are properly identified. There is wide variation among states and districts in reclassification policies and practices, and various criteria are used for the purpose (Council of Chief State School Officers, 1994a).

It may well prove desirable to allow NCES data users to create varying definitions of limited-English-proficient status to suit specific analytic purposes. English-language learners are not a homogeneous population. Attempts to understand their educational outcomes will benefit from consideration of their nativity, their educational and other experiences in English and a non-English language, and other factors related to language acquisition and the development of bilingualism.

Another complication in data collection is variation in data collection methods across districts and states. Some use a district survey of English-language learners, others have a state survey, and still others have a state census on the number of students in bilingual education and ESL programs. Administrative record data are often considered to be of poor quality and unreliable, partly because of this variation in methods.

Another concern is variation in data collection levels, that is, differences in the degree of aggregation of numbers. District counts are generally sent to state agencies, which then may aggregate them or not before sending them to federal agencies for reporting.

There is also variation in data collection purposes. Various agencies and divisions of the Department of Education have differing purposes for their data collection efforts. For OBEMLA, the primary purpose of data collection is to obtain an accurate count of students served by Title VII programs. For OCR, equity is a primary concern, as well as compliance with federal mandates in the area of civil rights and access. For OUS, policy analysis is the primary concern. For NCES, collecting valid and reliable data that will enable reporting to the U.S. public and the Congress on the status of American education is the prime purpose, and policy analysis is only a secondary purpose.

Other data collection issues raised include the costs and feasibility of collecting the data. Because survey costs are often prohibitive and new federal monies are not expected, agencies have recently been conducting computer-assisted phone surveys as a cost-cutting measure. NAEP has gone to a matrix sampling design, so that each student does not have to take a 4-hour test. The ongoing Early Childhood Longitudinal Study (see National Center for Education Statistics, 1995b) plans to administer individual assessments to kindergartners; this will be very expensive and may limit the number of children that can be sampled. In addition, the feasibility of administering the early childhood assessments in languages other than English and Spanish is questionable, since about 75 percent of all English-language learners speak Spanish. Thus, the 25 percent of English-language learners who speak a language other than Spanish will most likely be excluded unless assessment accommodation procedures are used for these children. Only a few states currently provide assessments in a language other than English, and only two provide alternative assessments in languages other than Spanish.

Content Coverage: Variables of Interest

For organizational purposes, we categorize variables of interest according to the five issue areas identified in *Education Counts* (National Center for Education Statistics, 1991a). In addition, we add a sixth area on demographic issues. The six areas or domains of interest, then, are the following:

- Readiness for school
- Demographics
- Social support for education
- Quality of educational institutions and teaching
- Learner outcomes
- Education and economic productivity

Annex 9-2 shows the variables of interest within these six areas.

As noted earlier, information and data on variables of interest regarding English-language learners are collected at the federal level by various agencies and departments for their own reporting purposes or because of monitoring mandates (Council of Chief State School Officers, 1994a). However, many important data are missing or addressed inadequately. Major gaps in the data needed to monitor the progress of English-language learners are found in the following areas: readiness-for-school indicators in general; English proficiency level (by grade); length of instruction in the second language in years; content and topic coverage of ESL/bilingual classes; type of instruction given in special classes for English-language-learners; and number of English-language learners by grade, school, and district. Another variable of interest is proficiency in the native language.

OBEMLA and OCR collect data from states about numbers of English-language learners, languages spoken, and services provided. The Bureau of the Census collects somewhat detailed data on language use in households. Information on language usage and ability was collected in the 1980 and 1990 censuses and will probably be collected in the year 2000 census. The Census Bureau's Current Population Survey collected information on language usage and ability in 1979, 1989, 1992, and 1995. The Census Bureau does not have an English proficiency variable per se, although it collects data on language spoken at home and respondent's ability to speak English (from not at all to very well). Respondents reported on their own and other household members' language usage and ability. The census does not collect data on the English proficiency status of individual children. For confidentiality purposes, the various data systems cannot be linked as they do not have ways to associate persons with households or common identification numbers. The coverage of variables of interest in each of the six issue areas identified earlier is discussed in the following subsections.

Readiness for School In the area of readiness for school, there are very few data on English-language learners currently available. The National Household Education Survey has collected data on preschool program participation and on reading materials and literacy activities in the home (e.g., reading, newspapers). However, it does not collect data on the English proficiency status of children. The Prospects study collected data for first and third graders on language use in primary and second language, but data on first graders do not really address "readiness" for school. Prospects also collected data on students' English proficiency level and literacy activities in the home. NCES' planned Early Childhood Longitudinal Study (National Center for Education Statistics, 1995b), which will be field tested in 1996, plans to collect data on children's health, such as birth weight and immunization record, preschool program participation, motor development, physical well-being, social and emotional well-being, language usage, literacy activities in the home, and general knowledge and skills. NCES plans to assess the children individually, using various checklists, activities, and nonverbal language and aptitude tests. There are currently no plans to assess students in Spanish, although it may be possible to use Spanish-speaking test administrators for some students.

Demographics The Title I program collects data on students living in poverty, as does the Census Bureau. The Census Bureau collects data on parent English proficiency levels, language spoken in the home, and most frequently used language (collected once in 1989). The language usage information that is collected is used to create a measure of linguistic isolation of the household. Almost all current surveys collect data on race/ethnicity, and many collect data on family income (U.S. Census, National Household Education Survey, NELS). Many agencies collect data on home language (U.S. Census, OBEMLA, Schools and

Staffing Survey, NAEP, National Household Education Survey, NELS), but the data are collected at different levels (e.g. student, school, household). OUS and OBEMLA collect state- and federal-level data on number of English-language learners, and the Schools and Staffing Survey has recently started collecting data on the number and percentage of these students in sampled schools. Several agencies have data on student participation in bilingual/ESL programs (OBEMLA, OCR [Prospects and the Descriptive Study of Services to LEP Students], NCES [NELS and the Schools and Staffing Survey]). Prospects also collected data on parent English proficiency and home language.

Social Support for Education   Social support includes the involvement of families and communities, as well as cultural and financial support. There has been little systematic definition of issues and data needs in the area of community and cultural support for learning and little or no data collected in this area. There are some data on per pupil expenditures, mainly at the local and state levels, but there is a problem with comparability of definitions for such terms as programs offered and administrative costs.

The National Household Education Survey has collected data on several indicators in this issue area, including parent involvement in school activities, reading materials in the home, and parent participation in ESL programs. High School and Beyond and NELS have collected data on parent involvement in school activities, on parental educational attainment, and on school cooperation with community agencies. The Census Bureau collects data on parental educational attainment. The CCD at NCES collects data on per pupil expenditures. Prospects is collecting data on parental involvement, literacy activities in the home, and parental education levels.

Quality of Educational Institutions and Teaching   In the area of school quality, the Schools and Staffing Survey covers most of the topics listed in Annex 9-2, including class size, pupil-teacher ratio, instructional time, course offerings, availability of bilingual/ESL programs, existence of various special programs, and availability of teacher aides. NELS collects data on instructional time, class size, availability of science laboratories and computers, secondary course offerings, homework given, and availability of special programs. No information is currently available on content/topic coverage in ESL/bilingual classes, although the Prospects study has some information about ESL/bilingual classes in the early grades. The Descriptive Study contains data on the availability and characteristics of ESL and bilingual instruction and the number of teacher aides.

In the area of teacher quality, Schools and Staffing teacher surveys collect data on years of experience, educational background, degrees, teacher salary, percentage certified in bilingual education/ESL, percentage teaching English-language learners, minority status of teachers, and enrichment activities. It also collects information from all teachers about whether they have any training to teach English-language learners (over and above ESL/bilingual certification), whether they have any English-language learners in their classes, and if so, what percentage of the class these students represent. The Descriptive Study has data on number of teachers certified in bilingual education and ESL and percentage teaching English-language learners.

Learner Outcomes   NAEP and NELS collect data on math and reading achievement, as well as on grades, academic course taking, and out-of-school activities. NELS also collects data on self-concept, retention and high school graduation, participation in extracurricular activities, English-language proficiency (self- and teacher-reported), engagement in school, and teachers' judgment of student ability. Although NAEP and NELS collect extensive data on student outcomes, a major problem is that the surveys exclude most English-language learners, so it is not possible to assess these students' achievement levels and disaggregate the data by English proficiency status. NELS can disaggregate by language minority and by English proficiency status. However, since only part of the total sample took the achievement tests, the data available on English-language learners reflect the performance of those who are judged by teachers and local school administrators to be capable of taking the test, and these students may not be representative of the pool of English-language learners. The Census Bureau collects data on English proficiency, but they are generally at the level of the household respondent and not the child. It also collects information about educational enrollment and educational attainment for each family member. Prospects is collecting data on student achievement in reading (in Spanish and English) and math, school grades, teacher judgments of student ability, student self-assessment of ability, grade retention, and teachers' reporting of English proficiency. As noted earlier, Prospects collected data on educational achievement from first and third grade students. However, 36 percent of the first grade and 45 percent of the third grade English-language learners were not given an achievement test in English; more than 27 percent of all English-language learners were not administered any achievement test.

Education and Economic Productivity   NELS student surveys collect data longitudinally on most of the indicators in this issue area: school attendance, tardiness, retention in grade, dropout status, degree completion, alternative certification, transcripts (from which it is possible to determine completion of key classes), college enrollment, persistence, college completion rate, and employment record. The Schools and Staffing Survey student record supplement collects data on attendance, tardiness, and retention.

Assessment Issues

The two major and conceptually different reasons given for including more English-language learners in federal studies are (1) to improve the quality of both the data and overall population estimates by including all relevant subpopulations, and (2) to examine equity issues through disaggregation of how various subgroups (e.g., English-language learners) are doing in comparison with the overall population. The first purpose is satisfied by including English-language learners in a study whenever they are encountered in a sample such that their probability of inclusion is no different from that of other individuals. The second purpose requires oversampling of English-language learners to enable statistically reliable estimates of characteristics of this population. OBEMLA funds have typically paid for both of these functions.

In either case, tensions arise over how to define data quality. The traditional definition is based on the reliability and validity of the observations. From this perspective, data on English-language learner achievement in content areas are suspect regardless of the language in which the testing is done. If the testing is in English, the scores reflect English proficiency as well as content knowledge and skills; if it is in the students' native language, the equivalence between the English and native-language versions of the tests is an issue (see also Chapter 5). Thus, the prudent option from the perspective of guarding the psychometric properties of the data would be to exclude data from English-language learners or include only data for those whose scores might be reliable and valid. On the other hand, data quality can also be defined in terms of the representativeness of the sample, which, as suggested earlier, is threatened whenever portions of the population are systematically left out of the sampling process. This definition of data quality is the one preferred by advocates for English-language learners and by OBEMLA, which is interested in the disaggregation of data on various subgroups as a way of comparing those subgroups with the overall sample. The tension between maintaining rigorous psychometric standards on the one hand and including all students on the other has been the focus of discussions between NCES and advocates for English-language learners (see August and McArthur, 1996). This dialogue, in addition to the passage of the Perkins Act, the reauthorization of the Improving America's Schools Act (P.L. 103-382), and the passage of Goals 2000 (P.L. 103-227), has created a climate in which NCES has begun to recognize the importance of these issues.

The following is an example of how excluding English-language learners from national studies results in inaccurate population estimates. In 1992, NCES funded a follow-back study of the NELS base year (1988) students who had been found to be ineligible because of limited English proficiency. The purpose of the study was to ascertain the status of these students (enrolled in school or dropped out), as well as their current eligibility for inclusion in the NELS sample in 1992. About 70 percent of the students deemed ineligible in eighth grade because of limited English proficiency were found to be eligible by twelfth grade (4 years later). Some were added to the NELS study at this point. The results of the follow-back study showed that when data on English-language learners (and students with disabilities) were included, the dropout rate for grades 8-10 was higher than originally estimated (6.8 vs. 6 percent). A technical report describing this effort was released in 1995 by NCES (Ingels, 1995, draft).

As discussed in Chapter 5, the validity of assessments administered to English-language learners is a central concern tied to the purpose of the assessment. A long-standing exclusion of English-language learners has created problems in estimation and in comparisons between these and other students. Advocates for English-language learners agree that rather than being excluded from assessments, these students should be "appropriately" assessed.

A majority of states currently use modifications for their English-language learners in at least one of their assessments. Such modifications can help make test content more comprehensible to these students (Hafner, 1995). As noted in Chapter 5, the most common modifications allowed are flexible scheduling, small-group administration, use of dictionaries, simplification of directions, reading of questions aloud, and extra time (Hafner et al., 1995). Allowing extra time has, however, been shown to advantage those students with more time, and this may be problematic.

In NCES' *Statistical Standards* (National Center for Education Statistics, 1992), there is a standard on educational tests. The Checklist for Educational Tests includes the following under special testing conditions:

- Test modifications should be provided for those with handicapping conditions or language differences.
- When feasible, validity, reliability, and other indices of test integrity should be investigated for special populations.

Thus, NCES appears to be condoning or recommending the use of modifications for English-language learners.

The validity issues that arise in testing English-language learners include the following:

- Is it valid to assess these students in English if they are not fully English proficient?
- At what point is it valid to test these students in English?
- If it is not feasible to assess English-language learners in their native languages, what modifications can be made to give them opportunities to be assessed in English?
- How do test modifications influence test reliability and validity?
- Is it possible to assign (impute) scores for these students based on background and language information?

As previously discussed, the American Institutes for Research is conducting several studies for NCES on procedures for incorporating English-language learners and using test adaptations in NAEP. In one substudy, NAEP assessments will be individually administered, and student performance on them will be compared with performance on group-administered assessments. Results from these studies will help answer some of the questions raised here.

The Prospects study, which would appear to be an optimal longitudinal database for researching factors associated with English-language learner achievement over time, is of somewhat limited usefulness, as over 25 percent of the students in the first year took no achievement test in either English or Spanish. In addition, there are large amounts of missing data. Sample attrition in longitudinal studies, especially in those that involve highly mobile populations such as English-language learners, is a serious concern in the design, implementation, and analysis of such studies. This problem was emphatically noted in a previous NRC report that looked at two large longitudinal studies in detail (Meyer and Fienberg, 1992).

RESEARCH AND INFRASTRUCTURE NEEDS

Coordination

9-1. To coordinate federal statistics, we recommend convening an interagency forum or working group composed of agencies responsible for producing, disseminating, and analyzing federal statistics about the status of English-language learners and bilingual youth to examine gaps, overlaps, and possible links in the overall system. Oversight responsibility for this group could lie with an agency such as the National Center for Education Statistics (NCES), and agencies to be involved would include NCES, the Office of Bilingual Education and Minority Language Affairs (OBEMLA), the Office of Educational Research and Improvement (OERI), the Office of the Under Secretary, the Department of Health and Human Services, and the Bureau of the Census (as well as other interested groups such as the Council of Chief State School Officers [CCSSO] and states with large English-language learner populations).

The LEP Student Count Study (Council of Chief State School Officers, 1994b) recommends that federal agencies coordinate to ensure that data are of good quality and that duplicate data collections are not conducted. In addition, a recent National Research Council (1995) report on a workshop addressing the integration of federal statistics on children recommends improved cross-agency planning and coordination and the development of opportunities for linkages with existing data collection efforts.

Population coverage (ensuring that a representative sample is included) is an example of a topic that holds great potential for interagency coordination. Besides NCES, this topic is central to the mission of OBEMLA, the Office of the Under Secretary, two OERI Institutes (the National Institute for Student Achievement, Curriculum and Assessment, and the National Institute for Students at Risk), and the states.

Standard Definition of Limited English Proficiency

9-2. *Different agencies and offices within the Department of Education that collect data on English-language learners in collaboration with states with large numbers of such students should agree on and use common definitions of basic concepts (limited English proficiency, linguistic isolation) consistent with definitions in the CCSSO Student Data Handbook for Early Childhood, Elementary and Secondary Education (National Center for Education Statistics, 1994). Furthermore, federal and state staff who work with local representatives should ensure that they are aware of and use the definitions and common usages in this handbook.*

There are currently a number of obstacles to collecting data on English-language learners, aggregating data across administrative levels, and allowing states to share data. One major issue is that there is no common definition of limited English proficiency that would yield commonality across studies, states, or even districts within given states. Similarly, other indicators are not consistently defined.

Common Framework

9-3. *NCES should evaluate whether the Common Care of Data (CCD), with its current limitations, is able to serve as a basic sampling frame. CCD should collect quantitative data on English-language learners (e.g., number and percent by school and district in the Administrative Survey). CCD is the best candidate for this purpose as it is annual, and its data can be combined with census data and other databases.*

9-4. *To make it possible to aggregate and share data, NCES should create a student-based record system. This measure has been recommended by several groups, including the Cooperative System[5] and CCSSO, but never initiated.*

9-5. *States might explore the use of the Speedee/Xpress system to allow consistency in data definitions and use and the exchange of data.*

9-6. *Districts should have individual student record systems that allow summaries or aggregations of data (e.g., number of English-language learners receiving services by type of service, number of English-language learners reclassified as fully English proficient).*

---

[5]The Cooperative System is a group organized by NCES and includes representatives from all states. It meets in Washington periodically to discuss common issues.

This chapter has pointed out that not all data of interest for our present concerns are complete and of good quality, and there is some duplication in data collection. In addition, it has noted a lack of linkage among data collection efforts, although with some exceptions (e.g., the U.S. Census and CCD, and the National Assessment of Educational Progress [NAEP] and the National Educational Longitudinal Study [NELS]).

Inclusion of English-Language Learners in Assessments

9-7. An intensive research effort is needed to develop strategies for including English-language learners in all federal and state education data collection activities.

Such an effort should be broad in several senses. First, it should be responsive to the intent of the laws that explicitly call for full inclusion (the Perkins Act, P.L. 98-524), and the Improving America's Schools Act, P.L. 103-382) by proposing accommodation and other strategies that are feasible in the short term; however, it should also recognize the difficulty of the challenge and develop a long-term strategy that would result in a psychometrically defensible system of inclusion. Second, it should recognize the diversity of the English-language learner population, including the range of languages represented and varying degrees of formal education and familiarity with formal testing. Finally, it should be responsive to the possibility that different issues may arise in different content areas being assessed (see Chapters 3 and 5) and that optimum inclusion strategies may differ depending on the knowledge area being measured.

9-8. Since assessments based on translations into a second language have questionable validity, research is needed to determine the equivalence of these materials.

9-9. The Department of Education might develop a checklist to help states and local administrators determine which English-language learners should be included in surveys and assessments and which should participate in alternative procedures.

9-10. The effects on test scores of excluding various subgroups and the validity and comparability of achievement measures in different languages should also be studied.

9-11. In its longitudinal studies program, NCES should oversample English-language learners to get adequate numbers.

A major issue for data on English-language learners is population coverage. Our analysis has suggested two problems in this area. The first is inadequate representation of these students in samples for the general population, resulting in general population estimates that are biased. Inadequate representation occurs mainly because the standard subject matter assessments in English are not appropriate for English-language learners, and there are few alternatives. This problem can be addressed by developing and investigating the validity and reliability of alternative assessments, including assessments in non-English languages and modifications to English-language assessments (see Chapter 5). The second problem arises from the need to conduct studies that disaggregate the data on English-language learners for various purposes. This issue can be addressed by sufficiently oversampling these students. A main obstacle in this case is financial: Who pays for the additional data collection? Our recommendation on this latter issue is presented in Chapter 10.

Research on strategies for including English-language learners in data collection activities would initially be through smaller-scale special studies. These studies would develop new assessment techniques that would allow full inclusion of those students and in the process would test the validity of alternative test modifications. One such modification would be native-language assessments; others might include modifications in test administration or test items (see Chapter 5). Special studies should also be conducted to develop standard procedures for incorporating English-language learners into assessments. Specifically, such studies should be conducted to determine which of these students should take the standard English assessments and which should take alternative versions, and what these alternative versions might be. This determination would be based in part on ascertaining the best predictors of student achievement in the various content areas (e.g., time in country, length of time in English instruction, first-language proficiency, English proficiency, linguistic isolation, language of parents). These smaller studies would be followed by field tests of regular assessments such as NAEP to explore the use of accommodations in tests and modified assessments.

Data Coverage

9-12. A common set of indicators for English-language learners such as those listed in Annex 9-2 should be developed by NCES, in consultation with other offices and advocacy groups. Data on indicators identified as important and currently not being covered should be collected, and those indicators that are being covered should be carefully reviewed for their appropriateness. This framework should be the base against which samples for all Department of Education research with English-language learners are compared. In addition, this information should be made available for use by OBEMLA and the Secretary of Education in preparing their reports to Congress.

Our review of variables of interest for monitoring the progress of English-language learners (Annex 9-2) uncovered a number of areas where data are either unavailable or inadequate. Major gaps identified were in the areas of school readiness; English proficiency; native-language proficiency; length of instruction in second language; content and topic coverage in ESL and bilingual education programs; type of instruction given in ESL and bilingual education classes; status of programs designed to help English-language learners and language-minority students in postsecondary institutions; and number of English-language learners by grade, school, and district. In addition, information on criteria for participation in and exit from bilingual programs and provisions for assessing content knowledge and skills are of interest.

ANNEX 1
NATIONAL SURVEYS AND DATA COLLECTION EFFORTS

Table 9-1 shows the various national-level surveys and data collection efforts as of 1995.

The first column in Table 9-1 lists the major cross-sectional surveys. The Common Core of Data (CCD) is NCES' major elementary-secondary sampling frame for public and private K-12 schools and districts in the country. It is conducted annually and provides basic information and descriptive statistics on public elementary and secondary schools. Three types of information are collected: general descriptive information, student data, and fiscal data.

Schools and Staffing is a cross-sectional survey of teachers and administrators on a nation-wide basis conducted every 3 to 5 years. Information collected includes teacher demand and shortage, programs and services offered, student characteristics, student-teacher ratios, school climate, demographic characteristics of teachers, and some administrative records on students. In 1993-1994, a new student record component collected data from class rosters of a subsample of teachers (10,326 students). The survey asked for information on the students' English proficiency status, home language, services received, courses taken, grades, and other outcomes.

The Fast Response Survey System is a one-time vehicle for special-topic surveys, with a methodology that allows quick response and data availability. It collects data from state agencies, local education agencies, schools, teachers, and adult literacy programs. One recent survey included a kindergarten teacher survey on children's readiness for school.

The Current Population Survey (CPS) is a monthly household survey conducted by the Census Bureau to provide information on employment, English-language proficiency of adults, frequency of use of non-English language, and other population characteristics. NCES funds an annual CPS supplement on school enrollment, educational attainment, and other educational items.

The National Household Education Survey is a cross-sectional household-based survey done every 2 years on various topics related to parents, children, and education, including preschool activities, participation in adult education, and school readiness.

Lastly, a one-time survey sponsored by OUS and funded by OBEMLA, the Descriptive Study of Services to LEP Students, was conducted in 1991-92. It collected data on number and characteristics of English-language learners, instructional services, administrative procedures, and instructional staff qualifications from state agencies, districts, schools, and teachers of these students.

In the second column of Table 9-1 are postsecondary surveys (all cross-sectional). Many of these collect data on minority participation in higher-education programs. The Integrated Postsecondary Education Data System collects data annually from postsecondary institutions on institutional characteristics, en-

TABLE 9-1 National Surveys and Data Collection Efforts, 1995

Cross-Sectional Surveys	Postsecondary Surveys	Surveys That Include Assessments
Common Core of Data (CCD)	Integrated Postsecondary Education Data System	National Assessment of Educational Progress (NAEP) (C)
Schools and Staffing	Recent College Graduates	
Fast Response Survey System	National Postsecondary Student Aid Survey	National Adult Literacy Survey (C)
Current Population Survey (CPS)	National Survey of Postsecondary Faculty	National Educational Longitudinal Study of 1988 (NELS) (L)
National Household Education Survey	Survey of Earned Doctorates	High School and Beyond (L)
Descriptive Study of Services to LEP Students	Postsecondary Faculty Quick Information System	High School Transcript Studies (C) National Longitudinal Survey (NLS)-72 (L) Beginning Postsecondary Student Longitudinal Survey (L) Baccalaureate and Beyond Survey (C and L) Early Childhood Longitudinal Study (L) Prospects (L)

NOTE: C = cross-sectional; L = longitudinal.

rollment, completions, salaries, finances, libraries, and staff. Recent College Graduates surveys this population on various topics, including field of study and employment status (especially in teaching). The National Postsecondary Student Aid Survey surveys college students every 3 years on financial aid, income, employment, demographics and costs, and special-population enrollments. The National Survey of Postsecondary Faculty provides data about postsecondary faculty characteristics and is conducted periodically. The Survey of Earned Doctorates is an annual survey filled out by all students who complete a doctorate; topics include demographics, field of study, time spent, financial support, and educational plans. The Postsecondary Education Quick Information System is a new survey system similar to the Fast Response Survey System. It collects timely data on focused issues, such as financial climate, status of deaf and hard-of-hearing students, and programs for disadvantaged students.

In the third column of Table 9-1 are the cross-sectional and longitudinal surveys that include assessments. NAEP is the largest of the agency's surveys/assessments and is conducted every 2 years. It consists primarily of cognitive tests and student, teacher, and school administrator questionnaires.

The National Adult Literacy Survey, conducted once in 1992, assessed adults nation-wide on demographics and on various types of literacy.

The National Educational Longitudinal Study of 1988 (NELS) is a longitudinal study that began with eighth graders in 1988 and will follow them for 10 years or longer. It consists of student, dropout, parent, teacher, and school administrator questionnaires; high school transcripts; and cognitive tests. In the initial survey, those among the cohort of eighth grade students whose English-language ability, as judged by the teacher, would prevent them from participating in an English-language program were excluded from the survey and the assessment. The first follow-up, conducted when these students were generally tenth graders, included those students who had been excluded in the initial survey, but whose language ability had improved sufficiently to participate in an English-language survey, or who could answer the survey translated in Spanish. Also, additional students were added to the sample to make it representative of all tenth graders. By the second follow-up, when these students were generally twelfth graders, all previously excluded students were included if possible. In addition, transcripts were collected for all sampled students, regardless of previous exclusion status.

High School and Beyond was a longitudinal study carried out among two cohorts: the sophomore and senior cohorts of the class of 1980. Several follow-ups were conducted through 1992. The study consisted of student, school, second-language, and parent questionnaires and a student test.

High School Transcript Studies are conducted periodically by NAEP, High School and Beyond, and NELS.

The National Longitudinal Survey (NLS)-72 was a longitudinal study that began in 1972; it followed the cohort for 14 years and five follow-ups. It consisted of student questionnaires, student tests, and high school transcripts.

The Beginning Postsecondary Student Longitudinal Survey began in 1990. It is a national longitudinal survey of postsecondary students designed to track correlates of their progress in college. It consists of a student survey, a parent survey, and a cognitive test.

The Baccalaureate and Beyond Survey is a postsecondary survey (both cross-sectional and longitudinal) consisting of a graduating student survey, a parent survey, and a cognitive test.

The newest longitudinal survey, which is currently in the planning stage, is the Early Childhood Longitudinal Study (National Center for Education Statistics, 1995b). It will be field tested in 1996 and will consist of individual student assessments and parent and teacher checklists. Plans call for the teacher and parent checklists to be translated into Spanish. Hispanics and Asian students will be oversampled, as will private schools. Oversampling of English-language learners is not planned, although these students will be substantially represented within the Hispanic and Asian oversamples and the Head Start supplements.

An additional study funded by the Planning and Evaluation Service and OBEMLA in the Department of Education—Prospects—is also listed here. Congressionally mandated, it is a 6-year longitudinal evaluation study on the impact of Chapter 1 (now Title I) programs—the first longitudinal study designed to measure the effects of Chapter 1 programs on language-minority students and English-language learners. It began in 1991 and collects data annually. In addition to collecting information on student demographics and educational services provided to English-language learners, it administers achievement tests to students—either the California Test of Basic Skills or its Spanish version (SABE). Three student cohorts from grades 1, 3, and 7 are being followed over time, and descriptive and achievement data are being collected to examine the sampled students' progress. As the longitudinal data become available, more valuable analyses will be possible. In 1995, the Department of Education published Prospects: First Year Report on Language Minority and LEP Students (Office of Policy and Planning, 1995). Findings to date indicate that English-language learners who attend public schools are particularly disadvantaged; many students are not receiving the quality instruction and services they need; most schools use several criteria, including measures of proficiency in English and non-English, to determine entry into and exit from these programs; and English-language learners receive lower academic grades, are judged by their teachers to have lower academic abilities, and score below their classmates on standardized tests of reading and math.

ANNEX 2
VARIABLES OF INTEREST FOR MONITORING
ENGLISH-LANGUAGE LEARNER PROGRESS

Readiness for School

- Birth weight
- Immunizations
- Preschool program participation
- Motor development indicator
- Physical well-being indicator
- Social and emotional well-being indicator
- Native-language proficiency
- English proficiency*
- Literacy activities in the home
- General knowledge and skills

Demographics

- Percentage of English-language learners in poverty
- Percentage of English-language learners in linguistically isolated households*
- Race/ethnicity
- Family income
- Parental English proficiency level*
- Home language
- Access to health and human services
- Length of instruction in second language (years)
- Most frequently used language*
- Number of English-language learners
- Student participation in bilingual/ESL programs

Social Support for Education

- Parent involvement in school activities
- Reading materials in the home
- School per pupil expenditure
- Average parental educational attainment
- School cooperation with community agencies

Quality of Educational Institutions and Teaching

School Quality
- Average class size
- Student-teacher ratio
- Instructional time
- Availability of computers
- Course offerings (secondary)
- Amount of homework given
- Availability of bilingual/ESL programs
- Existence of special programs (Title I, reading, math, tutoring)
- Content coverage of ESL/bilingual classes*
- Number of teacher aides

Teacher Quality
- Years of experience
- Educational background/degrees
- Average teacher salary
- Number certified in bilingual education/ESL
- Minority status
- Enrichment activities
- Percentage teaching English-language learners

Learner Outcomes

- English-language proficiency*
- Math achievement
- Reading achievement
- Achievement in other areas
- Grades
- General self-concept
- Grade retention
- Participation in extracurricular activities
- Academic course taking
- Teachers' judgments of student ability

Education and Economic Productivity

- School attendance, tardiness
- Retention in grade
- Dropout status (grades 8-12)
- Degree completion
- Completion of key classes (algebra)
- College completion rates
- Employment record

*May require new items in federal surveys.

REFERENCES

Abedi, J., C. Lord, and J. Plummer
1995 *Language Background Report.* Los Angeles: UCLA Graduate School of Education, National Center for Research on Evaluation, Standards, and Student Testing.

August, D., and E. McArthur
1996 *Proceedings of the Conference on Inclusion Guidelines and Accommodations for Limited English Proficient Students in the National Assessment of Educational Progress* (December 5-6, 1994). Washington, DC: National Center for Education Statistics.

Bradby, D.
1992 *Language Characteristics and Academic Achievement: A Look at Asian and Hispanic Eighth Graders in NELS:88.* Washington, DC: National Center for Education Statistics.

Council of Chief State School Officers
1991 *Summary of State Practices Concerning the Assessment of and the Data Collection about LEP Students.* Washington, DC: Council of Chief State School Officers.
1994a *The Feasibility of Collecting Comparable National Statistics about Students with Limited English Proficiency.* Washington DC: Council of Chief State School Officers.
1994b *LEP Student Count Study.* Washington DC: Council of Chief State School Officers.
1995 *Implementation Guide for SPEEDEE/Xpress.* Washington, DC: Council of Chief State School Officers.

Hafner, A.
1995 Assessment Practices: Developing and Modifying Statewide Assessments for LEP Students. Paper presented at the annual conference on Large Scale Assessment sponsored by the Council of Chief State School Officers, June. School of Education, California State University, Los Angeles.

Hafner, A., C. Rivera, C. Vincent, and M. LaCelle-Peterson
1995 Participation of LEP Students in Statewide Assessment Programs. Unpublished report, Division of Educational Foundations and Interdivisional Studies, George Washington University.

Hakuta, K., and G. Valdes
1994 A Study Design for the Inclusion of LEP Students in the NAEP State Trial Assessment. Paper prepared for the National Academy of Education Panel on NAEP Trial State Assessment. Stanford University, Stanford, CA.

Houser, J.
1994 *Assessing Students with Disabilities and Limited English Proficiency.* Washington, DC: National Center for Education Statistics.

Ingels, S.J.
1995 *Sample Exclusion and Undercoverage in NELS 88—Characteristics of Base Year Ineligible Students: Changes in Eligibility Status After Four Years.* Washington, DC: National Center for Education Statistics.

McLaughlin, M.W. and L.A. Shepard with J.A. O'Day.
1995 *Improving Education through Standards-Based Reform.* A Report by the National Academy of Education Panel on Standards-Based Education Reform. Stanford, CA: National Academy of Education

Meyer, M.M., and S.E. Fienberg, eds.
1992 *Assessing Evaluation Studies: The Case of Bilingual Education Strategies.* Panel to Review Evaluation Studies of Bilingual Education, Committee on National Statistics, National Research Council. Washington, DC: National Academy Press.

National Center for Education Statistics
1987 *Statistical Standards.* Washington, DC: National Center for Education Statistics.

1991a   *Education Counts: An Indicator System to Monitor the Nation's Education Health.* Special Study Panel of Education Indicators. Washington, DC: National Center for Education Statistics.

1991b   *A Study of Availability and Overlap of Education Data in Federal Collections.* Washington DC: National Center for Education Statistics/Council of Chief State School Officers.

1992   *Statistical Standards.* Washington, DC: National Center for Education Statistics.

1994   *Student Data Handbook: Early Childhood, Elementary, and Secondary Education.* Washington, DC: National Center for Education Statistics.

1995a   *Improving the Capacity of the National Education Data System to Address Equity Issues: An Addendum to a Guide to Improving the National Education Data System.* Washington, DC: National Center for Education Statistics.

1995b   *Early Childhood Longitudinal Study: Kindergarten Class of 1998-99 Brochure.* Washington, DC: National Center for Education Statistics.

National Education Goals Panel
1991   *Potential Strategies for Long Term Indicator Development, Reports by Six Technical Planning Subgroups.* Washington, DC: National Education Goals Panel.

National Forum on Education Statistics
1990   *A Guide to Improving the National Education Data System: A Report by the National Education Statistics Agenda Committee of the National Forum on Education Statistics.* Washington, DC: National Forum on Education Statistics.

National Research Council
1986   *Creating a Center for Education Statistics: A Time for Action.* Panel to Evaluate the National Center for Education Statistics, Committee on National Statistics. Washington, DC: National Academy Press.

1995   *Integrating Federal Statistics on Children: Report of a Workshop.* Board on Children and Families, Committee on National Statistics, National Research Council. Washington, DC: National Academy Press.

Office of Policy and Planning
1995   *Prospects: The Congressionally Mandated Study of Educational Growth and Opportunity, First Annual Report.* Washington, DC: U.S. Department of Education.

Olson, J.F., and A.A. Goldstein
1996   *Increasing the Inclusion of Students with Disabilities and Limited English Proficient Students in NAEP.* NCES Focus on NAEP Series 2(1):1-5.

Shavelson, R. J. McDonnell, L. Oakes, J. Carey, N.L. Picus
1987   *Indicator Systems for Monitoring Math and Science Education.* Santa Monica, CA: Rand Corporation.

Strang, E.W., and E. Carlson
1991   *Providing Chapter 1 Services to Limited English-Proficient Students.* Final Report. Rockville, MD: Westat.

Spencer, B.D.
1994   A study of eligibility exclusions and sampling: 1992 Trial State Assessment. In G. Bohrnsted, ed., *The Trial State Assessment, Prospects and Realities: Background Studies.* Palo Alto, CA: Armadillo.

10

Issues Related to the
Research Infrastructure

This chapter departs from the discussion of specific research areas in Chapters 2 through 9 to examine issues related to the infrastructure within which the research is conducted. The following issues are addressed:

- Issues about process
  —Agenda setting and the development of Requests for Proposals (RFPs)
  —Review of research proposals
  —Consensus development and accumulation of results
  —Dissemination
- Cross-cutting issues
  —Basic versus applied research
  —The funding of research centers versus the funding of field-initiated studies
  —Lack of expertise in the agencies
  —Insufficient or incompetent inclusion of language variables in surveys
  —Need for collaboration and coordination
  —Limited availability of funds

As context for this discussion of infrastructure issues, Appendices A-C present the findings of a comprehensive study designed to consolidate for the first time information on the history, the numerous organizations and programs, and the specific activities that comprise the infrastructure for research on English-language learners and bilingual education. The information gathered in the course of that study served as the basis for the review of infrastructure issues in this chapter. The reader is referred to Appendix A for an explanation of the study approach, which included extensive review of the literature and various background documents, as well as interviews with key personnel at both the federal and state levels.

Earlier chapters of this report have assessed the state of knowledge about the linguistic, cognitive, and social development of English-language learners and about the programs and teachers that educate them and data collected on them; they have also offered observations on the quality of the research. This chapter assesses the infrastructure that produced much of that research and identifies the characteristics that seem to have facilitated or inhibited good research. Our principal judgment, resting largely on the reviews included in previous chapters, is that the infrastructure has often failed to produce the high-quality and relevant research needed, this despite a great expansion of research on LEP issues in the past 15 years and the strenuous and skilled efforts of many researchers and agency officials. The effectiveness of the infrastructure has been strongly influenced by some factors we cannot hope to change, such as the politics of bilingual education. But we can recommend changes in organization, procedures, and allocation of resources that might improve the infrastructure, and changes in training that might strengthen the skills of the people within that infrastructure in the future. The final section of this chapter, then, presents a set of recommendations for addressing the issues listed above, and thereby improving the infrastructure for research on English-language learners and bilingual education.

ISSUES ABOUT PROCESS

Agenda Setting and the Development of Requests for Proposals RFPs

Federal research funds for the study of education have always been very modest and unpredictable. Thus, the possibilities for rational agenda setting are constrained. Agenda setting in education research is always tentative; the major players are always changing; and the process is always vulnerable to interruption, undue haste, politics, and controversy. Even during periods when funding has been fairly level, as with the laboratories and centers, the agenda-setting process has been haphazard, sometimes mandated by Congress, sometimes left to internal agency staff, sometimes involving extensive participation by practitioners and other stakeholders, and sometimes left largely to the discretion of research center directors.

Congressional mandates relevant to agenda setting are of two sorts: substantive and procedural. An example of a substantive agenda provided by Congress is the 1978 reauthorization of the Bilingual Education Act, which specified eight areas of research to be conducted by the new Title VII: studies to determine and evaluate effective models for bilingual-bicultural programs; studies to determine language acquisition characteristics and the most effective method of teaching

English within the context of a bilingual-bicultural program to students who have language proficiencies other than English; a 5-year longitudinal study to measure the effect of this title on the education of students who have language proficiencies other than English; studies to determine the most effective and reliable methods of identification of students who should be entitled to services under this title; the operation of a clearinghouse on information for bilingual education, which would collect, analyze, and disseminate information about bilingual education and related programs; studies to determine the most effective methods of teaching reading to children and adults who have language proficiencies other than English; studies to determine the effectiveness of teacher training preservice and inservice programs funded under this title; and studies to determine the critical cultural characteristics of selected groups of individuals assisted under this title for purposes of teaching about culture in the program.

A National Center for Education Statistics (NCES) official reminded us that many of their studies are mandated by law. Of course, when we say that the agenda began with Congress, the question really goes back to who inserted the mandate in the bill and argued it through committees and in some cases the administration. The 1978 research agenda was fashioned by a planning committee from within the Department of Education (Rudolph Troike, personal communication).

In the case of evaluation, which is a form of research, an agency's agenda is often shaped by Congress in a piecemeal fashion. Such is the case with the Planning and Evaluation Service (PES) in the Office of the Under Secretary of Education or the evaluation group in the Administration for Children, Youth, and Families in the Department of Health and Human Services (DHHS). Many of their studies are mandated by law or otherwise initiated from outside the agency. When an evaluation unit's mission is to serve a variety of programs, it makes little sense to talk about coherent agenda setting within the unit. PES, for example, evaluates the programs for the Office of the Under Secretary, the Office of Elementary and Secondary Education, and other offices. Often evaluations are specified in legislation; at other times they are requested by the agency that administers a program. In the case of the evaluation group in the Administration for Children, Youth, and Families, their main task is evaluating Head Start, and various aspects of that ongoing evaluation task are specified in law.

Agenda setting is thus reactive, although some agencies are by their nature more reactive than others. Yet even these groups strive to bring some coherence to their activities. In the case of PES, one official (Valena Plisko, personal communication) said that having the recently promulgated Department of Education strategic plan has been helpful in setting an evaluation agenda. In the case of the evaluation group in the Administration for Children, Youth, and Families, in 1995 they began to develop a more coherent agenda to link their various studies and build on those done in the past (Michael Lopez, personal communication). One piece that was recommended by an outside panel and not mandated was a study of bilingual Head Start programs. In addition, in response to a request by the Head Start Office in the Administration for Children, Youth, and Families, the National Research Council (NRC), under the auspices of the Board on Children, Youth, and Families, convened a series of meetings—the Head Start Roundtable—to provide a systematic analysis of research needs relevant to the changing context Head Start faces as it moves into its fourth decade. The report issued as a result of these meetings (National Research Council, 1996) explicitly addresses issues of ethnic and cultural diversity. However, agencies' internal plans are always vulnerable to interruption as a result of outside demands and internal pressures, so previous blue-ribbon efforts of the Administration for Children, Youth, and Families have not succeeded very well.

The second form of Congressional input into agenda setting involves the establishment of required procedures for agenda setting by research agencies that receive funds. One example is the Individuals with Disabilities Education Act, which requires extensive consultation with stakeholders, including adult learners with disabilities and the parents of school students with disabilities. Another example is the recent reauthorization of the Office of Educational Research and Improvement (OERI) in the Goals 2000 legislation, which established the National Educational Research Policy and Priorities Board. This act instructed OERI to coordinate research and required the development of a National Research Priorities Plan for the Department of Education's research efforts.

While agendas may be developed internally by research agencies, the word "agenda" is perhaps too broad here. Kingdon (1984:205) makes a distinction between agenda setting and "alternative specification," a distinction akin to that made by the military between strategies and tactics. The White House and Congress, adjudicating the relative claims of politics, principles, priorities, and public opinion, are more likely to be involved in establishing the larger agenda. In the case of the education of English-language learners, agenda setting could establish the urgency for research on these students and their education, as in the 1970s, or it could raise questions about the appropriateness of various kinds of programming and call for counter-research, as in the 1980s, or it could demote the issue to a more silent priority, as seems to be the case in the 1990s.

Sometimes the research agencies have a role in this larger agenda setting. They are often called upon to testify to Congress about their main objectives and what they recommend as major emphases (Graham, cited in Kaestle, 1992). When centers or laboratories are recompeted en masse, the agencies play a key role in proposing a new roster of research concerns to Congress or the administration. When OERI recompeted virtually all of its centers in 1989-1990, its planning process spanned 1988-1989, involving public meetings with researchers, practitioners, and policymakers. Tentative agenda priorities were published for public comment. Then, under the new Assistant Secretary, Christopher Cross, a blue-ribbon panel reconsidered the priorities and confirmed them. RFPs proceeded from this agenda for the set of OERI centers that have just completed their work. Similarly, in the recent recompetition for the regional laboratories, extensive public hearings were held, and public comment was sought for the recent recompetition of the centers and for the field-initiated research.

In these agenda-setting exercises, one can see the impact of the American tradition of public control in education. In the case of OERI, the client of education research is often seen as the practitioners—the teachers and administrators of schools. In the case of the Office of Special Education and Rehabilitative Services, the client is more often seen as a student with disabilities or the parents of a student. The Individuals with Disabilities Education Act requires broad constituent input into research agendas by such clients. These stakeholders are involved at the early stages, identifying strategic targets for research, according to an official (Louis Danielson, personal communication). This is a different view of the field from that which prevails in scientific agencies, which in thinking of the field think of the researchers themselves, not the clients of the research (i.e., practitioners or students).

Once the broad agenda has been established, the initiative usually passes to the research agencies, in consultation with researchers in the field, to determine what sorts of studies and what specific studies should be done—what Kingdon (1984) calls the specification of alternatives. These detailed agendas can be done well or poorly, depending on the mix of procedures and personnel that constitute the infrastructure. At the Office of Bilingual Education and Minority Languages Affairs (OBEMLA) and other agencies, the failure to maintain an active relationship with the field, for example through the use of standing panels, is exacerbated by the lack of qualified researchers on the agency staff, sometimes resulting in poorly drafted RFPs and Grant Announcements. In cases where an agency, with the support of Congress, trusts the researchers in the field to initiate useful research without a great deal of specification from the government, agenda setting is of less importance. The National Institutes of Health (NIH) provides a striking contrast to education research agencies in this regard. In the National Institute of Child Health and Human Development, for example, about 90 percent of the research funds are devoted to field-initiated research. There are occasional Congressional mandates and targeted requests for applications on particular topics, but for the most part the agenda is left open and is determined, in effect, by the aggregate of projects successfully proposed from the field.

Education research is in a double bind. There has been little faith (and little money) in field-initiated studies, so an agenda is needed to guide research efforts; yet the infrastructure is unstable and ineffective in building agendas. The task of creating an overarching agenda for research in the Department of Education has now fallen to OERI and the new National Educational Research Policy and Priorities Board. Time will tell how successful that effort will be, but given the instability and fragmentation that have characterized the past, something of this nature is needed.

At lower levels of specification, the record has been mixed. Both insiders and outsiders believe that OBEMLA's agenda-setting attempts have been weakened by politicization, lack of leadership, turnover of key personnel, and lack of a conceptual plan. As for the specification of alternatives in setting agendas for research centers devoted to LEP issues, the record is also mixed. In the opinion of Amado Padilla (personal communication), codirector of the winning proposal for the second OERI language center in 1985, the RFP was quite good. In response to the RFP, Padilla says, his planning group started brainstorming, trying to match up existing researchers and ideas with the research and development specified in the RFP. This is typical of the specification of alternatives by prospective OERI research center planning groups. They try to balance the demands of the RFP with their view of the field and its problems, plus their judgments about who does good research, plus pressures to get the work out in a relatively short time and to recognize various constituencies with an interest in the domain being studied.

In the case of the third OERI language center, the National Center for Research on Cultural Diversity and Second Language Learning, its codirector believes the coherence of its proposal came from ideas that emerged in the group's proposal planning sessions, notably a Vygotskyan psychological bent and an interest in ethnographic studies of multilingual situations (Barry McLaughlin, personal communication). The group wanted to get some finished work out rapidly, according to McLaughlin, and in response to the grant announcement felt a need to include as many language groups and geographic areas as possible, a complication of working in the area of language diversity. Also, there was a great deal of emphasis on the word "national" in the center's title. They did not have the latitude to select a few things to do well; rather, they felt they were expected to conduct research representative of the whole field of practice in the education of English-language learners. As a result, they included some research already in progress, plus a relatively large number of new, small projects, resulting in a more diverse repertoire of small-scale studies than might have resulted had they felt neither of the above pressures.

Research on English-language learners and their education is an extreme case of the problems faced by education research at the federal level, and education research is an extreme case of the problems faced by most federal research agencies. In education, and on LEP issues in particular, the procedures and agencies are unstable, the funds are sparse, the agency personnel are often untrained in research, and the topics are controversial. Thus, agenda-setting efforts are ad hoc, reactive, fragmented, and political. The need is for commitment to a more stable, longer-term agenda that will survive more than the usual 2 years served by agency heads. To effect such agenda development, responsibility needs to be located at a high level within the Department of Education; moreover, participants need to distinguish among different levels of agenda setting—the basic program versus the specification of alternatives versus the selection of research projects—and then determine which stakeholders are appropriately included in each.

Presumably, practitioners and politicians should have more input at the more general level of establishing overall goals for research, appropriate to the needs of the field as well as influenced by the high-pay-off areas where research is likely to make significant progress. Researchers and agency officials with deep research knowledge should have more to say about the specification of alternatives and should have exclusive discretion to judge the technical merits of individual projects. At the same time, despite the appropriateness of having different players at different levels of the agenda-setting process, the whole process should have coherence. There should be enough feedback and accountability so that the research findings relate in helpful ways to the larger agenda, and the agencies providing the funds should have an ongoing, affirmative responsibility to monitor the whole enterprise, relating research findings to the larger mission of the agenda.

Review of Research Proposals

Procedures for the review of proposals for research projects funded by the federal government differ considerably depending on the agency, on what kind of research is involved, and on whether the proposal is individually submitted or part of a center's work. Agencies that fund work largely by contract, such as PES, rely on internal staff reviews. This seems to stem from various considerations. First, there are not very many competitors for large-scale contract evaluation research, so it might be difficult to find knowledgeable outside reviewers without a conflict of interest (John Chapman, personal communication). Also, contracts are tied more closely than grants to the specifications laid down by the agency; there is less emphasis on creativity and more on technical capacity. All of these research-related activities, however, may soon be subject to new routines and standards. The National Educational Research Policy and Priorities Board is currently overseeing the development of standards for the evaluation and conduct of activities carried out by OERI, including the review and selection of proposals and the monitoring of grants awarded.

The classic process of external peer review, often cited as an enviable model by leading education scholars, is exemplified by NIH and the National Science Foundation (NSF). When budgets are sizable and much of the research is initiated by individual proposals from the field, as in the cases of NIH and NSF, agencies develop the capacity to maintain two features missing in Department of Education research agencies: standing panels of experts from the field and research administrators in the agency with substantial research expertise. We return to the latter in the discussion below on expertise. As for the standing panels, National Institute for Mental Health panel members have terms of 3 to 4 years, and they meet three times a year to review proposals. Their proposal rankings are expressed in a ranking system, on the basis of scientific merit. There is also a national advisory council that includes both scientists and citizen members, but our source at the institute told us that the "role of the council differs across institutes," and at the National Institute for Mental Health, the council generally supports panel judgments of merit (Mary Ellen Oliveri, personal communication).

At the National Institute of Child Health and Human Development, the research administrator we interviewed said the peer review system is "very robust" (Norman Krasnegor, personal communication). A "highly educated and technically sophisticated group of scientists" comes to Washington three times a year to review applications. Their national advisory council looks at applications to examine policy implications or to handle appeals.

At NSF, all research grants of over $50,000 must be subjected to peer review. Some of this is done by mail, by ad hoc reviewers; some of it is done by standing panels, as at NIH.

In the Department of Education agencies that do substantial amounts of research on language issues—OERI and OBEMLA—there is no tradition of standing panels. According to some department staff (Edward Fuentes and Joseph Conaty, personal communication), competitions of the same type are infrequent in the Department of Education, and thus standing panels might not work as well as at NIH and NSF. Sometimes there has been thorough peer review that has been well regarded in the field; often the review process has gotten worse marks (Kaestle, 1992). The suspicion by some that education is a weak field in which things do not get done well cannot be adjudicated since so many other adverse conditions prevail: too little budget, too much leadership turnover, and too little proportion of the budget in field-initiated research, plus the fragmentation of competing research paradigms. With the new National Educational Research Policy and Priorities Board, the new research institutes, and a commitment to spending 20 percent of future funds on field-initiated research, OERI may have the opportunity to build more of a tradition of standing panels. At the Office of Special Education and Rehabilitative Services, also in the Department of Education, the research funds have been (until now) somewhat more stable; there all reviews are done by ad hoc panels of experts familiar with the particular population or disability being researched, and until now, all of these panels have been brought to Washington for face-to-face meetings. But the vulnerability of these arrangements, as with education researchers' hopes for the new OERI institutes, is abundantly clear in the present political climate.

Since most research in education, including that on LEP issues, is conducted in research centers, the processes by which projects are chosen within centers are of considerable interest; however, they are more loosely governed and variable than the processes for judging the merit of field-initiated proposals or proposals for initial funding of the centers themselves. Of course, the initial roster of projects accompanies the proposal for establishing the center, and those proposals receive intense scrutiny from the agencies and from peer reviewers. These reviews are watched intensely by researchers in the field, who occasionally protest decisions and question the fairness of the selection process.

This process, however, chooses among the *centers* proposed; it does not in general inquire about the possible alternatives to *individual projects*. In any case, the process by which researchers are included in the center proposals is not an open one. It is a matter of planning groups attempting to respond to RFPs and Grant Announcements, judging what researchers are doing good work relevant to the center's mission and who is available. Often these decisions are influenced by geographical considerations and networks of acquaintances. No doubt this often results in excellent work by groups of high competence, but the process by which the funding reaches individual researchers is strikingly different from that for peer-reviewed field-initiated proposals.

Consensus Development and the Accumulation of Results

It is widely charged that education research seldom adds up to much, that it is too equivocal to inform practice. Some people argue that in social science research, results are necessarily "messier" than in the physical and biological sciences. Nonetheless, education researchers have, for the most part, not done a good job of accumulating evidence and building upon past research. Emerson Elliott (cited in Kaestle, 1992:15), the recently retired Commissioner of Statistics at NCES, came to the National Institute of Education (NIE) in 1972 after working on health issues at the Office of Management and Budget. At the health institutes, he said, "there was a strong sense that there was science, and that it was cumulating to something." Education research was "discredited" by the lack of such a conviction. One center director said that when he sent off his final report to NIE, "I don't think they even opened the boxes" (Amado Padilla, personal communication).

This situation has not universally characterized LEP-related research. During 1990-1992, OBEMLA funded three symposia. The first, in September 1990, focused on topics including demographics, issues of method and pedagogy, language teaching and learning, early childhood education issues, assessment, and LEP exceptional issues (see OBEMLA, 1990). The second symposium (September 1991) addressed evaluation and measurement issues (see OBEMLA, 1992). The third (August 1992) addressed middle and high school issues (see OBEMLA, 1993). Compendia of the research papers were published and widely distributed. But instances of such synthesizing activities are outweighed in the historical record by complaints of inattention to results. There are two related problems: one is whether the agencies do anything with the research they have funded (read it, understand it, critique it, synthesize it, disseminate it); the second is whether researchers in the field have a sense of evidence being amassed, of new directions and questions coming from completed research, and of relatively secure knowledge accumulating. No doubt there is some of this cumulative process in education research, including work on LEP issues. Nonetheless, the frequent complaints about ignored reports and lack of synthesis are symptomatic of the weak infrastructure of education research in general and of research on English-language learners in particular. The politicization of the issues and rapid turnover of leadership in the research agencies exacerbate the problem of building a cumulative knowledge base.

Key figures in the agencies and the centers are very aware of this problem, and there has been much discussion of it in the past few years. The Center for Research on the Education of Children Placed at Risk (CRESPAR) holds an annual symposium at the American Association for Education Research to take stock of results, and they periodically produce a volume of papers that reviews research from their center and elsewhere on a particular topic. In addition, they began a peer-reviewed journal in 1996 called the *Journal of Education for Students Placed at Risk*, which is now published by Lawrence Erlbaum Associates (Robert Slavin, personal communication). And Judith Anderson (personal communication), former acting director of the At-Risk Institute, which funds CRESPAR, says they are developing institute-wide guidelines for the synthesis and dissemination of research. The Administration for Children, Youth, and Families is conducting a review of past work in preparation for the production of a more coherent research agenda for the future (Michael Lopez, personal communication). At NCES, Edith McArthur (personal communication) reports, they have branched out from their now traditional annual reports, *The Condition of Education* and *The Digest of Educational Statistics*, to include special reports on focused topics such as urban youth, the education of Hispanic students, and high school dropouts. There is also a set of reports to various audiences for each large data set they produce. Eugene Garcia (personal communication), until recently the head of OBEMLA, reminded our interviewer that the Department of Education cosponsored the NRC effort that produced this report, which itself was a form of literature review, consensus development, and agenda building.

The successful proposal for the new Southwest Educational Development Laboratory displays the capacity of the current research infrastructure to inform new projects of past results. It proposed convening experts in the field before designing applied research on bilingual programs. It also proposed keeping abreast of research and program developments through journals, conferences, and electronic communication, looking to research agencies such as the National Center for Research on Cultural Diversity and Second Language Learning (now the Center for Research on Education, Diversity, and Excellence) and the Center for Applied Linguistics as sources of new knowledge and synthesis of ongoing research (Southwest Educational Development Laboratory, 1995).

While the above efforts can yield an ongoing, informal sense of what has been learned and what research is needed, there are more formal procedures for exploring and stating consensus in complex areas of research. The procedures often cited come from NIH. Our source at the National Institute of Child Health and Human Development explained that there is a special office in NIH responsible for conferences on consensus formation. It is "a very elaborate process that takes several years" (Norman Krasnegor, personal communication). Experts confer, examining the literature in a given area and exploring and debating the levels of certainty about research findings according to an established procedure. Both Christopher Cross (cited in Kaestle, 1992), as Assistant Secretary of OERI, and Joseph Conaty (personal communication), as Director of Research in OERI, have recommended the NIH model for education research. Conaty commissioned some papers in preparation for a budget request to pursue consensus development on the health institutes model. However, as he said, "if you have no discretionary money, you can't do consensus panels," and he never got funding specifically for the purpose, despite repeated requests.

Dissemination

If there are two issues that make education researchers and research administrators grimace, it is coordination of research efforts and dissemination of results—not because they do not want to do these things, but because no one seems to have clear answers about effective ways of doing them. We speak to the coordination issue below; here we look at the dissemination issue.

The issue of dissemination will not go away. The old linear model of research and development—some people do research, others develop materials from it, and others distribute it and train practitioners how to use it—is regularly criticized. Over the past two decades, pressures have mounted to involve practitioners in the agenda setting and conduct of research and to have researchers involved in thinking about links to practice from the start of their work. For better or worse (worse, we think), governments support very little basic research on language-minority issues and bilingualism. Most research, therefore, is intended from the start to reach some conclusions directly relevant to policy and practice—whether case studies of best practices or statistical studies of large programs, evaluation work, or data gathering about relevant populations and their experiences.

Making the links takes more than good intentions and more than traditional dissemination modes; it takes imagination, high priority, and resources. Imagine, for example, how many education research agencies would have the resources to adopt the approach of the health institutes. Mary Ellen Oliveri of the National Institute of Mental Health (personal communication) reports that the health institutes concentrate much more on basic research than do the education agencies, so their dissemination efforts are generally through traditional academic venues—journals and conferences. But when special reports are needed for policy purposes, they typically are based on the deliberations of large numbers of outside scientists (Mary Ellen Oliveri, personal communication). Similarly, Norman Krasnegor of the National Institute of Child Health and Human Development (personal communication) reports that because his agency sponsors only basic research, the audience "is the scientific community"; but when they decided they needed to get scientific findings on dyslexia out to the public, they went through their rigorous consensus process and then held a big conference, attended by first lady Hillary Clinton and Secretary of Health and Human Services Donna Shalala.

Perhaps the new centers funded through the OERI institute structure can carry on some of these more aggressive dissemination activities, with budgets three to five times those of previous OERI centers. The director of CRESPAR, the first of these new centers, says they are "quite fanatical" about dissemination; their dissemination staff is larger than their research staff. The task is daunting, nonetheless. Richard Tucker (personal communication), who worked at the Center for Language Education and Research, points out that even if one focused at the level of state education agencies, they are set up very differently in different states, and they respond to different regulations about bilingual education. One has to know the people, the politics, the problems, and the procedures to disseminate research results that will matter. "You don't reach each of the 50 states in the same way....There are so many multiple audiences, and the cost of getting to them is so high."

Nonetheless, some innovative dissemination overtures are being made in OERI. The new Office of Reform Assistance and Dissemination (ORAD) is responsible for developing a dissemination system for the entire department. They expect to establish extensive review processes for identifying promising and exemplary programs, practices, and products. One early effort has been a collaboration with NSF on brochures for parents published by OERI on *Helping Your Child Learn*; some of these have Spanish-language versions (Eve Bither, personal communication). The National Center for Research on Cultural Diversity and Second Language Learning developed a newsletter with a mailing list of 3,000-4,000 people, mostly teachers. They also developed practitioner reports, as well as some videotapes. Gilbert N. Garcia (personal communication) reports that OERI staff, through the cooperative agreement, are working closely with the new Center for Research on Education, Diversity, and Excellence to ensure that there is adequate dissemination of the studies the center staff are conducting. Valena Plisko at PES (personal communication) says they have "idea books" on various topics, such as school-wide projects in Title I or how to engage parents in Title VII programs. She fears these innovative dissemination efforts will be cut when the budget shrinks and hopes that the new comprehensive technical assistance centers can pick up some of these dissemination activities. The National Clearinghouse for Bilingual Education, funded by OBEMLA, is also charged with providing educators with information about exemplary practices and research, in conjunction with the Education Resources Information Center Clearinghouse on Urban Education and the University of California's Linguistic Minority Research Institute (see the National Clearinghouse for Bilingual Education home page on the Internet at http://www.ncbe.gwu.edu/).

It is not within our purview to review the work of the regional multifunctional resource centers operated by OBEMLA from 1984 to 1995, but their mission, in the course of providing technical assistance to bilingual/multicultural school programs, was to keep practitioners in touch with the latest best research. As a result of the 1994 reauthorization of the Elementary and Secondary Education Act (ESEA), the work of the multifunctional resource centers, as well as other ESEA centers (such as the Title 1 technical assistance centers), was taken over by 15 comprehensive regional assistance centers. The latter centers were funded to help states, school districts, schools, tribes, community-based organizations, and other grant recipients with the administration, integration, and implementation of programs funded under the Improving America's Schools Act. More specifically, they are to provide comprehensive training and technical assistance to improve teaching and learning in a manner that supports local reform efforts. In addition, as previously mentioned, three new regional laboratories are focused on culture and language.

Perhaps victory in the effort to achieve good dissemination of education research results will be declared when the word "dissemination" disappears. At the Office of Special Education and Rehabilitative Services, Louis Danielson (personal communication) reports, "We've stopped using the word 'dissemination' because it sounds like such a top-down approach." They favor the word "'communicate' because it suggests a conversation." It would seem from our interviews that improvements in what has traditionally been called dissemination will involve more resources, further reversals of the linear assumptions about research and development, and experimentation with new electronic technologies.

CROSS-CUTTING ISSUES

Despite our concluding point about dissemination (that it ought not to be considered the last step in a linear process), we have described the research infrastructure as a group of processes in a sequence from agenda setting to dissemination. There are, however, several issues that cut across these processes. These include basic versus applied research, the funding of research centers versus the funding of field-initiated studies, lack of expertise in the agencies, insufficient or incompetent inclusion of language variables in surveys, the need for collaboration and coordination, and limited availability of funds.

Basic Versus Applied Research

The control of education in the United States is shared by local and state authorities; moreover, everyone feels qualified to debate education issues because everyone has gone to school and had some educational experiences that were more effective than others. This situation makes education very different as a field for federally funded research as compared with medicine, defense, or even poverty. Not only has this situation produced an infrastructure that involves substantial participation by stakeholders in agenda setting, but it has also created pressures for more applied and less basic research. In research on the education of English-language learners, this pressure has been exacerbated by the politicization of issues of practice: whether and how much native language should be used in the instruction of these students. This in turn has led to an emphasis on "horse-race" research on the effectiveness of program types, as discussed earlier.

At another level of politicization, the two-party system often divides the federal government on issues related to the education of English-language learners. Under these conditions of party politics, especially in recent decades when the two major parties have had well-defined and contrasting positions on education, funds for research tend to get very specifically earmarked, leaving little to discretion, little to field-initiated research, and indeed little room for the funding of basic research. This further distinguishes education from fields such as health and defense: while political parties often stipulate how research monies are to be spent in the treatment of disease or military training, the amount of political influence involved in shaping the research of these institutions is small relative to the magnitude of the total research programs, thus leaving more room for basic research and more latitude for professional judgment in the research agenda-setting process.

In a democracy, there is much to be said for public involvement in agenda setting for education research. However, it is doubtful that the field of education will ever attain the cumulative knowledge base and the reputation for dependable knowledge enjoyed by research in many other areas without more funding for basic research. The Army Research Institute, for example, operates under a model of seven levels of research, moving gradually from the basic level (for example, exploring theoretical perspectives), through intermediate stages (such as a pilot application in experimental settings), to testing in a natural environment, and finally to more applied research and development (Ray Perez, personal communication). In education research, the early stages are truncated; there are researchers doing some basic research in education, of course, but they are funded more often by foundations or universities than by government, and their work is not generally linked to a planned program of experimentation and application in the field.

Various critics and observers have called for more basic research at NIE and OERI over the years, but the realities of the research infrastructure militate against this.[1] And the vicious circle of low funds leading to unimpressive results tends to

---

[1] For a recommendation in favor of basic research, see Kiesler and Turner (1977), and the NIE advisory council's endorsement of that recommendation, see National Council on Educational Research (1978). The history of this critique and a renewed argument for basic reserach are found in Vinovskis (1993, 1995).

perpetuate the situation. While all research at the National Institute of Child Health and Human Development is defined as basic, all research conducted by the Office of Special Education and Rehabilitative Services is required to be applied. The dilemma for education research can be seen in statements by the current Assistant Secretary for OERI, Sharon Robinson (personal communication), who wants OERI's research to be "cutting edge" and "courageous," but also client driven, not researcher driven. Left to themselves, researchers might not produce a great deal of "cutting edge" and "courageous" research, but without some funds for researcher-driven inquiry, the field will lack basic research as compared with other fields.

The Funding of Research Centers Versus the Funding of Field-Initiated Studies

A parallel but distinct issue is the optimum balance between research funds devoted to university-based research and development centers and those devoted to field-initiated research proposed by individuals or teams on particular topics. In these two categories (leaving aside large-scale evaluation contracts, which belong to neither category), most research funds in education have gone to centers.

Very few researchers think the past balance has been the optimum one. The overwhelming preference for research funds earmarked for laboratories and centers has resulted from the political situation mentioned above, causing the majority in Congress to specify how funds should be spent when the White House is controlled by the other party. Also, the centers and laboratories have political constituencies because they are local institutions, and they have lobbied effectively to maintain their lion's share. There is not much of a political constituency for field-initiated research; however, most disinterested parties agree that in terms of gaining the best blend of diverse research from the best people, more field-initiated studies would be desirable. No other field has as great an imbalance in this regard as education research. Of course, if the funds were there, the research agencies would need staff with expertise in research to administer the programs, and they would need strong panels of researchers to advise on the development of RFPs and Grant Announcements and to rate the proposals. Although both OBEMLA and OERI have had small programs of field-initiated studies over the past few decades, many researchers (and many education research administrators in Washington) believe these efforts are understaffed and have weak traditions of peer review panels.

High-quality field-initiated research work also depends on having a corps of active, well-trained researchers in the field. This dimension is difficult to estimate with any precision, but some leaders in the field of LEP research believe the corps is weak, a problem to which we shall return below.

Under the recent reauthorization of OERI, 20 percent of all funds in the five new research and development institutes is mandated for field-initiated studies. This set-aside will increase to 25 percent by fiscal year 1998. As a result there will be a substantial increase in the amount of money going to researchers on LEP issues outside of the research centers. This in itself provides an occasion for rethinking the related issues: first, establishing panels to organize and judge the competitions; second, locating and hiring relevant experts within the department to staff that process; and third, determining whether there are researchers in the field sufficient in number and talent to provide enough fruitful proposals. If the answer on the latter point is no, OERI and OBEMLA might consider whether the government should do more to develop the corps of researchers. One model that bears on the question of field-initiated studies is found in the Office of Special Education and Rehabilitative Services. Louis Danielson (personal communication) reports that about two-thirds of the office's $20 million annual research budget is allocated to field-initiated studies, but the funds are divided among dissertation grants, grants to people in their first 5 postdoctoral years, and grants to senior researchers. Thus, the agency is not only supporting the production of research on a competitive basis, but also helping to attract and retain able people in the research corps. The Spencer Foundation is also investing heavily in the effort to train and support young scholars for education research, but Spencer cannot be expected to accomplish alone the creation of the next generation of education researchers.

Lack of Expertise in the Agencies

Knowledgeable critics both within and outside the education research agencies bemoan the erosion of staff who are substantive experts in research areas, such as existed in the early NIE and exist today in NIH, the Defense institutes, and elsewhere. This complaint was repeated in our interviews. One center director complained about his monitor's lack of knowledge of the field; another, an institute administrator, complained that only four people on the institute's staff have the capacity to manage research well. As the new institutes' budgets stabilize and as their acting directors are replaced with directors, attention will have to be given to the expertise of research administration staff if the research infrastructure is to improve. This issue arises again in our discussion of the next cross-cutting issue.

Insufficient or Incompetent Inclusion of Language Variables in Surveys

Throughout its existence, OBEMLA has attempted to persuade other agencies, particularly NCES, to include more language variables in surveys and data collection projects and has commonly paid the extra funds required when the agency agreed. As noted earlier, such data have sometimes been collected incompetently, rendering the results useless. The agency that does the most survey work, NCES, has little expertise in the subtleties of dealing with language variables. When experts are called in, it is sometimes too late to change the definition of variables or the collection of data. NCES is not oblivious to the issues, of course, but its recent performance on language variables is not consistent with its generally high reputation as a statistical agency.

The problems, to be sure, are very difficult. Definitions of limited English proficiency differ from state to state, and efforts to standardize have not yet taken hold (see Chapter 9). Earlier surveys did not carefully distinguish English-language learners from all language-minority students, some of whom speak fluent English (see the discussion on terminology in Chapter 1). When an assessment requires testing the subjects' cognitive abilities, practices of different schools in excluding English-language learners vary widely, and the development of Spanish-language alternatives proves difficult because of scaling problems. It is possible that NCES could profit from the experience of survey researchers working on international assessments, where efforts to compare results across languages have surmounted some problems of scaling. Inclusion of English-language learners in assessments of academic achievement is a major issue for NCES since they administer the National Assessment of Educational Progress. Thus they may put more emphasis on this issue than on the inclusion of descriptive language variables in the big longitudinal data sets that are becoming very important in research on students' schooling experience and school success (e.g., Jeanne Griffith, personal communication).

Aside from the question of whether agencies have the expertise to include language variables in their studies, some agencies remain relatively indifferent to the issue. The head of the evaluation group at the Administration for Children, Youth, and Families expressed the opinion that English-language learners are a small subpopulation in Head Start, and that issues related to their education are specific to them as a group and thus relatively unimportant to the general Head Start population (Michael Lopez, personal communication). However, estimates suggest that 20 percent of the children enrolled in Head Start nation-wide speak a language other than English (Jeanne Griffith, personal communication).

Efforts simply to persuade diverse agencies to pay more attention to language variables will probably have relatively little impact, despite OBEMLA's early successes in increasing the visibility of English-language learner experiences. There are disincentives: the variables are conceptually messy, so the job is difficult and consequently expensive; furthermore, the whole subject is politically controversial. As a result, there has been a general attitude in the past to "leave it to OBEMLA." Yet continuing to rely on OBEMLA is probably not a viable solution, for two reasons. First, having OBEMLA convince other agencies to include language variables as paid add-ons is obviously only a short-run solution designed to raise the visibility of the issues. Second, OBEMLA's capacity and budget for research have continually been vulnerable. The solution to this problem on a longer-term basis is connected to solving the more general problem of interagency collaboration on LEP research, to which we now turn.

Need for Collaboration and Coordination

Collaboration across research agencies is a well-known issue in Washington. It is a rational notion that goes against the grain of several agency realities: different schedules, different priorities, different approaches, too little time, and competition for budget.[2] Coordination activities in the federal research world are of three types. First, there are informal, ad hoc arrangements initiated by mid-level research administrators that grow out of initiatives by higher-level officials and/or routine reporting and evaluation requirements. Examples include coordination between the Departments of Labor and Education in school-to-work data collection, and consultation between the Department of Education and the Council of Chief State School Officers to develop summary information on state education policy and common data definitions (Jeffrey Rodomar, personal communication). Second, there are mandated, secretarial-level commissions that command agency attention, report, and go out of business, such as the Federal Coordinating Council for Science, Engineering and Technology, initiated by the White House and chaired by the Secretary of Energy, which examined science and math education (Office of Science and Technology Policy, 1991). Third, there are attempts by agency heads to coordinate research on a more systematic, ongoing basis. The chief example here, central to our interests (and discussed in detail in Appendix A), is the Part C Coordinating Committee empaneled more or less continuously from 1978 (through the Education Amendments of 1978) until 1984 (through the reauthorization of Title VII) in an attempt to coordinate research and evaluation work conducted with funds from ESEA Title VII. Its record is a mix of success and failure that tells much of the tale of federally sponsored research on LEP issues. Despite the turf battles and antagonism between PES and OBEMLA, various officials we interviewed in both agencies supported the committee's existence, thought it had done some good and necessary work, and supported its recent abortive revival.

Whatever the fate of the Part C Coordinating Committee, several factors are pressing research administrators in the Department of Education toward more coordination. Recent legislation established the National Educational Research Policy and Priorities Board and gave OERI a coordinating role on research across the department. It also called for a strategic plan for the department (which one PES official said was already helping to guide her agency's priorities) and for standards to guide the conduct and rate the quality of education research.

---

[2]On the general problem, see Atkinson and Jackson (1992); on the need for coordination in federal data-gathering activities, see Norwood (1995).

It is impossible to tell at this point what institutional shape these coordinating efforts will take in the next few years. Whatever that shape is, it will strongly affect the future development of an infrastructure for research on language-minority and bilingual education issues.

Limited Availability of Funds

The three Department of Defense services—Army, Air Force, and Navy—that deal with issues of human potential have laboratories that conduct research on education and training. Together these laboratories expend approximately $90 million annually. Recently, research center staff supported by the Department of Defense were criticized for flying personnel first class, matching employees' contributions to charities, and throwing office parties with federal funds, among other abuses (American Educational Research Association, 1996). It is difficult for education researchers to imagine budgets of that magnitude or to think about the kinds of problems that arise from having too much money. When the reauthorization of OERI was being discussed in 1993, writers advocating an institute structure with better-funded research centers, as well as more field-initiated research, pointed out what a small proportion of the money in education is invested in research. An NRC report (Atkinson and Jackson, 1992) notes that in fiscal year 1991, federal expenditures for education research and development were one-third of those for research and development in agriculture and transportation and only 4 percent of those for research and development in health. Moreover, this low investment in education research and development was not a function of total national expenditures for each activity. Federal education research was just 0.1 percent of total national expenditures for education, whereas federal transportation research was almost 0.6 percent of total national expenditures on transportation, federal agriculture research was 1.0 percent of total national expenditures on agriculture, and federal health research was 1.3 percent of total national expenditures on health care. In fiscal year 1995, the total research and development budget for defense was $35.3 billion, while that for education was $174 million (American Association for the Advancement of Science, 1996). In bilingual education, the Title VII funds for research have been reduced from approximately $6 million in 1981 to zero funding in 1996 (although a small amount of money will be available to continue the Benchmarks study).

Concluding Comments

The solutions to many of the problems with the infrastructure for research in education, and especially for research on LEP issues, would cost money. In our recent interviews, research officials from OBEMLA, NCES, and other agencies said that the limited amount of funding available is a major constraint to improving research on language-minority and bilingual education issues. To include more language variables and insert language issues in more studies would be expensive, as would rebuilding the agencies' research expertise and supporting centers and institutes. More federal money could easily be justified for research on English-language learners.

Federally sponsored research on English-language learners and bilingual education is at a crossroads. The institutional arrangements are being radically altered, with hopes for new coherence and improved quality centering on the institute structure, OERI's coordinating role, and the development of department-wide standards and priorities. Like all reorganizations, this one is disruptive. But it has the potential to improve upon the old arrangements, which were often competitive and sometimes hostile. More important, the funding will be more ample in some ways (at OERI at least) if a budget is put in place that honors commitments to the new institutes as well as the mandated 20 percent level of funding for field-initiated studies. If these features—institute budgets and the field-initiated studies set-aside—survive the budget process (and it is important to the future of research in this area that they do), it will be equally important that the work thus funded be done well. In our recommendations we suggest some ways to improve the infrastructure supporting such research. It should be noted that however tempting, the committee is not proposing a major overhaul in the infrastructure because we feel it would be unrealistic. Rather, we propose less dramatic changes in a number of areas that we believe can combine to improve the overall quality of research on English-language learners and bilingual education.

INFRASTRUCTURE NEEDS

Our recommendations for meeting the needs of the infrastructure for research on English-language learners and bilingual education fall into two broad categories: infrastructure needs regarding federally funded research on LEP issues, and roles for state education agencies and foundations.

Infrastructure Needs Regarding Federally Funded Research on LEP Issues

Infrastructure needs at the federal level relate to coordination of research, interagency staff collaboration, the relationship of research agencies to the field, the inclusion of minority language and LEP variables and expansion of language concerns in research agency programs, integration of the work of the regional laboratories into the research program, substantive research expertise within the agencies, the accumulation and dissemination of research and data, the next generation of researchers, and cultural versus structural change.

Coordination of Research

10-1. The Assistant Secretary for the Office of Educational Research and Improvement (OERI), in consultation with the Executive Director of the National Educational Research Policy and Priorities Board, the Director of the Office of Bilingual Education and Minority Language Affairs (OBEMLA), the Commissioner of the National Center for Education Statistics (NCES), and the Director of the Planning and Evaluation Service (PES), should request that the Secretary of Education appoint a Department of Education Advisory Committee on Research on English-language Learners. This committee should comprise the Assistant Secretary for OERI; the Executive Director of the National Educational Research Policy and Priorities Board; the Director of OBEMLA; the Commissioner of NCES; the Director of PES; and eight members from outside the government—four academic researchers and four practicing educators, all experts specializing in LEP issues. Department of Education personnel involved in administering grants on minority language and LEP issues should serve as advisors, as necessary. The nongovernmental members of the committee should have fixed terms of not less than 4 years.

The purpose of the committee would be to oversee and make recommendations in the following areas:

* *Agenda setting on language-minority and LEP research, evaluation, and data-gathering activities of the federal government, with an emphasis on including English-language learners in studies, as well as promoting fruitful studies that specifically target these students as subjects.*
* *The implementation of such agendas, including the balance of the research funds across agencies and across the different types of research settings (centers, laboratories, field-initiated research, and targeted Request for Proposals (RFP) research programs).*
* *Solicitation of an appropriate balance of advice about research issues from research experts in the field, educators, and agency staff.*
* *The uses of completed research, with focus on relationships among centers, laboratories, state education agencies, professional associations, and others involved in dissemination of the research results; the quality, modes, and extent of dissemination; and issues of synthesis and consensus development.*

Among the committee's activities would be the following:

- *Monitoring and reporting to the Department of Education, Congress, and the public on research activities that bear on English-language learners.*
- *Developing policy recommendations on the conditions under which inclusion of English-language learners in studies would be mandatory for reasons of scientific integrity (see recommendation 10-4 below).*
- *Convening conferences and other activities to highlight important advances in knowledge that can be gained through research involving these students.*
- *Recommending priorities for funding to the Assistant Secretary for OERI and the Executive Director of the National Educational Research Policy and Priorities Board for inclusion in the department's Research Priorities Plan (see recommendation 10-4).*

Our review of the research indicated that English-language learners are not incorporated into many studies that purport to be about all students. This is especially true outside the Department of Education, but even within the department there has been an absence of general commitment; OBEMLA was expected to pay for studies to include English-language learners in order to improve the accuracy of estimates of the entire student universe. In cases where a significant investment of research resources has been focused on these students, as in the case of the OERI Center for Cultural Diversity and Second Language Learning at Santa Cruz, there has ben no systematic connection between OBEMLA's interests in policy and practice and the basic research orientation of OERI. Thus, there has been a lack of coherence in the funding of research on English-language learners within the Department of Education.

A serious coordination effort is needed, and it must address two distinct problems. The first is that raised above of the inclusion of English-language learners in research that purports to be about all students. This is the responsibility of all agencies that fund research on school-age children, whether in the Department of Education or not. If the mission of an agency such as NCES is to collect national statistics on education, the accuracy of the information is compromised when English-language learners are not included. If the mission is to discover the bases of human development and learning, as in the case of OERI's new Centers on Achievement in School Mathematics and Science and Improving Student Learning and Achievement in English, or the National Institute of Child Health and Human Development, then it falls within that mission to ask how the presence of English-language learners might impact research findings. The second problem is the need to target resources deliberately and well toward understanding issues that are specifically about English-language learners. Responsibility for this domain of work most naturally rests with agencies whose mission is the study and advancement of these students' education and development.

For coordination to be appealing within a bureaucratic structure, the benefits must be emphasized. For those who fund research on all students, the obvious natural incentive is scientific accuracy. This is particularly true for research conducted in areas that recruit samples from subpopulations in which English-language learners are represented in large proportions: low-income samples, preschool and early elementary grade samples, urban samples, and samples from certain geographical regions. Another natural incentive for coordination for researchers whose work is on all students is that the inclusion of English-language learners might provide an opportunity to expand and possibly test their theories with a different population. In addressing literacy, Chapter 3 notes that researchers have typically avoided working with English-language learners even when second-language learners might be an ideal test case sample among whom basic questions about reading can be asked. In discussing content area learning, in particular the question of multiple representations of knowledge, Chapter 3 also highlights the value of testing these ideas with English-language learner samples.

For those who are interested in the development of English-language learners per se, the natural incentive for coordination lies in the potential for bringing rich theory about the larger population to bear on their particular concerns, settings, and conceptualization of issues. As Chapter 2 points out, the field of second-language acquisition has drawn considerable benefits, both theoretically and methodologically, from major developments in the study of child language acquisition. In turn, theories of second-language acquisition have played a prominent role in models of bilingual education, such as the California Case Studies discussed in Chapters 6 and 7. In the absence of rich theory, research within program offices, such as OBEMLA and PES, will be narrowly defined by programmatic categories (see Chapter 6). Given the highly political nature of bilingual education, there should be a strong incentive for agencies such as OBEMLA and PES to seek grounding for their work in the context of larger domains of research on language acquisition.

The best mechanism available for the coordination of research on LEP issues is the authority and responsibility of the Assistant Secretary for OERI, who, "with the advice and assistance" of the new National Educational Research Policy and Priorities Board, is charged to work with other assistant secretaries to "improve the coordination of education research, development and dissemination" (Educational Research, Development, Dissemination, and Improvement Act of 1994, Section 921(c)). Secretary of Education Riley (1995) added evaluation research to this understanding, noting that "we also intend to strengthen our efforts to coordinate our evaluation plans with our research and data collection activities."

In the conduct of research on LEP issues, as in education research more generally, research administrators have changed frequently over the past 20 years. Research agendas have been unstable and infrequently consulted. No single group has effectively overseen the relationships among different agencies in conducting research on language-minority and LEP issues. Moreover, no one has been responsible for assessing, synthesizing, and disseminating results across different research programs and building consensus concerning future research endeavors. Therefore, there has been little sense of cumulative accomplishment or the building of a knowledge base.

Interagency Staff Collaboration

10-2. The Department of Education should establish and encourage an informal discussion group on coordination of LEP research. Representatives who are charged with administering research on language issues within the Department of Education should confer and establish such a group which would meet periodically on issues of common concern. They should seek the participation of research staff from agencies outside of the Department of Education who deal with research on education and children, and they should ensure the participation of department staff who oversee the three new regional education laboratories that have language themes, as well as staff who oversee the new technical assistance centers.

A lack of collaboration is a common frustration in Washington. Frequently, agency personnel say that although it sounds like a good idea, it does not work because, among other things, agencies have different timetables, agendas, and budgets; no one has the time; and the effort is always delegated to low-level staff. Yet there are many examples of useful collaboration and coordination of research efforts across agency lines. The Part C Coordinating Committee sometimes operated effectively, but its effectiveness was compromised by competition for funds, by the politics of bilingual education, and by negative opinions about the research qualifications of some agency personnel. In the long run, federal research agencies in the field of education need to build internal research expertise because collaboration can be only as good as the collaborators. In the short run, however, the need for collaboration can be addressed by replacing the Part C Coordinating Committee with an interagency discussion group such as that proposed here. The above-recommended Department of Education Advisory Committee on Research on English-language Learners would provide high visibility and overarching oversight responsibility. But there are also examples of effective collaboration initiated by program staff on an informal basis because they wanted to do a better job by conferring with colleagues working on similar problems.

Relationship of Research Agencies to the Field:
Peer Review and Standing Panels

10-3. The National Educational Research Policy and Priorities Board is currently conducting a comprehensive examination of OERI's system of peer review. This is an essential activity to address the issue of research quality and help revitalize peer review as something much more than a bureaucratic instrument. The premise should be that peer review is a major vehicle of communication between funders and the field, a process through which principles about research priorities and technical quality of research are clearly articulated and applied to proposals. The current effort by the National Educational Research Policy and Priorities Board needs to be augmented by two additional efforts. One would involve examining the uses of peer review throughout the Department of Education, not just within OERI; such an expansion would be within the board's authority for advising on research activities throughout the department. The other additional effort would address the issue of how to ensure expertise on English-language learner issues throughout the peer review process; this effort could be undertaken by the above-recommended Department of Education Advisory Committee on Research on English-language Learners.

Many education researchers and agency personnel have mentioned with envy the use of standing panels of expert researchers to judge and rank proposals for research funds in more stable and higher-prestige agencies. The National Institutes of Health and the National Science Foundation are often noted as models. To adopt these models, however, would not be simple. First, representatives of those agencies point out the abiding problems in peer review, no matter how well executed, such as the balance between the expertise of ad hoc panels on focused topics and the stability and sense of ownership promoted by standing panels, and the dilemma of how and when to seek advice on social utility and other nontechnical criteria from nonresearchers.[3] Second, education research (and LEP research more particularly) suffers from special problems in trying to develop more effective peer review. The status of its research and its researchers is low, so there may not be unanimity on the need for rigorous peer review on technical grounds. Furthermore, education researchers suffer from an inability to agree on a common research paradigm. Education is a field of practice, and it enlists research efforts from people of very different disciplinary training and different philosophical perspectives; yet it elicits strong emotions, social commitments, and value judgments. This is perhaps inevitable, perhaps healthy in some regards, but it makes effective peer review more difficult. (See the discussion of these problems in Chapters 3 and 7.) Given the fragmented nature of education research paradigms (see Donmoyer, 1996), effective peer review must involve a very careful and balanced selection of panel members.

The need for effective peer review was strongly emphasized in the reautho-

---

[3]In 1994, the General Accounting Office issued a report on peer review in the National Science Foundation, the National Institutes of Health, and the National Endowment for the Humanities entitled *Peer Review: Reforms Needed to Ensure Fairness in Federal Agency Grant Selection.* See also E. Elliott's briefing paper for National Educational Research Policy and Priorities Board consultants (Elliott, 1996).

rization of OERI in 1994, and some of these concerns are being addressed for the department as a whole by the National Educational Research Policy and Priorities Board, which has developed and approved standards for peer review. Several principles are important for quality control across all topics of education research. Scholars from outside the department should participate in the review of proposals; in the building of consensus regarding what is known and what areas of investigation are most promising; in determining what combination of methodologies is best suited to the tasks defined; and in the developing Requests for Proposals, particularly ensuring that they set clear criteria for quality.

In addition, some aspects of peer review relate specifically to research on LEP issues. First, the need to include English-language learners in research whenever doing so would affect the scientific quality of the inferences drawn implies the value of having an expert on LEP issues on any peer review committee dealing with large-scale research on students in general. Second, the need to investigate English-language learners within a larger theoretical framework implies the value of including expert researchers on the larger contextual and conceptual issues (for example, literacy development or learning in content areas), along with those on English-language learners per se.

Research agencies in the Department of Education have infrequently used standing panels. More often they have used ad hoc raters, sometimes with face-to-face meetings and sometimes not. There are exceptions; NCES has standing panels for its survey projects. But the practice has been spotty over the years in the department. The result has been less expertise to support decision making in the agencies, less-supportive relationships from the research community, and less contact between agency specialists and researchers on a collegial basis. Some researchers in the LEP area believe that some poor-quality research has resulted from ineffective peer review. They believe there have been problems with the composition of review panels, with respect to both the mix of department staff and outside experts and the mix of researchers and nonresearchers. In addition, some have suggested that funding of projects through centers sometimes shields poor-quality projects from rigorous review.

Inclusion of Language-Minority and LEP Variables and Expansion of Language Concerns in Agency Research Programs

10-4. Coordinating committees should encourage research agencies to include LEP variables in data gathering and to conduct research focused specifically on English-language learners. The two groups recommended above—the standing advisory committee and the informal discussion group—should encourage increased attention to language issues in surveys and other data gathering. They should also encourage increased attention to language issues as a substantive focus in research, not only that sponsored by the department, but also that sponsored by agencies outside of the department that deal with childhood and education. In doing so, they should distinguish among three different and desirable forms of inclusion:

- *The incorporation of English-language learners into studies from which they are now excluded in order to obtain better population estimates. Adaptations of assessment instruments and procedures might be required to ensure inclusion.*
- *The disaggregation of data by LEP status, where possible and appropriate, in reporting and analyzing the data. This might help in understanding English-language learners in particular or in illuminating the status and experiences of students generally in some way. Oversampling might be necessary for such disaggregation.*
- *In funding of education research more generally, a requirement in Requests for Proposals to include English-language learners as subjects in research on a wide variety of topics where the language dimensions may earlier have been ignored. Perhaps necessary at some point would be a systematic inquiry by Congress into the extent of exclusion of English-language learners from federally funded research, followed by Congressional action if the situation should warrant. This action might include incentives for more work in this area.*

For some years there has been an attitude, reflected in the research infrastructure on English-language learner and bilingual education concerns, that agencies would leave those concerns to OBEMLA. One reason for this reluctance to initiate research and data gathering on English-language learners is that the inclusion of complex language variables in studies is expensive and difficult. Another is that the subject matter is politically controversial. Thus OBEMLA long had the role of persuading other agencies to incorporate language variables in their survey work and of providing the funds for doing so from the Title VII budget. This helped raise the visibility of language issues, but was not a good long-term solution. Too often the language component was added late in the process or with too little expertise, so the items added were not defined in useful ways.

The demography of language diversity in this country suggests that students' language abilities and histories will continue to be important variables for us to understand in studying education, and as noted above, studies that exclude part of the population from participation because of language are skewed scientifically. Therefore, it is important for agencies to develop the expertise and the incentives needed to include language variables routinely and competently in their education research.

It is also true that agencies outside of the Department of Education, such as the National Science Foundation and the Administration for Children, Youth, and Families, that deal with education issues seldom focus on the language diversity of students. It is important that they be persuaded to give more agenda priority to such issues.

Integration of the Work of the Regional Laboratories into the Research Program

10-5. The above-recommended Advisory Committee on Research on English-language Learners should ensure that staff from the three new regional laboratories specializing in language diversity participate in the department's research coordination activities. The directors of these laboratories should work with each other, with the above-recommended advisory committee, and with the above-recommended informal discussion group to ensure regular communication and collaboration, from the setting of agendas to the synthesis and dissemination of research.

Historically, the regional laboratories have operated more or less independently of the research and development centers. This has led to recurring complaints about fuzziness in the differentiation of the missions of the two groups. Two features of the present situation deepen our concern for the importance of integrating the work of the laboratories into an overarching agenda and collaborative network. First, three of the newly contracted regional laboratories have specialized missions involving English-language learner and multicultural issues, so there is a new opportunity for expanded and coordinated research work in these areas. Second, however, the laboratories are supervised by the Office of Reform Assistance and Dissemination (ORAD), not by the same institute that supervises the new Center for Meeting the Educational Needs of a Diverse Student Population.

Substantive Research Expertise Within the Agencies

10-6. Agencies in the Department of Education that have substantial responsibility for research on language-minority and LEP issues, such as OBEMLA, PES, and OERI (including the institutes, NCES, and ORAD), should allocate resources to train current staff and recruit staff with solid research experience so that there is substantive research expertise on English-language learners within the agencies. Agencies with incidental but important contact with such issues should find means to get the consultative expertise they need in a timely fashion.

10-7. The same key agencies should budget and implement internal senior research fellowships for scholars with expertise in LEP issues for periods of 6 to 12 months. These scholars would be involved in the ongoing research funding issues of the agency while engaging in some research of their own.

As noted earlier, many researchers and agency personnel bemoan the lack of research specialists within the agencies, both in general and specifically with regard to language-minority and LEP issues. We emphasize that OBEMLA's research staff and procedures need to be strengthened if it is to play a role in research management. There is currently little faith in the office's research capacity, a judgment that the committee unhappily shares. If the institute structure of OERI is to thrive, the institute staff must have more depth in the areas each institute covers. Typically, one person is given all responsibilities regarding English-language learners for a given office. Offices need more staff capacity to address complex language issues. One way to accomplish this would be through the employment of excepted personnel. Another would be through the Society for Research in Child Development Executive Branch Fellowships program. A third would be through training of existing staff on LEP issues, or conversely, training of OBEMLA staff on research issues.

Accumulation and Dissemination of Research and Data

10-8. The National Educational Research Policy and Priorities Board should charge the new Department of Education Advisory Committee on Research on English-language Learners with the development of a comprehensive system for integrating the review and synthesis of new knowledge into the dissemination and agenda-setting processes for LEP research. The committee could, for example, hold periodic meetings to assess the state of knowledge; it could adopt and sponsor consensus exercises such as those employed by the National Institutes of Health; and it could hold annual research symposia, as OBEMLA has done in the past. Through the board, the committee could consult the educators who use research results to develop priorities for the further accumulation of needed knowledge. The committee might also consider supporting the establishment of one or more additional juried research journals, with attention to achieving the most neutral or catholic stance on methodological and policy issues. But most important, the committee, working under the board, must be the locus of a coherent process of knowledge accumulation, from the genesis of research in agenda setting to the dual problematic processes arising from the conduct of good research: developing consensus on new knowledge and relating it to practice.

Research is a cumulative enterprise that depends on a tradition giving impetus to new studies. The usual process by which new knowledge is reviewed and archived is the publication of research findings in peer-reviewed journals; but in the field of language-minority and LEP issues, the political nature of the field has distorted even that process. *The Bilingual Research Journal*, publishcd by the National Association for Bilingual Education, and *READ Perspectives*, published by Research in English Acquisition and Development, Inc., both maintain editorial review boards of credible researchers. Yet each is eyed with suspicion by the other political camp, and many serious scholars are discouraged from submitting their work to such publications. Potential contributors may believe that judgments on their work depend on political orientation, as well as on the disciplinary orientation of the reviewers.

Moreover, many studies, particularly those funded through government contracts, never appear in the standard venues of publication and dissemination. Thus, the insertion of such work in the accumulating knowledge base—the process of archiving and reflecting upon the results—is left to the authors themselves, the funding agency, or the National Clearinghouse for Bilingual Education. Many of the investigators in charge of these studies do not work in a setting where publications are rewarded; thus relying on them to archive and disseminate on their own initiative is not effective. The agencies, to put it simply, have a very poor record of accumulating, synthesizing, reflecting upon, and disseminating research results from the studies they have funded, on LEP issues in particular and on educational research in general. The National Clearinghouse for Bilingual Education, funded by OBEMLA, is charged with being a broker between research and practice, providing information on effective practice to the field. As a part of the Department of Education's technical assistance and information network, the clearinghouse should continue to play a role in solving this problem, but it is not integrated into any coherent system for planning, evaluating, and disseminating research results.

Ideally, the building of a successful cumulative knowledge base can result only from a dynamic and coherent process that establishes priorities, funds projects, selects researchers, monitors research, coordinates work sponsored by different agencies, reviews and synthesizes results, disseminates new knowledge, and establishes new priorities. That this will not happen by itself in the infrastructure as currently configured is obvious from past performance. Resources are thin, and this challenging task is not anyone's clear-cut responsibility.

The Next Generation of Researchers

10-9. Research agencies should devote a substantial portion of their funds for research on minority-language and LEP issues to doctoral dissertation competitions and postdoctoral fellowships.

10-10. Congress should restore substantial funding of Title VII fellowships for doctoral training,[4] but allocate the grants to individuals studying LEP issues in any graduate department, rather than to those in programs in bilingual education per se.

Although we do not have systematic data on the issue, there is considerable concern among senior researchers and agency officials that insufficient talent exists at present, or in training, to accomplish the needed research in the

---

[4]Funding for the Title VII fellowships was discontinued in the fiscal year 1996 budget, but through a reprogramming request, funding has been continued for current fellows only. The budget for fiscal year 1997 also did not appropriate funds for fellowships, and a reprogramming request is under review.

language-minority and LEP areas. Through its work in doctoral training, dissertation support, and postdoctoral fellowships, the Spencer Foundation recognizes insufficient research talent as a general problem in education research. Its efforts have been crucial to attracting talented young people to work in education research, and some of them have worked on bilingual education and language-minority issues. Furthermore, in states with large language-minority populations, such as California, support programs (e.g., the Language Minority Research Institute) and training programs (e.g., that at the University of California at Santa Barbara) have helped to train and support researchers working on these issues. But federal research agencies, and others as well, also need to give attention to the problem of the future of the research corps. And the issue has special urgency for research relating to LEP issues because the area is politically charged, which may deter talented researchers from choosing it as a focus of their studies.

Models for the needed support abound. The Office of Special Education and Rehabilitative Services, for example, divides its considerable field-initiated studies funds among doctoral dissertation support, postdoctoral fellowships, and senior research grants, and various institutes of the National Institutes of Health support training programs. Title VII fellowships are a special case. They have been the major source of funding to develop research talent in bilingual education. Although the purpose of the fellowship program is to develop faculty for teacher training programs, the attainment of a doctorate, a teaching position at a university, and tenure at a university necessarily involves Title VII recipients in the conduct and use of research on LEP issues, and many of the active researchers in this area have been recipients of Title VII fellowships. On the other hand, Title VII fellowships tend to be restricted to students in schools of education and within these schools to students in bilingual/bicultural training programs. Many researchers in bilingual education received their degrees in educational areas outside of bilingual education and in disciplinary fields outside of schools of education, such as psychology, anthropology, and linguistics. Those researchers typically do not have access to Title VII fellowships. It might be more judicious and productive to award fellowships on an individual basis rather than to institutions, so that a broader range of students can have access to such support.

Cultural Versus Structural Change

10-11. All parties involved in developing the infrastructure for research on LEP issues should be aware that part of the problem is the need to escape a past history of interagency competition and mutual suspicion. The infrastructure is composed of attitudes as well as institutions.

The previous recommendations require resources, recruiting, and new institutional arrangements. But they are largely structural; if they are to work well, they must be accompanied by changing attitudes. When research budgets are low, issues are politically charged, agendas are volatile, leadership is constantly changing, and leaders believe they must continually reinvent their agencies, a vicious circle of low morale, low expertise, low performance, and low respect infuses the federal education research enterprise, and where good work is done in the agencies, it is done under great stress and without much reward. It is inevitable and understandable that under such circumstances, competitive and defensive attitudes are common. Even if new resources are forthcoming and new structures mandated, it will take an act of collective will to build effective collaboration across federal research agencies and between those agencies and their two "fields"—the field of educators who need to be involved in the agenda formulation, the conduct, and the uses of the research, as well as the academic field of researchers who work on LEP issues.

Roles for State Education Agencies and Foundations

Infrastructure Needs Regarding State Education Agencies

10-12. States should place some emphasis on the concerns expressed in recommendation 10-4 above—to include English-language learners in data gathering, to disaggregate the data by language status where possible in reporting, and more generally to be alert to the potential enrichment of research designs by attending to language issues. Specifically, states should collaborate with experts in institutions of higher education and district and school staff to learn more about the following areas:

• The incorporation of English-language learners into state assessment programs. Issues to be addressed would include how to decide which students get which assessments, as well as the development of alternative assessments for students unable to take the standard ones.

• The development of standard procedures for determining the English and native-language proficiency of English-language learners, best program placements, and the point at which these students should be exited from special programming.

• The development and evaluation of various theoretically driven models of instruction.

• The development of curricula that would enable English-language learners to meet high standards.

• The development and evaluation of teacher education programs and certification examinations for mainstream teachers who work with English-language learners and for teachers who work in English as a second language and bilingual education programs.

10-13. The Department of Education should consider providing financial support for some of these collaborative activities.

10-14. State universities in states with large numbers of English-language learners should consider establishing research and technical assistance programs to support faculty and students with interest in these issues. The University of California's Linguistic Minority Research Institute is an example of a state-wide research support network for language-minority and LEP issues.

Some states with large English-language learner populations are very conscious of the educational issues surrounding such students. Others, perhaps with smaller but growing numbers of English-language learners, are less active in gathering data and developing programs for these students. Our survey disclosed that even in the states with the highest concentrations of English-language learners, little research on LEP issues is conducted under the auspices of the state departments of education. However, there is a great deal of potential here for contribution to the research effort, because states conduct program evaluation and assessment of students and school-level performance, and they collect descriptive information on schools, teachers, and students.

Infrastructure Needs Regarding Research Support from Foundations

10-15. Foundations concerned with education research and reform should encourage grantees, where appropriate, to place some emphasis on the concerns expressed in recommendation 10-4 above—to include English-language learners in data gathering, to disaggregate the data by language status where possible in reporting, and more generally to be alert to the potential enrichment and generalizability of research designs by attending to language issues.

10-16. Foundations can facilitate a more coherent research agenda on LEP issues by setting up and supporting communication—ongoing networks or conferences—among people who do not otherwise work together. The work that led to this report is the kind of reflection and synthesis that can result from such support.

Foundations have the independence and the resources to be catalysts for research, brokers for tough-minded stock taking, and sponsors of research synthesis and agenda setting (as in the case of the present report, which was funded by a combination of foundation and federal funds). The Spencer Foundation's central role in sponsoring basic and applied research, as well as in supporting the recruitment and training of the next generation of education researchers, has been discussed above. With this notable exception, foundations interested in education tend to emphasize action, reform, and the development of effective educational programs, not research per se. However, because research on learning and its contexts is often intertwined with such activities, these foundations can foster excellent research and at the same time press researchers to relate their work to the world of practice. In our informal survey of the foundations most interested in education, we did not find as robust an interest in language issues as we had hoped. Perhaps this report may inspire shifts of emphasis in some agendas or suggest ways in which foundation-sponsored work can address language-minority and LEP issues without much additional cost.

REFERENCES

American Association for the Advancement of Science
  1996   *Research and Development FY 1997.* AAAS Report XXI. Washington, DC: American Association for the Advancement of Science.
American Educational Research Association
  1996   The grass is greener: Department of Defense Centers. *Research Policy Notes* (Dec. 1995-Jan. 1996):3-4.
Atkinson, R.C., and G.B. Jackson, eds.
  1992   *Research and Education Reform: Roles for the Office of Educational Research and Improvement.* Committee on the Federal Role in Education Research, National Research Council. Washington, DC: National Academy Press.
Donmoyer, R.
  1996   Educational research in an era of paradigm proliferation: What's a journal editor to do? *Education Researcher* 25(2):19-25.
Elliott, E.
  1996   *Briefing Paper on Peer Review for Consultants to the National Education Research Policy and Priorities Board.* Office of Educational Research and Improvement, National Educational Research Policy and Priorities Board. Washington, DC: U.S. Department of Education.
Kaestle, C.F.
  1992   Everybody's Been to Fourth Grade: An Oral History of Federal R&D in Education. Wisconsin Center for Education Research, University of Wisconsin-Madison.
Kiesler, S.B., and C. Turner, eds.,
  1977   *Fundamental Research and the Process of Education.* Committee on Fundamental Research Relevant to Education, National Research Council. Washington, DC: National Academy Press.
Kingdon, J.W.
  1984   *Agendas, Alternatives, and Public Policies.* New York: Harper-Collins.
National Council on Educational Research
  1978   *Fourth Annual Report.* National Institute of Education. Washington, DC: U.S. Department of Education.
National Research Council
  1996   *Beyond the Blueprint. Directions for Research on Head Start's Families.* Roundtable on Head Start Research, Board on Children, Youth, and Families, Institute of Medicine and National Research Council. Washington, DC: National Academy Press.
Norwood, J.L.
  1995   *Organizing to Count: Change in the Federal Statistical System.* Washington, DC: Urban Institute Press.
Office of Bilingual Education and Minority Languages Affairs
  1990   Proceedings of the First Research Symposium on Limited English Proficient Students, September. U.S. Department of Education.

1992   Proceedings of the Second Research Symposium on Limited English Proficient Students, August. U.S. Department of Education.

1993   Proceedings of the Third Research Symposium on Limited English Proficient Students, September. U.S. Department of Education.

Office of Science and Technology Policy

1991   *By the Year 2000: First in the World.* Prepared by the Committee on Education and Human Resources, Federal Coordinating Council for Science, Engineering and Technology, James D. Watkins, Secretary of Energy, Chair. Washington, DC: Office of Science and Technology Policy.

Riley, R.W.

1995   Letter from the U.S. Secretary of Education, to the Honorable John Porter, Chairman, Subcommittee on Labor, Health and Human Services, and Education, Committee on Appropriations, House of Representatives, September 18.

Southwest Educational Development Laboratory

1995   Task 7: Specialty Area Development/Language and Cultural Diversity. Proposal prepared by Southwest Educational Development Laboratory, Austin, Texas.

U.S. General Accounting Office

1994   *Peer Review: Reforms Needed to Ensure Fairness in Federal Agency Grant Selection.* Report to the Chairman, Committee on Governmental Affairs, U.S. Senate. GAO/PEMD-94-1. Washington, DC: U.S. General Accounting Office.

Vinovskis, M.A.

1993   Analysis of the Quality of Research and Development at the OERI Research and Development Centers and the OERI Regional Educational Laboratories. Unpublished report, Office of Educational Research and Improvement, June. U.S. Department of Education, Washington, DC.

1995   Changing Views of the Federal Role in Educational Statistics and Research. Office of Educational Research and Improvement, Preliminary draft, September. U.S. Department of Education, Washington, DC.

11

Priorities for Research

Our survey of research on English-language learners and programs designed to serve them has led to a broad range of recommendations for research directions and priorities based on the substantive and methodological strengths and weaknesses in each of eight topical areas (Chapters 2 through 9) and in the research infrastructure (Chapter 10). Worthy as these recommendations are in their own right, the process of priority setting for an overall research agenda requires examining their comparative merit in light of our present state of knowledge and educational needs. We begin by setting forth the principles that have guided our identification of research priorities and provide coherence to our proposed agenda. We then present the identified priorities that apply to each of these principles and steps that can be taken toward their implementation.

Principle 1: Extension of Existing Theories and Methodologies. Priority should be given to important topics to which insufficient attention has been paid, but for which there already exist promising theories and research methodologies so that sound research can be conducted in the immediate future.

Progress in research is often made through a relatively simple extension of the theories and methodologies developed within one domain to another. The field of second language acquisition, for example, evolved primarily through the application of developments in the field of first-language acquisition. The advantage of such a strategy is that progress can be rapid. In addition, this approach has the potential to attract new researchers into the field of language-minority education because it gives them opportunities to extend their work in new ways that are just different enough to be interesting.

Principle 2: Population Coverage. Priority should be given to addressing important gaps in population coverage, such as certain age or language groups, for whom the applicability of current findings from a more limited population can be tested.

The great majority of existing research is geared toward the early elementary grades and English-language learners of Spanish background. This distribution is a fairly accurate reflection of the realities of student demographics. However, research efforts should not be driven purely by the present demographic distribution of the subject population, since the demographics of immigration frequently change. More generally, our quest for knowledge should be geared toward understanding processes specific to particular subpopulations, as well as those that apply across subpopulations. By testing theories in different populations, we are better able to gauge their generality.

Principle 3: Questions of Strong Interest to Particular Constituencies. Priority should be given to legitimate research questions that are of strong interest to particular constituencies, such as educators, policymakers, and the public at large.

The interests of multiple constituencies that are concerned about the education of English-language learners should be incorporated into the selection of priority areas for research. We do not imply here that questions ill suited for empirical inquiry should be included or that technical issues related to theory, methodology, data analysis, and interpretation should be decided by nonresearchers. Rather, we believe that research on questions of high interest to those most involved with programs for English-language learners would stand the best chance of having a practical impact. We also believe research that is owned by a diversity of constituencies and not just by the research community or advocates for a particular viewpoint would have the best chance to thrive with respect to public confidence and, ultimately, funding.

Principle 4: Research Capacity Building. Priority should be given to endeavors that would build the nation's capacity to conduct high-quality research on English-language learners and programs designed to serve their needs.

Successful research efforts, in addition to providing answers to complex problems, would help build confidence among constituencies and funders in language-minority research, and in education research more generally. Infrastructure problems that pose barriers to the conduct of high-quality research are identified in Chapter 10 of this report. These include the capacity of both the funding agencies and the field more generally to develop and carry out a coherent and high-quality research agenda that is strong enough to rise above the politics of this area.

RESEARCH PRIORITIES

Principle 1: Extension of Existing Theories and Methodologies

Among the topics that are of high importance and to which existing theories and methodologies can be applied are content area learning, second-language English literacy development, intergroup relations, and the social context of learning.

Content Area Learning

Content area learning has been neglected in research on English-language learners, primarily because discussions about bilingual education typically put the issue of the language of instruction in the foreground and content area learning in the background. There is very little fundamental research on this topic with English-language learners, but our review, focusing on the areas of subject matter specificity, multiple forms of knowledge, and the role of prior knowledge, has raised some important hypotheses. The methodology in this area comes from cognitive science, attempting to understand deep representations of knowledge through a combination of procedures (e.g., observation, protocols, experimental manipulation), and it can be applied quite readily to the problem of content learning among English-language learners. This line of research would enable us to answer questions such as the following: What role does English-language proficiency level play in content area learning? Are there modifications to the language used by teachers that can make complex subject matters accessible even to second-language beginners? What are the effects of English-language learners on teachers of specific subjects and their classrooms? To what extent does learning complex material in a particular language require having content-specific structures in that language? In addition, the robustness of cognitive science as a field promises to bring an infusion of new talent into the study of language-minority education (Principle 4).

Second-Language Literacy

Second-language literacy has received somewhat more attention than content area learning, but certainly not enough to provide definitive answers about its predictors or other fundamental questions. As we have seen, the field of first-language literacy is in some disarray from internal paradigmatic divisions. Nevertheless, that work can provide a strong foundation for addressing important questions about second-language literacy, such as the necessary basis for its development and the optimal literacy instruction, given student background. Indeed, work on second-language literacy can have the beneficial effect of invigorating scholarship on literacy in general. Important questions include the following: What is the nature of the relationship between language proficiency and literacy skill, as well as between first- and second-language literacy skill? What is optimal English literacy instruction for children of different ages, those with different native languages, those whose native language is not written, or those whose parents are not literate in English? Can literacy be used as a route to language learning, and if so under what circumstances and with what consequences?

Intergroup Relations

The question of intergroup relations with regard to the social status of English-language learners has not received much attention, perhaps because the question is so controversial in bilingual education as a result of criticisms that bilingual programs segregate and stigmatize these students. This neglect is unfortunate because the social climate in schools can undermine even the best of academic programs. Existing research, based primarily on the relationship between African Americans and whites, indicates that curricular and pedagogical interventions can help break down categorization, create superordinate groups, and enable students to develop more positive attitudes and perceptions regarding students from different groups. Much of this research was done prior to the large influx of new immigrant groups from Asia and Latin America. Given the existence of theoretical and methodological frameworks for examining intergroup relations, the following sorts of questions might productively be explored: What are the consequences of status differences among the languages children speak for their intergroup and interpersonal relations? How do teachers' perceptions of the status of children's languages influence their interactions with, expectations for, and behavior toward those children? What roles do English proficiency level and choice of language use serve in social comparisons among language-minority students? Do children form perceptions of others based on native-language use or English proficiency?

Social Context of Learning

Research that has examined language-minority students in the context of their communities and homes has enhanced our understanding of the abilities and knowledge students bring to classrooms and the socialization practices that shape their development. Drawing on this work, many educators incorporate knowledge about students' homes and communities into their instruction to increase the students' academic potential. Much of the current knowledge is based on research using qualitative and interpretive frameworks. These methodologies need to be supported and amplified through studies using systematic sampling and quantitative measures. For example, studies of innovations that lead to stronger connections among language-minority parents, community members, and school personnel and the effect of these innovations on the attitudes and understanding of all involved have been developed primarily by those who hold interpretive perspectives. Further exploring these important developments from the perspective of quantitative evaluation, including an examination of social and educational outcomes, could extend this field in important ways.

It should be noted that this and indeed all four research areas applying Principle 1 have direct program application potential. As interventions are developed, the recommendations from Chapter 6, on program evaluation, will need to be applied: the interventions should be developed based on theory, they should be easy to distinguish, and they must be carefully studied, followed by rigorous evaluation of the outcomes.

Principle 2: Population Coverage

Incorporating particular subpopulations into research not only results in answers to questions of importance to those groups, but also allows us to see whether theories and principles established for certain populations apply to others. Even if they do not, theory is informed and improved. Underrepresented populations in research include young children in preschool and early programs, older students with little or no formal education, older students formerly classified as having limited English proficiency, language groups other than Spanish, and English-language learners with disabilities.

Young Children in Preschool

The linguistic, cognitive, and social/emotional development of children in preschool programs needs more attention. The second-language acquisition literature has not addressed this age group adequately because their native language is still developing, and therefore they are not considered pure cases of second-language acquisition (usually considered to be after age 5). Although the Administration for Children, Youth, and Families (Department of Health and Human Services) has addressed very young children, mostly through descriptive studies of Head Start programs, these children have been missed by most Department of Education research and evaluation efforts because they do not fall within the K-12 range. Given the large number of English-language learners in this age range, heavily represented in Head Start, this is a high-priority research area.

Older Students with Little or No Formal Education

One group of students not well represented in research is those who immigrate to the United States at a later age, such as in middle or high school. Of particular concern are those students who received little or no formal education in their country of origin. In recent years, schools have reported this to be a growing concern. The most important questions for this group are in the areas of English-language acquisition, the development of literacy, and content area learning.

Older Students Formerly Classified As Having Limited English Proficiency

Middle and secondary school students who are no longer classified as having limited English proficiency need to be studied. They are important for several reasons. First, we know very little about the academic and social needs of students who are exited from special programs, since most evaluations of programs stop at the point when students leave them. Information on students' long-term development can provide important insights into ways of providing them with continuing support. Second, if a school or community chooses to emphasize native-language maintenance, attention to these students is important because at this point they are bilingual, yet this is the age when social pressure strongly works against the native language. Most of the programs for the development and maintenance of the native language have focused on the elementary grades, but programs to support high levels of bilingualism at the middle and secondary levels may be just as important.

Language Groups Other Than Spanish

Language groups other than Spanish—roughly one-quarter of English-language learners—have been inadequately represented in research. Studies of basic learning processes, programs, and communities that examine linguistically heterogeneous samples, as well as in-depth inquiries into specific language groups other than Spanish, are needed. Increasing numbers of classrooms have multiple language groups; hence research and development conducted in all-Spanish settings may not apply. Moreover, it is possible that, at least initially, children's native languages can exert subtle effects on their learning of content.

For example, Spanish-speaking children score higher on National Assessment of Educational Progress vocabulary items that have Spanish cognates (such as "fiesta") than would be predicted by their overall performance on the assessment. Finally, teacher expectations and school effects are related to student characteristics, including ethnic background. Hence, research involving students of non-Latino ethnic backgrounds is needed to test various hypotheses about the relationship of various multicultural artifacts to schooling processes.

English-Language Learners with Disabilities

According to a recent report prepared by the Department of Education, Office of Special Education Programs (1993), there are very limited data on numbers of English-language learners with disabilities. The report estimates that 228,000 English-language learners could benefit from special education services.[1] Another estimate (Baca and Cervantes, 1989) suggests that approximately 1 million English-language learners also exhibit learning problems that may qualify them for placement in special education programs. According to Baca (1990), programs for English-language learners with disabilities have been refined and institutionalized since 1985. However, data from the Department of Education suggest that there are still gaps in meeting the needs of these students. Few states have established procedures and guidelines for delivering educational services to this population; very few data are available on effective assessment and instructional practices for these students; and studies conducted in California, Colorado, and Florida indicate a dearth of available bilingual special education and related services personnel. The Department of Education report concludes with the following statement:

> Additional data and studies would help to develop procedures that: distinguish LEP students from LEP students with disabilities, yield unbiased assessments of student need, and result in IEPs [individual educational plans] that assist LEP students with disabilities in reaching their potential. In addition, evaluative studies of materials and curricula developed specifically for LEP students with disabilities are needed in order to assist service providers in meeting the needs of this unique population (p. 30).

There is also a need for teacher education programs across the country that would offer courses specifically geared to educators who work with these children.

Principle 3: Questions of Strong Interest to Particular Constituencies

Principles 1 and 2 appeal to the researcher's perception of important problems. On the other hand, there are many questions about language-minority education that are of particular interest to various groups, including Congress, the administration, and state and local education administrators; the public and the media; advocates for equity; advocates for specific programs; foreign-language advocates; and teachers. It is important to note that these constituencies are not in a position to evaluate the relative technical merits of the research instrumentation; this is a matter to be addressed through a strong system of peer review, as addressed in our recommendations in Chapter 10. But constituency groups are

---

[1]The estimate of 228,000 comes from multiplying the Department of Education's estimate of 1.9 million school-age English-language learners by the department's estimate that 12 percent of all school-age children have disabilities.

critical in developing an awareness among the public and Congress that the questions being addressed by research are meaningful to people outside the research community.

Congress, the Administration, and State and Local Education Administrators

The key questions for Congress and education administrators are unlikely to change: How can we help English-language learners meet high performance standards? Are the programs effective? As our review has amply demonstrated, these are deceptively simple questions with no easy answers. Researchers need to reformulate the questions as follows: What programs, and more importantly what program components, are effective in a given context? How do we make existing programs better? In this report (Chapter 6), we have argued that evaluations of the relative efficacy of broad programs that are loosely implemented in a wide range of settings are likely to yield little information about what interventions are effective. Lessons drawn from the failures of past program evaluation practices point to the importance of strong theory, clearly articulated program goals, successful implementation of program components, comparison group equivalence, and measurement of outcomes. At the same time, we have urged that local evaluations focus on determining whether programs are properly implemented and on fine tuning those programs so they become more responsive to the needs of children, schools, and communities. Most of the components for successful evaluation are within reach of current knowledge, with the major exception of the assessment of content area learning, as discussed below in the section on assessment.

The Public and the Media

Embedded in questions about program effectiveness are larger questions raised by the public and the media about English-language learners and bilingual education. Are the children learning English? Are school programs doing all they can to accomplish this? Are bilingual education programs serving to segregate English-language learners rather than integrate them into the mainstream? Should public funds be used to support the development of ethnic languages, and if so, which ones? These are concerns frequently raised in newspaper editorials, op-eds, and letters to the editor.

Advocates for Equity

Advocates for equity are concerned about access to resources: Do English-language learners have access to good instruction and to resources such as Title I and Goals 2000 funding? Are there differences in opportunities to learn? What barriers are posed that interfere with the learning of English-language learners? Are students being given the optimum instruction for learning English and subject matter knowledge and skills?

Advocates for Specific Programs

Different parties in the debate about program types would emphasize different questions to be pursued, although all sides would acknowledge the difficulties of any endeavor that assumed program categories to be monolithic or static. Moreover, all stand to benefit from a less idealized and political view of programs, founded in research-based knowledge and emphasizing that the best programs will consist of a blend of approaches. There are large areas of commonality across advocacy groups: all parties are interested in how the children acquire English; they are also uniformly interested in finding out what happens to students who receive no special services. However, critics of bilingual education see a lack of research on effectiveness within the range of programs that use only English, while advocates for bilingual education would prefer to see such research in the context of bilingual programs, especially those that promote the full development of both languages.

Foreign-Language Advocates

Advocates for foreign-language education have a different set of priorities. Their concern is not the learning of English, but the development of national capacity in languages other than English. They see the bilingualism attainable by language-minority students as setting high standards for the level of proficiency desirable in foreign languages. Those taking this perspective advocate research focused on programs that fully develop the native languages of English-language learners as well as English and explore the optimum age at which such programs can be introduced. They also view language minorities as a resource for native speakers of English and advocate research on two-way bilingual programs and the social relationships that may form between the groups in such programs.

Teachers

The primary interest of educators immediately involved in teaching English-language learners is in getting helpful ideas and practical guidance for accomplishing their short- and long-term objectives. Questions noted above about language acquisition, content area learning, and intergroup relations are of interest to teachers, but framed around prototypes and examples of particular cases, rather than generalities and principles. The anthropological tradition in education research, especially the ethnographic work in classrooms, schools, and communities, has struck a sympathetic chord among those in everyday practice by vividly illustrating generalizations and by offering contradictions to conventional wisdom. Teachers are interested as well in knowing what programs work and under what conditions. Also useful to this group would be research on assessment addressing its purposes for placement and instruction.

Principle 4: Research Capacity Building

One approach to the development of research capacity and the improvement of quality is through the nurturing of new theoretical approaches, new methodological developments, or cross-fertilization among fields that would be exciting enough to draw fresh talent into research in this area or to create a productive mix of researchers from different theoretical and methodological orientations. As an example, we have mentioned above the problem of content area learning. Stated more generally, this problem belongs to the area of cognitive science, including cognitive psychology, artificial intelligence, linguistics, philosophy, neuroscience, and anthropology. Work in this intersection area, applied to language-minority students and English-language learners, would tap into the talent pool from a currently vibrant area of research.

One promising approach to research is the combining of interpretive analysis and traditional analytic paradigms. Another approach to developing research capacity is through the improvement of coordination and collaboration across institutional boundaries to solve complex problems. We identify six areas: early childhood education (preschool) and development, characteristics of effective practice, assessment, program evaluation, teacher education and professional development, and the distinction between student needs related to English proficiency and those related to poverty. Although the institutions specifically mentioned in this section are at the federal level or federally funded, state education agencies, and in some cases foundations, would also be interested in these areas.

Combining of Interpretive Paradigms with Analytic Paradigms

In many areas of research we have reviewed, there are important roles to be played by ethnographers and qualitative researchers, both as sources of new interpretations and as additional checks on the validity of the claims made by the research. For example, our discussion of content area learning (Chapter 3) points to the power of a multimethod, problem-oriented approach that includes detailed interpretive analysis. Complex problems require a clever combination of diverse methodologies. Likewise, our discussion of program evaluation (Chapter 6) and effective schools research (Chapter 7) emphasizes the important complementary relationships among theory-based intervention, documentation of program implementation, and rigorous measurement of outcomes. In the area of professional development, it is crucial to use a variety of methods to assess teacher competencies, including teacher assessments, as well as empirical studies to determine the relationship between knowledge gained in professional development and its implementation in the classroom. These and other areas provide fertile ground for collaboration between the interpretive and positivistic traditions and should be given priority as a potential means of attracting new research talent. In addition, the involvement of interpretive, case-oriented researchers would make the work more useful from the perspective of teachers and educators, as discussed above under Principle 3.

Early Childhood Education and Development

We have already mentioned the linguistic and social development of young children in preschool programs as a priority under Principle 2. Effective research on this topic would require collaboration between the Head Start Office in the Administration for Children, Youth, and Families and the Office of Educational Research and Improvement (OERI) Early Childhood Institute. In addition, basic child development research, such as extension of the child language database (CHILDES), could be supported by the National Institute for Child Health and Development or the National Science Foundation (NSF).

Characteristics of Effective Practice

Chapter 7 identifies ways of improving learning opportunities for English-language learners. This is the domain of interest of the OERI national centers and regional laboratories that specialize in cultural diversity and second-language learning, of the Office of Reform and Dissemination (ORAD) at OERI, and of the Office of Bilingual Education and Minority Languages Affairs (OBEMLA) through its basic programs. The National Center for Education Statistics (NCES) also collects information pertinent to the learning environment, for example, through its Schools and Staffing Survey and its longitudinal data sets. Finally, although the opportunity-to-learn provisions of Goals 2000 have been stifled because of political controversy, the law continues to provide the authority to offer grants for developing model opportunity-to-learn standards.

Assessment

Assessment of student achievement is discussed throughout this report and in particular in Chapter 5. Answering the questions raised in our discussion of assessment issues would require coordination of effort among a number of agencies, some of which are legally required to provide for the inclusion of English-language learners in assessments (NCES, under the Perkins Act, as discussed in Chapter 9, and OBEMLA, under Title VII[2]). Groups with an important stake in

---

[2]OBEMLA is required to ensure that all data collection by the Department of Education includes the collection and reporting of data on limited-English-proficient students.

a research and development effort on assessment include NCES; the OERI National Institute on Student Achievement, Curriculum, and Assessment; the Planning and Evaluation Service within the Office of the Under Secretary; and the National Institute on the Education of At-Risk Students.

Program Evaluation

The importance of improving the evaluation of programs for English-language learners was noted above under Principle 3 in the discussion of public interest in program accountability. Nurturing new approaches to evaluation would be in the interest of OBEMLA, both in its joint activities with the Planning and Evaluation Service on the evaluation of program categories and in its individual evaluations of grantee performance. Better program evaluation is also in the strong interest of ORAD, which requires program outcome data to certify programs as promising or effective.

Teacher Education and Professional Development

Chapter 8 indicates the importance of a research base on approaches to the preparation and development of teachers of English-language learners. Theoretical coherence is important not just in the development of teacher education programs, but also in the evaluation and continued development of teachers. Teacher education and professional development for teachers specializing in English-language learners are supported by Subpart 3 of Title VII and administered by OBEMLA. At the same time, Title I, through Compensatory Education Programs (Office of Elementary and Secondary Education), supports professional development. This program serves a large number of English-language learners, especially those in high-poverty schools. Finally, OERI does not have an institute directly addressing teacher development, but the functions cut across the institutes.

Distinction Between Needs Related to English Proficiency Development and Poverty

We have seen repeatedly that most English-language learners also live in families and communities with highly stressful economic and social conditions. The ways in which these overlapping conditions operate and interact need to be examined so that programs targeting poverty and those targeting limited English proficiency can be better coordinated. Within the Department of Education, this would involve coordinating the efforts of OBEMLA and the Title I Office. Across departments, the coordination would especially involve the Departments of Health and Human Services, Labor, and Housing and Urban Development.

IMPLEMENTATION OF THE PRIORITIES

Chapter 10 reviews infrastructure problems that have plagued research on language-minority education. The complex and serious questions that need to be answered in the area are in severe imbalance with the human resources available to address them. Providing opportunities for cutting-edge work on an important problem is one of the best ways to bring fresh talent into a field. Thus, the field of language-minority education would be well served by investments in promising areas of research that would attract new talent by highlighting exciting questions, by offering resources to develop networks of researchers, by making funding available for work in the area, and by offering predoctoral and postdoctoral opportunities for young scholars.

We have also seen ample evidence of poor coordination and collaboration across research funding agencies. Almost any complex problem in this area cuts across the functional categories of basic and applied research, program evaluation, and statistical estimates of population parameters. Some of the work has immediate benefits, and some is long term and more indirect in its practical impact, but it is the full portfolio of work that gives society the real benefits of its investment in research. Issues in language-minority education must be addressed in the work of offices and agencies beyond OBEMLA, as well as that of states and foundations. Moreover, if we cannot agree on what good research is and what the priorities are, and if the major funders cannot coordinate their efforts, pressing problems will remain inadequately addressed. Improving the quality of the research will also require improvements in the way agendas are established, proposals are reviewed and selected, and results are synthesized and disseminated.

Aside from human resource and structural problems, our review suggests the importance of attitudinal changes in building a collective will to address the complex problems in the field in the face of a troubled history. Undoubtedly, excellence is a long-term goal. We now suggest some concrete steps that might be taken in the short term to develop a long-term vision.

1. As argued in our recommendations in Chapter 10, the coordinating lead in the field should be taken by a new Department of Education Advisory Committee on Research on English-language Learners that would develop a comprehensive system for integrating the review and synthesis of new knowledge into the agenda-setting and dissemination processes. Its charge would be Department of Education-wide, although it should also address and complement the work being funded outside the department; for example, it should foster coordination among the Early Childhood Institute at OERI, the Head Start Office, and the Administration for Children, Youth, and Families, as well as collaboration with states with large numbers of English-language learners. Immediate topics to be addressed by this committee would be the areas identified in this chapter that are ripe for coordina-

tion: early childhood (preschool) education, characteristics of effective practice, student assessment, program evaluation, teacher education, and the effects of limited English proficiency and poverty. The substantive topics for research to be pursued within each of these areas would be those identified under Principles 1 and 2 above.

2. It is difficult to influence the agendas of agencies outside the Department of Education, especially NSF; the National Institute for Childhood Health and Development; the National Institute for Mental Health; and the Administration for Children, Youth, and Families. Our review has revealed that very little research conducted by those agencies has involved explicit attention to the English-language learner population. As discussed earlier, the most positive way of achieving greater inclusion of these students in research is through the incentives of achieving greater scientific accuracy and expanding and generalizing current work. The proposed Department of Education Advisory Committee on Research on English-language Learners should sponsor conferences and other activities jointly with other agencies to bring these incentives to the attention of researchers. Less positive, but perhaps necessary at some point, would be a more systematic inquiry by Congress into the extent of exclusion of English-language learners from the research, followed by Congressional action if the situation should warrant. This action might include incentives for more work in this area.

3. Other areas the committee identified for strengthening include the peer review process used to fund proposals; the processes available for monitoring research, accumulating knowledge, and developing consensus in given fields; and mechanisms for the dissemination of research results. The National Educational Research Policy and Priorities Board is overseeing improvements in these areas. The proposed Advisory Committee on Research on English-language Learners should play an important role in ensuring that the funding and conduct of research on English-language learners are included in this department-wide agenda.

4. The National Educational Research Policy and Priorities Board is currently taking a comprehensive look at OERI's system of peer review. This is an essential activity to address the issue of research quality. As Chapter 10 suggests, the peer review system at the National Institutes of Health provides a good model, but before one could import this model wholesale, constraints that characterize the LEP area would need to be addressed, such as the heterogeneity of research paradigms, poor articulation of the relationship between theory and practice, and the small scale of funding. Moreover, peer review would have to be seen as much more than a bureaucratic instrument—as a major vehicle of communication between funders and the field, and a process through which principles about research priorities and technical quality of research are clearly articulated and applied to proposals. The current effort by the National Educational Research Policy and Priorities Board should be augmented by two additional efforts. One would be to look at uses of peer review throughout the Department of

Education, not just within OERI. Such an expansion would be within the board's authority to advise on research activities across the department. The other would address how to ensure expertise on English-language learner issues throughout the peer review process. This concern could be constructively addressed by the proposed Department of Education Advisory Committee on Research on English-language Learners.

5. Population coverage issues are relevant to any research agency that purports to generalize its findings, but fall most immediately within the interests of NCES. As recommended in Chapter 9, NCES should develop a common framework within which student and program data can be collected for national statistics. This framework could be extended to accommodate samples from all studies involving English-language learners and LEP programs. NCES could take the initiative to monitor the population representativeness of all funded research conducted by federal, state, and private agencies, and report to the Advisory Committee on Research on English-language Learners regarding important gaps in coverage.

6. NCES should work with states and with all offices that collect data on English-language learners to use a common definition of limited English proficiency. NCES should also lead an empirical effort to develop operational measures of limited English proficiency that can be used for a variety of purposes, ranging from large-scale assessment, such as the National Assessment of Educational Progress, to program-based and basic research studies, such as those funded through OERI. NCES should also take the lead in developing procedures for incorporating English-language learners into large-scale assessments, including modifications in assessments and assessment procedures.

7. OBEMLA has been a consistent and all too often lone voice in advocating research on English-language learners and LEP programs. Unfortunately, its capacity to manage research has been inconsistent and a frequent source of controversy. Nevertheless, OBEMLA is the valid channel through which the public-interest questions about English-language learners and programs that serve them, such as those identified above under Principle 3, are directed and filtered. OBEMLA should therefore take steps to identify itself as the conduit through which such public concerns are expressed. For example, OBEMLA could conduct consensus-building activities that would bring educators and advocates together with researchers to identify important questions for research investment. These areas for research could then be further developed in conjunction with the Advisory Committee on Research on English-language Learners.

8. OBEMLA provides major support for teacher education and professional development activities through Subpart 3 of Title VII. This report has shown a major need for research to improve the education of teachers who work with English-language learners. OBEMLA should take the lead in developing and evaluating theoretically informed approaches to the development of teachers who are specialists in teaching English-language learners, as well as those who are not

specialists, but nevertheless teach a large number of such students. Based on knowledge gained from this research, OBEMLA could take the initiative in working with the Office of Compensatory Education to develop guidance for professional development for those in Title I programs who teach these students. OBEMLA could also work with the regional educational laboratories and comprehensive regional assistance centers that provide support to teachers whose classrooms include English-language learners. OBEMLA should develop consensus-building activities with the OERI institutes, especially the Students-at-Risk Institute, to identify priority areas for research that would be pursued by the institutes toward the end of improving teacher education. OERI should fund research in these areas.

9. Another important function for OBEMLA is in the development of researchers on English-language learner issues. OBEMLA already conducts a significant share of activities in this area through its Title VII Bilingual Fellowship Programs. OBEMLA should leverage this valuable source of support to attract education researchers who have not previously worked with this population, as well as to attract researchers who have traditionally not worked in the area of education, for example by encouraging applications from both students in other educational fields and students in institutions outside of schools of education. OBEMLA should also take a lead role in coordinating with other agencies and foundations in an effort to attract and develop fresh talent in this area.

10. A more long-term role for OBEMLA is to position itself so it can better utilize information on programs and their effectiveness from its Subpart 1 programs. Over the years, thousands of projects have been funded under Title VII basic programs. These programs constitute a tremendous opportunity—not yet realized—to implement theoretically driven interventions and assess their effects in different contexts. For example, the law does not require programs to describe and justify the theories underlying their programmatic approaches. Moreover, although programs are required to conduct evaluations, these evaluations have tended to assess compliance with federal requirements, rather than to examine program effectiveness (which would, ideally, be related to theory). Given the paucity of information in the evaluations, it is difficult to use them to enrich the theory-program-outcomes process. OBEMLA should work with the Planning and Evaluation Service of the Office of the Under Secretary to implement the recommendations offered in this report for improving program evaluation (see Chapter 6). To avoid problems that have arisen in the past, the staff capacity at OBEMLA should include researchers with expertise in the use of evaluation for purposes of program development.

11. Agencies in the Department of Education that have substantial responsibility for research on minority-language and English-language learner issues, such as OBEMLA, the Planning and Evaluation Service, and OERI (including the institutes, NCES, and ORAD), should allocate resources to train current staff and recruit staff with solid research experience so that there is substantive re-

search expertise on English-language learners within the agencies. Agencies with incidental but important contact with such issues should find means to obtain the consultative expertise they need in a timely fashion.

12. States need information regarding the educational attainment of their English-language learners, how their performance compares with that of other students in the state, and which educational interventions are effective for these students. States should make efforts to include English-language learners in data gathering, to disaggregate by language status where possible in reporting, and more generally to attend to research that will improve instructional interventions for these students. States should also endeavor to improve teacher education and professional development. There are shared issues across states, and thus states would benefit as well from collaboration.

13. Foundations fund many school reform efforts, but they do not systematically attend to the inclusion of English-language learners in those efforts or to the assessment of outcomes for these students. Foundations might encourage those who conduct such efforts to address the needs of these students. In addition, foundations might fund projects that would specifically address the educational needs of English-language learners, as well as support the development of local, state, and federal policies that would enhance their education. Finally, foundations could facilitate a more coherent research agenda on English-language learner issues by setting up and supporting communication mechanisms, including ongoing networks or conferences among people who do not usually work together.

CONCLUSION

We began our report about research on the education of English-language learners with assumptions shared by this committee. To repeat, they are as follows:

• All children in the United States should be able to function fully in the English language.

• English-language learners should be held to the same expectations and have the same opportunities for achievement in the academic content areas as other students.

• In an increasingly global economic and political world, proficiency in languages other than English and an understanding of different cultures are valuable in their own right and should be among the major goals for schools.

We believe these assumptions represent broadly shared values. As we have applied our scientific expertise to evaluate the state of the art in the education of English-language learners and envisioned a research agenda for the immediate and distant future, we have been troubled by extent to which politics has constrained the development of sound practice and research in this field. Since the politics will persist, the demand placed on high-quality and broadly credible research becomes even more compelling. As this report has shown, considerable knowledge has already accrued, and there are ways of strengthening and building upon it. This vision can be realized through a strategic combination of theory, research, program development, evaluation, and monitoring. The committee hopes that the paths we have delineated can be followed with maximum intensity and minimum distraction.

REFERENCES

Baca, L.
  1990   *Theoretical and Applied Issues in Bilingual/Cross-Cultural Special Education: Major Implications for Research, Practice, and Policy.* Boulder, CO: BUENO Center for Multicultural Education.
Baca, L., and H. Cervantes, eds.
  1989   *The Bilingual Special Education Interface.* Columbus, OH: Merrill.
Office of Special Education Programs
  1993   *To Assure the Free Appropriate Public Education of all Children with Disabilities.* Fifteenth Annual Report to Congress on the Implementation of The Individuals with Disabilities Education Act. Washington, DC: U.S. Department of Education.

Appendices

APPENDIX

A

The Infrastructure for Research on English-Language Learners and Bilingual Education

Diane August and Carl Kaestle

This appendix presents the results of a comprehensive study of the infrastructure for research on English-language learners and bilingual education. The origins of that infrastructure are first examined. This is followed by an explanation of the approach used for this study. The third and fourth sections review the agencies involved in the research and their activities at the federal and state levels, respectively. The fifth section describes the efforts of the various foundations, and the sixth those of the national reform networks. The final section addresses the recruitment and training of researchers.[1]

THE ORIGINS OF AN INFRASTRUCTURE FOR RESEARCH

Bilingual Education in the Nineteenth Century

From the inception of free public education in the United States through the 1960s, most schools used English as their language of instruction, offering work in other languages only as second-language instruction. However, there were exceptions. In nineteenth-century New York City, St. Louis, Milwaukee, Cincinnati, smaller cities in Ohio, small towns in Wisconsin, and some communities in Louisiana, New Mexico, and elsewhere, school officials approved instruction in languages other than English as a response to the educational needs of immigrant children or as a reflection of the political strength of language-minority groups (see Castellano, 1983; Schlossman, 1983a; Jones, 1973).[1]

---

[1]Although there is no single source that consolidates perspectives on bilingual education, valuable information can be found in Crawford (1995); Zehler et al. (1993); Baker and de Kanter (1983);

The arguments used to support or oppose such programs were similar to those we hear today. Opponents argued that children needed English to function well as workers and citizens in America, that immigrants would remain isolated and clannish if they did not mix thoroughly with other children in the English-language environment of the common school, and that children would remain too long in the bilingual programs provided. Advocates variously argued that bilingual programs were needed to attract and retain immigrants' children in the public schools; that bilingual education was a reasonable accommodation; and that the purpose of these programs was a transition to English, which the children would learn soon enough.

Occasionally, research in favor of bilingual education was cited. John Peasley, superintendent of Cincinnati's schools, studied achievement test scores and concluded that "a child can study two languages at the same time and do as well in each, as he would if all his time were devoted to either language alone." And in St. Louis the head of German education persuaded William Torrey Harris, the famous superintendent of St. Louis schools, to provide classes in which German students were mixed with the other students. Harris approved a 5-year experiment comparing the mixed and segregated German-language classes. Achievement scores following the experiment suggested that "the Anglo-Americans will certainly learn more German" in the bilingual classes, while "the German Americans are not retarded in their progress by the presence of the Anglo-Americans," doing as well as those in segregated German bilingual classes (Schlossman, 1983a:156, 164). Usually, however, educators argued not from research, but from political conviction, common sense, or anecdote. Arguments were often expressed in terms such as "...rests on the soundest bases of public policy" or "as is well known." In a Milwaukee debate, both sides claimed that "expert" opinion supported their position (Schlossman, 1983a:174).

In 1837, New York City opened two German schools. These were public primary schools with German-speaking teachers, provided for German American immigrant children. The instruction was supposed to be in English, and the purpose was to prepare the children to pursue their education in the existing public schools and thus to become identified with our native population. After a year, 380 children had been admitted. The school board tried to limit attendance to a 1-year maximum, but the teacher said the children could not be prevailed upon to attend the other schools because of dissimilarity of language, dress, manners, and so on. The board compromised, but insisted that the aim was to make these children, though Germans by birth, Americans by education, which could be accomplished only by their attendance at the regular common schools.

Glenn (1996); and Hakuta (1986). A good historical perspective from the early phase of bilingual education can be found in a five-volume set published by the Center for Applied Linguistics (1977).

Critics on the board said in 1843, "When foreigners are in the habit of congregating together they retain their national customs, prejudices and feelings and are therefore not as good members of society as they would otherwise be" (Kaestle, 1973:144). The board repeatedly refused requests for similar Italian schools, and in 1850 they abolished the German schools. Yet when the New York City schools underwent a governance reform and allowed more decentralized control in the latter part of the century, some wards offered German instruction once again, illustrating the ebb and flow of foreign-language instruction in nineteenth-century public schools. In rural Wisconsin and Minnesota, where German or Norwegian immigrants sometimes constituted a majority of a town's population, local schools often had German and Norwegian teachers, and, despite state laws limiting foreign-language instruction to 1 hour, German or Norwegian often became the school vernacular.

Where the conditions were right, local schools in the nineteenth century often accommodated other languages. The extent of these practices cannot be precisely stated, but some estimates are quite substantial. Kloss (1977), for example, calculates that perhaps a million schoolchildren received some or all of their instruction in a language other than English in 1890. Some nonimmigrant politicians favored the accommodation as part of a strategy to attract immigrants, and some educators spoke positively about the outcome. The superintendent of Marathon County schools said that "if the children should first learn to express their thoughts in their mother tongue, they would later learn more of the English language in three months than they would learn, in the old way, in three years" (quoted in Schlossman, 1983a:144). In some midwestern cities with large German populations, various sorts of bilingual programs existed. William Torrey Harris argued that it was "in the interest of the entire community here that the German shall cultivate his own language while he adopts English as his general means of communication" (quoted in Schlossman, 1983a:151). Arguments of the opponents of these programs also sound familiar to the modern ear. In Milwaukee, dissenting board members argued in the 1890s that "instruction in German unnecessarily burdens these young children and retards their progress in other studies.... All means should be used to give them the best possible education in the English language, the language of their country" (quoted in Schlossman, 1983a:172).

It is not surprising that little research was conducted on the scattered bilingual programs of the period. Little research was conducted on any educational practice. State departments of education had modest staffs and budgets, and American universities had as yet established neither a tradition nor an infrastructure for research. At the state and federal levels, research consisted largely of gathering statistics that could be used in formulating education policies.

The Early Twentieth Century

Three developments of the late nineteenth and early twentieth centuries changed the above situation: the expansion of state departments of education; the rise of research universities in the United States, with the attendant development of the social sciences; and the launching of large philanthropic foundations, many of which had an interest in education. These developments portended an increase in education research. However, by the time the necessary infrastructure was in place, the scattered, fledgling programs in bilingual education had largely ended. Use of the native language in schools went into a long period of dormancy starting with public outcries about the waves of new immigrants in the early 1900s (Jones, 1960; Hakuta, 1986). The Dillingham Commission, set up by Congress to investigate the changing patterns of immigration, noted the low skill levels of new immigrants who had "congregated together in sections apart from native Americans and the older immigrants to such an extent that assimilation [had] been slow" (quoted in Jones, 1960:178). More pointedly, Francis Walker, president of Massachusetts Institute of Technology, expressed his concerns: "These immigrants are beaten men from beaten races, representing the worst failures in the struggle for existence....Europe is allowing its slums and its most stagnant reservoirs of degraded peasantry to be drained off upon our soil" (quoted in Ayres, 1909:103). Conditions had changed dramatically from the 1800s with respect to societal attitudes toward immigrants, in part as a result of the increased number of immigrants and in part as a result of the fact that the sources of immigration had changed from northern to southern and eastern Europe. Added to the anti-immigrant feeling was the hostility to German language and culture associated with World War I. In the wake of these combined developments, many states passed laws making English the sole language of school instruction in the first two decades of the century (Liebowitz, 1980).

Thus from the 1920s on, although there was more education research in general, there was less bilingual education in practice. This is not to say, however, that there was no research on the educational needs of language-minority children or on language-minority populations more generally. As Hispanic American educators entered the mainstream of university research and educational administration, they mustered research to argue against the massive discrimination experienced by Hispanic students.

The most famous of these researchers, George Sanchez, took his doctorate at Berkeley and held positions first as a researcher for the New Mexico state department of education and later as a professor of education at the University of Texas at Austin. Continually challenging discriminatory practices, Sanchez (1934:770) wrote about the subtle problems of translation for bilingual children taking mental ability tests. He argued that the "prostitution of democratic ideals to the cause of expediency, politics, vested interests, ignorance, class and 'race' prejudice" had led to inferior, segregated schooling, while standardized mental tests rested on an assumption of common culture and language. Schools "have the responsibility of supplying those experiences to the child which will make the experiences sampled by standard measures as common to him as they were to those on whom the norms of the measures were based." Like his mentor Herschel Manuel, Sanchez invested his energies in fighting the segregation of Mexican American children, not in arguing for separate bilingual programs (Schlossman, 1983b). In *Forgotten People* (Sanchez, 1940), he argued that New Mexico's public schools and other institutions had refused to accept and serve the needs of Mexican Americans, resulting in cultural lag and lack of opportunity to assimilate. Speaking of the teachers of Taos, Sanchez said, "Bilingualism and its problems, as a significant challenge and as an opportunity in education, is largely a closed book to them" (p. 78). "The educational policy followed in New Mexico is startling in its ineptitude," he declared (p. 33). A smattering of more general research on language minorities emanated from America's research universities from the 1920s to the 1960s, culminating in some important pieces of work, such as Fishman et al.'s influential *Language Loyalty in the United States* (1966). However, bilingual education was virtually absent from the policy agenda of American public schools, so the potential for research to shape policy and practice in this area remained to be seen.

The Latter Twentieth Century

Bilingual education did not significantly re-emerge until 1963, when a Ford Foundation grant set up an experimental program in Dade County, Florida, to accommodate the needs of the first wave of Cuban refugees, many of whom had intentions of returning to Cuba at the earliest opportunity (Mackey and Beebe, 1977). The goal of this program was to create fully functional bilingual students, and it enjoyed the privilege of including the elite among the Cuban refugee community and English-background students whose parents were interested in a bilingual education. The success of this program gave encouragement to the concept of bilingual education for students from less privileged backgrounds (see Hakuta, 1986).

Federal endorsement of bilingual education began in 1968 when President Johnson signed into law the Bilingual Education Act as Title VII of the Hawkins-Stafford Elementary and Secondary Education Act, authorizing funds to be made available to local school districts on a competitive basis to establish innovative programs for students of limited English proficiency. The law did not specify that these programs had to use the native language of the students, although in practice most of them did (Crawford, 1995:60, footnote 1). Funds could be used to support programs, train teachers and aides, develop and disseminate instructional materials, and encourage parent involvement in the programs. In fiscal year 1969, Congress made the first appropriation for bilingual education, $7.5 million, enough to fund just 76 projects serving 27,000 students. Congressional action was followed by a flurry of activity in state legislatures and in the courts. Many states, starting with Massachusetts in 1971, enacted their own laws requiring special services, including bilingual education, for English-language learners.[2]

In 1974, in a class action suit filed on behalf of Chinese-background students against the San Francisco Unified School District, the Supreme Court ruled that districts offering the same instruction to English-language learners as they did to English-speaking children were in violation of the Civil Rights Act (*Lau v. Nichols,* 414 U.S. 563, 1974). In agreeing with the plaintiffs, they wrote:

> There is no equality of treatment merely by providing students with the same facilities, textbooks, teachers, and curriculum; for students who do not understand English are effectively foreclosed from any meaningful education.

Importantly, the ruling did not require bilingual education:

> No specific remedy is urged upon us. Teaching English to the students of Chinese ancestry who do not speak the language is one choice. Giving instructions to this group in Chinese is another. There may be others. Petitioners ask only that the Board of Education be directed to apply its expertise to the problem and rectify the situation.

In response to this ruling, the Department of Health, Education and Welfare issued a set of proposed remedies (known as the *Lau* remedies) to be used by its Office for Civil Rights to negotiate compliance plans with school districts that did not provide special programs for English-language learners, and thus were in violation of *Lau.* These proposed remedies required the provision of transitional bilingual education in most instances and went beyond the literal interpretation of the *Lau* decision with respect to specific remedies.

The recommendations of the *Lau* remedies found three types of programs acceptable. We quote (excerpted in Baker and de Kanter, 1983:221):

> (1) *Bilingual/Bicultural Program.* A program which utilizes the student's native language (example: Navajo) and cultural factors in instructing, maintaining and further developing all the necessary skills in the student's native language and culture while introducing, maintaining, and developing all the necessary skills in the second language and culture (example: English). The end result is a student who can function, totally, in both languages and cultures.

> (2) *Multilingual/Multicultural Program.* A program operated under the same principles as a Bilingual/Bicultural Program *except* that more than one language and culture, in addition to English language and culture is treated. The end

---

[2]This action by Massachusetts was followed by similar actions by Alaska and California (1972); Arizona, Illinois, New Mexico, and Texas (1973); Michigan, New York, and Rhode Island (1974); Colorado, Louisiana, New Jersey, and Wisconsin (1975); Indiana (1976); Connecticut, Maine, Minnesota, and Utah (1977); and Iowa, Kansas, Oregon, and Washington (1979). California's state law was allowed to "sunset" in 1987.

result is a student who can function, totally, in more than two languages and cultures.

(3) *Transitional Bilingual Education (TBE).* A program operated in the same manner as a Bilingual/Bicultural Program, except that once the student is fully functional in the second language (English), further instruction in the native language is no longer required.

English as a second language (ESL), which the *Lau* remedies defined as "a structured language acquisition program designed to teach English to students whose native language is not English," was not considered appropriate "because an ESL program does not consider the affective nor cognitive development of students."[3]

The policy debate in the education of English-language learners in the early years of Title VII and the post-*Lau* period of the 1970s thus came to be defined in terms of how aggressively to pursue the use of the native language. The 1970s saw the active pursuit of bilingual and even bicultural education in both Congress and the courts and an administration eager to press for bilingualism (e.g., Gaarder, 1967). The first reauthorization in 1974 dropped the poverty criterion for eligibility and required schools to include instruction in the native language and culture. As noted earlier, many states followed suit by passing bilingual education laws that were modeled on Massachusetts law and on *Lau*, both of which set a specified number of students that would trigger a requirement for the provision of bilingual instruction.

Around this time a series of evaluations began, comparing different methods of instruction for English-language learners. The first major event was the release of a study by the American Institutes for Research, challenging the effectiveness of bilingual education as compared with "sink-or-swim" situations for these students (Dannoff, 1978; see also Chapters 3 and 6 in this volume). Nonetheless, during the late 1970s the federal government settled into a policy of transitional bilingual education, rejecting English immersion on the one hand and the maintenance of non-English languages on the other. Much of the subsequent politics of language instruction for English-language learners can be seen as efforts to change that policy, and much of the research of the next two decades has been generated and interpreted through this lens. Despite the government's repeated statements that the purpose of bilingual education was the transition to English, opponents saw bilingual education as a force for language pluralism and the maintenance of non-English languages.

If the 1970s was a period of advancement for proponents of instruction through the native language, the 1980s was one of hurried retreat. The *Lau* remedies, requiring native-language instruction, were broadly used by the Office

---

[3]Elaboration and discussion of the uses of the *Lau* remedies can be found in Crawford (1995) and in Birman and Ginsburg (1983).

for Civil Rights in negotiating with local school districts, but they had never been set in regulations. They were finally proposed as regulations in 1980 during the final months of the Carter administration and prior to President Carter's electoral loss to Ronald Reagan that same year. The proposed regulations were withdrawn early the next year by the Reagan administration for being "harsh, inflexible, burdensome, unworkable, and incredibly costly...an intrusion on state and local responsibility" (Education Secretary Terrel Bell, cited in Crawford, 1995:53).

Title VII also came under stern criticism for its requirement of native-language use. President Reagan took time to depart from his prepared address to a group of mayors:

> It is absolutely wrong and against American concept [sic] to have a bilingual education program that is now openly, admittedly dedicated to preserving their native language and never getting them adequate in English so they can go out into the job market (New York Times, March 3, 1981).

Secretary of Education William Bennett found much to attack in Title VII, specifically the restrictions on the proportion of funding for Special Alternative Instructional Programs, which do not use the native language. According to the Director of the Office of Bilingual Education at the time, Alicia Coro (personal communication), flexibility was needed because many school districts did not have the resources to provide native-language instruction for students from a myriad of backgrounds; ESL instruction was a more practical approach. The 1984 reauthorization had placed a cap on Special Alternative Instructional Programs of 4 percent of total program spending in Title VII. In a well-noted address in 1985, Bennett summed it up as follows:

> This, then, is where we stand: After seventeen years of federal involvement, and after $1.7 billion of federal funding, we have no evidence that the children whom we sought to help—that the children who deserve our help—have benefitted. And we have the testimony of an original sponsor of the Bilingual Education Act, Congressman James Scheuer of New York, that the Bilingual Education Act's original purposes were perverted and politicized; that instead of helping students learn English, the English has been sort of thinned out and stretched out and in many cases banished into the mists and all of the courses tended to be taught in Spanish [sic]. That was not the original intent of the program (U.S. Department of Education, 1985).

Following a vigorous legislative battle in which proponents of bilingual education tried to maintain the existing cap on Special Alternative Instructional Programs, the cap was increased from 4 to 25 percent in the 1988 reauthorization (Section 7002(b)(3) of Title VII of the Elementary and Secondary Education Act of 1965, as amended in 1988).

The shift in Congress from mandating of bilingual programs to increased acceptance of English-only programs has continued to this day. In the most recent reauthorization in 1994, the 25 percent cap was retained, but with a special provision for exceeding it if a grant applicant shows bilingual education to be infeasible because of the diversity of native languages or if bilingual teachers are not available despite documented efforts. At the state level, California allowed its aggressive state bilingual education law to sunset in 1987. Although no other states have allowed their bilingual education laws to lapse, these laws continue to generate controversy in state legislatures, most recently in states such as Massachusetts, Rhode Island, New York, and Connecticut.

With the erosion of the position of bilingual education advocates in Congress in the 1980s, as well as the decreased enforcement of *Lau* by the Department of Education, an important court decision emerged on the definition of what it means for a school to take appropriate action to overcome language barriers that impede equal participation by its students in its instructional programs. In this decision, the Fifth Circuit Court of Appeals offered an interpretation of Section 1703(f) of the Equal Educational Opportunities Act of 1974, which referred to appropriate action. *Castaneda v. Pickard* (648 F.2d 989, 1006-07, 5th Cir. 1981) is the leading case that establishes a school district's obligations. It requires that (1) the program pursued by the district be informed by an educational theory recognized as sound by some experts in the field, or at least deemed a legitimate educational strategy; (2) the program and practices actually used by the school system be reasonably calculated to implement that theory effectively; and (3) a school's program, although premised on sound educational theory and effectively implemented, produce results indicating that the language barriers confronting students are actually being overcome. Other court cases, including *Keyes v. School Dist. No. 1* (576 F. Supp. at 1519) and *Teresa P. v. Berkeley Unified School District* (724 F. Supp. 698, 716 N.D. Cal. 1989), have dealt with requirements for serving English-language learners under the Equal Education Opportunities Act, and in their interpretation have used *Castaneda* as a persuasive precedent (see August and Garcia, 1988). *Castaneda* is notable from the perspective of this report because of the burden it places on programs that they be informed by educational theory and the evidence upon which they are based (see Chapter 6).

The final leg of the history that brings us up to date begins with the national education reform movement that was punctuated most prominently by the 1983 publication of *A Nation at Risk* (National Commission on Excellence in Education) and the 1989 Education Summit in Charlottesville. The call to arms by the nation's governors (led by then-Governor Clinton) and President Bush led to a characterization of the entire national student body, not just particular groups of students, as being at risk. There was an ensuing call for explicit education goals, standards, and accountability, generically referred to as *standards-based reform* (see Chapter 5), to make the United States competitive in a global economy. Standards-based reform continues to define the debate over reform to this day (McLaughlin et al. 1995).

One by-product of these political battles was to strengthen the framework of debate and analysis, which saw the education of English-language learners as a contest between two alternative strategies—some use of the native language versus an English-only approach—whose coherence in practice was illusory (since they were implemented differently in each site), but whose electrical charge in politics was potent. Several influential researchers have bemoaned the inelegance, ineffectiveness, and narrowness of research conducted under such circumstances over the past 20 years and have urged the value of basic research in developing more adequate theory to underlie bilingual education programs (see, e.g., McLaughlin, 1985; Hakuta and Gould, 1987). Many other researchers, of course, have lent their talents and time to the large-scale program evaluation studies that have dominated the agenda (see Chapter 6).

The Bilingual Education Act of 1978 provided, for the first time, funds for a regular program of research on the education of English-language learners. There had been a few individual research projects on bilingual education funded by the old Office of Education and then by the National Institute of Education (NIE), which was established in 1972. But the 1978 legislation directed the Office of Bilingual Education (OBE) to lay out a 5-year plan of research. The law also required that the "Assistant Secretary of Education coordinate research activities of the National Institute of Education, with the Office of Bilingual Education, the National Center for Education Statistics, and other appropriate agencies, in order to develop a national research program for bilingual education (Elementary and Secondary Education Act, as amended 1978, Section 742(a)(3) of Title VII).

In response to this section of the law, and because OBE had no research staff at the time, while various other agencies in the Department of Education had research capacity and responsibilities, the department established a committee to coordinate research efforts on bilingual education department-wide. Named for the section of Title VII that provided the research money, the Part C Coordinating Committee envisioned a situation in which OBE would develop the capacity to fund and monitor research, but would also distribute funds to NIE for research on teaching and learning among English-language learners; to the National Center for Education Statistics (NCES) for data collection and survey efforts; and to the Department's Office of Policy, Budget, and Evaluation (OPBE) for the evaluation of bilingual education programs. The Coordinating Committee was chaired by a representative of the Assistant Secretary for Education; some original members of the committee were Ronald Hall, Leslie Silverman, Katherine Truex, and Lois-Ellen Datta.

For the first time, then, the federal government had created an infrastructure for research on language-minority student education. This infrastructure was a set of resources and institutional arrangements—funds, personnel, and procedures—intended to engage experts in surveying, analyzing, and evaluating the experiences of English-language learners and the programs designed to meet their needs, and thereby to improve practice. Now the ingredients for research-based educational policies existed, at least in theory: bilingual education was a growing feature of local school practice, but programs had very diverse characteristics and aims; bilingual education was becoming a hot debate; and the nation had at least a modest commitment to research in education. Researchers were challenged both to sort out the complexities of programs and results and to provide ammunition for the debates. In retrospect, however, the past 20 years has not been a heyday for research on this topic. Often, despite the existence of a research infrastructure, policy has been driven by the kinds of stereotypes, political preferences, and misconceptions that informed debates on bilingualism in the nineteenth century (see Hakuta, 1986). Nor did the research systematically contribute to improvements in practice, partly because of problems with the research methodology—an overreliance on large-scale evaluations and effective/nominated schools research, as well as faulty and weak mechanisms for oversight of the research enterprise.

The purpose of this appendix is to describe how that infrastructure developed, how well it has worked, and what obstacles have impeded the effective funding of research and evaluation in this field. To some extent, the infrastructure for research related to the education of English-language learners partakes of the inadequacies of education research in general (see Atkinson and Jackson, 1992; Kaestle, 1993; Dershimer, 1976; Sproull et al., 1978). The picture is further complicated by the fact that the infrastructure for education research in general, and for research on these students in particular, is being substantially restructured as we write this report. Issues related to the infrastructure and recommendations for its improvement are addressed in Chapter 10 of this report.

APPROACH TO THIS STUDY

Our central interest is in research on children with limited English proficiency and the programs designed to meet their educational needs, including bilingual education. We are also interested, however, in research on bilingualism as a cognitive and social phenomenon and research on language minorities and their relation to American schooling. As a shorthand for this set of concerns, we use the phrases "English-language learners" and "LEP issues" (see the discussion of definitional issues in Chapter 1). When deciding whether to include a given piece of research in our purview, we sometimes included research that specified a target group, such as Asian Americans or Hispanic Americans, having a large proportion of non-native speakers of English, even if the research did not directly address language acquisition; in contrast, we did not include studies that targeted "minority," "inner-city," or "disadvantaged" populations unless language was the specific focus. We looked not only at basic, intermediate, and applied research that directly addressed our topics, but also at studies that looked incidentally at language, those that included language as an explanatory variable, and data collection projects that included language variables.

We surveyed all of the federal research agencies that fund a significant amount of research on LEP issues. We gathered background documents on these agencies and, using a standard protocol, conducted interviews with 27 research administrators and others centrally involved in federal education research. We also surveyed the state education agencies for states with a population of English-language learners of 6 percent or more. That standard yielded nine states: Alaska, Arizona, California, Florida, Hawaii, New Mexico, New York, Rhode Island, and Texas.[4] In telephone interviews, we inquired about their research activities on this subject, using a protocol similar to the one that guided our federal agency interviews. Appendix B provides lists of those interviewed and the protocols used at the federal and state levels. Finally, we surveyed the annual reports of the philanthropic foundations that fund the most research in education, and we tabulated the grants devoted to LEP issues. Appendix C lists the research activities funded at the federal level and by the foundations. Given time and resource constraints, we were not able to assess the research and evaluation activities conducted by school districts, by university researchers working without extramural support, or by researchers who receive funds from sources other than those specified above. Nor were we able to survey and assess the role of professional associations in supporting the research enterprise.

We note that social scientists who study legislative processes and governmental agencies have constructed many theories about how political agendas are established, how laws are passed, and how agencies administer them (commonly cited examples include Kingdon, 1984, on agendas; Weiss, cited in Callahan and Jennings, 1983, on the research-to-policy nexus; and Cyert and March, 1963, for a critique of overly rational models of organizational behavior). It is not our purpose to construct new theories of this sort or to critique existing ones, except to note that the theorists' models, metaphors, and taxonomies for institutional processes are incomplete unless they also take into account human factors such as personality, ambition, and talent. The administration and conduct of research on education in general and the education of English-language learners in particular have been broadly affected by these human factors. Our interviews reflected both dimensions. Participants may not have expressed structural and bureaucratic concerns in the same terms as would theorists, but they voiced concern about the same organizational matters, such as windows of opportunity and instability of leadership. At the same time, they also testified that some successes and some failures are widely perceived as products of the talents, the personalities, and the commitments of the key players. We generally have left out of this account commentary about the participants' personalities; however, we do mention some aspects of ability as collective assets or liabilities of agencies or of the whole infrastructure when they appear to be key determinants of whether the infrastructure produces research effectively.

---

[4]We conducted interviews in eight of these nine states; we were unable to establish contact with the state director for Rhode Island.

THE WORK OF FEDERAL RESEARCH AGENCIES

This section reviews the history and research on LEP issues of the federal research agencies: the Office of Bilingual Education and Minority Languages Affairs (OBEMLA), the Office of Educational Research and Improvement (OERI), the Planning and Evaluation Service (PES) within the Office of the Under Secretary of Education, other agencies within the Department of Education, the National Science Foundation (NSF), the Department of Health and Human Services (DHHS), and the Department of Defense.

The Office of Bilingual Education and Minority Languages Affairs (OBEMLA)

This office evolved from the OBE in 1980. It administers the funds for grants to states and districts to conduct programs for English-language learners; from 1980 until 1995, it had a small research office to oversee the Title VII research funds authorized by the Bilingual Education Act. The current appropriation sharply curtails the research functions of OBEMLA. In fiscal year 1996, funds for research as well as professional development were zeroed out.[5] For fiscal year 1997, the Secretary is requesting $14.3 million for Support Services (Subpart 2), of which $1.2 million would be for research and studies. Despite the recent cuts, the office has been the principal source of funds for research on LEP issues (through the bilingual education appropriation), so it requires fairly extensive attention in this chapter. To some observers, OBEMLA seems to have been the lonely advocate for research and data gathering on these issues; to others it has seemed a problem, a program agency lacking adequate staff to administer and monitor first-rate research.

The 1978 reauthorization of Title VII quadrupled the amount of money authorized for research (to $20 million), required evaluation components for all Title VII grants, and set some directions for research (Castellano, 1983).[6] Congress called for efforts to discover effective models for bilingual education; to study language acquisition; to mount a longitudinal study of the effects of bilingual education; to study means of identifying eligible students; to study teacher training, as well as supply and demand; to examine inservice programs funded by

---

[5]However, the department is asking for reprogramming of funds to enable the Benchmarks study to continue. If granted, this will be the only research funded in fiscal year 1996. This is permissible because of report language in the appropriations bill allowing the department to request reprogramming of funds within the account.

[6]It should be noted that there is usually a discrepancy between what amount of funding is authorized and what is appropriated. For example, the amount authorized for Title VII in 1980 was $300 million, but Congress appropriated $167 million.

Title VII; and to study the cultural characteristics of various groups that should be integrated into the bilingual/bicultural education curriculum (Liebowitz, 1980).

The Part C Coordinating Committee was now in a position to develop and implement a substantial research program and to influence the attention given to language issues by other offices in the Office of Education (Department of Health, Education, and Welfare) that conducted research. With a budget of approximately $5.28 million per year, OBE planned to support about 20 new and continuing evaluation and research studies per year (Gilbert N. Garcia, personal communication). The agency summarized the Congressional agenda under three concerns: needs assessment (how many English-language learners, bilingual teachers, resources, program types); effectiveness (what programs are best, how to evaluate programs); and management of programs (how to meet legal requirements and determine success) (Kaestle, 1992). This research agenda was focused on very practical matters, such as program surveys and needs inventories.

Beginning in late 1980, the Director of OBE chaired the Part C Coordinating Committee,[7] although in practice that role was delegated to Ronald Hall, chief of the policy unit at OBE, and to OBE research analysts Gilbert N. Garcia and Dorothy Waggoner. While still chaired by the Assistant Secretary, the committee had developed a 5-year research plan for the 1978-1983 period (dated July 1979). The projects in the plan included a survey of teacher supply and demand, a study called Significant Bilingual Instructional Features, a project on the development of evaluation and data-gathering instruments, a study on the need for bilingual education in Puerto Rico, a study of parental involvement in Title VII programs, partial support for the High School and Beyond Study, and a study to devise a way of using 1980 census data to estimate the number of English-language learners in the nation. The plan also included an effort to develop and disseminate instructional models.

Garcia (personal communication) says the Part C Coordinating Committee worked well in some regards, at least in the early years. He adds that "the existence of an interagency committee to coordinate research on English-language learners and the development of a 5-year research plan were unprecedented and helped influence and advance policy." The committee enabled some high-quality research to be assigned to NIE, OPBE, and NCES through memoranda of understanding that spelled out the responsibilities of the offices managing the assigned work. Research administrators from those agencies sometimes discussed the construction of survey items for their projects in committee meetings. With Part C Coordinating Committee funds, the scope of important NCES studies, such as High School and Beyond, was expanded. Funds were used by the Census Bureau to create and apply the first census questions on language use in the United States. Garcia also points out some OBE successes in raising the

---

[7]Before 1980, the committee was chaired by the Assistant Secretary for Education.

visibility of language research issues. Both NIE, in its annual *Condition of Education*, and OPBE, in its annual reports, began including sections on LEP issues in the early 1980s. OBE also produced *Condition of Bilingual Education* reports in 1981 and 1983, which in part reported on research findings.

Before Garcia left OBE, he began working on a second 5-year plan for research, although he himself says it suffered from the absence of a conceptual framework and a lack of leadership at the agency. Starting around this time and extending into the second 5-year period (1984-1989) were such projects as the National Longitudinal Evaluation of the Effectivemess of Services for Language Minority Limited English Proficient Students (Longitudinal Study), the Longitudinal Study of Immersion and Dual Language Instructional Programs for Language Minority Children (Immersion Study), a Teacher Language Skills Survey, research on educational technologies in bilingual education, a study of Effective Approaches to In-Service Staff Development, and a feasibility study for a possible LEP supplement to the National Assessment of Educational Progress.

During this period, a policy unit for Research and Evaluation was created within OBE. However, Secretary Terrel Bell disbanded the Part C Coordinating Committee on June 14, 1984. According to an original member of the committee, John Chapman, the committee was disbanded because OBEMLA Director Jesse Soriano asserted that it was simply advisory and that he would make final decisions. This position ran counter to policy formulated by the presidential transition team in 1980, which had debated the issue of how the committee would operate when there was no longer an Assistant Secretary of Education. Their conclusion was that while the Director of OBEMLA would chair the committee, it would operate on a consensus basis; OBEMLA would not have veto authority over committee decisions (memorandum from Terrel Bell to Gary Bauer and Jesse Soriano, June 14, 1984; memorandum from Jesse Soriano to Part C Coordinating Committee principals, December 6, 1983).

The committee had accomplished some constructive work in its early days precisely because most of OBE's research money was being given to organizations such as NIE, OPBE, and NCES, so the research administrators from those offices were very willing to participate. According to Garcia, the committee was also successful because it had a research plan, and staff members got along well with each other. Even in the early days, however, there were tensions. They arose from three sources: simple competition among the agencies, different viewpoints on how English-language learners should be educated and programs evaluated, and a growing conviction among those outside OBE (particularly among officials at OPBE) that OBE did not have the experience and talent to fund and monitor first-rate research. Garcia (personal communication) adds that "things broke down" because subsequent OBE/OBEMLA directors did not understand research, OPBE wanted to prove that OBE/OBEMLA "didn't work," and OBE/OBEMLA staff had little support from bilingual education practitioners in the field. These strands of tension became intertwined in the increasingly contentious relations between OBEMLA and OPBE. The subsequent director of OBEMLA's research office was Edward Fuentes, who came to OBEMLA from OPBE in 1985 and stayed until 1989. Now that OBEMLA had a research capacity (at least on paper), its officials decided that more of the research should be administered in house. This had the side-effect of exacerbating existing tensions between PES and OBEMLA. We address the issue of coordination across agencies in detail in Chapter 10, but the struggles on the Part C Coordinating Committee and subsequently between PES and OBEMLA were so fateful for OBEMLA that they must be discussed here as context.

Garcia welcomed NIE's attempts on the early Part C Coordinating Committee to delegate some research money for basic research, in contrast to the very practical concerns of Congress and OBE. He was less positive about the methodological stance of OPBE on evaluation, which he considered rigid and traditional (interview of Garcia by Kaestle, 1991, in the National Research Council [NRC] project archived at the Hoover Institution, Stanford University). When bilingual education became highly controversial in the mid-1980s, the research on its effectiveness also became controversial, and the tensions that already existed on the Part C Coordinating Committee provided the backdrop for an OBEMLA defeat at the hands of OPBE.

Soon after he arrived at OBEMLA, Fuentes concluded that there was insufficient accountability and monitoring of the projects farmed out to other agencies; too many were delayed and not producing the "deliverable" reports required in their grants. So he decided both to get tougher about monitoring tardy contractors and to begin producing Requests for Proposals (RFPs) for work to be administered within OBEMLA. With millions of dollars potentially moving from the other agencies back to studies contracted and monitored by OBEMLA, tensions mounted (interview of Fuentes by Kaestle, 1991, in the NRC project archived at the Hoover Institution; see Kaestle, 1992). For a few years, Fuentes was protected by the Director of OBEMLA, but the director changed, and around late 1988 or early 1989, Fuentes was summoned by the Deputy Under Secretary for Planning, Budget, and Evaluation, Bruce Carnes, and told that anything relating to evaluation had to be approved by OPBE and that OPBE would decide which OBEMLA-proposed projects were research or evaluation. Fuentes was also told that anything with potential policy implications had to have OPBE approval. Fuentes felt that any research has potential policy implications, and thus virtually any OBEMLA research project would have to be cleared by OPBE. As a result he resigned.

From this point on, the research funds for bilingual education were virtually controlled by Alan Ginsburg, head of OPBE. The reputation of OBEMLA as a weak agency for research had become entrenched in an administration that was skeptical about the value of bilingual instruction and favored the kind of evaluation studies that had come from OPBE, challenging the superiority of bilingual education in contrast to other ways of responding to English-language learners

(Hakuta, 1986; Meyer and Fienberg, 1992). Early in this era of research on bilingual education, OPBE had sponsored a highly publicized report by the American Institutes for Research, challenging the effectiveness of transitional bilingual education programs (Dannoff, 1978). Then, early in the first Reagan administration, OPBE staff produced a review of the evidence, arguing again that the effectiveness of bilingual education was not supported by research (Baker and de Kanter, 1981; Willig, 1981-1982; McLaughlin, 1985). Two other large-scale studies initiated by the Part C Coordinating Committee in 1982-1983 reflected the dominance of OPBE in administering Title VII funds: the National Longitudinal Evaluation of the Effectiveness of Services for Language Minority Limited English Proficient Students (Longitudinal Study) and the Longitudinal Study of Immersion and Dual Language Instructional Programs for Language Minority Children (Immersion Study). These two studies established the "horse-race" framework for research on bilingual education; their results were hotly debated but inconclusive (Burkheimer, Jr. et al., 1989; Ramirez et al., 1991; Meyer and Fienberg, 1992). (These studies are reviewed in Chapter 6).

What are the implications of this history for the research infrastructure? First, the politics of immigration and language diversity and sharply differing views of American pluralism shaped the politics of the education of English-language learners, and the politics shaped Congressional legislation, administration policy, and interagency conflict over research related to these students. Second, efforts at coordination and collaboration that look good in principle cannot survive when the politics of research are as intense as they are on this topic. Various attempts to insulate education research from politics, such as the creation of the NIE, have proved ineffective. The health institutes (and NSF, with a few exceptions) have succeeded better at this than have education agencies. In our recommendations in Chapter 10, we address what structures might best promote a program of dispassionate, basic research that could survive alongside the directly applied research and evaluation that is necessarily shaped by current policy and programs.

Most recent federally funded research on LEP issues conducted outside the OERI-funded research centers has been aimed at assessing program effectiveness. The Bilingual Education Act, as reauthorized in 1988, provided for a program of research that continued into the Bush administration, and this program fell largely under the control of OPBE. From 1988 to 1990, about $2.6 million per year was expended on research and evaluation.[8] In addition to the two big comparisons of instructional techniques—the Longitudinal Study (completed in 1990) and the Immersion Study (completed in 1991)—other studies included an evaluation of Title VII evaluation assistance centers, contracted to

---

[8]Note that OBEMLA did not have the authority to give out grants, so most of the research it funded was through contracts.

Atlantic Resources Corporation; a set of case studies on effective migrant education practices, conducted by Development Associates; a study by Westat of how Chapter 1 services impact English-language learners; the augmentation of various surveys with English-language learner samples, funded by OBEMLA (the Congressionally mandated Prospects study on the long-term effects of Chapter 1, the National Educational Longitudinal Study of 1988 [NELS:88], the Schools and Staffing Survey conducted by NCES); and other studies (U.S. Department of Education, 1991). The full list of these projects reveals the status of Title VII research during the Bush administration: there was more evaluation than other research, and many resources were devoted to program effectiveness questions, shaped largely by OPBE and conducted primarily by contract research organizations.

It is not our task here to assess the quality of the research produced, but its uses and reputation are germane to understanding the weakness of the research infrastructure. After an expenditure of about $5 million a year, was practice influenced by research? Was there consensus on some matters that pertained to policy? To a great extent, of course, policy was argued and determined in the same mode as a century earlier—by cultural preference, political interest, and anecdote. But this was not unique to the topic of bilingual education. (On the weakness of the research-policy connection, see Weiss, cited in Callahan and Jennings, 1983; Lynn, Jr., 1978; Lindblom, 1990; and Weiss with Bucuvalas, 1980.) Nonetheless, Gilbert N. Garcia (personal communication) made a telling point when he remarked that even within OBEMLA, officials who worked in Title VII program administration were either unaware of research results produced in OBEMLA studies or unclear about their implications.

An even more discouraging conclusion was reached in 1992 by John Chapman (1992), a budget analyst in the Department of Education's Office of the Under Secretary. He determined that 91 research or evaluation studies had been funded with $47 million of Title VII money during the period 1980 to 1991, that is, approximately from the beginning of OBE's Title VII research efforts to the end of the Bush administration. He found that he could not review 40 of the 91 completed studies because no final reports remained. Most of the missing studies were smaller ones, totaling $4.7 million in support. Apparently, OBEMLA officials discarded all research files for the period 1978 to 1985—an implicit comment on their view of the value of cumulative research. Chapman reviewed 48 of the remaining 51 studies; he judged that 29 might be useful for policy formulation. Of these Chapman described 12 large-scale policy-relevant studies, 4 from each of the three supervising agencies—OBEMLA, OERI, and PES. His verdicts range from studies that were quite useful to others whose findings were severely limited by methodological flaws. If Chapman's selection of OBEMLA's four projects is itself representative, one would conclude that its attempts to mount large-scale in-house program evaluation studies had at best mixed success (see Chapter 6).

During the Clinton administration, OBEMLA was reorganized in conjunction with the federal government's restructuring effort. The research office was discontinued; the funding of research became a "team" effort (Eugene Garcia, personal communication, and OBEMLA's restructuring plan). As of 1993, the Office of Policy and Planning (OPP) (successor to the Office of Planning, Budget, and Evaluation in which PES was located) still had de facto control of the Title VII research funds (Campoverde, 1993).[9] During the next year, there were continuing discussions about the relative prerogatives and responsibilities of OBEMLA and OPP in conducting bilingual education research. There was some sentiment in favor of reviving the Part C Coordinating Committee, but OBEMLA's incoming director, Eugene Garcia, chose instead to emphasize continuing negotiations with the Assistant Secretary for OERI and the Under Secretary of Education to restore more OBEMLA control. Thus the Part C Coordinating Committee died with the change in administration (Valena Plisko, personal communication).

Meanwhile, OBEMLA continued to administer Title VII funds for research and evaluation, despite its subordination to OPP for approval of projects. Gilbert N. Garcia, Acting Director of Research, produced a framework for Title VII research. It included extensive plans for fiscal year 1994, reviewed Title VII research completed from 1991 to 1993, and attempted to project plans for new research under the reorganized agency (G. Garcia, 1994). Completed projects are included in the lists in Appendix C. Between 1991 and 1995, virtually all of this research fell into the categories of program surveys (for example, a Descriptive Study of Content-ESL Practices), program evaluations (for example, the Evaluation of Title VII Education Personnel Training Program, the Benchmark study), and LEP supplements to major data collection projects (for example, NELS:88).

In addition, considerable funds were expended for Small Business Innovation Research and the Special Issues Analysis Center. The Small Business Innovation Research program is intended to stimulate technological innovation in the private sector, strengthen the role of small business in meeting federal research and development needs, increase the commercial application of Department of Education-supported research results, and improve the return on investment from federally funded research aimed at providing economic and social benefits to the nation. Firms with strong research capabilities in science, engineering, or educational technology are encouraged to participate. The Special Issues Analysis Center, most recently located at Development Associates, Inc., provided three types of technical support to OBEMLA: the creation of databases on Title VII local and state grantees; the provision of advice on information collection and use; and, in response to a series of task orders, the preparation of special reports

---

[9]According to Valena Plisko, the name of the office in which the Policy and Evaluation Service is located has changed over time from the Office of Planning, Budget and Evaluation (OPBE) to the Office of Policy and Planning (OPP) and is now the Office of the Under Secretary.

(e.g., numbers and characteristics of English-language learners in the United States, use of information technology in language assessment), literature reviews (e.g., review of Department of Education-funded studies on English-language learners), and graphic materials, as well as the convening of panels of experts.

By definition, all of OBEMLA's research and evaluation deals with LEP issues. We now turn to agencies whose topical agenda is much broader. We are interested in the circumstances under which they conduct research on LEP issues and in their procedures for setting agendas and selecting and monitoring research. LEP issues may be urged upon these agencies by OBEMLA, Congress, or other external agencies; such issues may arise as the agencies address other educational questions; or LEP variables may be included incidentally in surveys or as explanatory variables in studies. The first of these agencies, OERI, is the Department of Education's main research arm. It addresses LEP issues in several ways; indeed, it has funded entire centers devoted to second-language learning, sometimes with moneys from Title VII and sometimes from its own research budget.

The Office of Educational Research and Improvement (OERI)

Created when the Department of Education was formed in 1980, OERI absorbed the functions of NIE, such as the research centers, in 1985. OERI has three major functions that involve research on issues pertaining to English-language learners and bilingual education: first, research conducted by the Office of Research until 1995 and now carried out by the five OERI institutes; second, surveys and analyses performed by NCES, located within OERI; and third, the research, development, and dissemination activities of the regional education laboratories, now supervised by the Office of Reform Assistance and Dissemination (ORAD). The research conducted by the Office of Research fell into two main categories: grants to create and maintain research centers and grants to carry out field-initiated proposals by individuals. The overwhelming majority of funds has gone to the centers, and the relative lack of funds to field-initiated studies is a recurring theme in discussions about the infrastructure of educational research (e.g., Atkinson and Jackson, 1992; see also Chapter 10). The same situation exists for OERI-sponsored research specifically on language issues; there has been little money for field-initiated studies, and most of the attention has been focused on research centers devoted wholly or in part to language diversity issues. For fiscal year 1997, 20 percent of OERI research funds has been allocated to field-initiated research, and 25 percent is expected to be earmarked in fiscal year 1998.

Research Funded by the OERI Research Centers

We examined the list of projects in all of OERI's research centers as of March 1995 (U.S. Department of Education, 1995). As of that date, there were 20 centers, listing approximately 277 projects. Of these, 40 projects related to

LEP issues. Of these 40 projects, 17 were in a single center—the National Center for Research on Cultural Diversity and Second Language Learning at Santa Cruz—which was devoted mainly to such issues. The remaining 23 projects on LEP issues were scattered among 10 centers (9 centers listed no such projects) (see Appendix C for a complete list). The contrast between the research done by the OERI research centers on the one hand and Title VII research conducted by OBEMLA, PES, or NCES on the other is dramatic: the center projects, which are funded by grants (rather than contracts), are smaller, often more qualitative in methodology, more complex conceptually, and less given to surveys and quantitative analysis.

We turn now to the studies on LEP issues funded by the four successive OERI research centers that over the years have been devoted mainly to these issues, and then to the studies of the center focused on at-risk students—the Center for Research on the Education of Students Placed at Risk (CRESPAR). The former four centers were, first, from 1979 to 1984, the National Center for Bilingual Research (NCBR), located at the Southwest Educational Development Laboratory; second, from 1985 to 1989, the Center for Language Education and Research (CLEAR), located at UCLA; third, from 1990 to 1995, the National Center for Research on Cultural Diversity and Second Language Learning (NCRCDSLL), located at the University of California at Santa Cruz (UC-Santa Cruz); and finally, the Center for Research on Education, Diversity, and Excellence (CREDE), the center contract just awarded, again to UC-Santa Cruz.

The National Center for Bilingual Research (NCBR)   This center grant was awarded to one of the regional laboratories established by OERI's predecessor agency, NIE. The creation of such a center had been advocated by Tomas Arciniega, a member of the National Council on Education Research (NIE's policy board) and the dean of education at California State-San Diego, who wanted to see bilingual education issues addressed at NIE. NIE had some research depth on language issues, with Michael O'Malley heading the section on language and Sylvia Scribner heading teaching and learning. Both were accomplished researchers. Others working on the RFP, either at NIE or as consultants, included Ramsey Selden, Richard Duran, Monte Penne, and Ricardo Martinez. However, the first director of the new center, Candido de Leon, was not himself a researcher, and the emphasis at the Southwest Educational Development Laboratory, as in all of the regional laboratories, had always been on development and technical assistance more than on research.

After the first year of operation, NIE officials appointed a panel to review the center's work. The panel members were not satisfied with the first year's work and decided to change the directorship. Amado Padilla, a psychologist from UCLA with a strong research record, became the new director. The concern at NIE was to bring research on bilingual education more into contact with developments in general education research. When Padilla arrived at NCBR, many projects were in motion, and most of the staff for those projects were not experienced researchers. One of the big projects was an attempt to survey and inventory English-language learners, which Padilla said took up a great deal of effort and money and yielded little knowledge. NCBR did another survey of how states were classifying English-language learners and a survey of the High School and Beyond data to see who these students were (Amado Padilla, personal communication). Unlike later centers, which recruited researchers and projects from various universities, NCBR did most of its work in house, although one project, on attitudes toward bilingual education, was contracted to David Sears at UCLA.

During the crucial first 5 years of substantial Title VII funding for research on bilingual education, then, neither OBEMLA nor NCBR was positioned to solicit, select, and monitor first-rate research on this topic. The fledgling infrastructure would not develop a strong reputation.

Center for Language Education and Research (CLEAR)   In 1984, a new RFP was issued for an OERI center on language research. Amado Padilla collaborated with Richard Tucker to form a center that would be located mostly at UCLA and the Center for Applied Linguistics in Washington, D.C, with subcontracts to some well-known researchers at other locations. Padilla was codirector for 3 years with Russell Campbell of UCLA; when Padilla went to Stanford, the center was directed by Campbell for another year, under reduced funding. Funding was terminated at the end of the fourth year, a year earlier than originally scheduled. This center had a team of more-experienced researchers than NCBR, with research projects scattered across many school districts in the United States. Their agenda was specified in eight task statements of the RFP. The center's research mission included second-language learning by native speakers of English. About one-third of its effort was in this language majority area; of that, about half was in research and about half in professional development. The projects located at the Center for Applied Linguistics, under the direction of Tucker, included a systematic 5 percent national sample of students' participation in foreign-language instruction, the development of an assessment instrument for English oral language proficiency, professional development projects in several public school districts across the country, and a project on how to integrate language and content in science for English-language learners (Richard Tucker, personal communication). At UCLA there were several projects: Russell Campbell and Kathryn Lindholm worked on language conservation efforts (for example, among the Korean community in Los Angeles), Lindholm did a project on two-way immersion programs in the Santa Monica area, Campbell looked at a Spanish immersion program in Culver City, Ann Snow studied sheltered instruction, Concepcion Valadez developed a language assessment center for new students in the Montebello school district, and Evelyn Hatch analyzed "scaffolding"[10] in class-

---

[10]The term "scaffolding" denotes methods to help make English more comprehensible to English-language learners by, for example, providing more context.

room discourse between teachers and English-language learners. There were also three subcontracts to other universities: at Yale, Kenji Hakuta was funded to work in the New Haven schools on the cross-language transfer of skills and the efficacy of young children as translators; Catherine Snow of Harvard worked on transfer of abilities across languages, using the distinction between contextualized and decontextualized abilities; and Richard Duran of UC-Santa Barbara had a project on reading and processing skills among adult university English-language learners (Amado Padilla and Richard Tucker, personal communication). (See Appendix C for a complete list of CLEAR projects.)

As noted above, OERI terminated CLEAR a year early, in 1989. While the center had a stronger repertoire of projects than its predecessor, elements of personality and politics came into play in this decision. OERI's Assistant Secretary, a close advisor to Secretary William Bennett, was Chester ("Checker") Finn; neither Finn nor Bennett nor Sally Kilgore, director of the Office of Research, was sympathetic to bilingual education, and they were thus skeptical of research on the subject. As President of the Center for Applied Linguistics, Tucker was in Washington and participated in several meetings to address the issues. In one case, the OERI team argued that sufficient research was being done on bilingual education by such agencies as the Army Research Institute and the Office of Naval Research; Tucker and CLEAR staff arranged to testify to a subcommittee chaired by Representative Major Owens that this research was related only tangentially to the needs of English-language learners in grades K-12. Yet despite some work that Tucker thought was first-rate and subsequently appeared in prominent journals, CLEAR closed its doors under adverse circumstances, in a tense relationship with its sponsoring agency. Bilingual education research had become as politicized as it was ever to be. With OBEMLA's research function virtually in receivership and CLEAR terminated, there was little left of the infrastructure for research on LEP issues. No center on language issues appeared on OERI's initial list of new centers. However, public commentary on the list forced the issue, and an RFP for a new center on language was developed.

National Center for Research on Cultural Diversity and Second Language Learning (NCRCDSLL)   NCRCDSLL at UC Santa Cruz, the third OERI center to deal with LEP issues, began in 1991 with 18 projects. Its agenda was shaped by a framework of Vygotskyan psychology[11] and ethnographic approaches to

---

[11]According to Vygotskyan theory, the developmental level of a child is identified by what the child can do alone. What the child can do with the assistance of another defines what Vygotsky calls the "zone of proximal development." Distinguishing the proximal zone from the developmental level by contrasting assisted versus unassisted performance has profound implications for educational practice. In Vygotskyan terms, teaching is good only when it "awakens and rouses to life those functions which are in a stage of maturing, which lie in the zone of proximal development" (Tharp and Gallimore, 1991).

classrooms and families; its project selection was influenced by the existence of a network of researchers in the University of California system called the Linguistic Minority Research Project (Barry McLaughlin, personal communication). The center's budget ranged from $.75 to 1.5 million per year according to codirector Barry McLaughlin, typical of the OERI centers of the 1980s. Most of the projects were conducted by researchers at University of California campuses; one project was in Boston, one at Arizona, and three at the Center for Applied Linguistics (see Appendix C for a list of NCRCDSLL research reports).

NCRCDSLL completed its work in 1995 and geared up to compete for the new center on language research.

Center for Research on Education, Diversity, and Excellence (CREDE)   As noted earlier, under the new structure mandated in the 1994 reauthorization of OERI, the agency has five institutes, each devoted to research, development, technical assistance, and dissemination in a single, broad area of educational practice. Each of these institutes conducts programs of research through targeted RFPs, open field-initiated studies, and the establishment and monitoring of research and development centers. The National Institute on the Education of At-Risk Students conducted a competition for a center on Meeting the Educational Needs of a Diverse Student Population, and this competition was won by the group at Santa Cruz. At a fiscal year 1996 budget of $3.9 million a year and similar projected amounts for the next 4 years, the new center's budget is about three times that of its Santa Cruz predecessor, though its agenda is also broader. The new center will have partners at 19 other sites, a number of them University of California and California State University campuses, studying not only English-language learners, but also other students at risk for reasons of poverty, geographic isolation, and race (*Education Week*, February 14, 1996). As part of its work, CREDE will conduct projects under six programmatic strands: (1) national quantitative studies will measure demographic shifts in student populations; (2) research on language-learning opportunities will highlight exemplary programmatic choices; (3) effective professional development practices for teachers, paraprofessionals, and principals will be explored; (4) the influence and interaction of family, peers, and community with regard to the education of linguistically and culturally diverse students will be explored; (5) the instruction of these students in different content areas, such as science and math, will be examined; and (6) successful school reform initiatives will be identified.

Center for Research on the Education of Students Placed at Risk (CRESPAR)
This center is a collaboration of Johns Hopkins and Howard universities, with subcontracts at ten other locations. With a budget of $4.7 million a year, it is the largest OERI center ever launched, and in that sense it is the showcase for the concept of the institutes: its large budget allows it to combine basic research with extensive dissemination, training, and program development activities. Of its 47

projects, 7 involve language issues, including several of the subcontracts. Richard Duran at UC-Santa Barbara, Kris Gutierrez at UCLA, Judith Marquez in Houston, and Grayson Noley in Arizona are each working on some aspect of LEP or language-minority issues. One of the centerpieces of the Johns Hopkins work, the Success for All program pioneered by director Robert Slavin, now has a program designed specifically for English-language learners, both in English and in a Spanish-language version developed by the Southwest Educational Development Laboratory. Nonetheless, the amount of CRESPAR research devoted to language minority and LEP issues is modest.

OERI Field-Initiated Studies

The Office of Research and now the new institutes have funded a modicum of field-initiated research. These studies tend to be small scale and thus usually focus on a single group or site. We surveyed the lists for fiscal years 1990, 1991, 1992, 1993, and 1994 (U.S. Department of Education, 1992, 1993, 1994, 1995). In fiscal year 1990, 4 of 12 projects funded addressed English-language learners. One looked at immigrant students in San Diego, another at gifted students among Pueblo Indians, another at first-generation Mexican immigrant high school students, and another at the education of Indochinese immigrants. The budgets of these studies ranged from $54,000 to $74,000. Of the 17 projects funded in fiscal year 1991, 3 were about LEP issues: a continuation of the gifted Pueblo student study, an action research project that gathered data on all language-minority students in four school districts, and a study of science teaching in ESL programs. In fiscal year 1993, OERI funded 11 field-initiated projects, of which 1 involved LEP issues obliquely—a study of decisions about postsecondary training and success among the children of migrant farmworkers. In fiscal year 1994, 1 of 10 funded projects dealt with non-English-language issues; it was a study of the choice of language used in Mexican American homes.

Because of their small scale, these projects, like the individual work within the research centers, do not fit the framework established by some government officials that relates massive program assessments to the politics of bilingual education programs. By their very nature, such studies are diverse in their methodologies and complex. Unlike the work of PES or NCES, their focus is not on evaluation or population estimates. They have a mix of goals that makes their mission more difficult to evaluate. In addition, some of the knowledge generated has been of more interest to the researchers than to practitioners. OERI needs to find better ways of improving the quality of its small-scale research. Under the new authorization, field-initiated grants are closely tied to the institutes. This should help OERI staff monitor the quality of the research.

Other OERI Studies

In addition to the work of the centers and the modest portfolio of field-initiated studies, OERI sponsored some research on LEP issues with Title VII funds transferred from OBEMLA. Chapman (1992) examines a selection of these in his review of the Title VII research. From 1980 to 1991, OERI administered 27 percent of Title VII research funds, or $11.2 million. Much of this money went to NCES to include language-minority and/or LEP variables in major data surveys. That operation is discussed below in the section on NCES. Other OERI projects included the large-scale Significant Bilingual Instructional Features study, contracted to the Far West Laboratory and completed in 1983. This study displayed some of the same weaknesses as OBEMLA's study of Special Alternative Instructional Programs, stemming from the fact that the programs for study were nominated from the field (Chapter 7).

National Center for Education Statistics (NCES)

NCES is the statistics-gathering agency for the Department of Education. Gathering statistics was the original rationale for a federal role in education, so it is a venerable tradition. School reformers from Henry Barnard (first U.S. Commissioner of Education) to the present have prefaced their proposals for change with data on how the present system operates. NCES was therefore a logical participant in the Part C Coordinating Committee on bilingual education research from its inception. By the 1970s, however, it had become apparent that the statistics operation in education was not up to the standards of such federal statistics agencies as the Census Bureau (see Chapter 9). After an NRC (1986) report and evaluation, the office was strengthened. Increased funding for NCES found favor with Republican administrations in the 1980s, and in the reauthorization of 1988 (Hawkins-Stafford Amendments to the Elementary and Secondary Education Act), the head of NCES became a commissioner with a 6-year term. NCES initiates and supervises the creation of many large data sets. Chapter 9 includes a full discussion of its activities and the limitations of its studies vis-à-vis English-language learners.

The Office of Reform Assistance and Dissemination (ORAD)

The regional education laboratories were created in the Elementary and Secondary Education Act of 1965 to complement the university-based research and development centers. The idea was that the centers would focus on cutting-edge research, while the laboratories would focus on dissemination, the development of materials for schools, technical assistance, and other partnerships with practice. Over the years there have usually been 10 regional laboratories, although there are currently 11. From the start, the envisioned collaboration between the centers and the laboratories failed to materialize.

The regional laboratories, then, are largely independent of the centers and carry on a mix of research, development, assistance, and dissemination activities within their regions (for evaluation of the laboratories, see Kaestle, 1992; Vinovskis, 1993; and Turnbull et al., 1994). Various specialties have been developed in the laboratories, depending on their leadership, their staffs, or regional needs. Until 1994, the laboratories were overseen by the Programs for the Improvement of Practice. When the five institutes were created, ORAD was also formed to oversee professional development programs, the National Diffusion Network, and other development and dissemination activities, including the regional laboratories. According to Eve Bither (personal communication), first acting director of the new office, some laboratories have ongoing projects that involve LEP issues; for example, the Southwest Educational Development Laboratory has a Border Colloquy Project attempting to develop common projects in education with Mexican educators, while the Far West Laboratory had a project examining how English-language learners are incorporated into school restructuring efforts.

In the recently completed competition, regional laboratories were required to develop special themes. Three of the funded proposals are for laboratories that will specialize in language and cultural diversity. One these will be in the Northeastern Region (serving New England, New York, Puerto Rico, and the Virgin Islands), hosted by Brown University; another will be in the Southwestern Region, at the current Southwest Educational Development Laboratory in Austin (serving Texas, Oklahoma, Louisiana, Arkansas, and New Mexico); and the third will be in the Pacific Region (serving Hawaii, Samoa, Guam, and the other Pacific islands with U.S. status), located in Honolulu (*Education Week*, January 10, 1996).

The Planning and Evaluation Service (PES), Office of the Under Secretary of Education

PES provides program evaluation services and other assistance to the Under Secretary. When it was located in OPBE, it was one of the original participants in the Part C Coordinating Committee, and in that venue became locked in a struggle with OBEMLA as described earlier. The discord continues to the present. Valena Plisko (personal communication), head of PES's elementary and secondary education evaluations, says relations between PES and the Office of Elementary and Secondary Education, as well as other offices, are generally collaborative and effective, while relations with OBEMLA have been "mixed and at times acrimonious," partly because of personalities and partly because of confusion about OBEMLA's mission. In the end, as we have seen, PES came virtually to control OBEMLA's Title VII research budget, not only having authority to approve almost all of OBEMLA's research projects, but also receiving outright the funds for many projects that PES initiated and monitored. From 1980 to 1991, PES received and monitored about half of the Title VII research funds, totaling $20.6 million (Chapman, 1992). These included the big "horse-race" evaluation studies of effective instructional program types (the Longitudinal and Immersion studies). Yet whatever the merits of PES's views of OBEMLA over the years, it is clear that PES projects on bilingual education did not escape reasonable criticism either (see Chapter 6).

PES's most recent large survey is called Prospects: The Congressionally Mandated Study of Educational Growth and Opportunity. The First Year Report on Language Minority and Limited English Proficient Students (Moss and Puma, 1995) presents descriptive information from the first 2 years of data collection (1991 and 1992) for two of the three cohorts examined in Prospects (the first and third grades), characterizing two groups of students—language-minority students and English-language learners. (See Appendix C for a list of all ongoing Title VII projects in PES.)

The future status of the relationship between PES and OBEMLA around the funding of research on English-language learners is not clear. The reauthorization of OERI calls for the Assistant Secretary, with the guidance of the new National Educational Research Policy and Priorities Board, to coordinate research across agencies. Secretary Riley (1995) has interpreted this to include evaluation work.

Other Agencies Within the Department of Education

The bulk of funding aimed at research on language-minority and LEP issues has to date been located in OBEMLA, PES, and OERI (including NCES). Many large program areas, such as the Office of Elementary and Secondary Education, fund programs (such as Title I) that serve significant numbers of English-language learners. But these offices do not have money designated for research, and some of them (including the Office of Elementary and Secondary Education) use PES for their program evaluation. We interviewed officials at two other offices to see whether they have funded research or evaluation of LEP issues.

The Office of Migrant Education

This office reports to the Assistant Secretary for Elementary and Secondary Education. It administers about $300 million in programs for migrant education, mostly in formula grants to state agencies and in technical assistance. For over 10 years there were three program coordination centers, located geographically in the midst of the three main migrant streams. These centers did some descriptive research. The New York center, for example, looked at migrant dropouts. But the Office of Migrant Education has little or no money for research per se, and its evaluations, funded sparsely, are done by PES. Its modest discretionary money is generally used for conferences or field-initiated program projects (Kristin Gilbert, personal communication).

Office of Special Education Programs (OSEP)

This office is within the Office of Special Education and Rehabilitative Services in the Department of Education. Unlike the Office of Elementary and Secondary Education, the Office of Special Education and Rehabilitative Services does its own evaluation work, in consultation with PES. Within OSEP, Louis Danielson directs the Division for Innovation and Development, which has a budget of about $20 million a year. Most of that money is loosely in what Danielson calls research, though by statute the research must all be applied. The other four divisions do less research, but together they may bring the total for research and quasi-research activities up to about $50 million (Louis Danielson, personal communication).

The principal legislation governing and funding special education activities at the federal level is called the Individuals with Disabilities Education Act, which may be slated for reauthorization in the 105th Congress. The House bill passed June 11, 1996. Included within the research program is a requirement that the secretary develop a comprehensive plan within 12 months of the bill's enactment. Research priorities within the House bill include projects that advance knowledge about teaching and learning practices and assessment techniques, instruments, and strategies, as well as the development and learning characteristics of children with disabilities; large-scale longitudinal studies; model demonstration projects to apply and test research findings; and projects that apply research and other knowledge to improve educational results by synthesizing useful research, and ensuring that it is in the appropriate format for use and available through various information sources. Both the House and Senate bills authorize level funding.

In the recent past, there has been a substantial budget for applied research on special education. Louis Danielson (personal communication) explained that his division funds projects for researchers at three different levels: studies by doctoral students, studies by researchers in their initial career (first 5 years beyond doctorate), and field-initiated research by more senior researchers (grants of up to $180,000 per year). He cited several projects addressing language issues in special education (that is, dealing both with students having limited English proficiency and those having some learning disability requiring that they have an Individual Educational Plan). One such project was Promoting Literacy Through Ecobehavioral Assessment, which addressed both types of students; another examined the perceptions of parents of Hispanic children with learning disabilities; another studied parental involvement and literacy among both types of students; another focused on comprehensive instruction for these students; another studied the transition from school to work for Asian American students with disabilities; and another was a dropout prevention project on Hispanic adolescents with emotional disturbances (for a complete list, see Appendix C). Most of these projects came from field-initiated competitions open to proposals on any topic dealing with special education. In the case of the dropout project, the agency held a competition focusing on that topic.

Previously, the agency held a direct competition for any projects dealing with LEP issues among children with disabilities. This competition provided funds for the selected researchers to meet twice a year; these meetings proved so useful that the researchers applied for and received a grant to continue the meetings for 2 years.

The Division for Innovation and Development also funds some policy research indirectly. For example, it funds forums and focus groups. Among these is the National Association of State Directors of Special Education, which has conducted policy research on the overrepresentation of minorities in special education programs.

It seems, then, that there is some substantial attention to LEP education research issues within the federal infrastructure for research on special education. It may also be noted as an impression of many education policy experts (including, for example, Marshall Smith, the current Under Secretary of Education) that research on special education carried out by the same agency that administers federal programs in the area has been a successful arrangement—more fruitful and less controversial than the case of OBEMLA, for whatever reasons (interview of Marshall Smith by Kaestle, 1991, in the NRC project). To the extent that this is true, the reduction of research funds within OSEP and the transfer of some authority over any future funds to OERI is a dramatic shift.

The National Science Foundation (NSF)

NSF is a federal agency governed by the National Science Board; it is not located within a department. It contains seven major units, called directorates. Six of these are in substantive areas such as engineering and the biological sciences; these directorates fund research and training in those fields. The seventh, called the Directorate on Education and Human Resources, funds research on math and science education in elementary and secondary schools. This directorate's Division on Research, Evaluation, and Communication, with a budget of about $50 million, has major action research projects, such as the State-wide Systemic Initiatives program. About $12 million goes for research and development on the uses of technology in education, $10 million for basic research on teaching and learning math and science, and $2 million per year for the new National Institute on Science Education at the University of Wisconsin. Neither the Director of the Division on Research, Evaluation, and Dissemination, Daryl Chubin, nor the codirector of the National Institute on Science Education,

Andrew Porter, is aware of any projects that have targeted English-language learners or dealt with language issues in math and science instruction. A search of projects in progress at NSF uncovered three that focus on English-language learners; however, only one could be considered research—a project to enhance the science education of elementary-age bilingual students (see Appendix C)

Department of Health and Human Services (DHHS)

The largest federal department relating to domestic policy, DHHS sponsors many programs that encounter issues related to language minorities and the education of English-language learners. We contacted officials in two department-wide offices that deal with research and evaluation, plus the National Institutes of Health (NIH).

Office of the Assistant Secretary for Planning and Evaluation (ASPE)

ASPE is responsible for policy analysis and advice, policy development, strategic and implementation planning, and the coordination and conduct of evaluation and policy research. As part of its overall mission, ASPE undertakes a variety of research and evaluation projects addressing issues affecting children and youth, especially those from disadvantaged backgrounds. The office operates a small research and evaluation program that focuses primarily on cross-cutting or emerging policy issues that are outside the scope of the program-focused studies conducted by the Administration for Children, Youth, and Families or other DHHS program units. Within ASPE, most studies on child and youth issues originate from the Division of Children and Youth Policy, a component of the Office of Human Services Policy.

ASPE encounters issues related to English-language learners and their families primarily as regards the health and human service areas that are the department's responsibility. In research, for example, ASPE is cosponsoring the first large-scale experimental evaluation of how child growth and development, mother-child relationships, and maternal functioning are affected by mothers' mandatory participation in welfare-to-work programs. This study—the Child Outcomes Study in the JOBS Evaluation—is cosponsored by the Administration for Children, Youth, and Families and the Department of Education. The sample in one site (Riverside, California) includes immigrant families, and the study uses a research strategy that addresses potential differences for these families. Children were aged 3-5 years when their mothers entered the study. Outcomes are assessed 2 and 5 years later using data obtained from home interviews with mothers and children, and, at 5 years, surveys of teachers. The study will provide data on developmental trajectories and outcomes in all domains, including physical health and safety, cognitive and social development, and school adjustment.

ASPE is also providing partial support to the Board on Children, Youth, and

Families of the National Academy of Sciences and the Institute of Medicine for a project examining the health and adjustment of immigrant children. The project is focusing on differential health and mental health outcomes of children from various immigrant groups, the varying trajectories that now characterize the development of immigrant children, and the delivery of services to these children and their families. It will synthesize the relevant research literature and support the secondary analysis of existing data sets.

Demonstration and Evaluation Branch, Administration for Children, Youth, and Families

This office formulates and contracts for evaluation work, principally on Head Start. There are two projects relevant to our interests: first, a descriptive study on demographic changes in the Head Start population and how these changes will affect multilingual and multicultural practices in curriculum and service delivery; and second, a study of the characteristics of families served by the 28 Migrant Head Start programs across the country. Other studies will touch on LEP issues by examining both language variables in data collection and program descriptions in case studies of best practice. There is a survey under way of all Head Start programs that will gather information about various populations and will include case studies of 30 programs, and there is an evaluation of the Comprehensive Child Development Program, which is aimed at low-income families.

The Administration for Children, Youth, and Families also just funded four university-based Head Start research centers (National Quality Research Centers). One of the main contractors is the Education Development Center in Newton, Massachusetts. This center has a subcontract at the School of Education at Harvard University (Catherine Snow, Patton Tabors, and Lilia Bartolome) for investigations that will deal exclusively with language diversity in Head Start classrooms and its impact on teaching, parent involvement, social service delivery, and administration.

National Institutes of Health (NIH)

NIH is a constellation of 22 institutes and centers. We spoke to research officials in two of the institutes that most often fund research related to education: the National Institute for Mental Health and the National Institute of Child Health and Human Development.

We found that a small amount of research is focused directly on the special populations in which we are interested, but that it is not a strong priority. There are some indications that NIH is becoming more interested in subpopulations; it can be hoped that language will occupy a significant place in these emerging priorities.

National Institute for Mental Health   With the help of a research administrator from the agency, we checked recent grants by the Behavioral, Cognitive, and Social Science Research Branch of the Division of Neuroscience and Behavioral Science, which funds only basic research. Of the approximately 280 projects funded in the past year, 11 had a primary focus on language (see Appendix C for a list of these projects). However, these studies focused on first-language acquisition and processing. The centers for behavioral science research funded through this branch do not address languages in a significant way (Mollie Oliveri, personal communication).

National Institute of Child Health and Human Development   The results were similar at the National Institute of Child Health and Human Development. This institute supports four centers on learning disabilities, training grants, individual field-initiated research grants, and a clearinghouse. The official we interviewed could not identify any projects dealing with language diversity. We located some, however, through a computer search of federally funded research. These included a study of language and literacy in bilingual children (Oller, in progress) and a study that examines the development of phonetic categories in bilingual children (Flege, in progress) (see Appendix C).

Department of Defense

The main research agencies funded by the Department of Defense are the Army Research Institute, the Office of Naval Research, and the Air Force Human Resources Laboratory. The armed forces helped pioneer methods for teaching second languages to native speakers of English after World War II. They also do some work on learning problems of limited-English-proficient recruits to the services' training programs. In addition, they fund quite a bit of research, both basic and applied, on linguistics and literacy in English. They do not, it seems, conduct much research that is relevant to the educational needs of language-minority students and English-language learners in elementary and secondary schools (Ray Perez, personal communication).

Conclusion

Federally funded research on language-minority issues and the education of English-language learners has, understandably, been centered in the Department of Education. It would be helpful in the future if language variables and language issues were considered more often in research conducted by other federal agencies, whether the primary focus is on reading, other cognitive processes, the delivery of social services, teaching techniques in math and science, or other topics of interest to the government. Furthermore, while the main task of designing the research agenda and conducting the research on the education of English-language learners falls appropriately to the Department of Education, it cannot do the job alone. Funds for research in the Department of Education have always been modest compared with those of other departments, and its infrastructure for research is not as effective as that in other departments. These two features interact: the relative paucity of funds and the relative ineffectiveness of research infrastructure create a vicious circle of low respect, low support, and modest results.

THE WORK OF STATE EDUCATION AGENCIES[12]

During January 1996, we conducted interviews with state education agency (SEA) officials who are responsible for bilingual education or other programs for language-minority students or English-language learners in eight states. As noted earlier, we chose the eight states that had an English-language learner population of 6 percent or more: Alaska, Arizona, California, Florida, Hawaii, New Mexico, New York, and Texas. (A ninth state, Rhode Island, met the threshold, but we were unable to connect with an interview respondent there.) The interviewer asked an official in each state to identify current and recent SEA research, entities that support the research, information services, and training grants on language-minority students or English-language learners or on bilingual education. The interviewer also asked about promising practices and obstacles in the sponsorship and future directions of research on these topics. Most respondents were state coordinators or directors of bilingual education (see Appendix B). The state respondents were assured that their states would not be identified by name; therefore, the identities of the states are masked in Appendix B, where the individual responses are detailed.

The questions were sent to the interviewees in advance of the interview. Interviewees were advised that information was sought not only on SEA-supported research in which the primary focus was English-language learners or language-minority children or bilingual education, but also on research where these children were a subpopulation by virtue of the design of the data collection; findings for this subpopulation may or may not currently be reported separately. Research was defined broadly (basic, applied, demonstrations, evaluations, and surveys).

For each question, we provide here a summary of the responses across the eight states.

Question 1: Does your SEA fund research on LEP and bilingual students, including basic research, applied research, demonstrations, evaluations, or survey research? Please elaborate on research funded in the past

---

[12]This section draws heavily on a report prepared for the committee by Lana Muraskin of the SMB Economic Research Organization, whose excellent research assistance we acknowledge.

five years and amounts of funding, if available, as well as identifying the administrative units within the SEA that fund this research.

SEAs engage in a limited amount of direct research on LEP or bilingual education issues, but many maintain student-level databases that could be used to conduct analyses. States also prescribe local evaluation requirements for state-funded programs. At present, the main direct research activities include the following:

- **Conducting annual (or other repeated) censuses of school districts** that obtain descriptive information on counts of English-language learners by various background and programmatic variables. These data are sometimes published by district or in aggregated form.
- **Analyzing data from state assessment programs** to determine the performance of English-language learners in relation to the performance of other students (or by LEP program or designation). A number of states maintain individual student record systems that provide background and performance data, although little is known about the quality of these data. The performance data are generally drawn from performance on English-language tests. Only a few states conduct testing in Spanish or another language.
- **Designing and monitoring local evaluations** of funded bilingual or other programs for language-minority students and English-language learners. States play a role in monitoring and evaluating Title VII programs. They also prescribe evaluation requirements for state-funded programs, monitor implementation, and provide technical assistance. State requirements appear to be similar to those of Title VII.
- **Designing teacher certification exams.** In the course of developing language proficiency and other certification exams, SEAs identify and study the skills teachers need and the links between exams and performance. They also perform various research tasks associated with test development. Most of this work is done on a contractual basis.

Question 2:   Does your SEA support centers, laboratories, or other entities that conduct research in the above areas? Please elaborate.

Development of teacher training programs appears to be the main research and development activity supported by SEAs in centers, laboratories, or other entities. Interestingly, curriculum development was not often mentioned as an activity of centers. In addition, it should be noted that there are other sources of state support for research on language-minority students and English-language learners—primarily state agencies that support faculty and researchers at universities. SEAs also make contributions to the federal regional educational laboratories, although they may not always be aware of specific research on English-language learners being conducted by these laboratories.

Question 3: Does your SEA support information services or training grants for scholars who work on the education of LEP and bilingual students? Please elaborate.

With a few exceptions, SEAs do not directly support information services or scholarly training of researchers who study these issues. It should be noted, however, that basic support of state university and college systems also supports the research activities of graduate students and faculty. As already noted, there are, in addition, university-based centers in several of these states that specialize in research on language-minority students and English-language learners.

Question 4: How does your agency decide what kinds of research to support, as well as which particular projects to fund?

Some respondents had a difficult time identifying the primary influences on decision making about research. In general, board of education and legislative mandates appear to play an important role. In addition, data requirements of state aid formulas are instrumental in data collections in some states (counts are needed to distribute funds). Title VII requirements and state traditions about what kinds of information and evaluation activities must accompany a grant award also appear important in establishing the planning and evaluation requirements for district-level programs that accept state aid. A few states noted that relatively new state standards for English-language learner performance are also having an effect on research priorities. The responses are notable for what they did not say as well as what they did. None of the respondents saw themselves as having a major role in decision making on research.

Question 5: What is your perception of promising state efforts in the sponsorship and conduct of research on these students?

The movement toward greater accountability for educational outcomes seems to be the major development setting the direction for research on English-language learners. Respondents in several states noted that these students are now being included in state assessment programs (sometimes with tests in native languages) and that state-wide standards for their performance are being established. This development promises to increase attention to tests and other measures for assessing the performance of these students, as well as to research that examines the best approaches and programs for improving performance.

Question 6: What is your perception of obstacles at the state level in the sponsorship and conduct of research on these students?

Lack of resources is clearly a strong theme among the responses, but other important obstacles to research were noted. Several states mentioned lack of staff; this generally means numbers, but it also means people with the technical and research skills necessary for the task. Some SEAs have offices of research (or the assessment office serves that purpose), but issues of English-language learners and bilingual education need to be state priorities for these offices to focus their resources on those issues.

Data quality is also a concern in some states. SEAs are often dependent on districts to supply both student-level and aggregated data. There are sometimes problems in the quality of those data, both evaluation data from projects and data from regular state-wide data collections. Resources for following up with districts are critically important when data quality is an issue.

Finally, SEAs are administrative entities, but they are administered by or experience oversight from elected officials or their appointees. The responses to the question about the locus of decision making for research make clear that these political influences are important in deciding what research gets done. As a result, research questions may be narrowly framed or may reflect a hidden (or not so hidden) political agenda.

In sum, SEAs do not conduct a great deal of research on English-language learners and their programs because SEAs do not conduct a great deal of research on any subject. But to varying degrees, they do assess the academic achievement of English-language learners, gather data on program and student characteristics, and evaluate programs. The data they muster could be useful to researchers funded from other sources, and some level of coordination would be desirable. The relationship between these data sources and federally funded research efforts might fruitfully be a topic of discussion for the federal Department of Education Advisory Committee on Research on English-language Learners recommended in Chapter 10.

THE WORK OF FOUNDATIONS

We constructed a list of foundations that gave substantial support to education research in 1989, based on a review of funding sources for education research prepared by the National Academy of Education (Kirst and Ravitch, 1991) (see Table A-1).

We obtained copies of the 1994 annual reports of all of the foundations shown in Table A-1. We then compiled lists of the projects they funded that appeared to deal with language-minority, LEP, or bilingual education issues.[13] We made these judgments on the basis of project descriptions, and categorized the projects as either research or nonresearch and as either explicitly about LEP

---

[13]We acknowledge the research assistance of Joshua Rubin of the University of Chicago on this section.

TABLE A-1 Foundations Supporting Education Research

Foundation	Total grants, 1994 or 1995 (millions of dollars; compiled from annual reports)	Rank among foundations, on education research (from Kirst and Ravitch, 1991)
The John D. and Catherine T. MacArthur Foundation	735.9	4
Ford Foundation	285.7	12
Pew Charitable Trusts	172.8	3
Andrew W. Mellon Foundation	119.5	7
Lilly Endowment	98.3	5
David and Lucile Packard Foundation	62.7	—
Exxon Education Foundation	53.8	2
Carnegie Corporation of New York	53.2	6
William and Flora Hewlett Foundation	39.3	8
James S. McDonnell Foundation	21.8	11
Spencer Foundation	13.0	1

NOTE: The Clark Foundation was ninth in support of education research in 1989, and The Rockefeller Foundation was tenth. We did not receive their annual reports and so did not include them in this survey.

issues or implicitly or indirectly so. Some projects required guessing since some annual reports are more specific than others. Our aim was simply to determine what sorts of projects the foundations supported in our area of interest and how robust the roster of those projects is, not to assess the relative commitments of the foundations to these issues. The complete list of relevant projects, by foundation, is found in Appendix C; here we summarize and give examples for each foundation.[14]

The John D. and Catherine T. MacArthur Foundation

The MacArthur Foundation provided funds for this report, which is, of course, both explicitly about research and explicitly about LEP education issues. The foundation's 1994 annual report showed it to be active in language projects and engaged with language-minority groups. Those projects that might implicitly involve English-language learners and that include some research are a small grant to Hispanic Human Resources of West Palm Beach, Florida, for a socioeco-

---

[14]It should be noted that many of these foundations provided support for the project that produced this report, including The John D. and Catherine T. MacArthur Foundation, the Pew Charitable Trusts, the Carnegie Corporation of New York, the Spencer Foundation, and the Mellon Foundation.

nomic study of the Hispanic community, and a very large grant to Youth Guidance of Chicago to assess the Comer project schools in that city. Other grants related to these issues went to the U.S. Committee for Refugees in Washington, D.C., to protect the rights of refugees in the United States by monitoring, among other things, public education; to a Chicago group for developing leadership among high school parents in a largely Hispanic area; to a Los Angeles group for developing leadership among Latino men and women; and to a school board in Florida for developing a conflict resolution program in English, Spanish, and Creole. As a result of current planning, however, the foundation has shifted its focus to professional development and is unlikely to fund future research in this area.

Ford Foundation

The annual report of the Ford Foundation gives no information about projects themselves, only the amount of funding and the names of the organizations receiving it. Among the grantees most clearly associated with LEP language issues were the Multicultural Education and Training Advocacy Project, the National Community College Hispanic Council, the National Coalition of Advocates for Students, and the Mexican American Legal Defense and Education Fund. Although the information is imprecise, the grant amounts are sizable. Some research-related activities might be generated by these grants, even though they seem to be addressed to groups that provide services and advocacy rather than research, as is typical of foundation funding on education issues.

Pew Charitable Trusts

The Pew Charitable Trusts funded a number of action projects that addressed language-minority or LEP issues in education. Some of these directly addressed education, such as the grant to Accion Comunal Latino Americana of Norristown, Pennsylvania, to provide supplementary education to low-income Latino children, and the grant to the New England Board of Higher Education to increase the number of Latinos, African Americans, and Native Americans in the teaching professions. Other Pew grants seemed likely to be concerned more incidentally with language, such as the grant to California Tomorrow of San Francisco for the dissemination of the Education for a Diverse Society Project.

Andrew W. Mellon Foundation

The Mellon Foundation gave a number of grants for research on language issues. Several grants were given to Michigan State University, The Johns Hopkins University, and San Diego State University for research on the adaptation of the children of recent immigrants; another, to Leadership Education for

Asian Pacifics, Inc., was for policy research on Asian Pacific immigrants. Program grants included five sizable awards (to California State University at Long Beach, California Tomorrow, the Center for Applied Linguistics, the Intercultural Development Research Association, and the University of Maryland, Baltimore County), all for programs on immigrant education. A large program grant to Teachers College of Columbia University supported work with suburban school districts in demographic transition. Two grants to Brown University supported school superintendents in their work with English-language learners.

David and Lucile Packard Foundation

The Packard Foundation did not fund any research per se on language issues, but did support a number of education programs relating to language. They gave modest-sized grants to Big Brothers/Big Sisters of Santa Cruz County for bilingual after-school tutoring; to the Self-Reliance Foundation of Santa Fe, New Mexico, to develop Spanish-language radio programs about family planning and women's reproductive rights; to the Sequoia Union School District of Redwood City, California, for immigrant education programs; and to others. They also awarded a large grant to Stanford University to improve translation services in health care settings for non-English-speaking Americans.

Carnegie Corporation of New York

Carnegie Corporation of New York supported this report. Two of the foundation's grants programs—Education and Healthy Development of Children and Youth, and Special Projects—provided significant support for research programs, model development, policy linkage, and community-organizing projects that benefit language-minority children, youth, and families. For example, the corporation provided support for research on effective parenting education and school reform models targeting Latino families, for legal advocacy to secure language-minority citizens' rights to equitable educational opportunity, for policy linkage activities that provide research-based analyses of language issues to federal and state lawmakers, and for voter education and outreach to strengthen the participation of Latino and Asian Americans in the democratic process.

William and Flora Hewlett Foundation

The Hewlett Foundation provided four grants related directly or indirectly to language issues in education, though not for research. Among these were support to the Ravenswood City School District to purchase native-language library materials, to Arizona State University to sponsor a conference on minority opportunities programs, to California Tomorrow for its Education for a Diverse Society project, and to Morgan Hill Unified School District for a diversity training program.

Spencer Foundation

The Spencer Foundation devotes virtually its entire grants budget to education research. Thus, although its total grants budget is smaller than that of many other foundations, Spencer is the largest supporter of education research among all the foundations, and its work is of great importance to the future of the education research enterprise. Among its projects relating to LEP issues in its 1994-1995 annual report were a grant to Marcia Farr to study literacy practices among Mexican immigrant families; a grant to Robert Fullwinder to study multicultural education as moral education; a grant to Sara Harkness and Charles Super to study parental ethnotheories, cultural practices, and the transition to school; a grant to Lucinda Pease-Alvarez and Kenji Hakuta to study language maintenance and shift in early adolescence; a grant to Alejandro Portes to study the adaptation process of second-generation immigrants; and a grant to Sandra Schecter and Robert Bayley to study family language environment and bilingual development. Through its Small Grants Program, a grant was made to Irene-Anna Diakidoy and Stella Vosniadov to study Lakota/Dakota children's knowledge acquisition in astronomy. Spencer postdoctoral fellowship awards last year included one to Judith Moschkovich to study the construction of mathematical meaning in bilingual conversations, and Spencer dissertation fellowships went to Cynthia Brock to explore a second-language learner's opportunities for literacy learning in a mainstream classroom and to Jane Herman to study cross-linguistic transfer among bilingual kindergartners learning to read.

Other Foundations

This survey was informal. We did not find projects that were obviously about LEP education issues in the most recent available annual report of the Lilly Endowment, the Exxon Education Foundation, or the James S. McDonnell Foundation, although each of those foundations may have supported many research projects or action programs on other education issues, as they have in the past.

Summary

There is a substantial amount of support flowing from the philanthropic foundations to projects aimed at language-minority, LEP, or bilingual education issues. Not very much of this support is for research, as is true of the foundations' general stance toward a world full of problems needing solutions. In our recommendations in Chapter 10, we suggest that the foundations, like the government, should be mindful of opportunities to include language variables and issues in projects while continuing to emphasize applications to practice. Furthermore, we urge the foundations to support synthesis or networking activities that might foster the improvement of research and policy on such issues.

NATIONAL REFORM NETWORKS

Since the mid-1980s, thousands of efforts have been launched to reform or restructure U.S. schools. Perhaps a dozen of these efforts have expanded to form networks that have gained national prominence and are frequently reported or cited in research, professional, or popular outlets. For the most part, these networks are not research oriented, but many have begun conducting evaluations of their projects. Moreover, most of these projects do not specifically target English-language learners. But since English-language learners have become an increasingly prominent component of the school population, many of these projects have, at a minimum, implicitly had to address the needs and issues of these students in local contexts.

There is enormous variability in the manner and the degree to which these projects have responded to the presence of language-minority students in U.S. schools. At one extreme is Success for All, a project based at The Johns Hopkins University and headed by Robert Slavin. Success for All did not begin as a program for English-language learners; it began in inner-city Baltimore with largely African American schools. However, it has been implemented in a small number of schools with substantial language-minority populations. The program has maintained its essential characteristics, but it has also been explicitly adapted for English-language learners. There are in fact two adaptations—an ESL adaptation for students who receive all instruction in English, regardless of their primary language, and a Spanish bilingual adaptation for students in a Spanish primary-language program. Success for All's unusually systematic evaluations indicate that both adaptations are highly effective in promoting higher levels of reading achievement among English-language learners in project schools.

A roughly analogous effort by the National Board for Professional Teaching Standards is under way. The board has been working to develop standards and assessments for certifying highly qualified teachers; eventually, teacher certification will be available in more than 30 areas. One of those areas is "English as a new language," and certification will be available to any teacher who wishes to be board certified for teaching in ESL or bilingual contexts. Employing the general framework used to develop certifications in other areas of teaching, the board will offer certification for teachers of English-language learners by September 1998. In addition, although minimal, standards for dealing with these students are included in the standards for all other areas of certification.

In contrast to Success for All and the efforts of the National Board for Professional Teaching Standards, some programs make no adaptations for or simply have not included English-language learners in their activities. For example, the National Paideia Center is based on the explicit assumption that the program "works with all students" and that there is no need to differentiate for specific groups. The Core Knowledge Foundation is similar in that it, too, promotes a common, core curriculum for all students, although it encourages schools to devote half of their curriculum to topics and skills deemed relevant and meaningful locally. In both cases, there is a rejection of the differentiation of educational treatment by language or cultural group membership. Project Zero has done no work with English-language learners.

More typically, however, reform efforts reviewed here attempt to deal with LEP issues through a subtle and complex interplay between the framework of the overall program and the particulars and exigencies of local contexts. Thus, Accelerated Schools, the Center for Educational Renewal, the Coalition of Essential Schools, Effective Schools, New American Schools Corporation, and the School Development Program have for the most part well-articulated core philosophies and principles. But they believe in the need to adapt curriculum, instruction, and other aspects of student experiences and school operations to the linguistic and cultural characteristics of the student population. How schools do this is left largely up to them, but the assumption is that local sites will attempt to synthesize the core principles of the network or project they have joined with the instructional and curricular features required by their student populations.

For the most part, these projects have not examined their effects on English-language learner outcomes; in many cases, they have not examined effects on student outcomes at all. Although conceptually the idea of "general principles locally adapted to English-language learner populations" makes great intuitive sense, generally these projects have yet to demonstrate the viability of this idea empirically. To this end, we would encourage projects to disaggregate outcome data by LEP status in order to compare the performance of English-language learners with that of other students. Moreover, we would encourage them to field test and evaluate adaptations of their programs for these students.

RECRUITMENT AND TRAINING OF RESEARCHERS

As noted in the discussion of recommendations 10-9 and 10-10 in Chapter 10, there is considerable concern among senior researchers and agency officials that insufficient talent exists at present, or in training, to accomplish the research that is needed on language-minority and LEP issues. Recognizing the problem of insufficient research talent across the whole field of education research, the Spencer Foundation has supported doctoral training, dissertation fellowships, postdoctoral fellowships, and small grants on a large scale (see Patrick, 1991, on the Spencer postdoctoral fellowship program). Those efforts have been crucial to attracting talented young people to work in education research, and some of them have worked on bilingual education and language-minority issues. Since 1992, five dissertation fellowships, one postdoctoral fellowship, and seven small grants[15] have been awarded for research on English-language learners and related language-minority concerns (from a total of approximately 135 such grants per year during the period).[16] In states with large language minority populations, support programs such as the Language Minority Research Institute of the University of California have helped train and support researchers working on these issues.

At the federal level, the Title VII fellowships, provided in various reauthorizations of the Bilingual Education Act, have been the major source of funding for the development of research talent in bilingual education. Between fiscal years 1979 and 1987, a total of 1,721 fellows participated in the fellowship program; another 316 participated between 1990 and 1991. Of the fellows participating between 1979 and 1987, 1,432 were pursuing a doctoral degree, 104 were postmaster's students, and 185 were enrolled at the master's degree level. Although the purpose of the fellowship program is to develop faculty for teacher training programs in bilingual education, not all recipients have followed this course. Even so, all Title VII recipients have necessarily been involved in the conduct and uses of research on LEP issues, and in some cases the attainment of a doctorate and the acquisition of a teaching position (27 percent of those studied) or university administrative position (8 percent of those studied) and receipt of tenure at a university. Thus many of the active researchers in this area have been recipients of Title VII fellowships. On the other hand, Title VII fellowships tend to be restricted to students in schools of education. Some notable researchers who work on LEP issues received their degrees in disciplinary fields outside of schools of education, such as psychology, anthropology, and linguistics. However, these researchers typically do not have access to Title VII fellowships. The 1996 appropriation provided no funds for Title VII fellowships, but the Department of Education reprogrammed $1.1 million to cover continuation grants to 100 fellows.

As we emphasize in Chapter 10, we believe federal research agencies need to give more attention to the problem of the future of the research corps for LEP issues. The concern has special urgency for research relating to LEP issues because the area is politically charged, and this may deter talented researchers from choosing it as a focus of their studies. Numerous models for the needed support exist. The Office of Special Education and Rehabilitative Services, for example, divides its considerable Field Initiated Studies funds among doctoral dissertation support, postdoctoral fellowships, and senior research grants. Various National Institutes of Health institutes support training programs. We urge more opportunities of this sort in our recommendations in Chapter 10.

Among those highly qualified and rigorously trained researchers needed to

---

[15]The small grants are heavily used by pretenured faculty.

[16]The topics are listed in the annual reports of the Spencer Foundation.

conduct research on LEP issues, we would hope that a substantial number would represent minority groups. This is a separate issue from the quality of the research corps as a whole; we raise it because of the role-model potential of minority scholars and, more important, the experience, insights, and networks they can bring to the enterprise. Although there are a large number of minority scholars and/or scholars from language-minority backgrounds currently doing work on LEP issues, senior people in the field need to nurture such participation among the younger potential scholars (see Padilla, 1994). Note that of the 13 Spencer awards for dissertations, postdoctoral fellowships, and small grants for work on LEP and related issues since 1992, 6 were awarded to minority scholars, a larger proportion than is usually the case.

Some notion of the potential pool of minority scholars can be gleaned from the annual reports on minority group members in higher education published by the American Council on Education. Figures for doctorates received in education are imperfect indicators of the pool because, as noted above, researchers on LEP and related issues are often trained in anthropology, psychology, linguistics, or other departments. Conversely, very large numbers of education doctorates are awarded to candidates headed for practice, such as school administrators, and among those trained for research careers, only a small minority will work on LEP issues. However, the broad parameters of minorities receiving the doctorate in education are as follows: of the 5842 U.S. citizens receiving a doctorate in education in 1994, 36 (.62 percent) were Native American, 80 (1.37 percent) were Asian American, and 225 (3 percent) were Hispanic American (Carter and Wilson, 1996). It is among these small groups and the equally small numbers of minorities in related disciplines that we must look for future minority scholars on LEP issues.

REFERENCES

Atkinson, R.C., and G.B. Jackson, eds.
    1992   *Research and Education Reform: Roles for the Office of Educational Research and Improvement.* Committee on the Federal Role in Education Research, National Research Council. Washington, D.C.: National Academy Press.
August, D., and E.E. Garcia
    1988   *Language Minority Education in the United States: Research, Policy, and Practice.* Springfield, IL: Charles C Thomas.
Ayres, L.P.
    1909   *Laggards in Our Schools.* New York: Russell Sage Foundation.
Baker, K., and A. de Kanter
    1981   *Summary Report of a Review of the Literature on the Effectiveness of Bilingual Education.* Washington: U.S. Department of Education.
Baker, K., and A. de Kanter, eds.
    1983   *Bilingual Education: A Reappraisal of Federal Policy.* Lexington, MA: Lexington Books.

Birman, B., and A. Ginsburg
    1983   Introduction: Addressing the needs of language-minority children. Pp. ix-xxi in K. Baker
            and A. de Kanter, eds., *Bilingual Education: A Reappraisal of Federal Policy*. Lexing-
            ton, MA: Lexington Books.
Burkheimer, Jr., G.J., A.J. Conger, G.H. Dunteman, B.G. Elliott, and K.A. Mowbray
    1989   *The Effectiveness of Service for Language-Minority Limited-English-Proficient Students*.
            2 volumes. Research Triangle Park, NC: Research Triangle Institute.
Callahan, D., and B. Jennings, eds.
    1983   Pp. 31-46 in *Ethics, The Social Sciences and Policy Analysis*. New York: Plenum Press.
Campoverde, R.O.
    1993   Memorandum from the Director of the Executive Secretariat, Office of the Secretary, to
            the Deputy Secretary, January 12. U.S. Department of Education.
Carter, D.J., and R. Wilson
    1996   *Minorities in Higher Education: 1995*. Fourteenth Annual Status Report, June. Wash-
            ington, DC: American Council on Education, Office of Minorities in Higher Education.
Castellano, D.
    1983   *The Best of Two Worlds: Bilingual-Bicultural Education in the U.S.* Trenton: New
            Jersey State Department of Education.
Center for Applied Linguistics
    1977   *Bilingual Education: Current Perspectives*. 5 volumes: *Linguistics, Social Science,
            Education, Synthesis, Law*. Washington, D.C: Center for Applied Linguistics.
Chapman, J.
    1992   Office of Management and Budget (now Office of the Under Secretary), unpublished
            paper, May 28. The Department of Education Bilingual Research Program. Washington,
            DC.
Crawford, J.
    1995   *Bilingual Education: History Politics Theory and Practice*. Los Angeles: Bilingual
            Educational Services, Inc.
Cyert, R., and J. March
    1963   *A Behavioral Theory of the Firm*. Englewood Cliffs, NJ: Prentice Hall.
Dannoff, M. N.
    1978   *Evaluation of the Impact of ESEA Title VII Spanish-English Bilingual Education Pro-
            grams*. Technical Report. Washington, DC: American Institutes for Research.
Dershimer, R.A.
    1976   *The Federal Government and Educational R&D*. Lexington, MA: Lexington Books.
Education Week
    1996   E.D. Awards 5-Year Grants to 10 Regional Research Labs. January 10:
    1996 $107 Million over 5 Years Awarded to 7 Research Centers. February 14:20.
Fishman, J., V. Nahirny, J. Hofman, and R. Hayden
    1966   *Language Loyalty in the United States*. The Hague: Mouton.
Gaarder, A.B.
    1967   Teaching in the mother tongue. Congressional testimony, U.S. Senate, Committee on
            Labor and Public Welfare, Special Subcommittee on Bilingual Education. (May 18,
            1968) Pp. 50-54 in Hearings on S. 428, 90th Congress, 1st Session. Washington, DC:
            U.S. Government Printing Office. (Excerpted: pp. 325-329 in J. Crawford, ed., Lan-
            guage Loyalties: A Sourcebook on the Official English Controversy. Chicago: Univer-
            sity of Chicago Press, 1992.)
Garcia, G.
    1994   Strategic Framework for Bilingual Education Research and Evaluation Studies Funded
            under ESEA, Title VII. OBEMLA, U.S. Department of Education, Washington, DC.

Glenn, C.L., with E.J. de Jong
   1996   *Educating Immigrant Children: Schools and Language Minorities in 12 Nations.* New
           York: Garland.
Hakuta, K.
   1986   *Minor of Language: The Debate on Bilingualism.* New York: Basic Books.
Hakuta, K., and L.J. Gould
   1987   Synthesis of Research on Bilingual Education. *Educational Leadership* 44 (March):38-
           45.
Jones, J.
   1973   Cultural Conflict in Rural Public Schools: The Case of Wisconsin, 1848-1890. Unpub-
           lished paper, Department of History, University of Wisconsin.
Jones, M.A.
   1960   *American Immigration.* Chicago: University of Chicago Press.
Kaestle, C.F.
   1973   New York Public School Society, Executive Committee Minutes, 1839, 1843. Pp. 143-
           144 in *The Evolution of an Urban School System: New York City, 1750-1850.* Cam-
           bridge, MA: Harvard University Press.
   1992   Everybody's Been to Fourth Grade: An Oral History of Federal R&D in Education.
           Wisconsin Center for Education Research, University of Wisconsin-Madison.
   1993   The awful reputation of education research. *Educational Researcher* (January-Febru-
           ary):23-31.
Kingdon, J.W.
   1984   *Agendas, Alternatives, and Public Policies.* New York: Harper-Collins.
Kirst, M., and D. Ravitch
   1991   *Research and the Renewal of Education.* Stanford, CA: National Academy of Education.
Kloss, H.
   1977   *The American Bilingual Tradition.* Rowley, MA: Newbury House.
Liebowitz, A.H.
   1980   *The Bilingual Education Act: A Legislative Analysis.* Rosslyn, VA: National Clearing-
           house for Bilingual Education.
Lindblom, C.E.
   1990   *Inquiry and Change: The Troubled Attempt to Understand and Shape Society.* New
           Haven: Yale University Press.
Lynn, L.E., Jr., ed.
   1978   *Knowledge and Policy: The Uncertain Connection.* Study Project on Social Research
           and Development, National Research Council. Washington, DC: National Academy
           Press.
Mackey, W.F., and Von Nieda Beebe
   1977   *Bilingual Schools for a Bicultural Community. Miami's Adaptation to the Cuban Refu-
           gees.* Rowley, MA: Newbury House.
McLaughlin, B.
   1985   *Second-Language Acquisition in Childhood. Vol. 2: School-Age Children.* Hillsdale, NJ:
           Erlbaum.
McLaughlin, M.W., and L.A. Shepard with J.A. O'Day.
   1995   *Improving Education through Standards-Based Reform.* A Report by the National Acad-
           emy of Education Panel on Standards-Based Education Reform. Stanford, CA: National
           Academy of Education.
Meyer, M.M., and S.E. Fienberg, eds.
   1992   *Assessing Evaluation Studies: The Case of Bilingual Education Strategies.* Panel to
           Review Evaluation Studies of Bilingual Education, Committee on National Statistics,
           National Research Council. Washington, D.C.: National Academy Press.

Moss, M., and M. Puma
   1995   Prospects: The Congressionally Mandated Study of Educational Growth and Opportu-
           nity. First Year Report on Language Minority and Limited English Proficient Students.
           Prepared for Office of the Under Secretary, U.S. Department of Education by Abt Associ-
           ates, Inc., Cambridge, MA.
National Commission on Excellence in Education
   1983   A Nation At Risk. A Report by the National Commission on Excellence in Education.
           Washington, D.C.: U.S. Department of Education.
National Research Council
   1986   Creating a Center for Education Statistics: A Time for Action. Washington, DC: Na-
           tional Academy Press.
New York Times
   1981   Reagan Defends Proposed Budget and Asks Mayors' Group for Help. March 3:1.
Padilla, A.M.
   1994   Ethnic Minority Scholars, Research, and Mentoring: Current and Future Issues. Educa-
           tional Researcher (May):25-27.
Patrick, C.L.
   1991   Spencer postdoc fellowships give young scholars "a chance to look at the taller moun-
           tains." Educational Researcher (October) 20(7):29-32.
Ramirez, D.J., S.D. Yuen, D.R. Ramey, and D.J. Pasta
   1991   Final Report: National Longitudinal Study of Structured-English Immersion Strategy,
           Early-Exit and Late-Exit Transitional Bilingual Education Programs for Language-Mi-
           nority Children, Vol. I-II, Technical Report. San Mateo, CA: Aguirre International.
Riley, R.W.
   1995   Letter from the U.S. Secretary of Education, to the Honorable John Porter, Chairman,
           Subcommittee on Labor, Health and Human Services, and Education, Committee on Ap-
           propriations, House of Representatives, September 18.
Sanchez, G.
   1934   Bilingualism and mental measures: A word of caution. Journal of Applied Psychology 8
           (December):770.
   1940   Forgotten People: A Study of New Mexicans. Albuquerque: University of New Mexico
           Press.
Schlossman, S.L.
   1983a   Is there an American tradition of bilingual education? German in the public elementary
           schools, 1840-1919. American Journal of Education (February) 91(2):139-186.
   1983b   Self-evident remedy? George I. Sanchez, segregation, and enduring dilemmas in bilin-
           gual education. Teachers College Record 84 (Summer):871-907.
Sproull, L., S. Weiner, and D.Wolf
   1978   Organizing an Anarchy: Belief, Bureaucracy, and Politics in the National Institute of
           Education. Chicago: University of Chicago Press.
Tharp, R., and R. Gallimore
   1991   The Instructional Conversation: Teaching and Learning in Social Activity. Research
           Report No. 2. Santa Cruz, CA: National Center for Research on Cultural Diversity and
           Second Language Learning.
Turnbull, B., H. McCollum, M. Bruce Haslam, and K. Clopy
   1994   Regional Educational Laboratories: Some Key Accomplishments and Limitations in the
           Program's Work. Final Report (December). Washington, DC: Policy Studies Associ-
           ates.
U.S. Department of Education
   1985   Address by U.S. Secretary of Education William J. Bennett to Association for a Better
           New York. Press release, September 26. U.S. Department of Education.

1991   *The Condition of Bilingual Education in the Nation: A Report from the Secretary of Education to the Congress and the President.* Office of the Secretary. Washington, DC: U.S. Department of Education.

1992   *Field Initiated Studies Program. Abstracts of Funded Projects, 1990 and 1991* (Spring). Office of Research, Office of Educational Research and Improvement. Washington, DC: U.S. Department of Education.

1993   *Field Initiated Studies Program. Abstracts of Funded Projects, 1992.* (Spring). Office of Research, Office of Educational Research and Improvement. Washington, DC: U.S. Department of Education.

1994   *Field Initiated Studies Program. Abstracts of Funded Projects, 1993.* (Spring). Office of Research, Office of Educational Research and Improvement. Washington, DC: U.S. Department of Education.

1995   *Directory of National Education Research and Development Centers.* Office of Educational Research and Improvement. Washington, DC: U.S. Department of Education.

Vinovskis, Maris A.

1993   Analysis of the Quality of Research and Development at the OERI Research and Development Centers and the OERI Regional Educational Laboratories. Unpublished report. Washington, DC: U.S. Department of Education, OERI, June.

Weiss, C.H.

1983   Ideology, Interests, and Information. Pp. 213-245 in Carol Weiss, D. Callahan, and B. Jennings, eds., *Ethics, Social Service, and Policy Analysis.* New York: Plenum.

Weiss, C.H. with M.J. Bucuvalas

1980   *Social Science Research and Decision-Making.* New York: Columbia University Press.

Willig, A.C.

1981-   The effectiveness of bilingual education: Review of a report. *NABE*

1982   *Journal* 6 (Winter/Spring).

Zehler, A.M., P. DiCerbo, C. Greniuk, L.K. Lathrop, A.M. Schwartz, P.J. Hopstock, W. Strang, and C. Heid

1993   *Literature Review of Federally Funded Studies Related to LEP Students. Final Analytic Report.* Arlington, VA: Development Associates.

APPENDIX
B

Federal and State Interviews

This appendix provides information on the interviews conducted at the federal and state levels as input to the discussion of research infrastructure and related issues in Chapter 10 and Appendix A. It presents a list of those interviewed and the interview protocol used with people who know about federal and state research.

LIST OF INTERVIEWS: FEDERAL

Judith Anderson
National Institute on the Education of
  At-Risk Students
Office of Educational Research and
  Improvement
U.S. Department of Education

Eve Bither
Acting Director of Office of Reform
  Assistance and Dissemination
Office of Educational Research and
  Improvement
U.S. Department of Education

John Chapman
Senior Budget Analyst
Budget Office
Division of Elementary, Secondary,
  and Vocational Analysis
U.S. Department of Education

Daryl Chubin
Division of Research Evaluation
  and Communication
U.S. National Science Foundation

Joseph Conaty
Acting Director
National Institute on Student
  Achievement, Curriculum and
  Assessment
Office of Educational Research and
  Improvement
U.S. Department of Education

Lou Danielson
Division of Educational Services
U.S. Department of Education

James English
Office of Migrant Education
U.S. Department of Education

Eugene Garcia
Director
Office of Bilingual Education
  and Minority Language Affairs
U.S. Department of Education

Gilbert Garcia
Office of Educational Research and
  Improvement
U.S. Department of Education

Kristin Gilbert
Education Program Specialist
Migrant Education
U.S. Department of Education

Alan L. Ginsburg
Director, Planning and Evaluation
  Service
Office of the Under Secretary
U.S. Department of Education

Norman Krasnegor
Human Learning and Behavior
  Branch
National Institute for Child Health
  and Development
U.S. Department of Health and
  Human Services

Preston Kronkosky
President
Southwest Educational Development
  Laboratory
Austin, TX

Michael Lopez
Branch Chief, Research,
   Demonstration & Evaluation
   Branch
Office of the Commissioner
Administration on Children, Youth,
   and Families
U.S. Department of Health and Human
   Services

Edith McArthur
Acting Program Director
Data Development
National Center for Education
   Statistics
U.S. Department of Education

Denise McKeon
Director of Outreach
American Educational Research
   Association
Washington, DC

Barry McLaughlin
Former Co-Director
Center for Research on Cultural
   Diversity and Second Language
   Learning
University of California, Santa Cruz

Martha Moorehouse
Office of Planning and Evaluation
U.S. Department of Health and
   Human Services

Mollie Oliveri
Branch Chief
Behavioral, Cognitive and Social
   Sciences Research Branch
National Institute of Mental Health
U.S. Department of Health and
   Human Services

Amado Padilla
School of Education
Stanford University

Ray S. Perez
U.S. Army Institute for the
   Behavioral and Social Sciences
U.S. Department of Defense

Valena Plisko
Policy and Evaluation Services
U.S. Department of Education

Sharon Robinson
Assistant Secretary
Office of Educational Research and
   Improvement
U.S. Department of Education

Jeff Rodamar
Planning and Evaluation Service
U.S. Department of Education

Edward Simermeyer
Director, Office of Indian Education
Indian Fellowship Program
U.S. Department of Education

Robert Slavin
CSOS-CRESPAR
The Johns Hopkins University

Gerald Sroufe
Director of Governmental &
   Professional Liaison
American Educational Research
   Association
Washington, DC

G. Richard Tucker
Department of Modern Languages
Carnegie-Mellon University

INTERVIEW PROTOCOL FOR THE FEDERAL GOVERNMENT

Organization and Administration

1. What are the mission and objectives of your office (unit, division, etc.)?
2. How is your office (division, unit, etc.) organized and administered? (Please provide an organizational chart.)
3. If your office (etc.) is responsible for activities other than research—provision of services, processing and monitoring of grants, statistics—how do the research activities relate to these other activities?
4. Have there been major organizational changes in the last five years that would affect research on bilingiual/LEP students? If so, what are they?

What Is Funded

For each of the following areas, for the past five years, please elaborate on what was funded, including amount and principal investigators/organizations for funded work. If you haven't done so already, can you provide us with a list of these projects and any other written information you might have describing these projects?

1. Does your office (department, agency, etc.) support research related to the education of limited-English-proficient and bilingual students including:

- basic research on the linguistic, cognitive, and social processes involved in the education of limited English proficient and bilingual students;
- applied research looking at effective instructional practices and schooling;
- demonstrations, evaluations; and
- survey research to find out about demographics, educational context, and student outcomes, including the supply of educational researchers and teachers?

Please elaborate on the above.

2. Does it support centers, labs, or other entities that conduct research in the above areas on bilingual/LEP students? Is so, please elaborate.
3. Does it support information services (clearinghouses) or resource centers? If so, please elaborate.
4. Does it support training grants for scholars who work on the education of LEP and bilingual students? If so, please elaborate.
5. Was any of this work field-initiated? If so, please elaborate (how much? what?).
6. Was any of this work intramural? If so, please elaborate (how much?

what?). Are there staff with expertise in this area working in your office (unit, division, agency, etc.)?

Development of Research Agenda

1. Do you have a research agenda? How is the research agenda in your agency, office determined? Who is involved in determining the agenda, and what is the process by which it is developed? How are priorities determined?

2. How much is determined within the agency? How much is determined by legislation or other outside entities? What legislation or entities?

Procurement

1. What is the process for developing the RFPs? Is it a formal or informal process? Are there standards? If so, what are they? Who is involved? How are decisions made?

2. What is the process for soliciting proposals and making the awards? Do you have a peer review process? Are there explicit standards? If so, what are they?

Monitoring

1. What is the process for monitoring the projects, both while they are implemented and before the final reports are released (i.e., are there report review and clearance procedures)?

Accumulation of Results

1. Are there any mechanisms in place to provide for review and syntheses of the research that is funded? If so, please elaborate.

2. Are there mechanisms in place for consensus development of the research literature? If so, what are they?

3. Is there an archiving system in place? If archiving mandatory? If so, with whom?

Collaboration

1. Do you collaborate (coordinate) with other offices, divisions, departments, institutions in the process of carrying out of research on bilingual/LEP students? If so, can you comment on benefits, drawbacks regarding this collaboration/coordination?

Dissemination/Linkages

1. Is there a mechanism, process for dissemination?
2. If so, to whom and how are research findings disseminated?
3. Are there any efforts to connect the research efforts/findings to practice? If so, what are they? Strengths? Weaknesses?
4. Are there any efforts to connect the research findings to policy? If so what are they? Strengths? Weaknesses?

Obstacles/Barriers to the Sponsorship of Research in This Area

1. Can you comment on obstacles/barriers to the sponsorship of research in this area? For example, are any of the following responsible to creating obstacles or barriers:

- amount of money available;
- infrastructure issues—control of money, coordination/collaboration across funders, leadership, process for development of RFPs, for making and monitoring awards;
- political climate; and
- quality and quantity of applicants?

Promising Efforts

1. What are some promising efforts in the sponsorship of research (i.e., coordination both across offices and across types of research, larger and longer commitments for study and experimentation on critical issues, more field-initiated research)?
2. What do you see as the three most significant research endeavors in the last five years? Why?

Supply of Educational Researchers

1. Does your unit support the training of educational researchers who work on language-minority education issues, through grants directly to colleges and universities or to students in the form of fellowships? Please elaborate.
2. Is there any information on the effectiveness of these efforts? Please elaborate.
3. Do you have any ideas or can you think of any examples of particularly effective efforts to train educational researchers, to increase the number of minorities working in this area?

Supply of Teachers

1. Does your unit support the training (preservice and inservice) of teachers of language-minority students? Please elaborate.

2. Is there any information on the effectiveness of these efforts?

3. Do you have any ideas or can you think of any examples of particularly effective efforts to:

- train teachers to work with language-minority students or
- increase the number of teachers who work with language-minority students, especially language-minority teachers who are themselves bilingual?

LIST OF INTERVIEWS: STATE

Ms. Lupe Castillo
Title VII Coordinator
Department of Education
New Mexico

Mr. Bernardo Garcia
Director, Office of Multicultural
    Student Language Education
Florida State Department of
    Education

Mr. James Greco
Manager, Office of Bilingual/
    Dicultural Education
California Department of Education

Ms. Anne Kessler
Program Manager
Bilingual Education Program
Alaska State Board of Education

Ms. Josephine Pablo
Director, Title VII, ESEA
General Education Branch/Languages
    Section
Hawaii State Department of
    Education

Ms. Verma Pastor
Bilingual/Migrant Program Director
Arizona Department of Education

Ms. Carmen Perez
Director, Bilingual Education
New York State Department of
    Education

Ms. Maria Seidner
Interim Director
Division of Bilingual Education
Texas Education Agency

STATE DEPARTMENT OF EDUCATION (SEA)
RESPONSES TO QUESTIONNAIRE

Question 1:   Does the SEA fund research on LEP and bilingual students, including basic research, applied research, demonstrations, evaluations, or survey research? Please elaborate on research funded in the past five years and amounts of funding, if available, as well as identifying the administrative units within the SEA that fund this research.

State A: The SEA does not conduct research per se, although it does collect information on student performance on statewide achievement tests. Achievement testing is conducted in grades 3, 5, and 8, and students are also required to pass a tenth grade competency examination in order to graduate. It is possible to identify ethnicity (broadly defined—e.g., Hispanic, Native American), as well as gender in these state performance data. At present, these data are not reported separately by ethnicity in a state report.

State B: The main state-supported research efforts are (1) evaluations of state-funded programs, (2) a census that includes counts and descriptions of English-language learners, and (3) analysis of data from the state performance testing program. With respect to evaluation, any project with state funds must conduct an evaluation. Any district that accepts state (formula) aid for bilingual education must use state-prescribed tests (the state mandates a pre/post-testing program), as well as develop program plans and evaluate its programs (not all districts accept aid, but most with significant numbers of English-language learners do). Using these data, state officials do analysis and issue an annual report to the State Board. They also provide technical assistance to districts. There is some concern about the quality of the testing data from some districts, however. There is also a state categorical funding program for bilingual education. This program has a competitive awards process, and the evaluation requirements are similar to those of the formula aid program.

In addition, the state conducts a census of language-minority children, which is used to distribute state formula aid for English-language learners. From this exercise, it is possible to identify such students, as well as the type of educational programs in which they are enrolled. The state maintains individual student records data, as well as extensive information on the districts and their programs.

The state's performance testing program data make it possible to identify English-language learners, as well as the programs in which they are enrolled. Performance testing is conducted at grades 3 and 6. There are also competency tests administered at intermediate and high school levels that can yield similar data. A new policy approved by the state board of education requires that the state measure English-language learner growth separately in the state assessment program (for many years these students were exempted from statewide testing, but under the new policy, districts must use tests in native languages, if available).

Although not currently a research activity, SEA staff anticipate that it will soon be necessary to develop new teacher certification examinations (this will probably be a Request for Proposals process).

State C: The main state research activity is district-level data collections to develop a state report card. The state prescribes the data elements and definitions (including an LEP definition), and districts provide reports to the SEA. The SEA produces a state summary. Among the data districts are required to submit are data about English-language learners: performance on state assessment (see below) and ethnic/linguistic background. The state maintains a student-level data records system. At present, the data on English-language learners are not aggregated at the state level in a report. They are used, however, to allocate state aid funds to districts.

The state assessment system requires tests at grades 4, 8, and 11. Many districts test students at all grades, however. The data collected by the state allow for the identification of English-language learners by school. It is also possible to isolate the performance of students in bilingual and bicultural programs.

In addition, the state received Title VII funds to work with districts. State officials monitor projects and do site evaluations. There is an Academic Excellence site in the state that has conducted research on English-language learner performance.

State D: This state conducts an annual (fall) district-level survey, yielding data by school and by individual student for its state management information system. These fall surveys provide data on enrollment, race, ethnicity, and language. It is possible to identify LEP, LEP/bilingual, LEP/special education, and LEP/parental denial status. An individual student-level record system is maintained by the state. (There is a weight in the state aid formula for English-language learners, and this data collection is used to assist in the distribution of formula aid.)

From this data collection, the SEA publishes "snapshots" of district-level data. Aggregated program data on English-language learners are currently published by grade and region of the state, but it would be possible to disaggregate these data further.

The state's performance assessment system collects school-level data. Information on attendance and dropout rates, as well as achievement data, are analyzed by the state. There is also an annual criterion-referenced third grade testing program in reading and math, as well as other grades in some years. The state receives school-level data and can separately examine the performance of schools with concentrations of language-minority students.

There is a state testing program in Spanish for grades 3-6 for English-language learners in math, reading, and writing. The program is currently undergoing new test development and beginning to implement new criterion-referenced tests. At present, some of the tests are being "benchmarked," and standards are being developed. Others are being field tested. Districts that receive state program funding for bilingual education are required to do pre- and post-testing of students using these tests.

Under contract, the SEA is also developing a new language proficiency test for bilingual teacher certification. The development process involves identifying skills needed by teachers and assessing the strengths and weaknesses of the current test.

The SEA research and evaluation division has conducted various evaluation studies, including a study of pre-K programs for English-language learners.

State E: This state has undertaken two specific research studies in the recent past with a focus on bilingual education. First, it issued a contract to a university in the state to develop an English as a second language (ESL) curriculum manual. To develop the manual, the university researchers undertook a "best practices" study, as well as a survey of districts and professional organizations. The aim was to develop ways of identifying levels of English proficiency of English-language learners. The results will be published soon. Second, the assessment and bilingual offices of the SEA cooperated to conduct two symposia, bringing together experts on assessment, surveys, and legal issues on English-language learners and bilingual education programs.

This state also compiles an annual report on the status of English-language learners and their programs. The report provides district-level data on the participation and performance of English-language learners by type of program, assessment status, former English-language learners (i.e., those who have exited the program within the past 2 years), and non-English-language learners. Background data shown include native language, country of origin, and race/ethnicity. This report is based on individual student records submitted by districts (under an automated state student information database), but only aggregated district-level data are currently published.

State F: The SEA conducts needs assessments, evaluations, and on-site monitoring of Title VII projects and sends reports to OBEMLA. In addition, the state-funded LEP program requires districts to develop evaluation plans and collect achievement data on the English-language proficiency of participants. Several years ago, the state conducted a specific research activity to examine the relative benefits of pull-out and self-contained classrooms.

The state assessment program's regular achievement testing applies to English-language-proficient students only. Some districts also give native-language proficiency tests for diagnostic purposes. Through school-level data submitted to the state from the regular testing program, it is possible to estimate, by school, the percentage of English-language learners (by ethnicity) achieving at grade level.

State G: The state conducts an annual census of public school districts (and cooperating private schools) that collects school-level data on a wide variety of variables. The data are analyzed in the bilingual office, and results are published in a yearly report. They include (by school) the number of English-language learners (based on a state legal definition), the number of students reassessed, the number of languages spoken, the types of programs in which students are participating, the number of qualified bilingual teachers, and what tests are used.

The SEA used to collect dropout data by ethnic group, but the respondent was unsure whether these data are still being collected.

For the past 5 years, the state has operated a performance-based testing program. Tests were developed by the SEA in Spanish, but they are no longer in use. At present, testing is taking place in grades 4, 8, and 12 in reading, writing, and math, but the program is being reexamined. However, districts also conduct standardized testing in grades 4, 7, and 11 using nationally known standardized achievement tests, and it is possible to identify English-language learners by program from the test results (which are submitted to the state). Last year, the SEA analyzed district-level state-wide testing data and found that English-language learners in bilingual programs did better than those in ESL (i.e., overall, their gap with English-proficient students was smaller, and in some districts they performed better on average).

State H: This state has conducted several research studies in the recent past. It published a volume that provided a theoretical framework on schooling and language-minority children to which key researchers in the field contributed. A Title VII grant was used to identify five schools in which to implement a theoretically sound program with extensive evaluation. Results of the pilot program were published, and a major city in the state revised its program based on the research.

The state is currently supporting a research program examining staff development for teachers who work with English-language learners (see the entry for this state under question 2 below).

In addition, the statewide assessment program (which is currently being revised) requires standardized achievement tests in grades 2 through 10. Spanish versions of tests are currently being requested of publishers who seek to have their tests approved for the statewide program. Providing such tests will enhance the publishers' chances of test adoption, but they are not required of all publishers, so some will probably not submit them. The state can analyze achievement data to determine, for example, whether English-language learners who are fluent in English do better.

The state maintains a demographic database by school. This database includes the results of a home language survey and English-language assessments, as well as teacher counts. These data are used in compliance reviews, and a state report is issued each year.

The state has a legal requirement to monitor districts on education for English-language learners every 3 years, following up where problems are identified. There is state funding for bilingual education, which is allocated by formula (weights for poverty, transiency, ethnicity).

Summary: SEAs engage in a fairly limited amount of direct research on English-language learners/language-minority students or bilingual education, but many maintain student-level record databases that could be used to conduct sophisticated analysis (at least cross-sectionally). States also prescribe local evaluation requirements for state-funded programs. At present, the main direct research activities include the following:

• **Conducting annual (or other repeated) censuses of school districts** that obtain descriptive information on counts of English-language learners by various background and programmatic variables. These data are sometimes published by district or in aggregated form.

• **Analyzing data from state assessment programs** to determine the performance of English-language learners in relation to the performance of other students (or by LEP program or designation). A number of states maintain individual student record systems that provide background and performance data, although little is known about the quality of these data. The performance data are generally drawn from performance on English-language tests. Only a few states conduct testing in Spanish or another language.

• **Designing and monitoring local evaluations** of funded bilingual or other programs for English-language learners/language-minority students. States play a role in monitoring and evaluating Title VII programs. They also prescribe evaluation requirements for state-funded programs, monitor implementation, and provide technical assistance. State requirements appear to be similar to those of Title VII.

• **Designing teacher certification exams**. In the course of developing language-proficiency and other certification exams, SEAs identify and study the skills teachers need and the links between exams and performance. They also do various research tasks associated with test development. Most of this work is done on a contractual basis.

Question 2: Does the SEA support centers, labs, or other entities that conduct research in the above areas? Please elaborate.

State A: The state does not support any other entities engaged in research.

Although the program is categorical, all funds for bilingual education are distributed by formula to districts, so there are no discretionary funds for use by other entities.

State B: There are technical assistance centers in the state that help the SEA obtain state-requested data from districts as one function, but they do not do research.

The state does work with universities to develop teacher training programs. The SEA is beginning a dialogue with several universities about research needed to design new programs for bilingual and ESL teacher certification. There is a considerable demand for additional qualified teachers. The state currently issues provisional certificates, and teachers have several years to obtain certification. In conjunction with universities, the state has spent $1 million to develop the courses necessary to enable provisional teachers to qualify and pass the test certification exam. The state has conducted a needs assessment to determine how many teachers are needed (based on the numbers of provisional certificates it has issued).

State C: This state supports a language center at a branch of the state university system. The center conducts a wide variety of research on native languages and their survival (this center dates back to the Lau Centers). The results of this research are important in state policy supporting the teaching of native languages. The center publishes monographs and booklets with SEA funding.

State D: There are a number of regional service centers in the state, some focusing on bilingual education. There are also university-based teacher training centers. It was not known how much research takes place at either type of facility.

State E: There are no entities supported on an ongoing basis to conduct research in these areas, but sometimes there is support on an ad hoc basis for a specific research activity requested by the SEA.

State F: The state helps support a federal regional educational laboratory that also receives Title VII funds.

State G: There are no such entities supported by the SEA to conduct research in these areas. The SEA does keep in touch with university-based researchers who conduct research on English-language learners.

State H: The state supports a language-minority program at a campus of the state university system; the program brings together scholars from several campuses. The SEA sometimes provides guidance on specific studies. For example, under the auspices of this program, researchers from several campuses are currently examining the question of what is the most appropriate staff development for teachers who work with English-language learners.

Summary: Development of teacher training programs appears to be the main research and development activity supported by SEAs in centers, laboratories, or other entities. Interestingly, curriculum development was not often mentioned as an activity of centers. In addition, it should be noted that there are other sources of state support for research on language-minority students and English-language learners—primarily state agencies that support faculty and researchers at universities. SEAs also make contributions to the federal regional educational laboratories, although they may not always be aware of specific research on English-language learners being conducted by these laboratories.

Question 3: Does the SEA support information services or training grants for scholars who work on the education of LEP and bilingual students? Please elaborate.

State A: The SEA supports a project that is designing and revising the teacher examination for bilingual education teacher certification. An evaluation of the previous examination was conducted, and it concluded that a change was needed. The new exam is being developed by a committee of researchers and teachers and is currently undergoing prepiloting at one university. The project cost is $85,000.

State B: The SEA is not now supporting such efforts, but there is a large need in the state.

State C: The state staff development network receives funds from the SEA for training grants. The funds support research and teacher training in districts. Many of the districts that receive these funds use them in projects for native-language students. As noted previously, a state-supported university-based center conducts a variety of research functions, including training of researchers.

State D: The SEA does not support such activities directly, but regional service centers in the state provide staff development.

State E: The SEA supports a variety of teacher training and curriculum development projects that are related to language-minority students and involve research. It has recently developed a 300-hour inservice program on ESL and is conducting training of trainers for the program. The program has an evaluation component and supervised implementation. University researchers at a center for applied linguistics were heavily involved in the development of this program. The state also funded the development of a K-12 language arts program involving pilot testing and formative evaluation in a major school district in the state.

State F: As noted under question 3 above, this state supports faculty at a university-based language center that conducts a variety of research activities. In addition, it makes specific grants to the university system to support research by Ph.D and M.A. candidates, as well as faculty, on issues affecting language-minority students.

State G: The state pays tuition for teachers who are seeking certification in bilingual education. It is possible that some of these persons are doing research as part of their education.

State H: The SEA supports teacher training, but not scholar training per se.

Summary: With a few exceptions, SEAs do not directly support information services or scholar training on English-language learners. It should be noted, however, that basic state support of university and college systems also supports the research activities of graduate students and faculty. As already noted, there are, in addition, university-based centers in several of these states that specialize in research on language-minority students and English-language learners.

Question 4: How does your agency decide what kinds of research to support, as well as which particular projects to fund?

State A: In general, the State Board of Education decides what research to undertake, but occasionally legislative requirements drive research (e.g., a decision to revise teacher exams was made after complaints to legislators by persons taking the test).

State B: The decision to require district-level planning and evaluation for state-funded bilingual programs follows the pattern established for most state-funded programs. Furthermore, the SEA has supported the decision strongly because data from these evaluations are used to decide which programs to continue to fund. The data are also used to identify low-performing schools, which then must develop plans to improve performance (schools that continue to perform poorly face takeover). In the past, English-language learner performance was not a factor in the identification of low-performing schools, but that is now changing, and LEP performance will be a separate criterion in state review.

Another current consideration in research decision making is that senior state officials and the board of education want to streamline reporting. They want fewer reports and simple reports that are user-friendly. The state may adopt school report cards in which the performance of English-language learners would be identified.

State C: SEA activity on standards and curriculum frameworks is driving the research currently being done. In that activity, standards for English-language learners/language-minority students are being identified. Also affecting current research is an initiative by the governor's office to reexamine the distribution of state aid. A task force is examining the foundation funding formula and has identified districts with funding gaps (e.g., large English-language learner population, but little tax base). The task force is exploring new ways to allocate state funds.

State D: Most data collections result from legislative mandate. For example, the new education code calls for research on teacher training and learning. Availability of resources also plays a role.

State E: Specific research is undertaken based on needs indicated by districts. For example, a symposium on assessment of English-language learners was offered because of district interest. District directors get together once a year to discuss priorities. Overall data collections are usually driven by legislative requirements.

State F: State funding requirements play an important role in defining what research is undertaken. In addition, the state superintendent is "graded" on student performance, which also affects what research is conducted. For example, one current performance standard is that 25 percent of English-language learners will exit each year. As a result, the SEA is currently studying the efficacy of the 25 percent figure and cutoff scores for achievement tests.

State G: The annual census of public school districts is the result of legislative mandate. In addition, Title VII grant rules require information on English-language learners.

State H: There are three ways that research is likely to be undertaken: (1) a specific legislative mandate (e.g., the legislature wants to examine the efficacy of year-round schools); (2) a state board of education mandate (e.g., one board member wants the SEA to compare the results of English-only as opposed to transitional bilingual education); (3) staff initiative (e.g., staff bring together a consortium of university scholars to address an issue).

Summary: Some respondents had a difficult time identifying the primary influences on decision making about research. In general, board of education and legislative mandates appear to play an important role. In addition, the data requirements of state aid formulas are instrumental in data collections in some states (counts are needed to distribute funds). Title VII information requirements and state traditions with respect to what kinds of information and evaluation accompany grant awards also appear important in establishing the planning and evaluation requirements for district-level programs that accept state aid. A few states noted that relatively new state standards for English-language learner performance are also having an effect on research priorities. The responses are notable for what they did not say as well as what they did. None of the respondents saw themselves as having a major role in decision making on research.

Question 5:   What is your perception of promising state efforts in the sponsorship and conduct of research on these students?

State A: SEA staff have proposed a variety of research activities. For example, they have proposed a research project that would identify the achievement levels of all English-language learners, then identify the curriculum in which they are enrolled. The study would look at modalities and administration that make a difference. Studies that show the reasons for achievement (or its lack) would help justify the resources for bilingual education. The financial climate for such research is viewed as poor, however (see the entry for this state under question 6 below).

State B: Officials in this state have recently developed a research agenda on English-language learners. They have posed a series of research questions. They have not yet identified sources of financial support, however. The questions suggested by the respondent during the interview included the following: How long do students (with different characteristics) need bilingual or ESL instruction? Is it possible to construct student profiles for different levels or kinds of service? Are instruments that test performance measuring what we want them to measure? Are test translations fair? Are tests appropriate for recent immigrants with little prior schooling? What programs are most appropriate for recent immigrants? How do we diagnose students' real needs—not just their LEP status? What are the relative advantages of phonics as opposed to other approaches?

This is a period of massive change in the SEA. The current push is for greater accountability, and there is a strong need to answer the question, "What have we accomplished?" Research that supports accountability (e.g., examining LEP performance as part of school report cards) would fit with the change in direction.

State C: The current superintendent and senior SEA staff are interested in carrying research to the student level (not just aggregated to schools or districts). Also, the SEA has been reorganized to merge data collection and assessment with teacher training in the same division. This is seen as beneficial to research.

State D: The current effort to establish benchmarks and state standards for performance tests in Spanish is an important, positive development. Once the tests are fully implemented, it is likely that initial scores will be lower for English-language learners than for English-language students. It is hoped that analysis of these data will then be conducted and will lead to efforts to improve instruction. Better assessments should also be able to show instructional effects. Further, the performance assessment system is designed to identify whether students taking the test in English were formerly LEP (the previous year only), which should enable additional analysis of instructional effects. Districts can opt out of the assessment program for a year or so, but eventually they must participate.

State E: Awareness of the need for research on English-language learners is high. There is a clear perception that new SEA policies will affect these students. The RFP to overhaul the state assessment program specifically mentions the needs of these students (testing accommodations, waivers, disaggregation of data for this population, alternative assessments). New curriculum framework development plans also refer to English-language learners' needs. In addition, there has been a legislative change; English-language learners are now encouraged to participate in compensatory education, so they will be included in research on compensatory programs.

State F: The emphasis in the SEA is on collecting data that show how students are performing. The respondent believes that there is now a need to identify and study effective classroom strategies. In supporting professional education, the state encourages students in advanced-degree programs to conduct classroom research. It also encourages similar research through innovation grants to schools, some of which are being used to study programs for English-language learners (although much of the funding is used for increased services or inservice education).

State G: The respondent did not identify new research efforts on the horizon.

State H: There is a strong movement in the state toward greater accountability and research that supports it. One positive development is the push for state-level standards for programs serving English-language learners. Creation of such standards will require assessment to develop and then track students into various programs and approaches. Districts will have to present plans for how they will achieve the standards and then conduct research to show the results. All of these requirements promise a greater emphasis on research on English-language learners.

Summary: The major development that seems to be setting the direction for research on English-language learners is the movement toward greater accountability for educational outcomes. Respondents in several states noted that these students are now being included in state assessment programs (sometimes with tests in native languages) and that statewide standards for their performance are being established. This development promises to increase attention to tests and other measures for assessing the performance of English-language learners, as well as to research that examines the best approaches and programs to improve performance.

Question 6: What is your perception of obstacles at the state level in the sponsorship and conduct of research on these students?

State A: The biggest obstacle to research is money. State officials (SEA, legislature, state board) are all supportive of research by the SEA, but there is simply not the money to do it. In general, the governor is inclined to give new resources to districts directly. In part, this is due to conflicts between the board and the governor, but it is also a function of resource scarcity.

State B: The obstacles are both money and sufficient state staff to conduct research.

State C: Money is quite limited at present because industries in the state are in a slump and because federal dollars are likely to decrease. Under those circumstances, it is difficult to justify additional dollars for research. In addition, shifting state leadership makes it difficult to sustain longer-term research efforts.

State D: There is considerable fear among educators who deal with English-language learners about state performance assessment. They do not want to be told that the students they work with are not performing well. This fear of assessment translates into a fear of conducting research.

State E: Lack of resources is the main obstacle to research. It would also help state efforts if there were a clear federal message to conduct research. The development of a centralized research function at the federal level would send an important message. Also, there should be more opportunities for states, especially large states with sizeable English-language learner populations, to conduct joint research. Such collaborations have proven beneficial in the past.

State F: A major obstacle is the inability to obtain high-quality data from schools. In using state data for research purposes, there is an SEA clearance process. It is easier for the bilingual office to facilitate access to data for SEA or district staff, more difficult for graduate students. In general, the state should do more to encourage research, especially research on learning styles. At present, activities are undertaken only when there is sustained individual initiative.

State G: Lack of money and staff are the chief obstacles to research. The SEA would like to conduct research on what is working (programmatically) in bilingual education.

State H: A major obstacle to research is that the whole field of bilingual education is politically charged. There are some political officials seeking research simply to prove that bilingual education is or is not effective. It is difficult to find research that is not conducted by a "hired gun" with a particular viewpoint. In this politically charged atmosphere, it is difficult to examine programs honestly and critically.

Summary: Lack of resources is clearly a strong theme among the responses, but other important obstacles to research were noted by respondents. Several states mentioned lack of staff; this generally means numbers of staff, but it also means persons with the technical and research skills necessary for the task. Some SEAs have offices of research (or the assessment office serves that purpose), but issues of English-language learners and bilingual education need to be state priorities for these offices to focus their resources on those issues.

Data quality is also a concern in some states. SEAs are often dependent on districts to supply both student-level and aggregated data. There are sometimes problems in the quality of those data—both evaluation data from projects and data from regular state-wide data collections. Resources are critically important to allow follow-up with districts when data quality is an issue.

Finally, SEAs are administrative entities, but they are administered by or experience oversight from elected officials or their appointees. The responses to the question about the locus of decision making for research makes clear that these political influences are important in deciding what research gets done. As a result, research questions may be narrowly framed or may reflect a hidden (or not so hidden) political agenda.

Funded Research Activities

This appendix details the funded research activities related to English-language learners and bilingual education. It includes the following activities:

- Research funded by the Department of Education, 1980-1995
- National educational research and development centers
- The Center for Language Education and Research (1987-1988)
- Publications of the National Center for Research on Cultural Diversity and Second-Language Learning
- Research on English-language learners funded by the Office of Special Education Programs
- A project of the National Science Foundation
- Fiscal year 1995 grants to the National Institute for Mental Health and the Department of Health and Human Services
- Projects of the other National Institutes of Health
- Activities funded by foundations
- Activities funded by the Spencer Foundation

RESEARCH FUNDED BY THE U.S. DEPARTMENT OF EDUCATION, 1980-1995

The following table lists the research activities funded by the Department of Education during 1980-1995.

Name	Years Funded	PI/Organization (Principal Researcher)	Total Amount (Dollars)	Managing Office
Bilingual Fellows	1988, 1991-92	Mayatech	434,712	OBEMLA
Inservice Training	1981, 1983-84	ARAWAK Consulting Group	768,385	OBEMLA
Benchmark Study	1995	Institute for Policy Analysis and Research	448,221	OBEMLA
Field-Initiated Studies[a]	1995		683,979	OBEMLA
Development of Teacher Training Models	1993		500	OBEMLA
An Analysis of LEP Students Grant Analysis Study	1991	Atlantic Resources Corporation	20,523	OBEMLA
An Aggregation and Analysis of the Title VII Local Education Agency Database	1991	Amerind	45,873	OBEMLA
Analysis and Reporting of SEA Data LEPS	1990	Atlantic Resources	258,781	OBEMLA
Analysis of the Level of Demand for EACS	1988	Atlantic Resources	140,048	OBEMLA
Review of ESL Literature	1984	InterAmerica Research Associates	35,000	OBEMLA
Outlying Territories	1984	Development Associates	24,000	OBEMLA
Recent Immigrant Study (HOPE)	1984	Hope Associates (Esperanza Medina)	164,373	OBEMLA
Dean's Grant Program	1984	Carolyn W. Ebel (Carolyn W. Ebel)	10,000	OBEMLA
Descrip. Anal. of Title VII SEA Activities	1983	SRA Technologies	195,433	OBEMLA
Native Americans (MESA)	1983	MESA Corp.	167,143	OBEMLA
Bilingual Education in Pacific Islands	1983	U.S. Human Resources	159,953	OBEMLA
Educational Technology	1983	COMSIS	130,170	OBEMLA
Head Start Evaluation Strategies	1981	Juarez and Associates (Regino Chavez)	49,750	OBEMLA
Capacity Building Study	1981	NTS Research Corporation (Liz Reisner)	80,000	OBEMLA
Projections Study (Interamerica)	1980	Interamerica Research Associates	32,640	OBEMLA
Pacific Island Language Groups	1980	Interamerica Research Associates	25,000	OBEMLA
A Descriptive Study of the ESEA Title VII Education Services for High School Students	1994-95	Development Technologies, Inc.	299,893	OBEMLA

Name	Years Funded	PI/Organization (Principal Researcher)	Total Amount (Dollars)	Managing Office
Bilingual Fellows Supply and Demand	1991-92		100,720	OBEMLA
Updating a Database on LEA Participation	1990-91	Amerind	180,557	OBEMLA
SEA/LEA Capacity Building	1989-90	ARC and Ass. (Yungho Kim, Tamara Lucas)	411,050	OBEMLA
Family English Literacy Program Evaluation	1989-90	Atlantic Resources	490,773	OBEMLA
Educational Personnel Training Evaluation	1989-90	Research Triangle Institute	735,466	OBEMLA
Exemplary Alternative Programs	1988-89	Southwest Educ. Development Lab (Tikunoff)	794,395	OBEMLA
Definization of Letter Contract	1985-86	Novcom Systems, Inc.	205,989	OBEMLA
Teacher Language Skills Survey	1980-82	InterAmerica Research Associates (Michael O'Malley)	601,962	OBEMLA
Special Issues Analysis Center (SIAC)	1992-95	Development Associates	2,359,013	OBEMLA
Descriptive Study of Content-ESL	1991-94	Center for Applied Linguistics (CAL)	929,338	OBEMLA
Innovative Approaches	1987-90	Development Ass.	2,596,378	OBEMLA
Special Issues Analysis Center (SIAC)	1985-89	COMSIS	927,482	OBEMLA
NAS	1994-95		200,000	OBEMLA/ OERI
Small Business Innovation Research (SBIR)	1991-95		1,505,979	OBEMLA/ OERI
Recent College Graduates	1985, 1987, 1990	Research Triangle Institute	128,850	OERI
Schools and Staffing	1987	SRI International	98,606	OERI
Causal Relationships	1983	Dept. of Psychology, Yale	45,000	OER
LM&AI Instrument Validation (NCBR)	1983	National Center for Bilingual Research (Daniel Ulibarri)	59,974	OERI
English Tense Marking in Vietnamese	1983	Center for Applied Linguistics	50,891	OERI
Literacy in Inglewood	1981	Department of Education, UCLA (Kathleen Rockhill)	4,716	OERI
Improving the Functional Writing	1981	Center for Ethnographic Research (Trueba and Moll)	125,000	OERI
Improving the Functional Writing/Urban	1981	University City Science Center, Philadelphia (Morris and Louis)	136,000	OERI
Hispanic and Anglo School Post Office Sy.	1981	Jennifer Greene (Jennifer Greene)	31,420	OERI

Name	Years Funded	PI/Organization (Principal Researcher)	Total Amount (Dollars)	Managing Office
Comparison Cognitive Monitoring Skills	1981	Department of Psychology, Stanford (John Flavell)	14,776	OERI
Acquisition of Literacy Skill in L1-L2	1981	Department of Education, UC Santa Barbara (Susan Goldman)	32,966	OERI
Organization of Chicano Narrative Behavior	1981	Educational Testing Service (Richard Duran)	40,955	OERI
Cross Language Research	1981	Department of Psychology, UC Riverside (Ovid J. Tzeng)	50,000	OERI
Cognitive Flexibility and Social Skill	1981	Department of Psychology, Yale (Kenji Hakuta)	65,165	OERI
Mathematics Learning Style Chinese	1981	ARC and Associates (Sau-Lim Tsang)	31,645	OERI
Algebra Clinical Interview Tech.	1981	Physics and Astronomy Department, University of Mass., Amherst (Gerace and Mestre)	31,680	OERI
Language Function 3rd Grade Reading Lessons	1981	ARC Associates (Larry Guthrie)	61,001	OERI
Development of Writing	1981	Department of Education, Arizona State University, Tempe (Carole Edelsky)	52,318	OERI
English Language Use Adolescent Vietnamese Refugees	1981	Center for Applied Linguistics (Wolfram and Christian)	64,891	OERI
Lang. Behavior of Puerto Ricans in the U.S.	1981	Centro de Estudios Puerto Riquenos (Pedraza Pousada and Bennet)	62,180	OERI
Development of Writing Native American	1981	Program in Lang and Lit, College of Education, Univ. of Arizona/Tuscon (Yetta Goodman)	70,000	OERI
Nonverbal Factors in the Educ. of Chinese	1981	Asian American Studies, SF State University (Malcolm Collier)	14,478	OERI
Interdependence and Management in Bil C1	1981	School of Education, Stanford (Elizabeth Cohen)	51,999	OERI
Nonverbal Comm. Amerind Children and Teach	1981	Native American Research Institute (Paul Greenbaum)	64,767	OERI
Report Series on Local Bil. Ed. Programs	1981	E.H. White and Company (Regina Kyle)	82,893	OERI
Assessment of 2nd Language Skills in Puerto Rico	1980	Southwest Educational Development Laboratory (Silvia Viera)	49,433	OERI

	Years Funded	PI/Organization (Principal Researcher)	Total Amount (Dollars)	Managing Office
Inservice Training Needs Puerto Rico	1980	InterAmerican University (Eduardo Rivera Medina)	242,718	OERI
Bilingual Inst. Pract. Non-Public Schools	1980	Educational Testing Service (Elford and Woodford)	133,000	OERI
Synthesis of Results of SBIF Study	1980	E.H. White and Company (Regina Kyle)	31,000	OERI
Adult Working Class Speakers	1980	The Huron Institute (Cancino and Hakuta)	15,000	OERI
School Communicative Competence	1980	Graduate School of Education, Fordham (Brause and Bruno)	60,145	OERI
Bilingual Education Strategies	1983-84	Ventriglia (Ventriglia)	152,180	OERI
Learning English Through Bilingual Instruction	1980-81	School of Education, UC Berkeley (Lily Wong Fillmore)	436,000	OERI
Language and Literacy in Bilingual Instruction	1980-81	Southwest Educational Development Laboratory (Domingo Dominguez)	538,794	OERI
Social Context of Learning in Bil. Class	1980-81	Graduate School of Education, U.C. Berkeley (Donald Hansen)	402,000	OERI
Language Diversity and Classroom Discourse	1980-81	Center for Applied Linguistics (Shuy and Kovac)	104,830	OERI
Bil. Comm. Skills in Classroom Context Pro	1980-81	Center for Human Information (Luis Moll)	103,720	OERI
Significant Instructional Features Study	1980-82	Far West Laboratory (William J. Tikunoff)	2,829,609	OERI
National Assessment Educ. Progress (NAEP)	1983-87	WESTAT	818,005	OERI
Small Business Innovat. Research (SBIR)	1987-93	Various	379,344	OERI
National Educational Longitudinal (NELS)	1984-92	National Opinion Research	2,500,000	OERI
(NELS) High School and Beyond	1981-82, 1984	National Opinion Research (S. Peng, R. Valdivieso)	890,000	OERI
Secondary Students Study	1983, 1985	Naomi Gray	645,790	PES
Chapter 1 LEP Students	1983, 1985-86, 1990-93	WESTAT/ABT	798,618	PES
English Language Proficiency Study (ELSP)	1980, 1982-85	Decision Resources/Bureau of Census (Chester Bowie)	2,671,150	PES

Name	Years Funded	PI/Organization (Principal Researcher)	Total Amount (Dollars)	Managing Office
Multifunctional Centers Study	1986	Policy Studies Assoc.	38,881	PES
Indian Add On	1985	Development Assoc.	438,591	PES
Evaluation of EDACS	1984	Pelavin Associates	104,324	PES
DISTAR	1984	Pelavin Associates	83,716	PES
Synthesis of Ed Research I	1984	Pelavin Associates	97,229	PES
Longitudinal Analysis of the IMPA	1984	University of Oregon	82,157	PES
National Long. Descriptive Phase	1983	Develop Ass./Research Triangle Institute (Mal Young)	789,000	PES
Clearinghouse Evaluation	1983	Pelavin Associates	92,328	PES
NonTitle VII Districts	1983	Advanced Technology	57,681	PES
Bilingual Education Formula	1981	Applied Urbanetics	75,000	PES
Parental Involvement in 4 Federal Ed. Pro.	1980	Systems Development Corp. (Al Robbins)	310,300	PES
Training for Student Placement System Res.	1980	Southwest Educational Development Laboratory (Mashito Okada)	203,708	PES
Descriptive Study of Svcs. to LEP Students	1991-92	Development Assoc.	709,000	PES
National Academy Review	1990-91	National Academy of Sciences	200,000	PES
Parent Attitude Study	1985-86	Educational Testing Service	694,822	PES
META Analysis	1981-82	National Center for Bilingual Research	393,000	PES
Study of Teaching Training (RMC)	1981-82	RMC Research Corporation (David Kaskowitz)	146,258	PES
Development of Data Gathering Models	1980-81	InterAmerica Research Associates (Ray Perez)	410,000	PES
Eval. of Classroom Component (CLIC)	1980-81	Development Associates (Rene Cardenas)	82,893	PES
Identifying Model Strategies	1991-93	Public Studies Associates (PSA)	477,000	PES
Immigrant and Refugee	1989-91	COSMOS	473,240	PES
Evaluation Models Study	1985-87	SRA Technologies	940,753	PES
Selection Procedures	1984-86	Pelavin Associates	431,209	PES
Local Evaluation and Improvement Practices	1989-92	Development Assoc. (Hopstock, Young, Zehler)	471,125	PES
Immersion Study	1983-88, 1990	SRA Technologies/ Aguirre Intl.	4,545,919	PES

Name	Years Funded	PI/Organization (Principal Researcher)	Total Amount (Dollars)	Managing Office
National Long. Evaluation Impact Phase	1983-84, 1986,	Development Assoc./ Research Triangle Institute (Mal Young)	4,663,390	PES
Synthesis of Ed. Sponsored Research II	1988-89	Pelavin Associates		PES

NOTE: Information used to compile this table came from the U.S. Department of Education, Office of the Under Secretary.

*a*Following are the projects included and total amount for each: Cambridge School System—Amigos Research Project—S118,241; Arlington Public Schools (VA)—Alternative Assessment in two-way bilingual immersion programs—S84,035; University of Chicago—Learning at Home—$108,106; George Washington University—Oasis Oral Assessment of Students in Spanish—$69,893; Arlee Montana—Writing Assessment—$45,968; Bernalillo Public Schools (NM)—Talking Life Experiences and Stories—$130,074; IDRA (San Antonio) Early Childhood Model Development—S127,662.

NATIONAL EDUCATIONAL RESEARCH AND DEVELOPMENT CENTERS (1990-1995)

National Center on Adult Literacy
Director: Daniel Wagner
University of Pennsylvania
3910 Chestnut Street
Philadelphia, PA 19104-3111

- The Families and Literacy Learning Project
- Adult Literacy Programs for Bilingual Populations

National Center for Research on Cultural Diversity and Second Language Learning
Director: Barry McLaughlin
University of California at Santa Cruz
141 Clark Kerr Hall
Santa Cruz, CA 95064

- Matches and Mismatches in Family and School Discourse: Consequences for School Achievement in Hispanic and Anglo Children from Low-Income Families
- Parent-Child Conversations and Children's Linguistic and Conceptual Development: Effects of Language and Culture

- Socialization of Scientific Discourse in Samoan-American Households
- The Development of Effective Education in Native American Culture
- Assisting the Literacy Development of Spanish-Speaking Students
- Funds of Knowledge for Teaching
- Korean-American Literacy Practices
- Language Instruction for LEP Children
- Two-Way Bilingual Education: Learning and Understanding Two Different Languages in the Same Sociocultural Context
- Discourse Strategies in Cooperative Learning Settings
- The Academic Consequences of Untracking Low Achieving Students
- The Role of Sociocultural, Instructional, and Motivational Factors in the Development of Higher Order Cognitive Processes in Mathematics Among Language Minority Students
- Integrating Language and Culture in Social Studies
- Cheche Konnen: Case Studies in Scientific Sense-Making
- Diagnostic and Dynamic Assessment of Comprehension and Reasoning Skills
- Assessing Academic Language of Language Minority Students
- Context-based and Interactive Approaches to Assessment Study

Center for Research on the Education of Students Placed at Risk
Co-Director: Robert E. Slavin
Johns Hopkins University
CSOC, 3505 North Charles Street
Baltimore, MD 21219

Co-Director: A. Wade Boykin
Howard University
Department of Psychology
Washington, D.C. 20059

- Effective Bilingual Education
- Effective American Indian Education

Center on Families, Communities, Schools and Children's Learning
Co-Directors: Don Davies and Joyce Epstein
Boston University
605 Commonwealth Avenue
Boston, MA 02215

- National Support Systems: Impact on Puerto Rican Families, Communities, and Schools

The National Research Center on the Gifted and Talented
Director: Joseph Renzulli
University of Connecticut
362 Fairfield Road U-7
Storrs, CT 06269-2007

- An Investigation of Giftedness in Economically Disadvantaged and Limited-English Proficiency Students

National Research Center on Literature Teaching and Learning
Director: Arthur N. Applebee
State University of New York at Albany
School of Education
1400 Washington Avenue
Albany, NY 12222

- Teaching the Process of Literary Understanding
- The Role of Literature in the School Experiences of 4- to 7-Year-Old Children: A Longitudinal Study

- Multicultural Awareness in Multiethnic Schools: Linking Organizational and Individual Perspectives in Literature
- Cross-Cultural Responses to Literature

National Center for Research in Mathematical Sciences Education
Director: Thomas Romberg
University of Wisconsin
Wisconsin Center for Education Research
1025 West Johnson Street
Madison, WI 53706

- Implementation of Reform

The Policy Center of the Consortium for Policy Research in Education
Director: Susan Fuhrman
Rutgers University
86 Clifton Avenue
New Brunswick, NJ 08901-1568

- Categorical Programs

National Reading Research Center
Co-Directors: Donna E. Alvermann and John T. Guthrie
University of Georgia
318 Aderhold Hall
Athens, GA 30602-7125

  • Extending the Classroom Use of Shared Reading to the Home Environment of Culturally and Linguistically Diverse Students
  • Literacy Behaviors in a Kindergarten Bilingual Classroom
  • Portfolios Across Sites and Cultural Contexts

National Center for Science Teaching and Learning
Co-Directors: Arthur L. White and Michael H. Klapper
Ohio State University
1929 Kenny Road
Columbus, OH 43210-1015

  • Japanese Sojourners' Learning Strategies
  • Hispanic Culture and Science Learning
  • Construction and Validation of an Articulated Assessment Package to Evaluate Achievement and Attitudes Related to Integrated Science and Mathematics Education for Anglo and Hispanic Elementary School Students

National Center for Research on Teacher Learning
Co-Directors: Robert E. Floden and G. Williamson McDiarmid
Michigan State University
College of Education
116 Erikson
East Lansing, MI 48824-1034

  • Learning About Diverse Learners

National Center for the Study of Writing and Literacy
Director: Sarah W. Freedman
University of California at Berkeley
School of Education
5513 Tolman Hall
Berkeley, CA 94720

  • Diversity and Literacy Development in the Early Years
  • The Oral and Written Language Growth on Non-English Background Secondary Students
  • Literacy Learning/Writing in the Multicultural Secondary Classroom
  • Cultural Models of Literacy: A Comparative Study

CENTER FOR LANGUAGE EDUCATION AND RESEARCH
(1985-1989)

Academic Knowledge Base

Improving Reading Instruction and Text Comprehension for Language Minority Students.   C. Valadez, (University of California, Los Angeles); A. Padilla, UCLA.

Reading Achievement Among Language Minority Students.   R. Duran, UC-Santa Barbara.

Dialogue Journals as a Research and Pedagogical Tool with Language Minority Students.   J.K. Peyton, (Center for Applied Linguistics, CAL).

Improving Reasoning Skills.   R. Duran, UC-Santa Barbara.

Language and Problem Solving in Secondary School Science Classes.   G. Spanos, CAL; J. Crandall, CAL.

Processes and Significant Features of Cooperative Learning Programs.   E. Jacob, CAL.

The Adjunct Model of Language Instruction for Language Minority University Students.   M.A. Snow, UCLA; D. Brinton, UCLA.

Written and Spoken Language Differences in Bilingual Elementary School Children.   V. Flashner, UCLA.

Scaffolded Classroom Interaction and Its Relation to Second Language Acquisition for Language Minority Students.   B. Hawkins, UCLA.

Professional Development

Preparation and Implementation of the Professional Development Program.   C. Valadez, UCLA; J. Crandall, CAL.

Developing an Information and Support Network of Educators of Language Minority Students.   J. Crandall, CAL; D. Christian, CAL.

Helping Pre-Service Teacher Training in Bilingual Education and ESL Credential Programs to Meet the Needs of Teachers in the Field.   C. Valadez, UCLA.

Improvement of Content of Materials, Curricula, and Programs

Materials, Curriculum, and Programs for Language Minority Educators.   C. Valadez, UCLA.

Materials, Curricula, and Programs for Second Language Education.   D. Christian, CAL.

Linguistic and Metalinguistic Underpinnings of Academic Learning

Cross Language Transfer of School Skills and Metalinguistic Skills in Bilingual Program Students.   K. Hakuta, UC-Santa Cruz

Contextualized and Decontextualized Language Skills. C. Snow, Harvard.

Question Strategies in a Second Language: Learning and Teaching Effective Question Strategies. K. Lindholm, UCLA.

Academic Language Talk: Significant Features in the Responses of L1/L2 "Effective Communicators." C. Simich-Dudgeon, CAL.

Syntactic and Semantic Processing in Second Language Learners. E. Cascallar, UCLA.

Second-Language Instructional Programs

National Survey of Elementary and Secondary Foreign Language Programs. N. Rhodes, CAL.

Definition of an Immersion Methodology. J. Galvan, UCLA.

Comparison of FLES and Immersion Programs. N. Rhodes, CAL.

Development of Assessment Instruments. C. Stansfield, CAL.

The Effects of Proficiency-Oriented Adaptation of Textbooks and Instructional Practices on Student Foreign Language Learners. C. Stansfield, CAL.

Language Attrition

Follow-up of Spanish Immersion Program Graduates. J. Galvan, UCLA.

Extent and Nature of Language Skill Loss Following Training Programs. C. Stansfield, CAL.

Relations Across Linguistic Minority and Second-Language Programs:

Survey of Bilingual Immersion Programs. K. Lindholm, UCLA.

The "Good Learner" of English in Two Settings. M. McGroarty, UCLA.

Evaluation of Existing Interlocking Programs at Elementary and at High School Levels. K. Lindholm, UCLA.

Implementation and Evaluation of New Language Education and Academic Progress Programs. K. Lindholm, UCLA.

PUBLICATIONS OF THE NATIONAL CENTER FOR RESEARCH ON CULTURAL DIVERSITY AND SECOND-LANGUAGE LEARNING

Sociological Foundations Supporting the Study of Cultural Diversity by H. Mehan.

Instructional Conversation: Teaching and Learning in Social Activity by R.G. Tharp and R. Gallimore.

Appropriating Scientific Discourse: Findings from Language Minority Classrooms by A.S. Rosebery, B. Warren, and F.R. Conant.

Untracking and College Enrollment by H. Mehan et al.

Mathematics and Middle School Students of Mexican Descent: The Effects of Thematically Integrated Instruction by R. Henderson and E. Landesman.

Moving in and out of Bilingualism: Investigating Native Language Maintenance and Shift in Mexican-Descent Children by L. Pease-Alvarez.

Two-Way Bilingual Education: A Progress Report on the Amigos Program by M. Cazabon, W. Lambert, and G. Hall.

Literacy Practices in Two Korean-American Communities by R. Scarcella and K. Chin.

Teachers' Beliefs about Reading Assessment with Latino Language Minority Students by R. Rueda and E. Garcia.

Tracking Untracking: The Consequences of Placing Low Track Students in High Track Classes by H. Mehan, L. Hubbard, A. Lintz, and I. Villanueva.

Students' View of the Amigos Program by W. Lambert and M. Cazabon.

Enacting Instructional Conversation with Spanish-Speaking Students in Middle School Mathematics by S. Dalton and J. Sison.

Verbal Comprehension and Reasoning Skills of Latino High School Students by R. Duran, R. Revlin, and D. Havill.

"This Question Is Just Too, Too Easy!" Perspectives from the Classroom on Accountability in Science by B. Warren and A. Rosebery.

Conceptualizing Academic Language by N. Rhodes and J. Solomon.

Syncretic Literacy: Multiculturalism in Samoan American Families by A. Duranti and E. Ochs.

OFFICE OF SPECIAL EDUCATION PROGRAMS RESEARCH ON ENGLISH-LANGUAGE LEARNERS

Development and Validation of an Evaluation Instrument to Measure Instructional Effectiveness of Bilingual Special Education Programs
   Principal Investigator: Carmen Arreaga-Mayer
   Beginning Date: 8/1/90
   Ending Date: 7/31/93

A Comparative Study of Language and Learning Disabilities Across Chinese and Hispanic Language Minority Groups
   Principal Investigator: Ji Mei Chang
   Beginning Date: 9/1/91
   Ending Date: 2/28/93

Program Effectiveness for Culturally and Linguistically Different Exceptional Students
   Principal Investigator: Jozi DeLeon
   Beginning Date: 10/1/91
   Ending Date: 3/31/93

The Language Minority Student and Special Education: A Multi-Faceted Study
   Principal Investigator: Russell Gersten
   Beginning Date: 9/15/90
   Ending Date: 9/14/93

A Descriptive Study of Collaboration Between Bilingual and Special Educators
   Principal Investigator: Kathleen C. Harris
   Beginning Date: 10/1/91
   Ending Date: 3/21/93

Parent-Professional Partnership: Minority Parents' Participation in the Educational Process
   Principal Investigator: Elizabeth Harry
   Beginning Date: 7/1/89
   Ending Date: 6/30/92

Enhancing the Delivery of Services to Black Special Education Students from Non-Standard English Backgrounds
   Principal Investigator: Elizabeth Harry; Margaret McLaughlin
   Beginning Date: 8/1/90
   Ending Date: 7/31/93

Alternative Special Education Assessment of Urban Minority Students
   Principal Investigator: Jacqueline Jones
   Beginning Date: 10/1/91
   Ending Date: 12/31/92

Proactive Schooling: Preventing Dropout in Highest Risk Adolescents
   Principal Investigator: Kathy Larson
   Beginning Date: 10/1/90
   Ending Date: 8/31/95

Literacy Intervention in At-Risk Hispanic Learning Handicapped Inner-City Adolescents: A Pilot Study
> Principal Investigator: Agnes Lin
> Beginning Date: 10/1/91
> Ending Date: 11/30/92

Reducing Cultural Misunderstanding in Schools and Related Service Settings
> Principal Investigator: Cheryl Mattingly
> Beginning Date: 9/1/90
> Ending Date: 8/30/93

Promoting Literacy Through Ecobehavioral Assessment and Class-wide Peer Tutoring for Racial/Ethnic Limited English Proficient Minority Students with Disabilities
> Principal Investigator: Carmen Arreaga-Mayer
> Beginning Date: 6/01/94
> Ending Date: 7/31/97

Parental Involvement in Literacy Instruction: Perceptions of Hispanic Parents of Children with Learning Disabilities
> Principal Investigator: Marie Hushes
> Beginning Date: 8/15/94
> Ending Date: 8/14/95

Comprehensible and Comprehensive Instruction for Language Minority Students with Learning Disabilities
> Principal Investigator: Robert Jimenez
> Beginning Date: 6/01/94
> Ending Date: 5/31/95

Influences Affecting Southeast Asian Perceptions of Special Education in the U.S.
> Principal Investigator: Juan C. Rodriguez
> Beginning Date: 9/01/93
> Ending Date: 8/31/95

NATIONAL SCIENCE FOUNDATION

Language Acquisition in Science Education for Rural Schools
Principal Investigator: Patricia L. Stoddart
Associate Investigators: Roberta M. Jaffe; Lucinda Pease-Alvarez
Performing Organization: University of California-Santa Cruz, Department of
Studies in Education, Santa Cruz, CA 95064

Summary: This project focuses on implementing systemic change in the
teaching of elementary school science to bilingual students so that they
have access to a challenging science curriculum that builds on their
cultural and linguistic resources. In achieving this aim, the program will
become a vehicle for integrating, restructuring, and enhancing the science curriculum and language development programs in seven school
districts and for establishing links to the Latino families and rural agri-
cultural communities from which students come. The locus of the
project activities will be the school site. The staff development program
will be tailored to address school and district priorities, and will support
teachers in the implementation and planning of a comprehensive science
curriculum that addresses content and language development goals. In
addition, the evaluation of the project will include a research component
designed to gather information that will help teachers forge links between learning science and doing science in an authentic context that
relates to students' scientific conceptions, language, and culture.

NATIONAL INSTITUTE FOR MENTAL HEALTH
FISCAL YEAR 1995 GRANTS

Grammar and Processing Anaphoric Pronouns
   William J. Badecker
   The Johns Hopkins University
   Baltimore, MD
   Award: $88,413

Working Memory in Visual Reasoning and Language
   Patricia A. Carpenter
   Carnegie-Mellon University
   Pittsburgh, PA
   Award: $101,936

Biological Foundations of Vocal Learning
    Robert J. Dooling
    University of Maryland, College Park
    College Park, MD
    Award: $89,891

Affective and Linguistic Functions of Prosody
    Anne Fernald
    Stanford University
    Stanford, CA
    Award: $172,281

Early Changes in Lexical Processing
    Lisa Gershkoff-Stowe
Indiana University
Bloomington, IN
Award: $13,008

Privileged Information in Linguistic Communication
    Boaz Keysar
    University of Chicago
    Chicago, IL
    Award: $65,797

Study of Sentence Processing
    Reiko Mazuka
    Duke University
    Durham, NC
    Award: $112,355

Causes and Consequences of Lexical Activation
    Arthur G. Samuel
    State University of New York
    Stony Brook, NY
    Award: $113,637

Normal and Disordered Language Processing
    Mark S. Seidenberg
    University of Southern California
    Los Angeles, CA
    Award: $101,745

Prosodic and Syntactic Structure in Sentence Comprehension
    Shari R. Speer
    Northeastern University
    Boston, MA
    Award: $102,300

Phonetic Category Structure and Lexical Access in Aphasia
    Jennifer A. Utman
    Brown University
    Providence, RI
    Award: $13,008

OTHER NATIONAL INSTITUTES OF HEALTH

The Development of Phonetic Categories
Principal Investigator: James E. Flege
Performing Organization: University of Alabama, Birmingham, Alabama
Sponsored by the National Institute on Deafness and Other Communication Disorders

It is widely believed that a critical period exists for second-language (L2) speech learning. However, the actual cause(s) of foreign accent remain uncertain. The research proposed here will evaluate a model that attempts to account for age-related changes in bilinguals' production and perception of vowels and consonants ("sounds") in their L2 and in their native language (L1).

Language and Literacy in Bilingual Children
Principal Investigator: D. Kimbrough Oller
Performing Organization: University of Miami Coral Gables, Coral Gables, Florida
Sponsored by National Institute of Child Health and Human Development

The proposed research will consist of a linguistically diverse, proactive investigation of the effects of social and linguistic backgrounds of children on learning under two widely different training methods.

FOUNDATIONS
(1994)

Grants are listed in the 1994 annual reports of these foundations.

The John D. and Catherine T. MacArthur Foundation

Research
Explicit

National Academy of Sciences, Washington, D.C.
$75,000

Implicit

Hispanic Human Resources, West Palm Beach, FL
Socioeconomic study of the Hispanic community
$20,000

Partial Research
Explicit

Youth Guidance, Chicago, IL
To test the Comer program in Chicago schools
$750,000 over 3 years

Implicit

U.S. Committee for Refugees, Washington, D.C.
To protect rights of refugees in the United States by monitoring, among other things, public education
$300,000 over 3 years

School Board of Palm Beach County, FL
Conflict resolution program in English, Spanish, and Creole
$182,000

Nonresearch
Explicit

ASPIRA, Inc. of Chicago, IL
Preparing parents as teachers and leaders in North Side High Schools with large Latino populations
$90,000 over 3 years

Hugo N. Morales, Fresno, CA
Radio Bilingue, the first bilingual public radio network in the United States
$30,000-$75,000

Implicit

NALEO Educational Fund, Los Angeles, California
Provides leadership development activities for Latino men and women
$50,000 over 2 years

Support Center of Chicago
To incorporate the Latino Capacity Building Program
$5,000

Mexican Fine Arts Center Museum, Chicago, IL
Nation's first Latin American performing arts festival
$225,000

Art Institute of Chicago
To improve its capacity to serve African-American and Latino audiences
$925,000

Hispanic Housing Development Corporation, Chicago, IL
Development of the Teresa and Hipolito Roldan Career Development Program
$45,000

Palm Beach County Literacy Coalition, Delray Beach, FL
Job specific literacy and English-language skills for health service workers
$102,000

Spencer Foundation

Research
Explicit

Marcia Farr
Language, Literacy and Gender: Oral Traditions and Literacy Practices Among
Mexican Immigrant Families
$265,000 over 3 years

Robert K. Fullwinder
Multicultural education as moral education
$86,500 over 18 months

Sara Harkness and Charles McAfee Super
Parental ethnotheories, cultural practices, and the transition to school
$442,650 over 3 years

Lucinda Pease-Alvarez and Kenji Hakuta
Language maintenance and shift in early adolescence
$187,500 over 3 years

Deborah A. Phillips
Partial support of the Committee to Develop a Research Agenda on the Education
of Limited-English-Proficient and Bilingual Students
$150,000 over 20 months

Alejandro Portes
Children of immigrants: the adaptation process of the second generation
$339,000 over 20 months

Sandra R. Schecter and Robert Bayley
Family language environment and bilingual development: toward an integrated
maintenance model
$90,200 over 18 months

Nancy A. Budwig
The impact of early language input on children's discourse: implications for
school participation
$12,000

Cynthia Brock
Exploring a second-language learner's opportunities for literacy learning in a
mainstream classroom

Jane Herman
Cross-linguistic transfer among bilingual kindergartners learning to read

Gigliana Melzi
Developing narrative voice: conversations between Latino mothers and their
preschool children

Cynthia Helen Brock
Literacy and second-language acquisition at the elementary level
$18,000

Implicit

Sophia A. Villenas
Latina immigrants in rural North Carolina: women constructing education in new communities

Spencer Postdoctoral Fellowships

Research
Implicit

Judith N. Moschkovich
The construction of mathematical meaning in bilingual conversations
$35,000

A.L. Mailman Family Foundation

Partial Research
Implicit

The Children's Foundation Washington, D.C.
Create and field test publications and materials for Hispanic child care providers
$20,000

Charles Steward Mott Foundation

Nonresearch
Explicit

Latino Institute, Chicago, IL
School reform project in the 132 Chicago public schools with Hispanic majorities
$50,000

Multicultural Education, Training and Advocacy, Inc., San Francisco, CA
To improve public education by empowering immigrant and native-born minority parents
$150,000

Pew Charitable Trusts

Nonresearch
Explicit

Accion Communal Latino Americana de Montgomery County, Norristown, PA
Providing supplementary education to low-income Latino children
$100,000 over 2 years

Implicit

Japanese American Cultural and Community Center, Los Angeles, CA
International cultural exchange in the performing arts
$55,000 over 9 months

Taller Puertorriqueno, Inc., Philadelphia, PA
To form a national network of Latino arts stores
$30,000 over 6 months

California Tomorrow, San Francisco
For the dissemination of the Education for a Diverse Society Project
$150,000 over 2 years

New England Board of Higher Education, Boston, MA
To increase the numbers of Latinos, African Americans, and Native Americans in the teaching profession
$400,000 over 3 years

David and Lucile Packard Foundation

Nonresearch
Explicit

Big Brothers/Big Sisters of Santa Cruz County
Bilingual after-school tutoring
$30,000

Implicit

Stanford University
To improve translation services in health care settings for non-English-speaking Americans
$300,868

Self Reliance Foundation, Santa Fe, NM
For U.S. national Spanish-language radio programs on family planning and women's reproductive rights
$13,300

Sequoia Union School District, Redwood City, CA
For immigrant education program at Sequoia High School
$57,014

Family and Community Enrichment Services, Belmont, CA
Las Familias Unidas program for Latino youth and their families in Sequoia High School District
$32,000

Hispanos Unidos, Redwood City, CA
Teatro Juvenil, an after-school theater program for Latino youth
$31,310

Santa Cruz Barrios Unidos, Santa Cruz, CA
To prevent violence and gang involvement among Latino youth
$55,000

Carnegie Corporation of New York

Research
Explicit

Stanford University
A report on federal education programs for limited-English-proficient students
$165,000 over 16 months

The Latino Institute, Chicago, IL
Toward the Latino Urban Policy Agenda Project
$225,000 over 3 years

Implicit

Yale University
To test both the Comer and Zigler methods
$350,000 over 2 years

Partial Research
Implicit

Puerto Rican Legal Defense and Education Fund, New York, NY
To make high-quality education available to Puerto Ricans
$450,000 over 3 years

National Council of La Raza, L.A., CA
For work with Hispanic school-aged children in increasing their educational success
$300,000 over 2 years

Big Brothers/Big Sisters of America, Philadelphia, PA
To plan a national strategy to reach and serve Hispanic children and adolescents
$25,000

Southwest Voter Research Institute, San Antonio, TX
Toward a citizenship project for Hispanic immigrants
$75,000

Nonresearch
Explicit

Avance, San Antonio, TX
Parent-child education program, including English-language classes
$350,000 over 2 years

National Board for Professional Teaching Standards, Detroit, MI
To offer certificates in 33 fields, including special certificates for work with limited-English-proficient children
$1,000,000

Implicit

Latino Issues Forum, San Francisco, CA
Toward public education to encourage naturalization among legal immigrants
$25,000

Puerto Rican Legal Defense and Education Fund, NY, NY
Toward institutional strengthening in public education and media advocacy
$25,000

Ford Foundation

Research
Explicit

National Coalition of Advocates for Students
$150,000

National Immigration Forum
$535,000

Partial Research
Explicit

Multicultural Education and Training Advocacy (META) Project
$160,000

Implicit

Refugees International
$150,000

National Community College Hispanic Council
$175,000

Nonresearch
Explicit

Mexican American Legal Defense and Education Fund
$1,425,000

American Bar Association Fund for Justice and Education
$190,000

Implicit

Congressional Hispanic Caucus Institute
$400,000

Cuban American National Council
$190,000

Institute for Puerto Rican Policy
$230,000

Latino Institute
$300,000

National Hispanic Leadership Institute
$75,000

National Puerto Rican Coalition
$340,000

National Puerto Rican Forum
$25,000

United Latino Fund
$200,000

Chicago Coalition for Immigrant and Refugee Protection
$175,000

Coalition for Humane Immigrant Rights of Los Angeles
$160,000

Coalition for Immigrant and Refugee Rights and Services
$145,000

Haitian Refugee Center/Sant Refijie Ayisyin
$250,000

Immigration and Refugee Services of America
$500,000

Massachusetts Immigration and Refugee Advocacy Coalition
$50,000

New York Immigration Coalition
$145,000

Andrew W. Mellon Foundation

Research
Explicit

Michigan State University
For research on the adaptation of the children of recent immigrants
$130,000

Implicit

American Historical Association
To create a guide to manuscript collections in U.S. repositories relating to Spanish colonial presence in the New World, 1492-1900
$125,000

Leadership Education for Asian Pacifics, Inc.
For policy research on Asian Pacific immigrants
$225,000

Association of Research Libraries
To coordinate a North American distributed network-based system of library acquisitions and document delivery in Latin American studies
$90,000

Partial Research
Explicit

California State University at Long Beach
In support of programs on immigrant education
$615,000

California Tomorrow
In support of programs on immigrant education
$615,000

Center for Applied Linguistics
In support of programs on immigrant education
$640,000

Intercultural Development Research Association
In support of programs on immigrant education
$506,000

National Coalition of Advocates for Students
In support of programs on immigrant education
$300,000

University of Maryland at Baltimore County
In support of programs on immigratn education
$433,000

Implicit

University of California, Berkeley
To develop a research network and linked electronic library system with five
Chilean libraries
$300,00

University of New Mexico
To create an online database relating to Latin American and Caribbean countries
$200,000

University of Texas at Austin
To develop its Latin American Network Information Center
$500,000

Nonresearch
Explicit

Brown University
To support activities for school district superintendents working with limited-
English-proficient populations
$150,000

Implicit

University of Houston
To improve publishing operations and organizational capacities of Arte Publico
Press
$380,000

New York Community Trust
To assist immigrants and related groups in New York
$50,000

New York Immigration Coalition
For its project Improving Newcomer Access to City Services
$50,000

William and Flora Hewlett Foundation

Nonresearch
Explicit

Ravenswood City School District
To purchase native-language library materials
$100,000

Implicit

Arizona State University Foundation
For the Expanding Minority Opportunities program
$5,000

California Tomorrow
For the Education for a Diverse Society/School Restructuring project
$75,000

Center for Third World Organizing
For the multicultural leadership development project
$50,000

Summary

Foundation	Total Grants	Education Grants
Ford	$285,700,000	$46,300,000
Pew	172,815,600	31,275,000
Mott	49,031,000	
Lilly	98,300,000	27,500,000
Carnegie	53,152,574	22,866,033[1]
Packard	62,746,000	
Exxon	53,759,042	23,894,867[2]
Russell Sage		
MacArthur	735,900,000	47,800,000[3]
Spencer	12,990,000	12,990,000[4]
Mott		
Mailman	967,340	
Mellon	119,480,950	53,801,550[5]
Hewlett	39,330,008	10,713,000
McDonnell	21,791,551	6,000,967[6]

[1]Figure is for programs on children and youth.

[2]Breaks down into $3,504,511 for higher education, $962,989 for precollege education, and an additional $19,427,367 from the Exxon Education Foundation.

[3]Figures for MacArthur are for the period 1990-1994.

[4]It seems that all of the Spencer Foundation's grants went to education-related efforts.

[5]Figure is for higher education and scholarship ($45,683,700) plus literacy ($8,117,850).

[6]These figures may be inaccurate, since the relevant information was not clearly labeled.

SPENCER FOUNDATION:
SMALL RESEARCH GRANTS AND FELLOWSHIPS RELATING TO
LANGUAGE/LITERACY AND EDUCATION

1992

Small Grants
*Lourdes Diaz Soto, Lehigh University
Bilingual Families as Educators
$7,500

Dissertation-Year Fellowships
Angela R. Wiley, Clark University
Parental Values and the Child's Creation of a Culturally Relevant Self: Language as Mediation
$15,000

1993

Small Grants
*Aydin Durgunoglu and P. David Pearson, University of Illinois at Urbana
Language and Literacy Development of Spanish-Speaking Students
$7,500

Lucia A. French
Language Demands Associated with Schooling: A Perspective From Korea
$7,500

Dissertation Fellowships
Margaret Bender, University of Chicago
Contemporary Uses of the Cherokee Syllabary: The Meanings of Writing and of the Written Word in Cherokee
$15,000

*Miguel Lopez, University of California, Berkeley
English Literacy Acquisition Among Southeast Asian Children in Classroom Contexts
$15,000

1994

Small Research Grants
Denise A. Davidson, Loyola University of Chicago
Bilingual Language Development in Young Children
$9,250

John W. DuBois, University of California, Santa Barbara
Analyzing Bilingual Children's Understanding of Reading Comprehension: Questions Involving Source of Knowledge and Perspective
$5,000

William E. Nagy and Erica F. McClure, University of Illinois Urbana-Champaign
Linguistic Transfer and the Acquisition of English Vocabulary by Spanish-Speaking Students
$8,110

Dissertation Fellowships
*Thomas Mario Kalmar, Harvard University
Adult Biliteracy: The Case of the Cobden Glossaries
$15,000

Postdoctoral Fellowships
*G.Genevieve Patthey-Chavez, Los Angeles City College
School and Home Language Socialization: Understanding the Experiences of Latino Children
$40,000

1995

Small Grants
*Irene-Anna Diakidoy and Stella Vosniadov, University of South Dakota
Lakota/Dakota Children's Knowledge Acquisition in Astronomy
$12,000

Dissertation Fellowships
Cynthia Brock, Michigan State University
Exploring a Second-Language Learner's Opportunities for Literacy Learning in a Mainstream Classroom
$15,000

Jane Herman, Harvard University
Cross-Linguistic Transfer among Bilingual Kindergartners Learning to Read
$15,000

---

*Indicates minority scholar.

APPENDIX
D

Committee Sources

In addition to the literature reviewed and the knowledge and experience of committee members, the committee's work benefited from commissioned papers that were presented and discussed at a workshop, an open meeting at which representatives of professional and advocacy organizations presented their views, and technical reviewers. This appendix lists those papers, organizations, and reviewers.

COMMISSIONED PAPERS

Rethinking Culture, Community, and Schooling: Implications for the Education of Bilingual Students
Luis Moll, Rosi Andrade, Norma Gonzalez, University of Arizona

State Education Agencies and Research on Limited English Proficient or Language Minority Children and Bilingual Education
Lana Muraskin, Consultant, SMB Economic Research, Inc., Washington, DC

Second Language Acquisition and Preschool Education:
Research Findings, Methods, Implications, and Future Directions
Patton O. Tabors, Research Associate, Harvard University

Effective Schooling for LEP Students: The School Domain
National School Reform Efforts and LEP Students
Dr. Claude Goldenberg, Associate Professor, California State University, Long
  Beach

Preparation and Development of Teachers Serving Limited English Proficient
Students: A Research Agenda
Miriam Gonzales, Policy Studies Associates, Inc., Washington, DC

Estimating Population Parameters
Anne Hafner, Associate Professor, California State University, Los Angeles

Parental and Community Involvement in the Education of Limited English
Proficient and Bilingual Students
Nitza M. Hidalgo, Westfield State College, Goshen, MA

ORGANIZATIONS THAT PARTICIPATED IN OPEN MEETING

Julia Lara
Council of Chief State School Officers
Washington, DC

David Kamer
Mexican-American Legal Defense and Education Fund
Washington, DC

Rick Lopez
National Association for Bilingual Education
Washington, DC

Ben Louie
National Association of State Boards of Education
Alexandria, VA

Joel Gomez
National Clearinghouse for Bilingual Education
Washington, DC

Denise McKeon
TESOL
Alexandria, VA

ORGANIZATIONS INVITED TO THE OPEN MEETING
BUT UNABLE TO ATTEND

Ms. Gail Donavan
National Association of Elementary School Principals
Alexandria, VA

Mr. Timothy Dyer
National Association of Secondary School Principals
Reston, VA

Ms. Lorraine Edmo
Executive Director
National Indian Education Association
Alexandria, VA

Mr. Arnold Fege
National Parent Teachers Association
Washington, DC

Ms. Isabel Garcia
National Education Association
Washington, DC

Ms. Mary Hahn
National Association of Elementary School Principals
Alexandria, VA

Mr. Mark Rigdon
National Governors Association
Washington, DC

Ms. Mary Reece
National Association of School Administrators
Arlington, VA

Mr. Gerald Sroufe
Executive Director
American Educational Research Association
Washington, DC

Ms. Carol Vega
National Association of State Boards of Education
Alexandria, VA

Several associations that were unable to participate in the open meeting, submitted written materials. They include The National Association for Asian and Pacific American Education, The Institute for Research in English Acquistion and Development (READ), The Council of Great City Schools, and the Aspira Association.

TECHNICAL REVIEWERS

John Chapman, Office of the Budget, U.S. Department of Education (Ch. 10)

Joseph Conaty, National Institute on Student Achievement, Curriculum and Assessment, Office of Educational Research and Improvement, U. S. Department of Education (Ch. 10)

Alicia Coro, Office of Educational Research and Improvement, U.S. Department of Education (Ch. 10)

James Crawford, Consultant, Takoma Park, MD (Ch. 10)

Ed Fuentes, Office of Educational Research and Improvement, U.S. Department of Education (Ch. 10)

Claude Goldenberg, Associate Professor, California State University, Long Beach (Ch. 6, 7)

Arnold Goldstein, National Center for Education Statistics, U.S. Department of Education (Ch. 9)

Rene Gonzalez, Office of Educational Research and Improvement, U.S. Department of Education (Ch. 10)

Anne Hafner, Associate Professor, California State University, Los Angeles (Ch. 5, 9)

Julia Lara, Council of Chief State School Officers, Washington, DC (Ch. 5, 9)

Edith McArthur, Acting Program Director, Data Development, U.S. Department of Education (Ch. 9)

John Olson, Senior Research Scientist, American Institutes for Research/Education Statistics Services Institute, Washington, DC (Ch. 5, 9)

Jeff Owings, National Center for Education Statistics, U.S. Department of Education (Ch. 9)

Cindy Ryan, Office of Bilingual Education and Minority Languages Affairs, U.S. Department of Education (Ch. 8)

Robert Slavin, Center for Research on the Education of Students Places at Risk, Johns Hopkins University, Baltimore, MD (Ch. 6, 7)

Gerald Sroufe, Director of Governmental and Professional Liaison, American Educational Research Association, Washington, DC (Ch. 10)

Biographical Sketches of Committee Members and Staff

KENJI HAKUTA (*Chair*) is professor of education at Stanford University, where he teaches in the Program of Language, Literacy and Culture and the Program of Psychological Studies in Education. An experimental psychologist by training, his current research is on the linguistic development of bilingual children. His publications include *Mirror of Language: The Debate on Bilingualism* (Basic Books, 1986) and *In Other Words: The Science and Psychology of Second Language Acquisition* (Basic Books, 1994). He serves as cochair of the National Educational Policy and Priorities Board for the U.S. Department of Education. Dr. Hakuta has a Ph.D. in experimental psychology from Harvard University.

DIANE AUGUST is a senior program officer at the National Research Council and study director for the Committee on Developing a Research Agenda on the Education of Limited English Proficient and Bilingual Students. Previously, she was a public school teacher and school administrator in California, a legislative assistant in the area of education for a U.S. Congressman from California, a grants officer for the Carnegie Corporation of New York, and director of education for the Children's Defense Fund. Dr. August has also worked as an educational consultant in evaluation and testing, program improvement, and federal and state education policy. She has a Ph.D in education from Stanford University.

JAMES A. BANKS is professor of education and director of the Center for Multicultural Education at the University of Washington, Seattle. He is president-elect of the American Educational Research Association and is a past president of the National Council for the Social Studies. Professor Banks has written or edited 16 books in multicultural education and in social studies education, including *Teaching Strategies for Ethnic Studies*; *Multiethnic Education: Theory and Practice*; and *Multicultural Education, Transformative Knowledge, and Action*. He is the editor of the *Handbook of Research on Multicultural Education*, the first published research handbook in this field. Professor Banks has received four research awards from the American Educational Research Association and an honorary doctorate of humane letters (L.H.D.) from the Bank Street College of Education. He has a Ph.D. in social studies education from Michigan State University.

DONNA CHRISTIAN is president of the Center for Applied Linguistics in Washington, D.C., where she is active in research, program development and evaluation, and teacher education. She has also taught at the university level, including two years as a Fulbright senior lecturer in Poland. Her work has focused on the role of language in education, including second language education, dialect diversity, and policy issues. Dr. Christian has consulted and written extensively on these topics, including recent publications on issues of language and culture in school reform, the integration of language and content for immigrant students, and two-way bilingual education. She has an M.S. in applied linguistics and a Ph.D. in sociolinguistics from Georgetown University.

RICHARD DURÁN is professor in the Graduate School of Education at the University of California, Santa Barbara. Previously, he served as a research scientist at Educational Testing Service in Princeton. His fields of expertise include assessment and instruction of language minority students, and design and evaluation of interventions assisting language minority students. He is a member of the Technical Design Committee of New Standards and a member of various national technical panels that advise the National Center for Education Statistics on the conduct of surveys, including those on language-minority children. Professor Durán has a Ph.D. in psychology from the University of California at Berkeley, specializing in quantitative and cognitive psychology.

CARL F. KAESTLE is professor of education at the University of Chicago. Previously, he was a professor in the Departments of Educational Policy Studies and History at the University of Wisconsin-Madison, as well as chair of the Department of Educational Policy Studies and director of the Wisconsin Center for Educational Research. He has also been a high school teacher and a principal. He has written extensively on the history of education, the role of the federal government in education, and adult literacy. He has been a visiting fellow at the Charles Warren Center for Studies in American History at Harvard, the Shelby Cullom Davis Center for Historical Studies at Princeton and the Center for Advanced Study in the Behavioral Sciences. His current research interests combine history and policy—the area of reading, assessment, and adult literacy and the role of the federal government in elementary and secondary education. Dr. Kaestle is the current president of the National Academy of Education and has served on the advisory committee of the National Adult Literacy Survey. He is currently a member of the Board on Testing and Assessment of the National Research Council. He holds a Ph.D. in education from Harvard University.

DAVID KENNY is professor of psychology at the University of Connecticut. Previously, he taught at Harvard, was a fellow at the Center for Advanced Study in the Behavioral Sciences, and a visiting professor at Arizona State and Oxford University. His initial research area was in the analysis of non-experimental data and more recently, he has investigated person perception in naturalistic contexts. He has published 4 books and over 50 articles and chapters. Dr. Kenny served as first quantitative associate editor of *Psychological Bulletin* and is currently editor of the Guilford series *Methodology for the Social Sciences*. He has a Ph.D. in social psychology from Northwestern University.

GAEA LEINHARDT is senior scientist at the Learning Research and Development Center and professor of education at the University of Pittsburgh, where she directs the Instructional Explanations Project and chairs the Cognitive Studies in Education Program. Dr. Leinhardt began her career teaching in inner-city schools. Her research interests have focused on a combination of ethnographic and cognitive approaches to the fine-grained analysis of classroom phenomena and the analysis of cognitive aspects of teaching and learning in specific subject matter areas, such as mathematics, history, and geography. Currently, Dr. Leinhardt is developing a model of the cognitive structure of instructional explanations across subject matters, and developing portraits of teachers and students who are involved with educational restructuring programs. She has also been intensely involved in state and national efforts to improve teacher assessment. Dr. Leinhardt's work has won awards from the American Educational Research Association and the National Council for Geographic Education. She has a Ph.D. in educational research from the University of Pittsburgh.

ALBA ORTIZ is Ruben E. Hinojosa Regents professor in education, associate dean for academic affairs and research in the College of Education at the University of Texas at Austin, professor and director of bilingual special education in the Department of Special Education, and director of the Office of Bilingual Education in the College of Education. Previously, she served as a speech, hearing, and language therapist in the San Antonio school district and as an instructional consultant and materials specialist for special education and migrant education in San Antonio. Prior to that, she was assistant professor of Special Education and Director of the Bilingual/Bicultural Education at San Jose State

University and assistant professor and director of Bilingual Chicano Studies at Southern Methodist University. She is past president of the International Council for Exceptional Children. Dr. Ortiz is a frequent presenter and invited speaker at local, state, and national meetings and conferences on topics related to special education and bilingual education and has published extensively on these topics. She has a Ph.D. in special education administration from the University of Texas at Austin.

LUCINDA PEASE-ALVAREZ is associate professor of education at the University of California, Santa Cruz. She has a varied background working with language-minority students as a teacher and researcher and has taught in bilingual and ESL (English-as-a-second-language) programs at both the primary and secondary level. As a teacher educator, she teaches courses on literacy development, bilingualism, and first- and second-language acquisition. Dr. Pease-Alvarez's research interests include children's uses of oral and written language in home, school, and community settings. She is currently involved in a multifaceted longitudinal study of native-language maintenance and shift toward English in bilingual children of Mexican descent. She is coauthor *of Pushing Boundaries: Language Learning and Socialization in a Mexicano Community*, which focuses on the language practices and perspectives of children and adults living in a Mexican immigrant community. She has a Ph.D. in education from Stanford.

CATHERINE SNOW is Henry Lee Shattuck professor of education at the Harvard Graduate School of Education. She is also codirector of the Home-School Study on Language and Literacy Development, a longitudinal study of literacy development. She has served as acting dean of the Harvard Graduate School of Education and is currently chair of the Department of Human Development and Psychology. Dr. Snow's early research focused on the features of children's social and linguistic environments that facilitated language development, on cross-cultural differences in mother-child interaction, and on factors affecting second language acquisition. She has done research on the factors affecting the acquisition of literacy and on relations between aspects of oral language development and later literacy achievement in both monolingual and bilingual children. Dr. Snow edits *Applied Psycholinguistics*, serves on the editorial staff of numerous journals, and has consulted and written extensively on a range of language development issues. She has a Ph.D. in psychology from McGill University.

DEBORAH STIPEK is professor in the Department of Education at the University of California, Los Angeles, and director of the UCLA laboratory school (Seeds, University Elementary School), and of the UCLA Urban Education Studies Center. She is also a member of the MacArthur Foundation Network on Successful Pathways in Middle Childhood. Dr. Stipek's research interests focus on the effect of classroom contexts and instruction on children's motivation and learning. She has done many studies on cognitions and emotions associated with motivation in academic settings, and her recent work has concentrated on early childhood education and the transition into school. She has a Ph.D. in developmental psychology from Yale.

Index

Other reports from the Board on Children, Youth, and Families

New Findings on Welfare and Children's Development: Summary of a Research Briefing (1997)

Youth Development and Neighborhood Influences: Challenges and Opportunities: Summary of a Workshop (1996)

Paying Attention to Children in a Changing Health Care System: Summaries of Workshops (with the Board on Health Promotion and Disease Prevention of the Institute of Medicine) (1996)

Beyond the Blueprint: Directions for Research on Head Start's Families: Report of Three Roundtable Meetings (1996)

Child Care for Low-Income Families: Directions for Research: Summary of a Workshop (1996)

Service Provider Perspectives on Family Violence Interventions: Proceedings of a Workshop (1995)

"Immigrant Children and Their Families: Issues for Research and Policy" in *The Future of Children* (1995)

Integrating Federal Statistics on Children (with the Committee on National Statistics of the National Research Council) (1995)

Child Care for Low-Income Families: Summary of Two Workshops (1995)

New Findings on Children, Families, and Economic Self-Sufficiency: Summary of a Research Briefing (1995)

The Impact of War on Child Health in the Countries of the Former Yugoslavia: A Workshop Summary (with the Institute of Medicine and the Office of International Affairs of the National Research Council) (1995)

Cultural Diversity and Early Education: Report of a Workshop (1994)

Benefits and Systems of Care for Maternal and Child Health: Workshop Highlights (with the Board on Health Promotion and Disease Prevention of the Institute of Medicine) (1994)

Protecting and Improving the Quality of Children Under Health Care Reform: Workshop Highlights (with the Board on Health Promotion and Disease Prevention of the Institute of Medicine) (1994)

America's Fathers and Public Policy: Report of a Workshop (1994)

Violence and the American Family: Report of a Workshop (1994)